CRUSADERS AND COMPROMISERS

CRUSADERS AND COMPROMISERS

Essays on the Relationship of the Antislavery Struggle to the Antebellum Party System

Edited by Alan M. Kraut

Contributions in American History, Number 104

GP

GREENWOOD PRESS
Westport, Connecticut • London, England

Library of Congress Cataloging in Publication Data

Main entry under title:

Crusaders and compromisers.

(Contributions in American history, ISSN 0084-9219 ;
no. 104)
  Bibliography: p.
  Includes index.
  1. Slavery—United States—Anti-slavery movements—
Addresses, essays, lectures. 2. United States—Politics
and government—1815-1861—Addresses, essays, lectures.
3. Political parties—United States—History—19th
century—Addresses, essays, lectures. I. Kraut, Alan M.
II. Series.
E449.C955   1983   324.275′09   82-21085
ISBN 0-313-22537-0 (lib. bdg.)

Library of Congress Catalog Card Number: 82-21085
ISBN: 0-313-22537-0
ISSN: 0084-9219

First published in 1983

Greenwood Press
A division of Congressional Information Service, Inc.
88 Post Road West
Westport, Connecticut 06881

Printed in the United States of America

10 9 8 7 6 5 4 3 2 1

For
My Daughter,
Julia Rose Kraut

Contents

Tables

Acknowledgments

This anthology has given to me the honor of associating with eight outstanding scholars and professionals. Their talent, patience, good humor, and spirit of cooperation considerably lightened my editorial burdens. Each one readily accepts responsibility for his own craftsmanship, but if this volume enhances our understanding of antebellum politics as well as reform, the accolades belong to them collectively as well as individually. The unifying theme of the volume and all efforts to impose an integrity upon the essays are the editor's responsibility.

James T. Sabin, editorial vice-president of Greenwood, and series editor Jon Wakelyn are valued colleagues but even more, warm friends. As editors, their trained eyes scanned every page of the manuscript; as friends, their generosity and consideration contributed substantially to the book's completion. Greenwood Production Editor Arlene Belzer guided the manuscript over the final hurdles to publication. The other essayists and I especially appreciate her willingness to respect each author's stylistic preferences even at the expense of uniformity among the essays.

Many others have invested their talents and skills in this manuscript. Lorman Ratner first stimulated my interest in antebellum reform in an undergraduate honors history course. His encouragement and support have been constant through the years. Allan J. Lichtman, a twentieth-century expert, demonstrated his scholarly versatility and his finely honed critical faculties in his comments on my own essay. Several contributors aided me in clarifying some of the thoughts in the introductory essay. Joel H. Silbey and Lawrence J. Friedman generously shared their ideas on antebellum historiography. James Brewer Stewart offered his talents as stylist and critic on the final draft.

Only old-fashioned scholars still type their manuscripts. Thoroughly modern folks "word process" the stuff. Sheila Bradford tackled the job for us. The coordinator of The American University Computer Services, James F. Kearney, and Mark Ambill provided timely advice when hardware and software were getting us nowhere.

Deborah Aviva Kraut is my wife and severest critic. She is adept at spotting boring prose, opaque arguments, clumsy sentence structure, and her husband's need for a movie. Suffice it to say that the editor loves her and finds her indispensable in all that he does. My daughter, Julia Rose Kraut, to whom I have dedicated this volume at her mother's insistence, contributed nothing to its completion. In fact, the toddler, now aged two, delayed its finish by making me chase her around the playground every afternoon during my sabbatical leave. Still, I am in her debt. Whenever I verged on holding my manuscript above swing, slide, or sandbox she promptly corrected me, always anxious to tutor her father in what really matters.

During the completion of this book my father died. Harry Kraut's craft was electroplating not history, but his love of the past and its rich lessons inspired and nurtured my own. To him I owe the greatest debt of all.

Introduction

There were abolitionists in the United States before there was an independent republic. And even as that republic was born, the founding fathers argued over slavery. In the Constitutional Convention and later, in the halls of Congress, slavery's future was debated and compromised by politicians. As politicians labored to curtail the divisiveness that slavery produced, reformers committed themselves to an organized movement, operated outside of politics, to abolish the institution. Seeking social regeneration, these reformers eschewed the give-and-take of political bargaining for the uncompromising integrity of moral suasion. In pamphlets and newspapers, from pulpits and podiums, with sermons and songs, they sought to persuade Americans that black slavery was iniquitous and ought to be ended. However, by the mid-1830's, some abolitionists began turning to partisan politics as a vehicle for change, hoping to marshal the coercive power of government to achieve what written and spoken appeals to conscience had not.[1]

This volume examines the interaction of abolition and partisan politics in the 1830–1860 period. Some of the historians whose essays follow are primarily interested in the immediatist abolitionists—those who demanded the immediate end of slavery. Other contributors are far more concerned with the impact of the reformers' performances upon the second and third party systems. Whatever their point of departure, all these scholars refuse to isolate reformers from the main currents of thoughts and events or to become bogged down in the all-too-familiar historical debates. Historians once treated the abolitionists only as precipitators of the great war that divided the nation. This preoccupation, in turn, had the result of permanently binding historians into a conceptual straightjacket.

The constraints that historians had long permitted the Civil War to impose upon their interpretation of abolitionism and much else that preceded the hostilities were only gradually severed. In 1964, Joel Silbey attempted to rescue the history of the Middle Period and political history, in particular, from this "Civil War Synthesis" that treated all events only as they related to the growing sectional conflict over slavery.[2] Ever since, many "new" political historians have studied antebellum politics while consciously refusing to use the Civil War's reality as a filter for screening the significance of campaigns, election results, legislative voting, and a wide range of other forms of political behavior.[3] Regrettably, abolitionists have not fared as well as politicians at the historian's typewriter.

Despite the innovations of Silbey and others, the opponents of slavery have largely remained bound by the original "Synthesis"; students of the antislavery movement have persisted in describing the history of abolitionism as the "growth of a dissenting minority."[4] This paradigm projects all abolitionists as beginning as a despised minority, and then evolving into the architects of a "broad-based Northern antislavery conscience, which, in turn, demanded and secured the eradication of Southern slavery."[5] With few exceptions, historians have accepted this paradigm and, regardless of their reasons for believing that the abolitionists grew in number and influence, scholars have discussed the reformers only in relation to the coming fury of war. They have largely neglected the broader context of American society and culture with which reformers had contact prior to the war.[6]

Abolitionists' *raison d'être* was to end slavery, and slavery's survival was certainly one of the issues at stake when North and South came to blows. Therefore, abolitionism cannot be hermetically sealed from the "reality" of the Civil War, but it can be treated as a dependent variable. The movement can be understood, on its own terms, as a factor in antebellum politics separate from whatever role it played in causing the Civil War.

In an essay published in another anthology, Ronald Walters called for putting the abolitionists "back into American history."[7] Some have already begun the task. James B. Stewart in *Holy Warriors* (1976) provided a brilliant synthesis of abolitionist scholarship. He concluded that abolitionism had not led "directly to the destruction of slavery," that warfare between irreconcilable cultures, not moral suasion, had intervened between master and slave.[8] However, it was not Stewart's purpose to determine how abolitionism had or had not affected American institutions other than slavery, such as political institutions. More recently, Anthony F. C. Wallace's study of Rockdale, Pennsylvania, Paul E. Johnson's of Rochester, New York, and Mary P. Ryan's of Oneida County, New York, have placed abolitionism into the context of community development.[9]

Thus, antislavery scholarship is hardly a well "run dry," as some have charged.[10] The 1980's agenda for students of abolitionism must include not only more community studies but also those that concentrate upon abolitionism's relationship to specific values, institutions, and systems not formally attached to organized reform movements. Many volumes will be required to adequately answer Walters' injunction and restore abolitionism to its proper place in the national past. This volume, focusing upon the intersection of abolitionism and partisan politics between 1830 and 1860 represents a clear beginning.

Abolitionists entered the political waters cautiously in the 1830's, fearing that the undertow of political avarice might swallow up their cause, drowning its righteousness in compromise. Therefore, they confined their initial efforts to petitioning Congressmen. Frustrated by the gag rule in 1836, some abolitionists turned to the questioning of Whig and Democratic candidates for office, hoping to barter their endorsement for promises of support against slavery's defenders in Congress, state houses, and on the floors of state legislatures. However, when candidates repeatedly broke their pledges of support, some abolitionists turned to third partyism. In the spring of 1840, they organized the Liberty Party, thereby creating a schism between those favoring direct political action and those opposed to it. The latter group preferred confining reformers' efforts to moral suasion. This schism over political action (along with other disputes) permanently divided the American Antislavery Society and the entire movement into "political" and "nonpolitical" abolitionists.

Between 1840 and 1860, many opponents of slavery—those who demanded its immediate abolition and those who were satisfied with its non-extension into new territories—pursued their respective agendas through partisan politics. All Liberty men were immediatist abolitionists, but in the Free Soil, Whig, Democratic, and Republican parties there were immediatists, non-extensionists, and those who cared little about the slave except insofar as his bondage affected economic and political relationships in the free white community. Liberty men demanded that the federal government cease all protection of slave property in areas under its direct control and called for a broad moral condemnation of slavery. Free Soilers, few of whom were immediatist abolitionists, were less concerned with the immorality of slavery than the influence of the institution upon both black and white races. Some Free Soilers were active advocates of political equality for free blacks and deplored slavery's expansion; others opposed slavery's extension only because of its potentially deleterious influence upon the country's free white labor force. The latter group envisioned a competition between unfree black labor and free white labor in the new states and territories as undermining the future of the country's white middle class.

Antislavery Whigs and the minority of slavery's opponents in the Democratic Party were occasionally moved by moral indignation. But many in these parties usually opposed slavery because of its volatility as an issue that could shatter the American party system. The Republican Party, a northern sectional party born in the wake of the political realignment, embraced some abolitionists but most Republicans were non-extensionists only. As candidate and President, Abraham Lincoln pledged to the South that he would not tamper with its institution where it already existed.

Whatever their motives and objectives, slavery's most serious adversaries met only frustration at the polls. Political abolitionists and those with more limited objectives rarely won elections and certainly did not achieve social change at the ballot box. However, if the criteria for success are expanded to include the broader influence that slavery's opponents exerted upon partisan politics, then the verdict that political abolitionists were failures must be overturned. Political abolitionists and antislavery politicians succeeded in propelling the slavery issue onto the national political agenda. Once there, it remained a divisive issue contributing to the unhinging of partisan loyalties and the general disassembling of the second American party system as a prelude to the realignment of the 1850's. The more general political turbulence stirred by antislavery reformers interfered with the functioning of partisan politics as a forum for compromise. Reformers increasingly presented anti-southernism and sectional animosity as substitutes for the partisan loyalties that had always before allowed officeholders to circumvent sectionalism. Whatever their contribution to the coming of the Civil War, political antislavery men and women of all stripes played leading roles in disrupting and recasting partisan politics.

In the end, political antislaveryites were no more successful than William Lloyd Garrison, Wendell Phillips, and other moral suasionists in abolishing slavery. Bloody war alone resolved the issue. Consequently, as a minority within a minority, political reformers have rarely captured the imagination of historians of the antislavery movement. Their dismal performance at the ballot box and uncertain influence upon elections led to a similar neglect from political historians. A historiographical overview suggests the pattern.

As with all abolitionists, the first historical treatment of those who pursued reform through politics came from the political abolitionists' own pens. William Goodell, John Greenleaf Whittier, and Henry Wilson wrote histories of the movement.[11] Others such as Henry B. Stanton wrote memoirs.[12] And many wrote each others' biographies. Elizur Wright, Jr., wrote on Myron Holley. Luther Marsh celebrated the efforts of his father-in-law, Alvan Stewart. Beriah Green sketched the life of James G. Birney, while Birney's son William also memorialized his father in print.[13] The most perceptive critical analysis of political abolitionist efforts prior to the Civil War was penned by Goodell in 1852, shortly after the demise of the Liberty Party.[14] Goodell's account, though hardly objective, illuminates the strength of partisan loyalties during the second party system even as it acknowledges the flaws in the abolitionists' own approach to politics:

The old party attachments of many who joined the Liberty party were not broken off. They were not steady in their adhesion to the Liberty party. Some voted, occasionally, with the old parties to accomplish particular objects. Some voted for Mr.

Clay, as they said, "to keep out Texas." Some voted with the old party to procure amendments in State Constitutions. Some, if they would confess the truth, to secure a "protective tariff." Thus, the Liberty Party was weakened, and confidence in its stability and even its integrity was undermined.[15]

The strength of partisanship that Goodell described and the impotence of the abolitionists to shatter the bonds of party is echoed in histories written after the Civil War, even those by historians favorably predisposed toward the reformers. In 1897, Theodore Clarke Smith published such a volume, *The Liberty and Free Soil Parties in the Northwest*.[16] Though largely a traditional narrative history distilled from the words and deeds of prominent leaders, it was also a harbinger of the new political history. Smith gathered Liberty and Free Soil state voting returns for the six states of the northwest (Ohio, Indiana, Michigan, Iowa, Illinois and Wisconsin). These statistics covered all the elections in which the two parties participated: state and local elections as well as national contests. The compilation of electoral data was not, unfortunately, followed by rigorous, systematic analysis, but the empirical direction of the work is unmistakable.

Until the 1930's, all abolitionists were generally hailed by historians as paragons of virtue. There were occasional exceptions, of course. Theodore Roosevelt, unable to envision circumstances in which anyone might sacrifice party discipline on the altar of principle, tendered a harsh appraisal of abolitionist third partyism. Years before his own Bull Moose candidacy, the righteous Republican wrote, "The Liberty Party in running [James G.] Birney, simply committed a political crime, evil in almost all its consequences. They in no sense . . . helped forward the Anti-slavery cause, or hurt the existing organizations."[17] One can only speculate whether or not T.R.'s bitter denunciation of third party abolitionism might not have been somewhat muted had he turned historian later in his career.

During the 1930's and 1940's there was a decided shift in the historiographical winds. Revisionists, concerned with tracing causes of the Civil War, now depicted the abolitionists as fanatical agitators disrupting the bonds of party and toppling the peace carefully constructed by compromisers in both sections.[18] Even Gilbert Barnes in *Antislavery Impulse* (1933), one of the first modern studies of abolitionism, mixed his admiration for the reformers with doubts about the soundness of their approach.[19] To Barnes, who was most impressed by the revivalist roots of reform, the Liberty Party seemed a "most pathetic residue of antislavery organization." Barnes was not a "revisionist," but like them, he heaped blame upon the reformers not for causing the Civil War but for failing to achieve their objective of racial justice despite the obstacles.[20]

Abolitionism was in vogue during the 1950's and 1960's. The latter decade, especially, was the golden age of abolitionist scholarship. The Civil War centennial (1961–1965) rekindled interest in all groups connected with the conflict, though the debate over repressibility versus irrepressibility had reached an impasse a decade earlier. Even more than the centennial, though, the civil rights movement seemed to charge scholars with the responsibility for uncovering the origins of the problems that plagued their own society. A generation of neo-abolitionist students and scholars, moved by the struggle of black and white activists in Selma, Montgomery, and Washington, D.C., now wanted to know more about all antislavery advocates. The achievements and failures of the reformers, their ideologies, tactics, strategies, motivations, and personalities became the subjects of numerous books, reams of articles, and countless doctoral dissertations and masters' theses.[21]

Surveys of the abolitionist movement by Dwight L. Dumond and Louis Filler were both laudatory and comprehensive.[22] Though some scholars thought that Dumond, especially, had abandoned his critical faculties because of his unqualified acclaim for the reformers, most joined him in singing their praises. Political abolitionists received their due in both studies, but much of what was learned of those who pursued change at the polls was derived from the sparkling biographies that appeared during the 1960's and early 1970's. Lewis Tappan, John P. Hale, Owen Lovejoy, George W. Julian, Benjamin F. Wade, John Gorham Palfrey, Charles Francis Adams, and Joshua Giddings was each the focus of such a volume.[23]

Even during the 1960's, though, the abolitionists were not without their detractors. If some sixties activists found felicitous models in the antebellum reformers, others, especially those of more radical persuasion, drew sharp distinctions between abolitionists who truly possessed radical consciousness and those who did not. Such scholars sought to identify a radical tradition in American history, linking contemporary radicals with Populists in the 1890's and abolitionists in the antebellum period. Aileen Kraditor praised William Lloyd Garrison for his spirit of radicalism, but found wanting those embroiled in partisan politics.[24] She characterized the Liberty Party as an organization that was "conceived in frustration and self-delusion, acted out a farce, and died by betrayal."[25] The "object lesson" that Kraditor claims to have derived from her examination of abolitionists in politics is "the futility of attempts to effect radical change through a political party system that by its nature protests radical change."[26]

As Kraditor inspected the abolitionists' radical credentials, others examined their psyches. Revisionists in the 1930's and 1940's had often denigrated the abolitionists as crazed or fanatical. In 1942, revisionist Avery Craven had suggested that the economic and social turmoil of the antebellum period had caused some northerners to respond irrationally, treating slavery and the South as scapegoats. Abolitionism, according to Craven, was a response to unconscious psychological pressures.[27] The debate over whether abolitionism was a psychologically abnormal response to unrelated social upheaval, or a healthy reaction to the social aberration of slavery sputtered along during the 1950's and 1960's. It also led some historians to methodological innovations as they sought to apply social scientific theory and new data in pursuit of reformers' motives.

David Donald was the first to test the hypothesis that abolitionism was a psychological response, a tension-reduction mechanism to resist outside pressure.[28] Donald argued that status anxiety was a source of tension among abolitionists. Without distinguishing among political and non-political abolitionists, Donald arbitrarily selected a sample of abolitionist leaders. He described the men and women in his sample as descended from "old and socially dominant Northeastern families." The 1830's and 1840's, when these individuals reached maturity, was a time when, "social and economic leadership was being transferred from the country to the city, from the farmer to the manufacturer, from the preacher to the corporation attorney."[29] Thus, the abolitionists were a displaced social elite, many of whom turned to reform movements as an outlet for their frustrations and anxieties. If they could not lead society as their forebears had done, Donald argued, at least they would be in the vanguard of those seeking the moral reformation of that society.

Donald's methodological carelessness left his arguments vulnerable to devastating critiques by Robert Skotheim, Robert Dougherty, and later, Gerald Sorin.[30] No evidence emerging from either aggregate or individual level data has yet shown that abolitionists were ridden with status anxiety.

Moreover, few psychologists still held to the tension-reduction formula. Many found that individuals can adapt new roles without experiencing frustration. There was even substantial doubt that frustration automatically produces aggression. Certainly advocating abolition when most others do not and voting for a third party such as the Liberty or Free Soil parties in a traditional two party system are deviations from the norm. However, it was questionable whether voting for a third party should be classified as an aggressive activity related to maladjustment or personality disturbances.

Of course, it is impossible to prove that abolitionists voted for a particular candidate or party to satisfy a psychological need. It is also impossible to disprove the relevance of psychological determinants. Martin Duberman was in the forefront of those who rejected a view of abolitionists as "psychologically homogeneous" or abnormal. However, even Duberman admitted that the motives of abolitionists were not necessarily "unrelated in any way to their own inner turmoil or conflict."[31] In his study of political abolitionist leaders, Gerald Sorin suggested that abolitionism may have been a perfectly healthy reaction to the injustice of slavery. By the mid-1970's Lewis Perry could quite correctly characterize antislavery as "almost a no-man's land for psychohistorians."[32] Though the sources available for doing a psychohistory of abolitionists are meager, the more profound failure appears to be that psychohistorians are able neither to formulate clear definitions of emotional health, nor even to agree upon adequate research designs.

While some historians of the 1960's tried to capture the abolitionists on "the couch," others were tallying their votes, checking their occupations, and calculating their net worth. The concepts and techniques that revolutionized antebellum political history in that decade and the following had a profound influence upon abolitionist studies as well. In 1961, the pioneering work of Lee Benson signalled the era of the clinometrician in the study of American politics. Now historians familiar with social scientific theory and methodology began to explore systematically the character and social composition of antebellum political parties. Following Benson's lead, Ronald Formisano, Michael Holt, Joel Silbey, and Paul Kleppner, among others, applied their new tools to the old task of illuminating the antebellum party system, including the role of political abolitionists and other opponents of slavery.[33]

The new political historians, armed with canned programs to calculate correlation coefficients and the latest in computer hardware, were able to determine with precision the influence of political abolitionists on state and local politics in various parts of the North. However, believing that the character of a political party is determined by the character of the social groups supporting it, many new political historians were also driven to understand the social roots of the abolitionist electorate.[34] They distinguished more precisely than did earlier scholars between leaders and the rank and file of the antislavery movement. In his study of the 1844 election in New York, Lee Benson described Liberty men as men of "considerable standing in their communities and much better than average character." Most, he said, shared a common set of "radical religious beliefs" involving righteous secular activity as the key to spiritual salvation and were ex-Whigs politically.[35]

Benson's profile was only of the leadership and was admittedly impressionistic, though he called for a "systematic, detailed study of the social composition of the Liberty Party in any state." As late as 1974, Eric Foner echoed a similar call from David Davis who lamented that, "little is known of the rank and file members . . . of a single reform movement."[36] However, since then studies by John L. Hammond, John B. Jentz, Reinhard O. Johnson, Judith M. Wellman, and Alan M. Kraut have pursued the social roots of political abolition through the demographic characteristics of rank and file reformers.[37] Hammond, especially, sought to link political abolition to the religious revivalism that Gilbert Barnes, Whitney Cross, Timothy Smith and others had earlier described as the lifeblood of antebellum reform.[38]

As these scholars pursued political abolitionism through the pages of petitions, poll books, tax assessors' lists, and state and federal census returns, others insisted that what reformers thought and felt was as important as whether they were farmers or tradesmen. Richard Curry warned that "one embarks upon a perilous voyage if he fails to consider seriously enough the perceptions of the actors themselves."[39] During the 1970's, Eric Foner, Lewis Perry, Richard Sewell, Ronald Walters, and Lawrence J. Friedman worked toward a fresh examination of antislavery thought. In *Free Soil, Free Labor,*

Free Men (1970), and a decade later, in a collection of his own essays, Eric Foner argued that during the first half of the nineteenth century, northerners and southerners came to believe in fundamentally different ideologies.[40] According to Foner, most northerners adhered to a "free labor" ideology that emphasized success through individual effort and self-discipline, equality of opportunity, economic liberty for the individual, and boundless economic, geographic, and social mobility. All "producers"—farmers, manufacturers and workers—enjoyed a harmony of interests. Foner linked these "modern" values to the ethnic and religious backgrounds of northern social groups that some of the new political historians had located within the Republican Party's coalition. Foner viewed the Democratic Party, on the other hand, as the coalition of pre-modern cultures in America, especially white Southerners and Irish immigrants. While most new political historians argued against the existence of such profound ideological divisions in the American electorate, Foner insisted that the parties mirrored this fundamental rift. There were abolitionists among those who formed the Republican coalition, though many conservative Republicans found "particularly offensive . . . the constant moralizing of abolitionists and radicals about the peculiar institution."[41] Opposition to slavery was inherent in the "free labor" ideology, and abolitionists and Republicans remained committed to it even though their naivete prevented useful coalition with labor radicals. Foner deplored abolitionism's narrowness, which derived, he argued, from its individualistic roots in Protestant revivalism. Abolitionists, he lamented, defined freedom only as the right to freely contract for labor or labor's products. Thus abolitionists accepted the inequalities of wealth as the consequence of character differences.[42] This "truncated definition of freedom" alienated the antislavery artisan from the organizations crafted by abolitionists.[43]

Foner's use of the term "ideology" has provoked considerable discussion. Some "new" political historians such as Ronald Formisano charged that Foner had defined ideology only in terms of "class, party or section," which was too narrow and rigid to be useful. According to Formisano, Foner viewed ideology "as though it came from outside of political culture," rather than as "a normal part of political life," thus preventing Foner from creating the "collective mind of Republican leaders." Instead, Formisano argued for "a pluralist-eclectic approach to social groups and belief-systems," one that would "differentiate between the more coherent, articulate, and informed ideologies of political leaders and the looser belief-systems of the average voter." Formisano advised against using ideology as a *deus ex machina* that would determine rigidly the range of sources. Instead, he advanced the "new" political historians' recipe for distilling ideology: "identify all politically relevant subcultures, then [attempt] to recreate their belief-systems and relate those to party images, policies, and ideologies, utilizing both traditional sources and quantitative data." Occasionally disputes over definitions of ideology have erupted into open antagonism in the pages of professional journals. Their hostile tone suggests the importance that historians attach to the proper explication of political ideology and the confusion that has persisted over the past two decades concerning both its definition and the appropriate methodological approach for its study.[44]

As Foner sought to "reintegrate the political, social and intellectual history"[45] through the study of ideology, other scholars, who defined ideology less rigidly or comprehensively than he, also sought to understand abolitionists through their belief systems. Lewis Perry, for one, drew critical praise for exploring radical abolitionist thought in the broader context of the general tension between anarchy, government, and religion in American culture.[46] Perry argued for the existence of "a doctrinal link between antislavery and anarchism."[47] That link was the sovereignty of God, which Perry treated as potentially anarchistic because it led abolitionists to seek out and attempt to purge different forms of "slavery," or repression, from all American institutions, politics and government included, as well as from church, voluntary associations, and even the family. In the 1830's the idea of the government of God increasingly caused conservative moralists such as the abolitionists to seek an end not only to slavery but to all impure human government. Perry contends that political abolitionists, "no less than the Garrisonians, shared the heady objective of evangelizing the people of the nation and bringing them under the government of God."[48] He cites the words of political abolitionists such as James G. Birney and Beriah Green to demonstrate that they, like many Garrisonians, held anarchistic assumptions that compelled them to shun compromise and expediency, the cornerstones of mainstream partisan politics.

As Perry plumbed anarchistic thought to comprehend how radical abolitionists differed from less radical reformers, Richard H. Sewell published the first narrative history of antislavery politics since Smith's study in 1897.[49] Primarily synthesis that does not make any "startling" conceptual or methodological departures, it is nevertheless a comprehensive and thorough treatment of the political antislavery movement.[50] The volume contributes most significantly by defining the sharp disagreements that frequently existed among antislavery politicians over strategies and tactics. Among these were disputes over whether the single issue of slavery could successfully undergird a third political party; whether abolitionists should associate, even compromise with party politicians for the sake of reform; whether advocacy of emancipation ought to be linked to a broader racial egalitarianism. Sewell's work, in general, is clearly biased toward the abolitionists, for he seeks to demonstrate how they transcended the racist culture surrounding them.[51]

Rather than pursuing the differences between abolitionists and ordinary white Protestant reformers, Ronald Walters set out to understand "the social and cultural matrix" that bound all such reformers together, abolitionists, temperance people, pacifists, communitarians, and so forth.[52] Arguing, contrary to Sewell, that the similarities among abolitionists outweighed the differences, Walters suggests that all shared a similar set of cultural values, summarized by the term "voluntarism"; the belief that individuals could structure a good society by acting on their own initiative as long as all were compelled to conform to a high standard of moral conduct. Thus abolitionists endorsed individualism and the individual's conscience as the best guide to right and wrong while insisting that the essence of civilization was society's ability to suppress the animalistic impulses lurking within each self. All antebellum reformers, and abolitionists not the least, embodied a cultural tension "between the innately moral self and the self needing to be controlled, between the human nature to be liberated and that to be repressed."[53] To abolitionists, slavery and southern plantation society were anathema because they completely suppressed individuals' freedom and spontaneity while plantation society exercised inadequate restraints upon the brutality and rapaciousness of owners and overseers. Slavery, then, had to be removed before a voluntaristic Christian commonwealth could be established.

Walters argues that differences between political abolitionists and "antipolitical" Garrisonians "dwindled into ideological insignificance." To the contrary, the similarities between the two "became more obvious as the years passed," and both groups shared a vision of "a more perfect society."[54] Finally, Walters insists, neither political abolitionists nor their adversaries were "quite certain whether the American political system was capable of bringing it about."[55] Sharply disagreeing with historians who regard the schisms among the abolitionists as significant, Walters claims that abolitionists were "bound together by beliefs and perceptions that went deeper than the issues they argued about." He claims that abolitionists, and later the historians studying them, inflated the significance of the division and "made the parting seem more serious than it was."[56]

When abolitionists parted, where did they go and with whom? Lawrence J. Friedman shares Ronald Walters' view that the reformers had more in common with each other than they did with those who were not benevolent reformers. However, unlike Walters, Friedman neither dismisses the distinctions among abolitionists nor labors to specify the bridges linking abolitionists to the culture that had spawned them. Like Perry, Friedman is interested in abolitionist thought. But unlike Walters, Sewell, or Perry, he is most concerned with the internal, self-contained worlds that groups or cliques of reformers created, often around the leadership of a single individual such as Lewis Tappan or Gerrit Smith. Friedman's is an exercise in social psychology. His "gregarious saints" are the first generation of white immediate abolitionists, he claims to manifest a "blend of conviviality and austere piety."[57] On the one hand, immediatists were gregarious because they "sought rapport with those whom they sought to proselytize," on the other, they pursued sainthood by uncompromisingly pressing for "full obedience to the divine command."[58] Similar social characteristics, and the quality of leadership and ideology, all determined whether or not an individual immediatist might be drawn to one or another clique, or circle.

In discussing political abolition, Friedman distinguishes between immediatists and radicals. The latter abandoned the former's view that the cultural voluntarism so frequently practiced by immediatists in their local strongholds such as New York's burned-over district, could be broadly applicable to northern and national political life. Instead, radicals accepted the necessity of acting in concert with Conscience Whigs, Free Soilers, and others who wished to capsize the slave system through organized partisan effort in politics. Immediatists and radicals had much in common according to Friedman; their differences were largely in emphases. Immediatists stressed that slavery was the worst of moral wrongs because it "precluded individual opportunity to pursue God's command," while radicals emphasized that slavery was "a system of economic oppression—one that denied its victims the opportunity to improve their social condition."[59] Friedman illuminates the world of immediatists and radicals, respectively, from inside itself. However just as neo-Marxist historians glorify pre-modern workers and their sense of class unity with other workers, so Friedman may overly romanticize the closed social systems that abolitionists built upon a shared understanding and appreciation of common values and goals.

Perry, Sewell, Walters, and Friedman have all opened windows upon the thought, culture, and social disposition of abolitionists. However, an even wider vista is required to appreciate the influence that these reformers brought to bear upon all that surrounded them and vice versa. Only Walters had demonstrated that the abolitionists were part of a larger reform culture. It remains, though, to chart the relationship between antislavery advocates and specific institutions. This anthology presents the efforts of eight historians to do just that: to elucidate the relationship between the reformers and the political system of the pre-Civil War era.

There have been other anthologies on abolitionism. The two most distinguished are *The Antislavery Vanguard* (1965), edited by Martin Duberman and *Antislavery Reconsidered* (1979), edited by Lewis Perry and Michael Fellman. These are state-of-the-art volumes, containing essays that reflect the general condition of antislavery historiography in the era when each was published. The methodologies employed by many of the contributors, too, are the most sophisticated of their era. However, these collections, unlike this one, display a broad-brush approach to the antislavery movement. The abolitionist reformers, in all their guises and roles, supplied the unifying theme (if any) of both collections. Not so this volume. It is focused consistently upon politics. It explores in depth through nine fresh essays the relationship of abolitionism and politics. While its scope has been intentionally narrowed, its goal is to broaden the perspective of the student of the nineteenth century toward abolitionism. This it will accomplish by recovering abolitionists from their isolation under the historian's microscope and restoring them to their place in the tumult of life, especially political life, in antebellum America, where they can (and ought to be) studied *in situ*.

The emphases selected by the contributors fall conveniently into three categories, each of which has become a separate section of the volume. One category includes all essays dealing with the mutual influence of political abolitionism and partisanship upon each other; a second concerns the role of anti-abolitionism in politics; and the third includes the impact of politically involved reformers upon other groups and institutions in the society aside from politicians and parties. In the first section, James Brewer Stewart, Edward Magdol, Alan Kraut, Richard Sewell and Phyllis Field deal with the efforts by abolitionists to voice *their* protest through the political system. James B. Stewart's essay treats the often neglected northern wing of the Whig Party. Stewart explores the paradox that even as the Whigs' northern wing was containing third party abolitionism and other threats to party unity posed by reformers, it became the vehicle for converting abolitionists' moral protests into disruptive political forces. These forces would eventually undermine the Whig Party and the national party system to which it belonged. One means of articulating the abolitionist message to politicians was the petition. Edward Magdol has constructed a profile of signers using petitions and demographic data from communities in New York and Massachusetts to demonstrate the relationship of political abolitionist protest to a broader economic transformation occurring in these communities. Magdol argues that the process of industrialization that altered occupational and social structures affected the composition of the political movement to abolish slavery.

When petitions failed to impress major party politicians, some abolitionists chose to abandon the major parties, but not the party system. Alan M. Kraut suggests that the abolitionist third party, the Liberty Party, was neither a thoroughly modern political vehicle, nor a vestige of pre-modern political associations. Liberty men practiced "political antipolitics" and it was this unique hybrid quality of their party that undermined any possibility of electoral success even as it permitted the third party men to leave a lasting impression upon antebellum political culture.[60] Despite dismal electoral returns, the Liberty men helped derange partisan loyalties as a prelude to the realignment of the 1850's and the escalating sectional divisiveness that overpowered national parties and ended in civil war.

Not all opponents of slavery were abolitionists, of course. The Free Soil Party, born in 1848, was a coalition of abolitionists, non-extensionists, and disaffected members of major parties. Of late, historians have criticized the Free Soilers for abandoning both the goals of political abolitionism and the basic rights of black Americans. Richard Sewell admits that most Free Soilers were not "impractical ultras," but he demonstrates that within the party system Free Soilers, far more than either Whigs or Democrats, actively supported both the non-extension of slavery into the West and the adoption of egalitarian racial policies in the North. Sewell also identifies the Free Soilers as the transmitters of abolitionist sentiment to the Republican Party of the 1850's.

Phyllis F. Field, who has studied the Republican Party in New York State reports that, indeed, many Liberty men and Free Soilers did find a home in that party. Using the issue of equal voting rights for black men as a test case, Field demonstrates how this emerging major party responded to the ideological and institutional pressures exerted upon it by both the friends and foes of slavery. The very birth pains of the Republican Party were produced by the strain of "managing" the black suffrage issue through a referendum so that the issue of reform was neither abandoned nor permitted to strangle the infant party.

Just as abolitionism was a factor in antebellum politics, so was anti-abolition sentiment. In a second section of the volume, Joel H. Silbey explores the general opposition of antebellum Democrats to political abolitionism. Democrats identified sectionalism and all antislavery movements, but especially political abolition, as divisive. Emphasis upon party as well as suspicion of federal power when used to regulate behavior and institutions inspired among Democrats, particularly ethnoreligious outsiders such as the Irish, a loathing of all who threatened their values. Liberty Party men were chief among the cultural interventionists that Democrats loathed.

The politics of abolition affected more than parties and politicians, however. In a final section of the book several scholars address themselves to the implications of political antislavery movements for sectors of society other than the party system; specifically, these essays deal with the struggle over reform in the churches; the efforts of women reformers; and, more generally, the role of abolitionism in a society that was undergoing the process of modernization. John R. McKivigan demonstrates the close relationship between abolition politics and antislavery church activities, particularly during the post-1840 period. Especially important, according to McKivigan, were the antislavery "come-outer" congregations and sects. It was largely these come-outers who not only supported political abolitionist efforts but also shaped new Christian but non-denominational religious institutions, "Union Churches." These Union Churches separated themselves from their coreligionists who had become contaminated by acquiescing to slaveholding. Others, not prepared to abandon their denomination and join a Union Church, launched new sects that retained denominational dogma but substituted abolitionism and advocacy of political abolitionism, especially, for the proslavery, anti-black prejudices of the groups they left.

Many of those congregants most taken with the slaves' cause were women. Distinguished historian Gerda Lerner has described women abolitionists as "an integral aspect of the antislavery movement."[61] Nancy Hewitt uses Rochester, New York, as a laboratory for an examination of how women reformers became divided by the advent of political abolition, though many political abolitionists opposed women's rights. Hewitt argues that differences in organization, appeals, and tactics among women's groups reflected differences in members' access to material resources as well as the social character of the women involved in each group. Thus, political abolition became a flash point for the more profound differences that were obstructing the creation of a unified women's rights movement.

McKivigan's and Hewitt's studies suggest that the entry of abolitionists into the political arena affected more than just the party system. In a concluding essay Lawrence J. Friedman suggests that distinctions between political abolitionists and moral suasionists must not be exaggerated in significance lest they obscure even broader transformations occurring in antebellum society. He offers a psychosocial approach that views abolitionism in relationship to modernism. By modern, Friedman means the development of systems, institutions, and patterns of relationships in American culture and society markedly different from those that had evolved from the colonial experience. Modernists replaced local institutions of production and distribution with regional and national ones. They abandoned the parochial experiences, ideas, and political institutions of their communities for new, more diverse ones that originated in other places. Industriously, they pursued new information that led to the more efficient use of time and material resources. They engaged in long-term planning and envisioned long-term goals. Always they expressed tolerance and moderation toward new ideas and those espousing them. Most of all, they were willing to abandon the past and its stale traditions for a world of ambitious innovation.

While Friedman sees distinctions between political and non-political abolitionists, he sees the greatest distinction between abolitionists and other northern modernizers because abolitionists felt alienated from the larger community. What distinguished all immediatists from other northern modernists according to Friedman was a social psychology that he labels as "pious fellowship." Using political abolitionist Elizur Wright, Jr., as a model to illustrate his point, Friedman demonstrates that Wright's differences from non-abolitionists are less significant than his personal movement away from the immediatist "world in ourselves" and toward a more "gregarious" posture from which he found himself able to work with Free Soilers and other northern antislavery modernists who lacked the immediatist's missionary zeal to destroy slavery. Wright was never completely accepted by more pragmatic politicians such as those in the Republican Party because even though he espoused modernist values, major party politicians continued to look upon him as a first generation immediatist, too imbued with moral piety for the give-and-take of partisan politics. Thus, according to Friedman, Wright and many others who had been political as well as non-political abolitionists could only pursue their protest from the rim of the partisan political arena by the 1850's.

Though all the essays in this volume address the relationship of politics and abolitionism, there was no predetermined perspective or methodology to which all contributors agreed to adhere. And the range is broad. Several scholars such as Magdol, Field, and Hewitt, employ the systematic, quantitative approach of the new political history. Silbey and Kraut have used concepts derived from the research of political scientists, investigating party systems, while Friedman borrows generously from the insights of sociologists who have studied the "modern personality." Others such as Stewart, Sewell, and McKivigan pursue more traditional methodological approaches.

Nor is there complete concurrence upon substantive issues. Field and McKivigan disagree on the extent to which Republicans sought to challenge racial prejudices. Kraut and Friedman disagree on whether abolitionists can be categorized as modernists without substantial qualification. And Friedman disagrees with several authors because he regards the distinctions between political and non-political abolitionists as obscuring at least as much as they clarify.

These arguments and the others that should be stirred by the appearance of these essays suggest that rather than a well run dry, the field of abolitionist studies remains verdant and well irrigated with fresh ideas and new approaches to old ones.

Lawrence J. Friedman has argued elsewhere that abolitionist scholarship has hit a dead end because historians have become enmeshed in a fundamental contradiction that they have allowed to remain unresolved. In attempting to explain abolitionists' role in Civil War causation, he argues, historians have "felt compelled to assume that abolitionists had power and influence." However, to explain why abolitionists failed to persuade their fellow Americans to emancipate the slaves and ensure blacks their civil rights, the same historians, Friedman observes, have had to assume that "abolitionists lacked power and influence."[62] The contradiction is present but hardly insurmountable as this collection of essays suggests.

The authors in this anthology have begun to resolve the contradiction by loosening the stranglehold that the Civil War Synthesis has had on antislavery men and women, just as political historians have done for antebellum parties and politicians. They have done this by examining from various perspectives abolitionism's and American politics' impact upon one another without constantly relating their findings to Civil War causation. As the authors suggest, reformers who entered the political arena brought with them an issue that tottered but did not immediately topple the national party system and the major parties within it. Abolitionists helped create instability within this system of national institutions that had served as an arena for the peaceful resolution of sectional conflict. Political abolitionists did force their partisan adversaries to choose sides on a highly divisive issue, which lessened their ability to seek areas of compromise. Finally, political antislaveryites of all persuasions, increasingly polarized the sections by promoting feelings of anti-southernism and attacking as immoral the South's cherished institution. In so doing they fueled fires already smoldering.

The abolitionists did not cause the Civil War, nor did they succeed in freeing the slaves, but neither were they impotent, albeit vocal, bystanders observing the drama that unfolded during the pre-war decades. Their activities, especially those of the politically active, helped condition the political milieu such that the second party system fell to realignment and was replaced by a third system; this system, less national in scope, was less able to sustain sectional compromises in an atmosphere of escalating distrust and hostility.[63]

No scholar burning with the fever of Civil War causation will be content to abandon the Civil War Synthesis for this conservative perspective on abolitionism that seeks to separate the reformers from the coming of the war. However, that is precisely what the eight scholars whose essays follow hope to do. And in so doing they will lift the scholarly quarantine that has separated abolitionism from the mainstream of nineteenth-century life. The essays in this volume are not intended to provide the final word on the influence upon each other of politics and abolitionism. They are merely an opening volley of ideas fired from fresh ground. Their purpose is to get others to return the barrage.

NOTES

1. The problem of slavery in the colonial and early national periods is best covered in two volumes by David Brion Davis, *The Problem of Slavery in Western Culture* (Ithaca: Cornell University Press, 1966) and *The Problem of Slavery in the Age of Revolution* (Ithaca: Cornell University Press, 1975). Never during the course of the debate over the Constitution was serious consideration given to total emancipation of black slaves. To the founding fathers, the concerns of union, property rights and racial superiority were of more immediate importance than the slave's freedom. See William W. Freehling, "The Founding Fathers and Slavery," *American Historical Review* 77 (February 1972): 81–93.

2. Joel H. Silbey, "The Civil War Synthesis in American Political History," *Civil War History* 10 (June 1964): 130–139.

3. The pioneering volume in this genre that preceded Silbey's essay is Lee Benson, *The Concept of Jacksonian Democracy: New York as a Test Case* (Princeton: Princeton University Press, 1961). Later volumes include: Michael Fitzgibbon Holt, *Forging a Majority: The Foundation of the Republican Party in Pittsburgh, 1848–1860* (New Haven: Yale University Press, 1969) and *The Political Crisis of the 1850's* (New York: John Wiley & Sons, 1978); Ronald P. Formisano, *The Birth of Mass Political Parties, Michigan, 1827–1861* (Princeton: Princeton University Press, 1971) and *The Transformation of Political Culture: Massachusetts Parties, 1790s–1840s* (New York: Oxford University Press, 1983); Paul Kleppner, *The Cross of Culture: A Social Analysis of Midwestern Politics, 1850–1900* (New York: The Free Press, 1970);

and *The Third Electoral System, 1853–1892: Parties, Voters and Political Cultures* (Chapel Hill: University of North Carolina Press, 1979). See also, Robert P. Swierenga, *Beyond the Civil War Synthesis: Political Essays in the Civil War Era* (Westport, Conn.: Greenwood Press, 1975).

4. The paradigm is based upon Merton L. Dillon, *The Abolitionists: The Growth of a Dissenting Minority* (De Kalb, Ill.: Northern Illinois University Press, 1974). It is developed by Lawrence J. Friedman, " 'Historical Topics Sometimes Run Dry': The State of Abolitionist Studies," *Historian* 43 (February 1981): 177–194.

5. Friedman, " 'Historical Topics Sometimes Run Dry,' ": 178.

6. Those who have abandoned the paradigm and pursued the development of a new one in their own research include: Irving H. Bartlett, *Wendell Phillips: Brahmin Radical* (Boston: Beacon Press, 1961); Lewis Perry, *Radical Abolitionism: Anarchy and the Government of God in Antislavery Thought* (Ithaca: Cornell University Press, 1973); Ronald G. Walters, *The Antislavery Appeal: American Abolitionism After 1830* (Baltimore: Johns Hopkins University Press, 1976); Bertram Wyatt-Brown, "New Leftists and Abolitionists: A Comparison of American Radical Styles," *Wisconsin Magazine of History* 53 (Summer 1970): 256–268 and *Lewis Tappan and the Evangelical War Against Slavery* (Cleveland: Press of Case Western Reserve University, 1969). Most recently has been Lawrence J. Friedman's own call for a new paradigm in " 'Historical Topics Sometimes Run Dry,' " and *Gregarious Saints: Self and Community in American Abolitionism, 1830–1870* (New York: Cambridge University Press, 1982).

7. Ronald G. Walters, "The Boundaries of Abolitionism," in Lewis Perry and Michael Fellman, eds., *Antislavery Reconsidered: New Perspectives on the Abolitionists* (Baton Rouge: Louisiana State University Press, 1979), p. 4.

8. James Brewer Stewart, *Holy Warriors, The Abolitionists and American Society* (New York: Hill and Wang, 1976), p. 16.

9. Anthony F. C. Wallace, *Rockdale: The Growth of an American Village in the Early Industrial Revolution* (New York: Alfred A. Knopf, 1972); Paul E. Johnson, *A Shopkeeper's Millenium: Society and Revivals in Rochester, New York, 1815–1837* (New York: Hill and Wang, 1978); and Mary P. Ryan, *Cradle of the Middle Class: The Family in Oneida County, New York, 1790–1865* (New York: Cambridge University Press, 1981).

10. Review of *The Abolitionists: The Growth of a Dissenting Minority* by Merton L. Dillon in *American Historical Review* 83 (June 1976): 662. Also, Friedman, " 'Historical Topics Sometimes Run Dry,' " passim.

11. William Goodell, *Slavery and Anti-Slavery; A History of the Great Struggle in Both Hemispheres; with a View of the Slavery Question in the United States* (New York: William Harned, 1852); John Greenleaf Whittier, *The Conflict with Slavery, Politics and Reform: The Inner Life Criticism* (New York: Houghton Mifflin and Company, 1889); and Henry Wilson, *History of the Rise and Fall of the Slave Power in America*, 3 vols. (Boston: James R. Osgood and Company, 1872).

12. Henry B. Stanton, *Random Recollections* (New York: Henry B. Stanton, 1885).

13. Elizur Wright, Jr., *Myron Holley and What He Did for Liberty and True Religion* (Boston: Elizur Wright, Jr., 1882); Luther Marsh, "Alvan Stewart," unpublished m.s., n.d. Alvan Stewart Collection, New York State Historical Association; Beriah Green, *Sketches of the Life and Writings of James Gillespie Birney*

(Utica, N.Y.: Jackson and Chaplin, 1844); William Birney, *James G. Birney and His Times* (New York: D. Appleton and Company, 1890).

14. Goodell, *Slavery and Anti-Slavery.*

15. Ibid., p. 472.

16. Theodore Clarke Smith, *The Liberty and Free Soil Parties in the Northwest* (New York: Longman's Green and Company, 1897).

17. Theodore Roosevelt, *Thomas H. Benton* (Boston: Houghton Mifflin and Company, 1899), p. 260.

18. These historians, known as the revisionists include Frank L. Owsley, Charles W. Ramsdell, Albert J. Beveridge, George Fort Milton, James G. Randall, Avery O. Craven, and E. Merton Coulter. For a discussion of their views of abolitionists and Civil War causation, see Thomas J. Pressley, *Americans Interpret Their Civil War* (Princeton: Princeton University Press, 1954). See also David M. Potter, *The South and the Sectional Conflict* (Baton Rouge: Louisiana State University Press, 1968), pp. 91–99 and David Donald, "American Historians and the Causes of the Civil War," *South Atlantic Quarterly* 59 (Summer 1960): 351–355.

19. Gilbert H. Barnes, *The Antislavery Impulse, 1830–1844* (New York: Harcourt, Brace and World, 1933).

20. Ibid., p. 176.

21. The best historiographical essay on this period is Merton L. Dillon, "The Abolitionists: A Decade of Historiography, 1959–1969," *Journal of Southern History* 35 (February 1969): 500–522.

22. Louis Filler, *The Crusade Against Slavery, 1830–1860* (New York: Harper & Row, 1960). Dwight L. Dumond, *Anti-Slavery* (Ann Arbor: University of Michigan Press, 1961).

23. Bertram Wyatt-Brown, *Lewis Tappan and the Evangelical War Against Slavery;* Richard H. Sewell, *John P. Hale and the Politics of Abolition* (Cambridge, Mass.: Harvard University Press, 1965); Edward Magdol, *Owen Lovejoy: Abolitionist in Congress* (New Brunswick, N.J.: Rutgers University Press, 1967); Patrick W. Riddleberger, *George Washington Julian, Radical Republican, A Study in Nineteenth-Century Politics and Reform* (Indianapolis: Indiana Historical Bureau, 1966); Hans L. Trefousse, *Benjamin Franklin Wade: Radical Republican from Ohio* (New York: Twayne Publishers, 1963). Frank O. Gatell, *John Gorham Palfrey and the New England Conscience* (Cambridge, Mass.: Harvard University Press, 1963); Martin Duberman, *Charles Francis Adams, 1807–1886* (Boston: Houghton Mifflin Company, 1961); James Brewer Stewart, *Joshua R. Giddings and the Tactics of Radical Politics* (Cleveland: Case Western Reserve Press, 1970).

24. Aileen Kraditor, *Means and Ends in American Abolitionism: Garrison and His Critics on Strategy and Tactics, 1834–1850* (New York: Pantheon, 1967).

25. Aileen Kraditor, "The Liberty and Free Soil Parties," in Arthur M. Schlesinger, Jr., ed., *History of the U.S. Political Parties* (New York: Chelsea House Publishers), 1:741.

26. Ibid.

27. Avery Craven, *The Coming of the Civil War* (New York: Charles Scribner's Sons, 1942), pp. 117–118, 124–130, 150.

28. David Donald, "Toward a Reconsideration of the Abolitionists," in David Donald, *Lincoln Reconsidered: Essays on the Civil War Era* (New York: Random House, 1956), pp. 19–36.

29. Ibid., p. 33.

30. Robert Allen Skotheim, "A Note on Historical Method: David Donald's 'Toward a Reconsideration of the Abolitionists,' " *Journal of Southern History* 25 (August 1959): 356–365; Robert W. Doherty, "Status Anxiety and American Reform: Some Alternatives," *American Quarterly* 19 (Summer 1967): 329–337; Gerald Sorin, *The New York Abolitionists, A Case of Political Radicalism* (Westport, Conn.: Greenwood Press, 1971).

31. Martin Duberman, "The Abolitionists and Psychology," *Journal of Negro History* 7 (July 1962): 188. See also, Duberman, "The Northern Response to Slavery," in Duberman, ed., *Antislavery Vanguard: New Essays on the Abolitionists* (Princeton: Princeton University Press, 1965), p. 407n.

32. Lewis Perry, "Psychology and the Abolitionists: Reflections on Martin Duberman and the Neoabolitionism of the 1960's," *Reviews in American History* 2 (September 1974): 318.

33. See note 4.

34. Frank J. Sorauf, *Political Parties in the American System* (Boston: Little, Brown and Company, 1964); Richard Hofstadter, *The Paranoid Style in American Politics and Other Essays* (New York: Random House, 1967), p. ix; Murray Edelman, *The Symbolic Uses of Politics* (Urbana: University of Illinois Press, 1964), pp. 166–167; Robert K. Lane, *Political Life, Why and How People Get Involved in Politics* (Glencoe: Free Press, 1959), pp. 299–300; Philip E. Converse, "The Nature of Belief Systems in Mass Politics," in David Apter, ed., *Ideology and Discontent* (Glencoe: Free Press, 1964), pp. 206–261.

35. Benson, *Concept of Jacksonian Democracy*, pp. 210, 212.

36. Eric Foner, "The Causes of the American Civil War: Recent Interpretations and New Directions," *Civil War History* 20 (September 1974): 208. David B. Davis, ed., *Ante-bellum Reform* (New York: Harper & Row, 1967), p. 10.

37. As early as 1970, Leonard L. Richards began using demographic data to describe the social characteristics of both abolitionists and those who participated in anti-abolition mobs during the 1830's. Leonard L. Richards, *"Gentlemen of Property and Standing": Anti-Abolition Mobs in Jacksonian America* (New York: Oxford University Press, 1970), pp. 131–155. Historians who focused their quantitative studies upon political abolitionists include: John L. Hammond, *The Politics of Benevolence Revival Religion and American Voting Behavior* (Norwood, N.J.: Ablex Publishing Corporation, 1979); John B. Jentz, "The Antislavery Constituency in Jacksonian New York City," *Civil War History* 27 (June 1981): 101–122; Reinhard O. Johnson, "The Liberty Party in New Hampshire, 1840–1848," *Historical New Hampshire* 33 (Spring 1978): 123–166 and "The Liberty Party in Vermont, 1840–1848: The Forgotten Abolitionists," *Vermont History* 47 (Fall 1979): 258–275 and "The Liberty Party in Massachusetts, 1840–1848: Antislavery Third Party Politics in the Bay State," *Civil War History* 28 (September 1982): 236–265; Judith M. Wellman, " 'Are We Aliens Because We Are Women?': Female Abolitionist Petitions in Upstate New York," paper presented at the National Archives Conference, Washington, D.C., April 1976; Wellman, "To the 'Fathers and Rulers of Our Country': Abolitionist Petitions and Female Abolitionists in Paris, New York, 1835–1845," paper presented at the Berkshire Conference on Women's History, June 1976; Wellman, " 'We Do Respectfully Pray': The Social Bases of Abolitionist

Petitions from Central New York, 1836–1839," paper presented at New York History Conference, April 1980; Alan M. Kraut, "The Forgotten Reformers: A Profile of Third Party Abolitionists in Antebellum New York," in Perry and Fellman, *Antislavery Reconsidered*, pp. 119–145.

38. Hammond, *The Politics of Benevolence;* Barnes, *The Antislavery Impulse;* Whitney R. Cross, *The Burned-Over District: The Social and Intellectual History of Enthusiastic Religion in Western New York, 1800–1830* (Ithaca: Cornell University Press, 1950); Timothy L. Smith, *Revivalism and Social Reform: American Protestantism on the Eve of the Civil War* (New York: Abingdon Press, 1957).

39. Richard O. Curry, "Romantic Radicalism in Antebellum America," review of Lewis Perry's *Radical Abolitionism in Reviews in American History* 2 (December 1973): 529.

40. Eric Foner, *Free Soil, Free Labor, Free Men: The Ideology of the Republican Party Before the Civil War* (New York: Oxford University Press, 1970); Foner, *Politics and Ideology in the Age of the Civil War* (New York: Oxford University Press, 1980).

41. Foner, *Free Soil, Free Labor, Free Men,* p. 188.

42. Foner, "Abolitionism and the Labor Movement in Ante-bellum America," in *Politics and Ideology,* p. 64.

43. Ibid.

44. See the exchange of letters to the editor between Eric Foner and Ronald Formisano in *Civil War History* 22 (June 1975): 185–190.

45. Foner, "Introduction" in *Politics and Ideology,* p. 9.

46. Curry, "Romantic Radicalism in Antebellum America," p. 524.

47. Perry, *Radical Abolitionism,* p. x.

48. Ibid., p. 169.

49. Richard H. Sewell, *Ballots For Freedom: Antislavery Politics in the United States, 1837–1860* (New York: Oxford University Press, 1976).

50. Richard Orr Curry, "The Political War Against Slavery," review of Richard H. Sewell's *Ballots For Freedom* in *Reviews in American History* 4 (December 1976): 546.

51. Lewis Perry, review of Richard H. Sewell's *Ballots For Freedom* in *Journal of Southern History* 43 (February 1977): 124–125.

52. Walters, *Antislavery Appeal,* p. 188.

53. Ibid., p. 99.

54. Ibid., pp. 16–17.

55. Ibid., p. 18.

56. Ibid.

57. Friedman, *Gregarious Saints,* p. 3.

58. Ibid.

59. Ibid., p. 230.

60. The term "political antipolitics" was coined by James Brewer Stewart, *Holy Warriors,* p. 97.

61. Gerda Lerner, "The Political Activities of Antislavery Women," in Gerda Lerner, ed., *The Majority Finds Its Past: Placing Women in History* (New York: Oxford University Press, 1979), p. 128.

62. Lawrence J. Friedman, "Abolitionists Versus Historians," review of James

Brewer Stewart's *Holy Warriors* and Ronald G. Walters, *Antislavery Appeal* in *Reviews in American History* 5 (September 1977): 342. Also, Friedman, " 'Historical Topics Sometimes Run Dry,' " passim.

63. Eric Foner has reminded historians and their readers that "those who viewed the war as a great divide often disregarded social and intellectual continuities spanning the decades preceding and following the conflict." Foner, "Yes Va., There Was A Civil War," *New York Times,* September 14, 1980.

I

POLITICS, PARTIES, AND ANTISLAVERY REFORM

1

Abolitionists, Insurgents, and Third Parties: Sectionalism and Partisan Politics in Northern Whiggery, 1836–1844

James Brewer Stewart

In July 1836, the House of Representatives adjourned, and Congressmen hurried home to begin the presidential elections. Many were eager to enter the canvass as Whigs, a new political label for a party still only partially formed. Taken together, Whigs seemed a conglomerate of interests so contradictory that some historians have termed their party at its inception "stillborn." Yet the clerks' records of voting in this session revealed the unmistakable fact that in the House the Whig and Democratic parties displayed, from the first moments of the second party system, dramatically different reactions whenever slavery questions arose. Representatives voted on these topics: (1) resolutions denying Congress' power to abolish slavery in the South, and in the District of Columbia; (2) bylaws to repeal the House's "gag rule" to prevent debate on antislavery petitions; (3) resolutions affirming the benefits of repressing abolitionist agitation; (4) bills to admit to statehood the territory of Arkansas, which had already legalized slavery; (5) motions to negotiate with the Republic of Texas, preludes, in some minds, to its future annexation as a slave state. Except for fugitive slaves and international slave-trade issues, here was a complete general catalog of the slavery-related questions that Congress was repeatedly to take up in the pre-Civil War decades.[1]

As Whigs and Democrats answered the roll, their votes created stark patterns of contrast. Nearly 90 percent of Democrats, Northern and Southern alike, voted for emphatic proslavery positions on all these roll calls. Whigs divided sharply along North-South lines. All Southern Whigs, (except one who soon departed Virginia for California) voted with the Democrats. But their Northern confreres, save two, assumed strong antislavery positions that consistently distinguished them from everyone else. Over 95 percent opposed curtailment of Congressional debates on antislavery petitions, slave trading, and the expansion of slavery. A few even went on record that Congress might have the power to legislate abolition in the slave states. From this date forward, until their party's collapse in 1854, Whig Congressmen continued to act out this sectional division as Democrats from North and South generally adhered to proslavery positions. From the first, Whigs found they had no choice but to disagree over slavery questions. While campaigning in 1836 on behalf of the three presidential candidates put up against Martin Van Buren, Northern Whig Congressmen clearly wished to emphasize that neither they nor their party were beholden to slaveholding interests. Southern Whigs, meantime, held up their own voting records and claimed the opposite.[2]

Stark portents of the Civil War cannot be read into this Whig division. Whig devotion to certain economic measures, to hating Jacksonian "despotism," to intersectional business connections, to two party partisanship on the state and local levels, and to common ideals of statesmanship and Unionism, all were too lasting to permit such extrapolation. The federated structure of the national party also encouraged variance between sections among Whigs on slavery questions.[3] Yet it is also clear that the Northern Whigs occupied a unique position in the second party system. In the South, their colleagues contested with the Democrats to convince voters of their greater devotion to slavery.[4] Since Northern Democrats gave every indication that they also supported slavery's interests, Northern Whigs, alone, offered a clear antislavery alternative.

Free state voters who wished to register their dislike for the peculiar institution began to gravitate toward the Whigs after 1836. Some, who were active abolitionists, soon found the party wanting in antislavery zeal and began to confront it with third party political challenges. In response, antislavery tendencies within Northern Whiggery also grew. Meanwhile, many other voters came to discover that the Whigs' offer of an antislavery alternative allowed them to harmonize their loyalty to an appealing national party with deeply held religious, social and economic values that could also prompt strong antislavery feelings. From the later 1830's through the 1840's the Whig party retained its national unity and was the principal agency for containing third party efforts against slavery. But judged by its unique ability to attract sectionally minded voters, the Whigs' Northern wing also became, during this same period, the most effective vehicle for translating abolitionism and more general Northern forebodings about slavery into increasingly powerful and disruptive political forces. An examination of this paradoxical process will occupy the remainder of this essay.

In the North at least, the cliché is misleading that the Whigs' only point of agreement for building a party was opposition to "King Andrew's usurpations." Likely recruits, voters as well as politicians, shared a constellation of social characteristics. (This despite the fact that some of the scholars who have done most to "reconstitute" their likenesses have also quarrelled so over details that they have threatened to reduce Whigs' profiles to caricatures.) One such profile, that of a Whig who might have been particularly inclined to hold strong antislavery views, might look something like this: more often than not, he hailed from native New England stock. He was inclined to live somewhere in latitudes that stretched westward from Massachusetts, through New York's "Burnt Over District," Ohio's "Western Reserve," and Indiana's northern tier of counties to the shores of Lake Michigan. But wherever he settled, in all likelihood he had taken up residence in a rapidly developing center of commercial enterprise and manufacturing or on farmland devoted to cash-crop agriculture. Here he found himself surrounded by expanding networks of trade, communication and education. He might have been found in any social class, but rising entrepreneurs, their skilled and semiskilled employees, and farmers involved in market production would likely have found him a congenial associate. He, like they, would probably have embraced evangelical religion and have been eager to recommend its principles, hoping to promote moral orderliness in individuals and spiritual harmony throughout society.[5] Through benevolent organizations and missions he was inclined to combat the "irreligion" that he judged responsible for the "stains" he believed had multiplied in the social fabric. He was prone to suspect, moreover, that Jacksonian "partyism" generated such "pollution," yet with no sense of inconsistency he often joined political crusades during the early 1830's against the Masons, "grog sellers," "papists," and "Sabbath breakers" whom he accused of undermining society's foundation. Politics, to him, involved the categorical imperative to reform people, to liberate their energies and to regularize community morals.[6]

This style of "political pietism" contained strong, if latent, possibilities for sectionalism. It reflected, for one thing, deep misgivings over the implications of mass politics as Jacksonians had first pioneered them and as they involved slavery. Suddenly, the Democratic national organization had swept away provincial barriers. As such Whigs viewed the process, ruffian immigrant Catholics and their urban bosses, haughty slaveholders, degraded and poor whites, rough-handed day laborers and hard-drinking urban mechanics, and the many Southern-born residents of the free states had been combined into a far-flung, disciplined engine for vote-getting. And each of its constituent parts consistently displayed pronounced class and ethnic hostilities to the pietists' impulses to liberate society and the economy through religious activity.[7] Committed to an inclusive vision of a Christian "free labor" America, anti-Jacksonians of this evangelical persuasion could only look with consternation on the appearance of a party that seemed to uphold in the name of laissez-faire every white subculture's peculiar "vices," while in the bargain shattering the nation's integrated banking system, its network of internal improvements and its "nationally beneficial" tariffs.

By 1836, two closely related trends were beginning to emerge from this yeasty brew of politics and social conflict. Democrats across the nation were putting their party foursquare in support of slavery and in opposition generally to "political pietism." Vital segments of the Northern Whig party were at the same time incorporating into their ranks religious and social groups who were the most intimately involved with legitimating free labor and consolidating an expansive new commercial-industrial order.[8] Such Whigs naturally reacted with aversion as Jacksonians showed unstinting support for a slave system whose primary tendencies seemed to prompt unnatural hierarchies, social atrophy and personal degradation.

To be sure, there were many Northern Whigs as individuals and groups, who embraced proslavery positions. Local Whig elites matched the Democrats in their leadership of the anti-abolitionist mobs of the mid-1830's. As several historians have shown, the more zealous an individual's commitment as a "courthouse" leader to either party, the more prone he might have been to endorse repression in order to preserve personal standing and neighborhood order against abolitionist disruption. Moreover, the great Whig merchants of New York City and Boston turned cultivation of Southern goodwill into high art and reaped the rewards in trade. Hence the "Cotton Whig" oligarchy periodically hounded abolitionists through the courts of Massachusetts, while high-toned New York Whigs let race-mongering editor James Watson Webb publicize their feelings. Few Whigs, antislavery or not, displayed any moral discomfort when touting "planter statesmen" like Clay, Harrison, and White as "presidential timber."[9]

But all these tendencies were small and secondary compared to the Democrats' uniform eagerness to embrace Southern interests. The nature of the Jacksonian coalition and the party's rules of organization were both resigned to yield the proslavery voting records posted by Democrats in Congress. That Jacksonian diplomacy and Indian policy also advanced slaveholders' interests was apparent to Whig and abolitionist critics by the mid–1830's. And when Jackson and his Cabinet moved directly to suppress abolitionism, Democratic politicians and voters, Northerners and Southerners alike, responded eagerly, taking after these "Bible-thumping," "teetotalling" "amalgamators" who threatened their local autonomy, racial supremacy, religious independence and cultural integrity. Completing the record of consistency, Democrats of the state level took the initiative everywhere except in Massachusetts in pushing for legislation to contain abolitionism.[10]

Agitation by the American Anti-Slavery Society had forced slavery questions directly into the second party system, and Democratic party responses had attempted to circumscribe their impact. Those vital segments of the Northern Whig party that were committed most strongly to "political pietism" and the values of "free labor" insisted, in turn, that voting the Democrats out and enacting Whig legislation were the only sure ways to preserve American freedom from Southern encroachments. Thus, early in the Whig party's history, partisan loyalty and antislavery feelings had begun to fuse and reinforce each other in the organization's Northern Whigs. In the now completed national party system, the North's most sectionally minded moral reformers had found a home in the Whig Party and had succeeded in identifying their enemy as all members of the Democracy, Northerners and Southerners alike. A potentially divisive sectional conflict was thereby redirected into a far more manageable partisan confrontation that Whigs could turn to their own advantage in the North. Not Southerners, but Democrats in general became the targets at which both Northern and Southern Whigs could take aim, albeit for different reasons. How long and how successfully the Whigs would be able to harness such volatile sectional prejudices for their party's benefit, even as such feelings grew and spread, ultimately was to determine the life span of the second party system itself.

By 1840, some of these trends were becoming obvious, and the Whig party was performing its antislavery task well. Its Northern wing was now drawing to it most of the grass-roots strength of the formally organized abolitionist movement and nearly all other voters whose opinions were less radical but sectionally antagonistic nonetheless. Veteran abolitionist Henry B. Stanton, one of the original Oberlin College radicals, sensed the situation correctly and was therefore very leery about proposals to establish an emancipationist third party. Such a party, he feared correctly, would get pitifully few voters because nearly everyone who hated slavery was voting Whig. He predicted that "49/50ths of our friends," would support William Henry Harrison for President, even though he owned slaves.[11] And in so doing, these "Whig abolitionists" sensed no moral inconsistencies or strains on their party loyalty. During these hard economic times, prospects of revised tariffs, distribution, a revived national bank, debtor relief and expanded internal improvements were all appealing measures among a wide spectrum of voters North and South. They were especially so to Whigs in these economically expansive Northern regions, so congenial to "political pietism."[12]

Martin Van Buren, Northern Whig voters were told, was "par eminence the slaveholders' candidate" because "all the policies of his administration," economic policies included, had been "controlled by Southern principles." Hence the Democracy had driven Northern yeomen and tradesmen to the brink of "ruin," while also "waging undisguised, systematic warfare against the abolitionists." Determined, in Stanton's colorful phrase, "to wade to their armpits in molten lava to drive Van Buren from power," these "abolitionist Whigs" clearly perceived victory for their party as achieving clear sectional gains as well as partisan economic goals all at the same time.[13]

This Whig appeal proved irresistible to most sectional voters in the 1840 Presidential canvass and vindicated Stanton's predictions. The newly formed abolitionist Liberty party received 0.3 percent of the ballots cast. Out of 70,000 to 100,000 male members in the Anti-Slavery Societies, not to mention the inestimable number of nonaffiliated antislavery voters, only 6,000 to 8,000 actively refused to support one of the two major candidates, voting instead for the Liberty party while crushing the "doughfaced" Democrats in the process. In New York State, for example, William Seward and Thurlow Weed employed such tactics with great success. So did influential Whig organizations in Vermont, Massachusetts, Ohio, and Michigan, and they too embellished the theme of "Harrison and Northern rights." In every pocket of abolitionist strength the "Whig whirlwind," as one stunned Liberty man reported, caused "truly amazing" defections of abolitionists to Harrison's banner.[14] Whether acting out of principle or partisan expediency, Whig politicians openly appealed to antislavery constituencies. They discovered that the great benefit of sectionalism was simultaneous advantage over the hated Democrats, the grasping slaveholders, and the nettlesome Liberty party.

After 1840, Northern Whig tactics heightened many voters' awareness of sectional issues. These Northerners now kept closer track of their representatives' behavior whenever such issues were raised, whether in Washington or in the state legislatures.

By 1840, then, some of the most antislavery minded of these constituencies had already begun to arm their representatives to Congress with specific mandates to speak for "Northern interests." And there was no mistaking the general social character of these Whig representatives who began in the later 1830's to join John Quincy Adams' struggles against the "gag rule." Joshua Giddings, William Slade, Seth Gates, Nathaniel Borden, and others less prominent were all particularly forthright embodiments of anti-Jacksonian "political pietism." Each had embraced revivalism and renounced colonization, and nearly all had pitted themselves in earlier years against the "Masonic conspiracy." Teetotallers all, each also engaged in various evangelical reforms. Slade's *metier,* universal public education, would one day lead him to become Vermont's first State Commissioner of Schools, and then his state's Governor. Gates mingled easily in the radical community that gathered around upstate New York philanthropist Gerrit Smith. Giddings proudly wore "reformers suits," claimed to be a nonresistant, loved to rub elbows with radical abolitionists and heartily endorsed women's rights.[15] Each wore his Whig allegiance proudly. But none of them could, at the same time, forget the intense interest in these causes taken by Anti-Slavery Societies, so active in their districts.

Congenial from the first to sectionalism, the Northern Whig party was in the early 1840's beginning to furnish a broad meeting ground for abolitionist radicals who were eager for political results and members of its own Congressional delegations who also shared deeply in the evangelical culture of antislavery. As the abolitionists' petition campaigns and their efforts to form a third party focused local attention on sectional issues in Washington, these insurgent antislavery Whigs in particular became increasingly alert to the tasks of upholding "Northern rights" and of identifying their party ever more closely with antislavery goals.

All these trends found expression in the trial of John Quincy Adams, Joshua Giddings' censure and re-election, and the many other attempts by vocal antislavery Whigs to agitate slavery questions in the house during the early 1840's. At every level of this familiar narrative abolitionist involvement was significant. Joshua Leavitt and Gamaliel Bailey, the Liberty party's two leading editors, and, of course, Theodore Weld, openly collaborated with Adams, Giddings and the other Whig insurgents. Although less dramatically involved, other prominent abolitionist leaders such as Gerrit Smith, Lewis Tappan, and even some "nonpolitical Garrisonians gave active encourage-ment.[16] Most significant of all, however, was the high degree of grass-roots support for the antislavery Whigs generated by the abolitionists' petition campaigns themselves, for those efforts attracted signatures by the hundreds of thousands. Otherwise quarrelsome supporters of the American Coloni-zation Society and various competing groups of immediate abolitionists could set aside differences and join with all other citizens who mistrusted slavery in affixing their names to petitions that demanded a ban on new slave states or the abolition of slavery in the District of Columbia. Here, in the words of one petition campaign leader, were issues upon which "all classes, Abolitionists, Colonizationists, Mongrels and Nothingarians" (in other words, anyone hostile to the South) were able to agree.[17] By this abolitionist-sponsored process, important pockets of active antislavery opin-ion in the early 1840's now began to express themselves more forcefully and more frequently than they had in the 1830's. It was therefore no accident that the Whig Congressional insurgency grew more active, even as these sectionally sensitized constituencies demanded clear, consistent resistance to all politicians, Northern as well as Southern, who upheld the interests of slavery.

The example of Giddings' censure by the House for introducing some "incendiary" resolutions against slavery highlighted, by the very drama of the event, the great potential strength of the antislavery constituencies which abolitionists had done so much to activate. A stormy but unsuccessful at-tempt to repress Adams for presenting antislavery petitions had already demonstrated to the House how disruptive the collaboration between anti-slavery Whigs and abolitionists could be. So, failing to silence the formidable ex-President after two weeks of tempestuous debate, Representatives turned on the lesser known, less articulate Giddings. But after his censure, Giddings resigned his seat and was then re-elected by an enormous majority. In his remarkably "abolitionized" district, the election prefigured in some respects the mighty antislavery consensus that would begin overtaking Northern politics over a decade later. Whigs, Liberty men, and even some Garrisonians as well, briefly became nearly indistinguishable parts of one larger electoral voice. So, too, did some Democrats whose token candidate received roughly 80 percent fewer votes when compared with other Congressional contests between 1836 and 1844.[18] Clearly, the landslide expressed an endorsement of Giddings, not of the Whig party in general. But, this vote also had the effect of reconfirming within the Whig party the place of a most volatile yet broadly representative configuration of local antislavery opinion. Meantime, Whig newspapers throughout the free states indicated that a similar tendency to legitimize antislavery was to be found in the party's Northern wing as a whole, at least among its leaders. Most editorialists distanced themselves from Giddings' "rash extremism." Yet they simultaneously declared it an article of party orthodoxy to condemn without reservation the slaveholders and "doughfaced Democrats" who had stifled the right of Giddings' constituents to his representation of them. The influential *Ohio State Journal* for example, called Giddings' behavior an "offense against prudence and patriotism" that was nonetheless far "overshadowed and swallowed up in the monstrous usurpation" of the censure itself, caused by "Southern men and loco-focos." Claiming Giddings' vindication as their party's first objective, the *Journal* also took pains to make sure that antislavery minded voters credited the Whigs for their fidelity to Northern rights: "If the affront to Mr. Giddings is to be resented, let it be done with Whig votes."[19] Similar editorials in the Boston *Atlas,* the Cleveland *Herald,* the Pittsburgh *Courier* and other papers confirmed that while the party's Northern elites held no brief for Giddings' radical doctrines, they also could not afford to restrain him, or others like him, who had been accorded legitimate standing as Whigs. Rather than daring to offend the significant body of active antislavery voters upon which the Northern party now depended, agitators like Giddings were to be tolerated, justified and even encouraged as integral parts of Whiggery.[20]

Similar considerations informed the voting records of Northern Whig Congressmen during the early and mid–1840's as the insurgents brought to the floor an enormous number of antislavery matters. The results, too, were similar as active antislavery partisanship became more acceptable to the Whig party even as it became in Congress more frequent, flamboyant and directly connected with abolitionists. Whatever his negative personal opinions of Adams, Giddings and the others, the free state Whig Congressman was rare who felt politically able to express them openly in his voting record. Hence Northern Whigs consistently refused from 1840 to 1845 to go before their constituents and oppose their own party's foremost spokesman for "Northern rights." The censure vote against Giddings, for example, which passed 125–69, surely pleased many Northerners from his own party, who also knew that combined Democratic and Southern Whig voters alone would be sufficient to seal his fate. Others clearly sympathized at least with Giddings' right to exercise free speech, if not with his antislavery views per se. But whatever the motives, the necessities of voting "abolitionist" were as obvious to Northern Whig representatives as were the political costs of not doing so. All voted against censure, just as they had on every crucial vote in the earlier attempts to silence John Quincy Adams, and just as they would continue to do with increasing regularity against the "gag rule" itself.[21]

The 1840–1844 sessions of Congress were unprecedented for the number, range and volatility of sectional questions thrust before them by the insurgent Whigs and their abolitionist associates. Yet throughout this period of turbulence, broad patterns of intersectional cooperation within both parties remained very strong. Even as antislavery feelings in politics began to deepen and spread, Southerners and Northerners much preferred to do partisan battle on most issues as Democrats and Whigs, rather than as sectional advocates and opponents of slavery. In this process the Whig party and its antislavery wing was now playing a paradoxical, if not ironic, role. Sectionalism in politics grew stronger precisely because the Northern wing of Whiggery, which contained antislavery-minded constituencies, was so receptive to abolitionist influence, and produced and legitimized militant officeholders. At the same time, the Whig party functioned effectively on the national level to contain the same sectional forces that it was helping to assemble. It insured that opposition to slavery in politics would not produce severe alienation in the North from the two party system itself, a principal function of which was to unite the sections along Whig-Democratic partisan lines. Especially when selecting their Congressmen, voters whose religious values and social circumstances predisposed them to defending "free speech, free soil and free labor" found the choice easy to make.

On the state level too, when sectional issues took the form of contests over personal liberty laws or modification of "black codes" that legalized Northern racial discrimination, the matter of voting was often equally clear-cut.[22] Few doubted that the Whig party offered the only attractive practical alternative on all these matters to the "dough-faced northern pawns" of the slave power who, it was said, filled every rank among the Democrats. With uninterrupted regularity, antislavery constituencies continued to vote for Whig candidates who were pledged to watch over the interests of the North but who also, as good Whigs, opposed the Liberty party and kept strong ties with Southerners in their party on a multitude of other issues.[23]

The ongoing strength of the Whigs' antislavery appeal was certainly not lost on political abolitionists who once again dared to challenge the structure of the two party system, this time during the election of 1844. In renominating James G. Birney to run against Clay and Polk, the Liberty party put forth its greatest possible effort to wean voters away from their "corrupting, proslavery" loyalties to the two major parties. Deeply suspicious that both Whig and Democratic organizations acted with criminal coercion upon their own members as well as being proslavery in their policies, Liberty men had nevertheless improved greatly their own capacity to get votes since the "Whig whirlwind" had blown their party away four years earlier. This time, they challenged the Whigs' dominion over the antislavery constituencies with

complete slates of third party candidates, well-edited newspapers and statements of antislavery principle that reverberated with the broader economic
and ideological themes of "free soil, free labor, and free men." Northern
Whigs were becoming increasingly preoccupied by such concerns, especially
since 1842, when Texas annexation began to emerge as a major issue in
the campaign. The Liberty party's vote totals had been increasing steadily
in state elections since 1840. These party organizers now entertained some
hopes of exercising a balance of power in various states as the Whigs and
Democrats had achieved virtual parity in their ability to amass popular and
electoral votes.[24] The Liberty party's failure to achieve any of these aims in
this crucial election provides ample documentation for the Whigs' success
in protecting the two party system from the politics of unalloyed sectionalism. The third party's simultaneous success in forcing Northern Whiggery
into more militant anti-Southern postures, however, illustrates that Liberty
men were now exerting a sectional influence on politics far in excess of their
meager numbers.

Reflecting on the prospect of critical voter defections to the Liberty party,
Northern Whigs acted predictably and as they always had, blending expedient tactics with their own antislavery feelings to promote and expand
party interests. James A. Briggs, a Whig State Central Committeeman from
Cleveland, captured the essence of this Whig response when arguing privately
to another powerful party operative that Giddings should be endorsed for
renomination. "It would give us the abolition vote of the district," he explained, "and exert a good influence throughout the state by out-trumping
the third party ultras." Giddings' radical presence on the ticket would, in
other words, enhance the Whigs' abolitionist image in Ohio well beyond
the borders of the Western Reserve. As Briggs pointed out in conclusion,
by supporting Giddings, "Whigs make no sacrifice of any principle or measure, as Mr. G. is a Whig, and a Clay man . . . who will do us most good
on the stump."[25] In short, the most extreme opponent of slavery holding
national office at that time had to be accorded full license to speak out,
without inhibition, in order to minimize feared defections from Henry Clay
to James G. Birney. Giddings responded with relish and great energy, claiming for Henry Clay every sort of antislavery position such as support for
abolition of slavery in the District of Columbia, repeal of the coastal slave
trade and, of course, foursquare opposition to Texas annexation, no matter
what the circumstances. His effect on Ohio's Liberty party vote was devastating. William Slade, by contrast, found himself placed in a similar role
by Vermont's Whigs and resented it, expressing "great indignation" at those
who had "not the slightest sympathy" for his abolitionism but who were
"willing to *use me* to keep down the third party." In upstate New York,
Seth Gates finally grew even more resentful, to the point that he defected
to the Liberty party in the midst of the campaign.[26]

Giddings' example, not Slade's or Gates', turned out to be far more typical in this election of Northern Whig behavior. Texas annexation was unpopular in all party circles, no less among "moss backs" than among "ultra Whig abolitionists." Daniel Webster's proposal to add no new territory to the national domain sounded sensible to many Whigs in both sections and candidate Clay's initial letter opposing annexation was meant to reassure antislavery voters that the Whig party would remain an effective guardian of "Northern rights." But with their party thus committed, ardent antislavery partisans within it now found themselves free to confront the Liberty party's challenges very aggressively. The election promised to be extremely close, not just for the Presidency, but on state and local levels as well. Wherever the Liberty men were strong, Whigs of all stripes lashed out simultaneously against them, against slavery and against those pro-Southern "doughfaces," the Democrats who, it was emphasized time and again, would be the only ones to profit if antislavery voters switched from Clay to Birney.[27]

In this manner, the politics of slavery and abolitionism remained just where they had since 1836, firmly fixed within the intersectional framework of the Whig party. Such was the case even though the Liberty party had increased its totals in 1844 tenfold compared to 1840, causing Whigs to charge that the Liberty party had "stolen" just enough New York votes from them to insure Clay's defeat. This claim, which historians have debated extensively since, is not sufficient evidence to conclude that sectional challenges to Northern Whigs were not actually undermining the party's stability.[28] Historian Michael Holt is correct in his judgment that "Texas was a party, not a sectional issue in this election," despite Whig suspicions at the time that abolitionist voters did them in. Regardless of the outcome, Southern Whigs for their own sectional reasons had joined their Northern counterparts in a common front against annexation, while Democrats professed forthright expansionism. Both wings of Whiggery feared war with Mexico and still greater additions of territory, slave or free, as consequences of annexation, and to this extent intersectional agreement balanced the mounting sectional espousals of Northern Whigs.[29]

Yet the election of 1844 constituted a watershed for the Northern Whig party regarding its own longstanding involvement with antislavery and the challenges of political abolitionism. Its significance lay not in Clay's loss, or in the Whigs' continued maintenance of intersectional unity, but in a significant redefinition of what constituted partisan loyalty in the North. Through a long process of mutually reinforcing interaction, and with the appearance of the Texas question, Liberty men and Northern Whigs were now contesting for antislavery constituencies on a sectional issue, slavery's possible expansion, that was far more compelling and far more widely shared than any heretofore. Northern Whigs in general, not just vocal antislavery Whigs like Giddings or Slade, therefore, emphatically presented their party as unstintingly in favor of "Northern rights," completely opposed to the "slave ridden" Democrats, and the irresponsible Liberty men who abetted them.[30] The tactics that shaped the direction of Whig partisanship in the North and the growing ideological imperatives to defend Yankee "freedom" from Southern expansionism were now becoming inextricably intertwined. While the national organization was far from rupturing, it was nevertheless becoming obvious as the campaign wore on that, like it or not, the rules governing party loyalty could no longer be completely reconciled with the antislavery sentiment of Northern Whigs.

Clay, for example, sensed the trend, feared losing Southern support and began to moderate his anti-Texas position. William Seward, whose deep loyalties kept him true to his party until 1854, took a longer view than did Clay, and his conclusions captured perfectly the significance of the 1844 canvass for Northern Whiggery. "The reckless folly of the Administration in regard to Texas and the unprincipled adoption of it by our opponents have loosed our tongue stays," he wrote. "Slavery is henceforth and forever among the elements of political action in the Republic. Let Mr. Clay treat it as he may, and be the results of this canvass what it may, the ground the public mind has traveled cannot be retraced."[31]

For several years, as we have seen, insurgent antislavery Whigs and political abolitionists together had busied themselves circulating within the party a political rhetoric that warned of a grasping "slave power's" threats to free labor and its blessings—social mobility, personal improvement and general moral progress. From the later 1830's onward, a clearly antislavery wing had also secured from the party, albeit grudgingly, ever greater legitimacy while transmuting dangerous sectional impulses into matters for partisan conflict. But also, as war with Mexico again brought the issues of "free soil" and the "slave power" to the foreground, it was to become increasingly difficult to reconcile with party orthodoxy the demands of voters and elected officials who embraced antislavery ideology. Increasing antislavery within the party, accompanied by a continuing ability to contain sectional politics, by 1844, were the contradictory effects on Whiggery of its long and close associations with political abolitionists, emancipationist agitators and antislavery constituents that had begun in the 1830's.

As an epilogue, familiar narratives document some of the longer term legacies of the antislavery Whig/abolitionist tradition discussed above: the rancorous divisions that appeared in Congress and on state levels about the extent to which Whigs should oppose the Mexican war; the complete collapse of North-South unity in Congress whenever facing a vote on the Wilmot Proviso; the frustrated efforts of moderate leaders like Clay, Corwin, Webster, and others to mute Whig divisiveness; the final bolt from the party by Giddings' Ohioans and the famous "Conscience Whig" leadership of Massachusetts—all of these developments certainly confirmed that now, among some Whigs in the North, sectionally minded definitions of political loyalty were often becoming too extreme to coexist with party norms.

Yet for all this uproar, the election of 1848, like 1844, witnessed no immediate dislocations in Whiggery, either in the North or across the nation. Continued party stability, paradoxically enough, constituted one continuing influence of the Whigs' tempestuous antislavery traditions. The party's most ardent "Northern rights" leaders had now departed to the Free Soil party and the range of sectional impulses within Northern Whiggery had been narrowed accordingly.[32] At the same time, however, as they faced the Free Soil party challenge, Northern Whigs remembered tactics and built upon the ideological imperatives that had inspired them in 1840 and 1844. As a result, third party inroads on the Northern Whig vote again proved to be minimal, nearly as unimpressive as the Liberty party's had been four years earlier. Victorious Zachary Taylor retained 98 percent of the national vote the Whigs had received in 1844, and over 95 percent of that total throughout the free states. Immediately following the election, moreover, the Free Soilers' independent organization, weak from the outset on state and local levels, collapsed and the party never regained its structural coherence. Northern Whiggery obviously continued to hold the devotion of a large voting public whose motives ranged from reflexive partisanship to an ever increasing deep concern for protecting the value and destiny of "free labor" in America.[33] For one last time, in a national campaign where the issue of slavery's expansion was emphasized as never before, Northern Whiggery demonstrated again that it was able to contain in its framework of two party conflict this most explosive ideologically laden question.

In the process, however, patterns of antislavery within the Whig party first provoked by abolitionists even before 1840 still continued to deepen and spread. Such was the case despite the departure of Giddings, Sumner, Julian and others like them and also despite the fact that the original, radical emancipationist aims of the Liberty party had now been subsumed under the Free Soil banner. As they had in 1844, the great names of Northern Whiggery reiterated that only their party would "rightfully claim the appellation of the *Free Soil* party." Votes cast for Free Soiler Van Buren would, they warned, simply guarantee that Democrats would again "steal" the election, replaying Polk's victory (thanks to Birney) over Clay four years earlier. Only a Taylor victory could keep slavery out of western territories, and assure "the triumph of free soil."[34] By applying the precedents of 1844, Northern Whiggery had again succeeded in blunting naked sectionalism in Yankee politics, helping the national party thereby to weather the subsequent crises of 1849–50.

Yet in terms of the Northern party's maintenance of ideological flexibility on slavery, the cost was certainly clear and the result of now well-established trends. Horace Greeley accurately sensed this continuing development, writing in the aftermath of the 1848 campaign that "the lagging majority" of voters and politicians during the election had been "brought up to the standards of devotion to free labor" demanded by the Free Soilers. And as

Greeley also knew, the spread of sectional ideology now involved Northern Democrats as well as Northern Whigs, for both parties now felt compelled to vie for "free soil" credentials in order to blunt the impact of the third party while also contesting with each other. Such circumstances, Greeley understood, only tended to reinforce sectional proclivities everywhere in the North's two party system: " 'Van Buren and Free Soil' have triumphed in making even the venal and time-serving, lip-deep Free soilers vociferous for 'Taylor and Free Soil or Cass and Free Soil.' "[35] The two-party system, Whiggery included, had endured. But the presidential election of 1848 had also shown that the spread of slavery in the future would be regarded as anathema, especially among Whigs whose party had now been so extensively and irrevocably influenced by ten years' experience with abolitionists, with sectionally motivated third party challenges, and with multiplying antislavery elements in its own ranks.

In the aftermath of the Compromise of 1850, events worked toward a final resolution of this mutually reinforcing tension in Whiggery between sectionalism and party coherence. An infinitely complicated mixture of issues and extended state-level coalitions between both major parties and the Free Soilers overtook politics in the North, obscuring and eroding parties' identities even as it mixed anti-Southern feelings with disruptive partisan conflicts over nativism, temperance, religion and other localized issues. Yet as this Byzantine process unfolded, the great antislavery architects of the Republican party, most from maverick antislavery Whig antecedents, also began to explore the pathways to high office.[36] The rising careers of Charles Sumner, Henry Wilson, Ben Wade, Salmon Chase, Thaddeus Stevens, George W. Julian and Zachariah Chandler, among others, now measured the extent to which antislavery ideology, through its long history as a part of Northern Whiggery, had now come to attach itself to the intricate multi-issue politics, post-1850, in the free states.[37] Thus, when the Kansas-Nebraska Bill was enacted with full support of the Southern Whigs in Congress, members of the Northern branch, now so exhaustively exposed to sectional pressures already weakened internally, and influenced by their party's antislavery history, spurned their Southern colleagues and cheered as political structures began to collapse.

In this manner, Northern Whigs finally resolved the paradoxical relationship with antislavery, which had for so long permitted their party to uphold order in the nation's politics by appropriating sectional ideology and incorporating anti-Southern voters and politicians into its ranks. As Whiggery fragmented and parties formed anew along sectional lines, political avenues to civil war suddenly became far more numerous and easier to explore. The day had finally passed when free state voters could look to the Whigs to advance "free labor's" crucial interests while maintaining a national party through which North and South could unite on common grounds.

The claim of some historians that the political collapse of the 1850's and even Lincoln's election can be linearly traced to the election of 1844, or even the "gag rule" struggles constitutes gross oversimplification.[38] It underestimates the complexities of antebellum politics on all levels and risks the fallacy of seeking the causes of events in their consequences alone. Yet for all these proper cautionaries, the Whig party's antislavery legacy, dating from the 1830's and 1840's, contributed substantially to the disruptions of the 1850's. After the Kansas-Nebraska crisis, the party's interaction with antislavery elements, which had been so long in building, could finally be contained no more within partisan boundaries. Centrifugal forces of sectionalism, first appearing in the 1830's, had, at last, become sufficiently powerful to overwhelm the Northern Whig's capacity to transmute antislavery politics into party loyalty.

NOTES

1. Lynn L. Marshall, "The Strange Stillbirth of the Whig Party," *American Historical Review*, 72 (January, 1967): 455–68. For voting patterns on slavery, see Thomas B. Alexander, *Sectional Stress and Party Strength: A Computer Analysis of Roll-Call Voting Patterns in the United States House of Representatives, 1836–1860* (Nashville: Vanderbilt University Press, 1967), pp. 11–15.

2. Alexander, *Sectional Stress*, pp. 11–15; Joel H. Silbey, *The Shrine of Party: Congressional Voting Behavior, 1841–1852* (Pittsburgh: University of Pittsburgh Press, 1967), pp. 35–66; William J. Cooper, Jr., *The South and the Politics of Slavery, 1828–1856* (Baton Rouge: Louisiana State University Press, 1978), chaps. 1–3.

3. For discussion of the various elements of continuing party unity, see David J. Russo, "The Major Issues of the Jacksonian Period and the Development of Party Loyalty in Congress, 1830–1840," *Transactions of the American Philosophical Society*, 62 (1975): 4–32; Herbert Ershkowitz and William Shade, "Consensus or Conflict? Political Behavior in the State Legislatures During the Jacksonian Era," *Journal of American History*, 58 (December 1971): 591–622; Thomas O'Connor, *The Lords of the Loom: The Cotton Whigs and the Coming of the Civil War* (New York: Charles Scribner's Sons, 1968), pp. 1–92; Silbey, *Shrine of Party*, pp. 1–66; Glyndon Van Deusen, "Some Aspects of Whig Thought and Theory in the Jacksonian Period," *American Historical Review*, 63 (March, 1958): 305–22; Michael F. Holt, *The Political Crisis of the 1850's* (New York: John Wiley & Sons, 1978), esp. pp. 17–33.

4. See Cooper, *Politics of Slavery*, passim, for the clearest exposition of this process and also William Barney, *The Road to Secession* (New York: Praeger Publishers, 1968), passim.

5. This composite characterization is drawn from a multitude of sources, but especially from Whitney Cross, *The Burnt Over District: The Social and Intellectual History of Enthusiastic Religion in Western New York, 1800–1850* (Ithaca: Cornell University Press, 1950), chaps. 1–3; Paul E. Johnson, *A Shopkeeper's Millenium: Society and Revivals in Rochester, New York, 1815–1837* (New York: Hill and Wang, 1978), pp. 15–135; David M. Ludlum, *Social Ferment in Vermont* (New

York: Columbia University Press, 1939), pp. 1–62; James Brewer Stewart, *Joshua Giddings and the Tactics of Radical Politics* (Cleveland: Press of Case Western Reserve University, 1970), pp. 1–36; Patrick Riddleburger, *George Washington Julian: A Study in Nineteenth Century Reform and Politics* (Indianapolis: Indiana Historical Bureau, 1966), pp. 1–45; Ronald P. Formisano, *The Birth of Mass Political Parties, Michigan, 1827–1861* (Princeton: Princeton University Press, 1971), pp. 3–55; Leonard Richards, *Gentlemen of Property and Standing: Antiabolition Mobs in Jacksonian America* (New York: Oxford University Press, 1970), esp. pp. 131–55; Michael A. McManis, "Range Ten, Town Four: A Social History of Hudson, Ohio, 1799–1840" (Ph.D. diss., Case Western Reserve University, 1976); James H. Stuckey, "The Formation of Leadership Groups in a Midwest Frontier Town, Canton, Ohio" (Ph.D. diss., Case Western Reserve University, 1975). Two works that concentrate on the social makeup of the Liberty party are also pertinent here, since the close political affinity between antislavery Whigs in the North and Liberty men is obvious. See Gerald Sorin, *The New York Abolitionists: A Case of Political Radicalism* (Westport, Conn.: Greenwood Press, 1971), passim, and especially Alan M. Kraut, "The Forgotten Reformers: A Profile of Third Party Abolitionists in Antebellum New York," in Lewis Perry and Michael Fellman, eds., *Antislavery Reconsidered: New Perspectives on the Abolitionists* (Baton Rouge: Louisiana State University Press, 1978), pp. 119–45.

6. See especially Bertram Wyatt-Brown, "Prelude to Abolitionism: Sabbatarian Politics and the Rise of the Second Party System," *Journal of American History,* 58 (April, 1971): 316–45; Formisano, *The Birth of Mass Parties,* pp. 103–64; Johnson, *A Shopkeeper's Millenium,* pp. 79–135; Steven C. Fox, "Group Bases of Ohio Political Behavior, 1803–1848" (Ph.D. diss., University of Cincinnati, 1973), passim; Lee Benson, *The Concept of Jacksonian Democracy: New York as a Test Case* (Princeton: Princeton University Press, 1961), pp. 186–207.

7. The term "political pietism" coined by John L. Thomas is cited in John Mayfield, *Rehearsal for Republicanism: Free Soil and the Politics of Anti-Slavery* (Port Washington, N.Y.: Kennikat Press, 1980), pp. 35, 207n.3. For discussions of anti-evangelicalism and its religious, ethnic, and class bases, see Wyatt-Brown, "Prelude to Abolitionism"; Formisano, *Birth of Mass Parties,* pp. 104–11, 137–94; Johnson, *Shopkeeper's Millenium,* pp. 73–77, 129–35; Alan Dawley, *Class and Community: The Industrial Revolution in Lynn* (Cambridge: Harvard University Press, 1979), pp. 36–44, 113–22; Leonard D. Richards, *"Gentlemen of Property and Standing,"* pp. 145–48; McManis, "Range Ten, Town Four," passim, and Stuckey, "The Formation of Leadership Groups," passim.

8. For a particularly enlightening work that develops this theme in relation to Whiggery see Daniel Walker Howe, *The Political Culture of the American Whigs* (Chicago: University of Chicago Press, 1980), pp. 96–122, 150–80, 181–209. More generally, see John L. Hammond, *The Politics of Benevolence; Revival Religion and American Voting Behavior* (Norwood, N.J.: Ablex Publishing Corporation, 1979), pp. 36–105. Some trenchant interpretations linking Whiggery to antislavery's "modernizing" tendencies are found in Jonathan Glickstein, "Poverty is not Slavery; Abolitionists and the Competitive Labor Market," in Perry and Fellman, eds., *Antislavery Reconsidered,* pp. 195–218; Eric Foner, *Free Soil, Free Labor, Free Men: The Ideology of the Republican Party Before the Civil War* (New York: Oxford University Press, 1970), and "The Causes of the Civil War: Recent Interpretations

and New Directions," *Civil War History,* 20 (September, 1974): 197–214, also explores the themes of modernization as related to antislavery as a broad movement in politics.

9. Richards, *"Gentlemen of Property and Standing,"* pp. 148–49; Theodore M. Hammett, "Ideology and Interest; Two Mobs of Jacksonian Boston," *Journal of American History,* 62 (December, 1976): 845–68; O'Connor, *Lords of the Loom,* pp. 1–92.

10. Ibid. See also Bertram Wyatt-Brown, "The Abolitionist Controversy; Men of Blood, Men of God: James Gordon Bennett, William Lloyd Garrison and John Brown," in Howard H. Quint and Milton Cantor, eds., *Men, Women and Issues in American History,* 2 vols. (Homewood, Ill.: Dorsey Press, 1975), pp. 216–30. All of these anti-abolitionist themes can be followed in the *New York Herald* issue for September-October, 1835. For treatments of the Democratic party's extensive structural involvement with upholding slavery, see Richard H. Brown, "The Missouri Crisis, Slavery and the Politics of Jacksonianism," *South Atlantic Quarterly,* 65 (Winter, 1966); 55–72; Leonard Richards, "The Jacksonians and Slavery," in Perry and Fellman, eds., *Antislavery Reconsidered,* pp. 99–118.

11. Henry Brewster Stanton to James G. Birney, March 21, 1839, in Dwight L. Dumond, ed., *Letters of James Gillespie Birney, 1831–1851,* 2 vols. (New York: D. Appleton-Century Co., Inc., 1938), 1:531–532; See also the *Emancipator,* June 10, 1841; *Philanthropist,* November 11, December 9, 1840.

12. Stewart, *Giddings,* pp. 53–56; speech of William Slade in the U.S. *Congressional Globe,* 26th Congress, 1st Session, VIII, *Appendix,* 401–3; Arthur B. Darling, *Political Changes in Massachusetts, 1824–1848* (New Haven: Yale University Press, 1925), pp. 268–73; *Boston Atlas,* June 20, 1840; Glyndon Van Deusen, *William Henry Seward: Lincoln's Secretary of State and the Negotiations of the Alaska Purchase* (New York: Oxford University Press, 1967), pp. 72–80; Van Deusen, *Horace Greeley, Nineteenth Century Crusader* (Philadelphia: University of Pennsylvania Press, 1953), pp. 41–45.

13. Henry Brewster Stanton to James G. Birney, March 21, 1839; Gamaliel Bailey to James G. Birney, February 21, 1840, in Dumond, ed., *Birney Letters* 1:531–32; 541–43; Joshua Giddings to John Crowell, March 21, 1840, William Henry Harrison Papers, Library of Congress; Seth Gates to Joshua Giddings, September 21, 1840, Giddings Papers, Ohio Historical Society.

14. Ludlum, *Social Ferment in Vermont,* pp. 128–30; Darling, *Political Changes in Massachusetts,* pp. 265–78; Richard H. Sewell, *Ballots for Freedom: Antislavery Politics in the United States, 1837–1860* (New York, 1976), p. 77 (quotations); Formisano, *Birth of Mass Parties,* pp. 27–30; Stewart, *Giddings,* pp. 53–56.

15. Richards, "Jacksonians and Slavery, in Perry and Fellman, eds., *Antislavery Reconsidered,* p. 115; Ludlum, *Social Ferment in Vermont,* pp. 80, 130, 230–31; Stewart, *Giddings,* pp. 62–65; Douglas A. Gamble, "Joshua Giddings and the Ohio Abolitionists: A Study in Radical Politics," *Ohio History,* 88 (Winter, 1979): 37–56; James M. McPherson, "The Fight Against the Gag Rule: Joshua Leavitt ` the Antislavery Insurgency in the Whig Party, 1839–1842," *Journal of Negr'* 58 (July, 1963): 177–95. See also the correspondence from Seth Gat' Smith and James Birney reprinted in Dumond, ed., *Birney Letters* 2:' 685–86 for the years 1840–1843, and Seth Gates to Gerrit Smith' 1841, Gerrit Smith Papers, Syracuse University Library.

16. McPherson, "Joshua Leavitt," Gamble, "Joshua Giddings and the Ohio Abolitionists"; James Brewer Stewart, "The Aims and Impact of Garrisonian Abolitionism, 1840–1860," *Civil War History*, 15 (September, 1969): 197–212; Gilbert Hobbs Barnes, *The Antislavery Impulse, 1830–1844* (New York: Harcourt, Brace and World, 1933), pp. 181–90.

17. James Brewer Stewart, *Holy Warriors: The Abolitionists and American Slavery* (New York: Hill and Wang, 1976), pp. 80–84; Barnes, *Antislavery Impulse*, pp. 109–45.

18. Stewart, *Giddings*, pp. 75–76; *Liberator*, April 1, 1842; *Philanthropist*, April 6, 1842; *Emancipator*, March 31, 1842.

19. *Ohio State Journal*, March 30, 1842.

20. *Cleveland Herald*, March 30, 1842; *Boston Atlas*, April 2, 1842; *Pittsburgh Courier*, April 1, 1842; see also *Boston Courier*, March 26, 1842; *New York Express*, quoted in the Ashtabula *Sentinel*, April 9, 1842.

21. Richards, "Jacksonians and Slavery," in Perry and Fellman, eds., *Antislavery Reconsidered*, pp. 107–10; Alexander, *Sectional Stress and Party Strength*, pp. 41–56.

22. Thomas Morris, *Free Men All: Personal Liberty Laws of the North 1780–1861* (Baltimore: Johns Hopkins University Press, 1974), pp. 71–130; Paul Finkelman, "*Prigg v. Pennsylvania* and the Northern State Courts: Anti-Slavery Use of a Proslavery Decision," *Civil War History*, 25 (March, 1979): 5–35; Alan M. Kraut and Phyllis F. Field, "Politics Versus Principles: The Partisan Response to 'Bible Politics' in New York State," *Civil War History*, 25 (June, 1979): 101–18; Edgar Allen Holt, *Party Politics in Ohio, 1840–1850* (Columbus: F. J. Heer Printing Co., 1930), pp. 244–45. As Field and Kraut demonstrate, Whig espousals of antislavery goals and racial egalitarianism were often made opportunistically with the aim of disrupting the Liberty party only, not of achieving stated reforms. Whatever the Whig motives, however, the effect of these politics on Liberty party strength was devastating.

23. Silbey, *Shrine of Party*, pp. 49–56.

24. Ibid., p. 19; Sewell, *Ballots for Freedom*, pp. 85, 109–10.

25. James A. Briggs to Oran Follett, July 26, 1843, Oran Follett mss., Cincinnati Historical Society.

26. Stewart, *Giddings*, pp. 96–98; *Emancipator*, September 11, 1844; William Slade to Joshua Giddings, June 6, 1844; Seth Gates to Joshua Giddings, October 2, 1844, Giddings mss., Ohio Historical Society.

27. Mayfield, *Rehearsal for Republicanism*, pp. 39–40; Theodore Clarke Smith, *The Liberty and Free Soil Parties in the Northwest* (New York: Longmans, Green and Company, 1897) pp. 69–84; "Pacificus" [Joshua Giddings], *Western Reserve Chronicle*, November 8, November 15, November 22, December 6, December 13, 1852.

28. For various points of view on the Liberty party's impact on the New York vote, see Benson, *Concept of Jacksonian Democracy*, pp. 260, 267 and passim; Hammond, *Politics of Benevolence*, p. 87; Smith, *Liberty and Free Soil Parties*, pp. 80–82.

29. See Holt, *Political Crisis of the 1850's*, pp. 42–43 for this judgment. The viewpoint of this essay, however, does not accord with Holt's further conclusion that because Texas annexation was presented as a partisan issue it automatically ·rengthened the intersectional two party system. Instead, it will be argued, the

manner in which Northern Whigs transformed anti-Texas annexation into a partisan issue simultaneously caused sectionalism to grow within their party, with consequences that were, in the long run, destabilizing as well as immediately unifying. Holt's related position, that political leaders generally manipulated sectional issues for conscious partisan ends is also questioned here to some extent. Among Northern Whigs, at least, it seems that antislavery constituencies and their spokesmen caused antislavery ideology and issues to have, from the first, a spontaneous and legitimate setting within the party. That many Whig leaders did manipulate antislavery issues, however, is beyond question.

30. See, for example, Robert F. Dalzell, *Daniel Webster and the Trials of American Nationalism* (Boston: Houghton Mifflin Company, 1973), p. 92; Van Deusen, *Seward*, p. 102; Kinley J. Brauer, *Cotton Versus Conscience: Massachusetts Politics and Southwestern Expansion 1843–1848* (Lexington: University of Kentucky Press, 1967), chap. 3.

31. William Seward to Edward A. Stanbury, September 2, 1844, quoted in Van Deusen, *Seward,* p. 103.

32. Holt, *Political Crisis of the 1850's,* pp. 60–64.

33. The best analyses of election results are to be found in Mayfield, *Rehearsal for Republicanism,* pp. 191–202.

34. Boston, *Atlas,* September 14, 1848; *New York Tribune,* October 7, 1848 (quotations). For general treatments of Whig antislavery and the 1848 elections, see Frederick J. Blue, *The Free Soilers: Third Party Politics, 1848–1854* (Urbana: University of Illinois Press, 1973), pp. 115–118; Joseph G. Rayback, *Free Soil: The Election of 1848* (Lexington: University Press of Kentucky, 1969), pp. 239–59.

35. Greeley quoted in Rayback, *Free Soil,* p. 309.

36. There is a growing literature on these shifting tides of state-level politics, and their relation to the slow erosion and sectionalization of both major parties. See, for example, Formisano, *Birth of Mass Parties,* pp. 210–38; Stewart, *Giddings,* pp. 172–79; Kevin Sweeney, "Rum, Romanism, Representation and Reform: Coalitional Politics in Massachusetts, 1847–1853," *Civil War History,* 22 (June, 1976): 116–37; Michael F. Holt, "The Politics of Impatience: Origins of Know-Nothingism," *Journal of American History,* 60 (April, 1973): 309–31. The most extended general discussion of this topic is found in Holt, *Political Crisis of the 1850's,* pp. 101–38.

37. See David Donald, *Charles Sumner and the Coming of the Civil War* (New York: Alfred A. Knopf, 1961), pp. 182–210; Richard H. Abbot, *Cobbler in Congress: The Life of Henry Wilson, 1812–1875* (Lexington: University Press of Kentucky, 1972), pp. 44–64; Hans L. Trefousse, *Ben Wade: Radical Republican From Ohio* (New York: Twayne Publishing, 1963), pp. 60–71; Riddleburger, *Julian,* pp. 91–109; Fawn Brodie, *Thaddeus Stevens: Scourge of the South* (New York: W. W. Norton Co., Inc., 1959), pp. 121–22; Formisano, *Birth of Mass Parties,* pp. 204, 278; Foner, *Free Soil, Free Labor, Free Men,* pp. 124–33.

38. See, for example, Gilbert Hobbs Barnes, *The Antislavery Impulse, 1830–1844* (New York: Harcourt, Brace and World, 1933), pp. 191–97; Dwight L. Dumond, *The Antislavery Origins of the Civil War of the United States* (Ann Arbor: University of Michigan Press, 1939), pp. 83–114; Stanley Elkins, *Slavery: A Problem of American Institutional and Intellectual Life* (Chicago: University of Chicago Press, 1959), pp. 115–90; Glyndon Van Deusen, *The Jacksonian Era* (New York: Harper & Row, 1962), pp. 149–50.

2

A Window on the Abolitionist Constituency: Antislavery Petitions, 1836–1839

Edward Magdol

Although many of the founding members of the American Anti-Slavery Society (AAS) abhorred party politics, they did not hesitate to launch a campaign of mass political protest against slavery. The key weapon in that campaign, which began in the 1830's, was the petition. Antislavery petitions, written appeals for change, were drafted by the AAS as well as by state societies and religious organizations. Many thousands of Americans signed these documents of protest that were submitted to legislatures and Congress prior to the Civil War. Petitions were sent to Congress advocating the abolition of slavery and the slave trade in the District of Columbia; opposing the annexation of slaveholding Texas; protesting the passage of gag rules to table petitions that arrived in Washington; and objecting to the further admission of slave states to the Union. Whatever their particular objection to slavery, citizens from many different walks of life could make known their protest with a stroke of the pen.[1]

The American Anti-Slavery Society in 1837 launched a well-organized and systematic massive petition campaign against slavery in the District of Columbia and on other issues in order to defeat a congressional ban imposed on such petitions a year earlier. Abolitionists hoped to embarrass Congress on the constitutional question, stimulate a national debate and focus attention on slavery in the nation and possibly even achieve emancipation in the capital, if no place else.

The managers of this effort, James G. Whittier, Henry B. Stanton, and Theodore Weld, took their job seriously, and so did the signers. The 1837 campaign made significant news and aroused slave owners who were already nervous and skittish because of the Nat Turner insurgency and the growing power of Northeastern capitalism. John C. Calhoun charged that the petitions came from "soured and agitated communities." Calhoun's and other southern legislators' alarms understandably increased as the 1837, 1838, and 1839 petition campaigns were completed. Northerners also shared their apprehension. In New York an Oneida County grand jury condemned the 1836 petitions as "dangerous nuisances." Representative Ely Moore feared that abolitionist petitions were being used by Federalists to attack Democrats and white workingmen. Neither of these criticisms nor the congressional gag diminished the abolitionists' enthusiasm for the campaign.[2]

The 1838–39 petition campaign exceeded even the well organized one of a year earlier. Extending beyond the ranks of the abolition societies, it garnered 2 million signatures on various antislavery issues. This was at a time when national membership in the American Anti-Slavery Society local organizations numbered only about 100,000. The progress of the campaigns may be judged from the average number of signatures per petition: 32 in 1836–37, 59 in 1837–38, 91 in 1838–39, and 107 in 1839–40. Half a million signatures were gathered in 1838–39 specifically for the abolition of slavery in the District of Columbia. However, abolitionists failed to translate that voluminous response into actual votes for their Liberty party in 1840. The mere 7,000 votes for its presidential candidate, James G. Birney, that year revealed how much abolitionists would have to learn before they could claim political success.[3]

Signature collectors seriously pursued, debated and agitated their subjects. Signing a petition after a session with an avid abolitionist affirmed the commitment adopted by the petitioner and momentarily identified him or her with the organized movement. On the other hand, the act of signing crystallized an amorphous antislavery sentiment without necessarily drawing the signer into an abolitionist society. One Providence, Rhode Island, correspondent, "Candor," reminded newspaper readers of a distinction to be made between "antislavery men" and their public.

The abolitionists . . . present their paper to many who are not with them on other points, but who believe that Congress has this power [to abolish slavery] and think it ought to be exercised. . . . Why hold up the names of some of the first men among us to reproach, merely because they have the magnanimity to *say* what we all think and feel, if we think and feel at all—viz: that slavery is a terrible evil, and we pray God and pray men to abolish it as speedily as possible.[4]

"Candor's" concern suggests that signers of abolitionist petitions could not have placed their names on the papers casually, capriciously or as mere tokens of friendship or familiarity. The petitions were serious instruments of political action.

As an instrument for political action, the antislavery petition has served the historian as a barometer for measuring the intensity of reform sentiment among antebellum Americans. However, such lists of signatures can also aid historians seeking to explore abolitionism's grass roots. During the last decade, especially, scholars have increasingly abandoned the approach to the abolitionists that all but exclusively focuses upon individual reformers and, most often, those in the vanguard of the movement. Instead, historians have begun the arduous task of identifying the movement's rank and file, who have remained anonymous in the absence of letters, diaries and other written sources.[5] Names on petitions provide a starting point for identifying those Americans who chose to express opposition to slavery.

Motives are another matter. Thus far neither the status anxiety hypothesis borrowed from social psychology nor the view of abolitionism as merely an extension of the Second Great Awakening have proven persuasive explanations of why some Americans demanded slavery's abolition.[6] Only a few historians have gone beyond the impressionistic applications of theories of mass behavior and attempted to systematically analyze the social character of abolitionism's rank and file.[7] The use of demographic data to sketch a social profile of the anonymous reformers who signed petitions can illuminate the social character of abolitionism's popular base, offering particular insight into the identity of those who sought relief for the slave through politics in the 1830's.[8]

Part of the difficulty in understanding the abolitionist who petitioned his government for change has been the historian's tendency to isolate antebellum reform from the larger social forces that were permanently refashioning the United States politically, socially and economically even as abolitionists were issuing their protest. Abolitionism did not exist in a vacuum, nor were abolitionists isolated from larger, dramatic socioeconomic changes taking place in the United States. Even as historians have become increasingly sensitive to the relationship of abolitionism to political realignment, the nature of the party system and women's struggle for political equality, there remains a dearth of studies linking abolitionism with antebellum economic change. Little has been written about the relationship of abolition to America's budding industrial revolution. There is abundant evidence that the abolitionists and their contemporaries were well aware of a link. In an era rich with anti-monopoly and anti-aristocratic rhetoric, and rich with assertions of equal rights and the labor theory of value, attacks upon slavery struck sympathetic chords among rising manufacturers, tradesmen, mechanics, and artisans. The New England labor leader and land reformer William West told abolitionist debaters that he and his followers believed in the slogan, "Down with all slavery, chattel and wages." And in New York City, artisans and shopkeepers increased their proportions of antislavery petition signers through the 1830's. Middle-class and mechanic and artisan class aspirations appear to have been encouraged by the political stage of abolitionism, beginning with the petition campaign.[9]

Pursuing the study of antislavery petition signers in four northeastern cities undergoing the beginnings of industrialization permits the political struggle over slavery to be viewed in its relationship to antebellum economic change. City directories, census rolls, tax assessments and church records have been used to create a statistical profile that includes petitioners' occupations, worth in real property, religious affiliations and nativity. Such statistical measures can never expose the individual motives of those who signed memorials to Congress over a century and a half ago. They can, however, suggest the kind of individual to whom antislavery activists turned for support in their political efforts.

This essay relies upon a sampling of 1,624 from among the three-quarters of a million signers of the abolitionist petitions that were showered upon Congress by the American Anti-Slavery Society branches from 1836 to 1839. Elimination of illegible, unidentified and duplicate signatures reduced the sample to 677 men in four cities, chosen because of their varying conditions of industrialization. Those cities were Utica, Rome, and Schenectady, New York, and Fall River, Massachusetts. They also differ in the strengths of their antislavery movements, and, for this study, in the availability of data. Much more social and economic information was available in the larger of the four, Utica and Fall River, and thus gave them greater weight in the resulting profile. One hundred and fifteen Utica men that I regard as leaders have been isolated from that total of 677 in order to permit a comparison with rank and file signers.[10]

The cities chosen for this study were in various stages of production of goods. Movement toward industrialization in some of them occurred during contemporaneous religious revivals, abolitionist agitation, social reform and workingmen's movements. Since these all claimed public attention and were woven into a web of concerns, few persons could have remained ignorant of these movements. Moreover, since improvement or changes in society were their objectives, these movements tended to intersect with one another. Thus the anti-aristocratic and anti-monopolistic workingmen's movement, prominent in New York City during the Jacksonian era seems to have been intertwined with a basically similar anti-aristocratic and anti-monopolistic abolitionist movement. This is also suggested by Leonard Richards' findings about the 1835 Utica anti-abolitionist riot. It appears to have been an occasion for physical conflict based on differing value concepts between the mob of anti-abolitionist "gentlemen of property and standing" and anti-slavery mechanics, free laborers, merchants (shopkeepers) and rising manufacturers. One "class-conscious" correspondent of Utica's antislavery *Friend of Man,* writing in support of the right of petition, stated, "We will say to the men in Congress, Our Government is a democracy. We, the farmers and mechanics, are the rulers. We are the governors—you, our servants."[11]

Utica, the first of the four cities studied, was the center of antislavery agitation for western and northern New York.[12] It was also a prospering preindustrial town of 10,000 people. Its men found opportunities in workshops, offices, banks, insurance companies, railroad and canal shipping and in their own stores as shopkeepers, wholesale merchants and clerks. Here William Goodell established the *Friend of Man;* Alvan Stewart, a wealthy abolitionist attorney, practiced; Beriah Green headed the Oneida Institute in nearby Whitesboro where Henry Highland Garnet, the future black leader, and Theodore Weld, the future abolitionist evangelical, were students. Missionary Methodist and Baptist newspapers were published in Utica in the 1830's. The New York State Anti-Slavery Society chose the city for its state convention in 1835 but a mob attack, inspired and led by "gentlemen of property and standing," violently dispersed the delegates. The affair became well known as the Utica riot of 1835. Six months later abolitionists received a far more sympathetic response from their fellow citizens.

In March 1836, Weld addressed hundreds of Utica citizens in a series of sixteen lectures with no serious opposition. There was no violent disruption of his abolitionist speeches as there had been in other towns. Instead, an enthusiastic response was evident in the report that 600 names had been added to the Utica Anti-Slavery Society membership. A petition of 1,200 names, "a majority of them men" and "probably a majority of the legal voters in the city," was sent to Congress.[13]

In addition, Utica had become a center of other social movements. Reform, anti-Masonic, and workingmen's political party activity made Utica a hub of social change in upstate New York. But its hectic prosperity was paling even before the 1837 economic crash. Conscious of even greater advances in population and prosperity in industrializing towns, Utica's commercial leaders decided to introduce large-scale manufacturing in the 1840's. Challenging examples of successful industrial, rather than mercantile, capitalism lay close at hand in the nearby factory towns of New York Mills, New Hartford, Whitestown and Saquoit. Utica's society, culture and economy were infused with energy, expectation and change; and with uncertainty as its leaders contemplated factories in its future.

Fall River, the second of the cities under study, had gone through its industrial boom a decade earlier than Utica.[14] By the time of the organized abolitionist crusade the city was in the center of the American industrial revolution and a major factory metropolis. By 1833, there were thirteen manufacturers of cotton, wool and calico; factories producing iron, nails and textile machinery. At least 40,000 spindles were in operation in this industrial town of 5,000 inhabitants. It grew from a population of 4,159 in 1830 to one of 6,738 in 1840. New housing had to be constructed and new streets were created. Quaker, Baptist and Calvinist churches informed the community's values. The city also proved to be fertile ground for immediatist abolitionism, equal rights ideology and the workingmen's movement of the 1840's. The wide-ranging kinship network among established families such as the Bordens, Bowens, Durfees and Chases maintained an important integrative influence over the community. The domination of Fall River life by these family groupings reinforced the hegemony of a burgeoning and enlightened industrial capitalist class.

Yet portents of disharmony and challenge to that hegemony appeared. One was the establishment of a worker's cooperative store in 1833 by the Fall River Mechanics Association. It was intended to break the monopoly of the manufacturers' mill stores. Another was the developing ten-hour-day movement among workers in the 1840's, aided by the abolitionist Reverend Asa Bronson. A man of "massive proportions," Bronson was pastor of the First Baptist Church and president of the Fall River Anti-Slavery Society. He was forced out of his church in 1844 for his ten-hour activity by "a few of our aristocratic manufacturers, who love wealth more than justice." It probably was no accident that in 1834 the antislavery society was organized at the First Baptist Meeting House with 1,000 persons present. Nor was it an accident that Bronson's was among Fall River's nine votes for the abolitionist Liberty party in 1840. With him in that small band were two mechanics, a calico printer, a clerk, a boss carpenter at the print factory, and a prominent local bookseller. The Baptist church appeared to be a haven for radicalism under Bronson's pastorate. The meeting house provided a concourse in the 1830's shared by Quaker and Baptist manufacturers, merchants and mechanics. If radicalism went with the smell of leather in Lynn and Haverhill, it appeared to go with the warp and woof of wool and cotton in Fall River.[15]

While Fall River was the most advanced in industrialization of the four cities under study, Rome and Schenectady were probably the least. They were primarily in a small-shop and handicraft stage of development. However, their forges and blacksmith shops helped to bring them into the orbit of nearby manufacturing centers. Above all, their proximity to canal and railroad routes linked them to emerging regional centers of manufacturing, such as Albany's stove and iron goods industries and the cotton and wool mills surrounding Utica. The latter was a major commercial metropolis on the Erie Canal system, its prosperity due to the carrying trade and the great diversity of craftmen's shops producing everything from combs to carriages.[16]

During the 1830's all four cities were involved in the transition from craftsman's shop to the factory system of manufacturing, from merchant capitalism to industrial capitalism. Artisans, mechanics and new industrial entrepreneurs were challenging the domination of bankers, merchants, lawyers and landed gentry. Many of these Jacksonians climbing the ladder to economic success and political influence were committed to equal rights ideals. Personal liberty and the abolition of slavery, aristocracy and special privilege would be the fruits of power when they acquired it. Toward that end some added their signatures to antislavery petitions.

The 677 signers in the four towns are 41.7 percent of the 1,624 names found on eight petitions selected from fifteen filed with Congress from the four cities between 1836 and 1839.[17] In addition, the names of Utica abolitionist leaders were compiled from the records of the Utica anti-abolitionist riot and antislavery proceedings. Some classes of data were found and linked to those petitioners: occupation (by far the most readily available), age, birthplace, real estate assessment and church affiliation. Not all of these data were found for each of the signers. However, a close approximation of social structure may be discovered in the occupational and property data. Information about petitioners' birthplaces and church memberships permits some additional inferences to be drawn about the cultural influences that might have shaped their attitudes toward reform.

It is clear that these signers were a small portion of the whole male population but a significant proportion of the voting population. If we count only the number of signers on the largest single petitions from each of the four cities, the total (825) constitutes a sample equalling 18 percent of all voters (4,475) in the towns. More significantly, the 677 signers identified in the study constitute 15 percent of the voters. The absence of poll books or other voter records prevents precise identification of individual petitioners as voters. Since turnouts at the polls were high among a newly enfranchised electorate, we may infer that these petitioners were similarly faithful voters. Therefore, the ratio of signers to voters could be considered close to the actual proportions.

The campaign served as the abolitionists' most far-reaching political action before the Liberty party emerged in 1840. The demands made in the petitions may be considered the planks in a "platform" of an incipient "party" and an indication of its potential polling power. The broadest response on a single issue in one locality was on the Texas annexation issue in Fall River. Although the local society claimed only 279 members in 1837 and 1838, its annexation petition bore the signatures of 363 men.[18] Fall River's response echoed a national trend during the 1837–38 campaign. Of the 412,000 petitions sent to the House on all abolition questions, 182,400 registered opposition to annexation. Petitioners for the abolition of slavery and the slave trade in the District of Columbia ran second with a total of 130,000. Petitioners appear to have been more alarmed by the acquisition of additional territory to which slaveholders could bring their bondsmen than by the continuing humiliation of slave trading on the streets of the nation's capital. The circulation of anti-annexation petitions by non-abolitionists as well as by antislavery society members suggests that at least on the annexation issue, the reformers had acquired allies who opposed annexation for reasons having little to do with a moral repugnance toward slavery but perhaps much to do with preserving western soil for free labor.

Merchants, ministers and mechanics were joined by clerks, draymen, lawyers, farmers and some laborers in petitioning against slavery. Although social classes are difficult to define in the fluid preindustrial and early industrial eras, men may still be classified by their occupations. By the nineteenth century a man's job or "calling" was already a time-honored American way of delineating his social rank. This relationship between occupation and status is reflected in nineteenth-century city directories, which scrupulously included all craftsmen, tradesmen, professionals and men of property but often omitted laborers and transient and casual workers. Social historians regard occupation as an approximation of social class in the rapidly specializing economy of the mid-nineteenth century. In this study I have adopted with modification the occupational structure used by Peter Knights in his study of antebellum Boston.[19]

The nine occupational categories that I have used begin with the unskilled and in ascending order include skilled, commercial and professional, managerial, entrepreneurial and official men, as well as some farmers found within city limits (see Table 2.1). Some such as "law student" and "medical

Table 2.1
OCCUPATION GROUPS OF PETITIONERS IN UTICA, ROME, AND
SCHENECTADY, NEW YORK, AND FALL RIVER, MASSACHUSETTS

Occupation Group	Fall River (268)	Utica (324)	Rome (17)	Schenectady (62)	Total (671)	Utica Occupations (1837–38) (1,888)
	Percentage of Total					
1. Unskilled-Menial Service	10.1	4.3	—	1.6	6.3	13.2
2. Semiskilled & Service	3.4	4.6	—	4.8	4.0	5.3
3. Proprietor-Manager-Official	21.6	23.8	29.4	16.1	22.4	19.2
4. Skilled	41.4	40.1	41.2	61.3	42.6	42.6
5. Commerce and Sales	4.9	8.6	—	—	6.1	10.3
6. Semiprofessional	0.4	0.3	—	—	0.3	0.7
7. Professional	3.7	6.5	17.6	8.1	5.8	5.2
8. Farmer	9.7	4.6	5.9	—	6.3	1.5
9. Miscellaneous	4.9	7.1	5.9	8.1	6.3	1.9

SOURCES: Occupations were found in: *Utica City Directory, 1834, 1835, 1837, 1839*; Manuscript census, 1850, Utica, Rome, Schenectady, and Fall River; *Schenectady City Directory, 1841–42*; *Fall River City Directory, 1853*; Daniel E. Wager, *Our City and its People, A Descriptive Work on the City of Rome, N.Y.* (Boston, 1896).

student" and others defying precise classification inhabit the "miscellaneous" niche. A man's occupation was more readily available than other bits of information about him, thus yielding data on that item of the profile for 671 of the 677 in the sample population.

The skilled men—carpenters, blacksmiths, tailors, shoemakers, painters, printers, moulders and the like—comprise the largest group (286) and 42.6 percent of the signers in all four cities. It corresponds precisely with the proportion of artisans in Utica's occupational structure, 42.6 percent (Table 2.1). I have compiled that male occupational census from Utica's 1837–38 city directory as a standard with which to compare occupations because it was in a city passing from commercial entrepôt and small-scale preindustrial production to industrial, i.e., factory production. It may be regarded as roughly midway between Rome's and Schenectady's and Fall River's stages of industrialization.[20]

The second largest group consisted of 150 proprietors, managers and government officials (22.4 percent). Grocers and merchants such as shoe dealers, merchant tailors, builders and contractors, manufacturers and town and city civil servants and elected personnel filled this middle-class category. They were joined by 41 clerical, commercial and sales people (6.1 percent); by physicians, lawyers, editors, publishers and clergymen (5.8 percent), and a tiny proportion (0.3 percent) of semiprofessionals such as artists, dentists, and architects. This "white collar" group accounted for 34 percent of the 671 men identified by occupation.

The more commercial character of Utica and the more industrial character of Fall River may be reflected in the ratio of middle-class signers who fall into groups 3, 5, 6, 7 in Table 2.1. Uticans are overrepresented as a whole in these groupings while Fall River petitioners are underrepresented. Among the merchants are small manufacturers who worked at the bench or the forge and who also doubled as sellers of products. Among Utica signers, for example, 77 men are in group 3 (see Table 2.1). Ten were manufacturers and 14 were grocers. The merchants were the largest component of the group, 32 men and among them "maker/sellers." These probably were counterparts of those rising manufacturers who tended to support abolition in Leonard Richard's analysis of the Utica riot victims.

The one-dimensional nature of an occupational structure raises further questions. How can we distinguish employing and master craftsmen from journeymen, especially since we lack journeymen society membership lists? How can we distinguish between employed and employers among sales and commercial people? The answer may be found in adding the dimension of property ownership (see Table 2.2).

The $500-mark as assessed real estate furnishes a dividing line between lower and upper property-owning classes. Some problems are created by the presence of otherwise economically well-off occupational groups in the

Table 2.2
REAL PROPERTY ASSESSMENTS OF OCCUPATION GROUPS
(IN PERCENTAGES)

Occupation Group	No Real Estate	Less than $200	$201 to $500	$501 to $1,000	$1,001 to $5,000	$5,000 and over	Total (N = 563)	Percentage
Unskilled and Menial Service	91.9	0	5.4	2.7	0	0	37	6.6
Semiskilled and Service	86.4	4.5	9.1	0	0	0	22	3.9
Proprietor, Manager, Official	54.9	1.5	13.5	20.3	4.5	5.3	133	23.6
Skilled	73.3	0.8	13.7	9.4	2.0	0.8	255	45.3
Commerce and Sales	73.7	2.6	10.5	7.9	2.6	2.6	38	6.7
Semiprofessional	50.0	0	50.0	0	0	0	2	0.3
Professional	78.4	0	0	13.5	5.4	2.7	37	6.6
Farmer	60.6	0	12.1	27.3	0	0	33	5.9
Miscellaneous	83.3	0	16.7	0	0	0	6	1.1
TOTALS	70.3	1.1	11.9	12.3	2.5	2.0	563	100.0

SOURCES: Utica, *Tax Assessment Book*, 1835 (Utica Public Library); Fall River, *Tax Assessment Roll*, 1838 (Fall River Historical Society).

lower property class—some professionals, proprietors (petty merchants) and small farmers. Nonetheless, the division helps to indicate who might have been a journeyman and who a master craftsman or employer.

The most striking finding is the large proportion of propertyless men in all occupations. Ninety-one percent of the unskilled and 86 percent of the semiskilled owned no real estate. These were boarders, renters and itinerant laborers of the antebellum period. The larger number of skilled men and the 28 "commerce and sales" persons without real estate probably were journeymen dependent on wages and clerks in stores and offices unable to acquire ownership of a house and lot, and of materials and machines. Thirty-one of the 38 men in the "commerce and sales" group in Table 2.2 were clerks. In addition, 90 percent of the tailors, 77 percent of the shoemakers, 78 percent of the grocers, 90 percent of the laborers and 62 percent of the carpenters owned no property. Artisans, merchants and grocers with real estate tended to cluster in the $500–$1,000 and $1,000–$5,000 categories. The artisans and proprietors above the $500-mark probably were master craftsmen or employers and wholesale and large retail merchants. However, if the dividing line between master and journeymen were raised to $1,000 of real estate, we might introduce a bias toward journeymen.[21]

Two-thirds of the proprietors, managers and officials and all of the professionals with real estate were in the higher brackets, from $501 to more than $5,000. On the other hand the manual labor, skilled, semi-, and unskilled men were predominantly in the modest $201–$1,000 level. There may be yet another indicator of master-journeymen differences among "artisans" in these data. Only 10.6 percent of those with real estate in this group fall in the upper brackets of $1,000 and over. These men probably were the owners of their shops and the employers of the others in the artisan category.

Most of the farmers with real estate were in the middle ranks, $201–$1,000. They appear to have been family farm proprietors or sons of farmers without property of their own and not involved with large-scale commercial agriculture. Like the artisans, they appear to fit in the abolitionists' cherished constituency of "the bone and sinew of society."

An antislavery constituency among middle and lower economic groups emerges from the occupational and real estate data for 563 men (Table 2.2). This partly affirms Richards' uncovering of a preponderance of rising manufacturers and tradesmen among abolitionists in Utica. The data also affirm findings by Alan Kraut about Liberty party votes in the 1840's. And they support John Jentz's study of New York City artisans in the late 1830's. There, too, craftsmen were between 36 and 47 percent of the signers in the late 1830's, when the petition campaign was highly organized and reached the largest number of signers. In New York City, "laborers and other unskilled" comprised between 3.6 and 8.3 percent of the signers during those years.[22] Similarly the cross section of our four cities shows considerable underrepresentation of men in the lowest occupational ranks. Nevertheless, that such men did sign the petitions should be taken seriously as a corrective to the belief that abolitionists appealed only to middle classes, the propertied, educated, skilled and economically successful.

The importance of workers to the abolitionist movement and its petition campaign did not escape William Goodell. His *Friend of Man* reprinted two editorials from newspapers in shoemaker territory. One, in the *Essex Gazette*, voiced its defense of and appreciation of "the real worth of the mechanic[s]" against the imposition upon them by the "aristocracy." The second, in the *Haverhill Gazette*, linked workingmen and abolitionism by addressing the question "Aristocracy vs. Abolition." The editor asserted that the "Aristocracy of the North" stood against the "middle interest men." These were the "mechanics, farmers, and laboring classes" that filled "our ranks of abolition." The question before the nation in the summer of 1836 when this editorial appeared, wrote the editor, was "the right of the laborer, whether white or black, to the fruits of his hard toil."[23]

If the editor appeared to shy away from explicit endorsement of the labor theory of value, he nevertheless pointed to an important contemporary social relationship. The interests of the people of New England, including manufacturers and some merchants, coincided with the interests of mechanics and artisans, as opposed to those of "aristocrats" North and South—"the Lords spiritual of Andover, and the Lords temporal of Boston" and the slave owners arrayed themselves against the emancipationists.[24] Indeed, it was some of those Boston men of property who had attempted to lynch William Lloyd Garrison only a year earlier. Could some of them also have been those Boston bankers—owners and guardians of money and credit—who wielded a tightfisted control over capital necessary to make a large manufacturer out of a rising craftsman? Could they have been men who forced Lynn shoe manufacturers to establish their own "Mechanics Bank," or Fall River textile mill owners to provide their own capital resources and summon the support of mechanics and artisans to harmonize their interests with them? These are speculations prompted by the concordance of journeymen and manufacturers on the antislavery question, the symbolic issue of individual freedom and opportunity.

In Utica, Goodell also sought to erect a bridge between free laborers and abolitionism. His editorials revealed some of the tension between labor spokesmen and abolitionists. The *Boston Weekly Reformer* had given priority to the cause of the "white slave—the mechanic—operative—day laborer, that suffers much from the *same cause* that galls the southern slave." Goodell advocated an opposite priority—"when the heavier oppressions of slavery are removed, the way will be prepared to remove more effectively the lighter burdens that press on the free." He called on all northern free laborers to espouse the cause of their sorely oppressed brethren of the South. These are early signs of the sharp break to come in the 1840's between northern workingmen and moral suasionist abolitionists.[25]

When we turn to the abolitionist leadership, however, marked differences emerge between them and the rank and file in this study. This is illustrated by separating Utica's 83 leaders with known occupations from the total (see Table 2.3). Unskilled and semiskilled men do not appear among these leaders. Thus, the three manual laboring groups increase their share of the remaining 588 rank and file petitioners. Thus, too, artisans and mechanics now dominate the petitioners and exceed the skilled portion of the Utica occupational structure. But skilled men, while still the largest group among the leaders, fall farther behind the combined groups of manufacturers, proprietors, merchants, professionals and commercial men among all petitioners. The combined middle-class groups comprise more than half of the leadership but only 32 percent of the rank and file. The strong middle-class character of the abolitionist movement was expressed in the overrepresentation of these occupational groups (see Tables 2.1 and 2.3). Moreover, the articulate and assertive leadership clearly was dominated by them.

Table 2.3
COMPARISON OF UTICA LEADERS' OCCUPATIONS WITH ALL OTHER
PETITIONERS' OCCUPATIONS

Occupational Group	Utica Leaders		Other petitioners	
	(N)	%	(N)	%
Unskilled	0		42	7.1
Semiskilled	0		27	4.6
Proprietor—Manager—Official	30	36.1	120	20.4
Skilled	31	37.3	255	43.3
Commerce and Sales	5	6.0	36	6.1
Semiprofessional	0		2	0.3
Professional	9	10.8	30	5.1
Farmer	0		42	7.1
Miscellaneous	8	9.6	34	5.8
TOTALS	83		588	

The statistics in Table 2.3 represent a leadership group in Utica that can be defined by its activities. Of the four cities, Utica was the only one in which an elite could be reconstructed from available data. Leadership was assigned to men who had been among the riot victims in 1835, most of them delegates to the state antislavery convention. Some also were officers of the Utica Anti-Slavery Society, the New York State Anti-Slavery Society and/or the Utica Wesleyan Anti-Slavery Society of the Methodist Episcopal Church. Some wore several hats: riot victims, organization officers, and signers of two and three petitions. They appear to have played leading roles in abolitionism as well as in church, temperance, political and cultural affairs. They were economically successful. Of 35 leaders for whom there are official property assessments, 62.8 percent owned from $501 to well over $10,000 of real estate. Thirty-four percent were assessed at between $1,000 and $5,000; and 17 percent over $5,000 (see Table 2.2).

Among them was Samuel H. Addington, a riot victim, vice-president of the Utica Anti-Slavery Society and a delegate to the 1837 American Anti-Slavery Society Convention. Addington was a stoneware manufacturer and merchant with houses, lots, and a pottery assessed at $7,100. He was a Presbyterian church member and a signer of three of the petitions in this study. A fellow churchman and riot victim was Phillip Thurber. He was a partner in a family dry goods, grocery and hardware business with property assessed at $12,300. One of the wealthiest leading men was fifty-two-year-old John Bradish, Esq., lawyer, member of the New York State Anti-Slavery Society Executive Committee, a Presbyterian and owner of tenements, lots and houses valued at $11,750. Harry Bushnell, blacksmith (in partnership), owned his shop, two houses and two lots, all valued at $1,800. Bushnell was an officer of the Utica and Wesleyan antislavery societies and signed two of the petitions in this study. Abijah Crane, a clergyman and riot victim, was corresponding secretary of the Central Agency of the Home Missionary Society. James C. DeLong, forty-six years old in 1836, was a morocco leather manufacturer and wool dealer, president of the Wesleyan Anti-Slavery Society, a riot victim and executive committee member of the state antislavery society. His real estate was assessed at $3,000. However, Joel P. Bishop, secretary of the Utica Anti-Slavery Society, was a propertyless clerk and a boarder.

Among Fall River petitioners, too, we find middle-class men of wealth, property and standing. In the late 1830's, Quaker and Baptist manufacturers, mill mechanics and artisans in that factory town seem to have found common ground in protesting against slavery and the annexation of Texas. This was before the bosses resisted the ten-hour day for their operatives and adamantly broke their strikes and blacklisted their leaders. Among the petitioners we find Richard Borden, Congregationalist, agent and treasurer of the Fall River Iron Company and president of the Bay State Steamboat Company. His personal and real property was assessed at $34,683, making him probably the wealthiest man in this study. We also find Oliver Chase, the Quaker cotton-thread manufacturer and founder of the giant Troy Mill. He had been raised and trained as a carpenter and wheelwright and was one of those legendary versatile and enterprising Yankee mechanics. With them is David Anthony. "Deacon Anthony" of the First Congregational Church for thirty-three years, Anthony was president of the Fall River Bank and treasurer of the Fall River Rail Road. Not all were men of wealth, however. Danforth Horton was a mason with no real estate but $300 in savings. He was a boarder and a member of the First Baptist Church. Daniel Gifford was a machinist and calico printer, a Baptist, and with Asa Bronson, one of the nine Liberty party voters in 1840. Benjamin C. Luther who owned no real estate was a clerk at the Pocasset Mills.

Schenectady's petitioners included leading men like John P. Beckly, vice-president of the Anti-Slavery Society, a merchant tailor, and a Methodist; Albert Brown, also a vice-president of the society, a chair and cabinetmaker and an elder of the Presbyterian Church; Obed Chandler, a master wheelwright, member of the temperance society, a Presbyterian; his son Daniel, member of the temperance society and a Presbyterian elder; Dr. Alexander G. Fonda, a member of the Reformed Dutch Church, member of the temperance society and recording secretary of the county agricultural society; Dr. James C. Magoffin, president of the County Medical Society, a Presbyterian elder and a temperance man; and Sidney Ross, president of the antislavery society, who was a coach-maker, a Presbyterian deacon and a temperance man.

Tradesmen and artisans in Schenectady included men like William Cameron, carpenter and Presbyterian; Thomas Houston, coppersmith and member of the Reformed Dutch Church; Ahasueras Lightall of the same church and a shoemaker; Caleb Lyon, senior and junior, coach-makers, temperance men and Presbyterians; Peter Schermerhorn and Albert Van Brunt, butchers, the first, a member of the Christian Episcopal Church and the second, a Presbyterian and a furnaceman who would later become a machine shop owner and manufacturer employing fifteen men.

Rome's small list of signers included John Edy, blacksmith and Congregationalist; Sanford Adams, who owned a foundry and machine works in 1835 at the age of thirty; Seth B. Roberts, prominent lawyer, Whig politician and Congregationalist; Asa Smith, supervisor of the Town of Rome in 1821; and three Methodist class leaders—L. E. Elmer, William McPhee, and T. S. Edgerton, whose occupations could not be determined.

These men of the "middling sort" were dominant in the leadership and were also found among the rank and file. Their stake in stable and moral communities was large. Their concern over temperance, as in Schenectady, and over slavery in the nation as a sin and a political cancer appears to have reflected their traditional beliefs in freedom of the individual and in the values of sobriety and industriousness. Slavery for them was a variant of the abhorrent profligacy of aristocracy and monopoly. The annexation of Texas, the imposition of the gag rule on petitions and the stain of bondage on the nation marred their ideal of liberty and were perceived as threats to their personal fulfillment.

These men, especially those in the upper economic ranks of Fall River signers, sometimes behaved in a contradictory fashion. There was an increasingly wide gap between their sympathy for the slave and their sympathy for their employees. Another contradiction was their opposition to slavery even as they purchased slave-produced cotton for their mills. Their actions may better be understood as flowing not from hypocrisy, although some may have held a double standard, but from the flaws in the "free labor ideology."[26]

The petitioners were overwhelmingly native born, heirs to the national ideals, and especially in New England, highly self-conscious of their region's role in the revolution of 1776. Table 2.4 shows 85 percent of the signers for whom birthplaces were found to have been native born and native to their states when they signed the petitions. They persisted in their communities and through their past and their present held a great stake in them. Those for whom birthplaces were found were overwhelmingly New Yorkers (and Oneida County men) in Utica and Massachusetts and Rhode Island men in Fall River, which embraced bordering Tiverton, Rhode Island. Descendants of the Puritan settlements, the Great Awakening, and the Revolution, they were a rising generation of movers and shakers themselves. They were young men, mainly in their late twenties and thirties, seeking places in the fast-moving world of change (see Table 2.5).

The signers tend to be identified with those churches in their cities most active in antislavery and temperance work (see Table 2.6).

Table 2.4
BIRTHPLACES OF PETITIONERS

State or Nation	(N)	Percentage
New York	44	14.5
Maine	1	0.3
Vermont	1	0.3
New Hampshire	4	1.3
Massachusetts	140	46.2
Connecticut	15	5.0
Rhode Island	54	17.8
England	17	5.6
Scotland	7	2.3
Ireland	11	3.6
Wales	9	3.0
TOTAL	303	

SOURCE: Manuscript census, 1850, Utica, Rome and Fall River; Index of 1850 manuscript census for Schenectady in Schenectady County Historical Society.

Table 2.5
AGES OF PETITIONERS

Age Group	All Petitioners		Utica Leaders		Rank & File Petitioners	
	(N)	%	(N)	%	(N)	%
Under 18	7	2.3	1	6.3	6	2.1
19–29	96	32.0	2	12.5	94	33.1
30–39	104	34.7	9	56.3	95	33.5
40–49	62	20.7	3	18.8	59	20.8
50–59	27	9.0	1	6.3	26	9.1
60 and over	4	1.3	0		4	1.4
TOTALS	300		16		284	

SOURCE: Manuscript census, 1850, Utica, Rome and Fall River; Index of 1850 manuscript census for Schenectady in Schenectady County Historical Society.

In Fall River, Baptist signers comprise 40 percent of those for whom church affiliation has been found.[27] It will be recalled that the Baptist church under Asa Bronson's ministry played a leading antislavery role. Baptist signers were notable groups in Utica and Rome as well.

There were many Quakers in the Fall River area, led in antislavery activity by the large clans of Buffums, Buffintons, Chaces and Wilburs. But rank and file Friends appear to be underrepresented in the data. A Quaker history of longtime antislavery activity, dating back to John Woolman and Anthony

Benezet, prompts an expectation of greater petition activity in the 1830's. Quakers had been among the earliest to file abolition petitions with the first Congress in 1790. On the other hand, by the 1830's they appear to have been reluctant to participate in nonsectarian petition activity. They probably filed petitions of their own, some of them from neighboring communities such as Swansea and Seekonk, but these have not been located. Friends were missing from the Fall River petitions but not from abolitionist activity.

Table 2.6
CHURCH AFFILIATIONS OF PETITIONERS

	(N)	Percentage
Baptist	55	22.0
Christian Union	18	7.2
Congregational	40	16.0
Methodist	19	7.6
Presbyterian	89	35.7
Dutch Reformed	16	6.4
Episcopal	7	2.8
Roman Catholic	1	0.4
Quaker	4	1.6
TOTAL	249	

SOURCE: Church Records, Fall River, Rome, Schenectady and Utica.

Utica:
   Articles of Faith and Practice of the Second Baptist Church of Christ in Utica (Utica: Bennett & Bright, 1835); *A Brief History of the First Presbyterian Church and Society in Utica, Creed and Members* (Utica, 1829); Isaac S. Hartley, *Historical Discourse of the Semi-Centennial of the Reformed Church* (Utica, 1880); Second Baptist Church, Record Book 1820–1839, Oneida Historical Society; Second Presbyterian Church, Roll Book, Oneida Historical Society; Daughters of the American Revolution, "Bible, Cemetery and Church Records" typescript at Utica Public Library; also manuscript church records at Old Trinity Episcopal Church, Utica, and Calvary Episcopal Church.

Rome:
   Manuscript records at the following churches: First Presbyterian, First Baptist, First United Methodist, and the Episcopal Church.

Schenectady:
   J. Trumbull Backus, *History of the Presbyterian Church, Schenectady* (Schenectady, n.d.); Willis T. Hanson, Jr., *A History of St. George's Church in the City of Schenectady*, 2 vols. (Schenectady, 1919); records of the following churches at the Schenectady County Historical Society: Methodist Episcopal, Protestant Episcopal and First Baptist.

Fall River:
   Manuscript records of the Methodist Episcopal Society; *Manual of the First Baptist Church* (Fall River, 1873); *Brief History of the First Congregational Church;* Membership lists of the Society of Friends, Swansea, Massachusetts, Monthly Meeting, and Fall River Meeting, 1837–38.

Presbyterians were well represented among the petitioners and just as forward and outspoken in Utica and Schenectady abolitionism as New England Quakers. Utica's Presbyterians, led by the 1835 riot victim Reverend Oliver Wetmore, contributed 69 percent of that city's petitioners with known church affiliations. In Schenectady, 36.8 percent of the church-identified signers reflected the preeminence of the Reformed Dutch Church there. Schenectady's second largest denomination, the Presbyterian, is represented by 47.4 percent of the city's church-identified signers.

Finally, it is difficult to account for the small Methodist rank and file presence in these data. Methodist petitioners, including eight Utica leaders, comprise 7.6 percent of the church-identified petitioners. Many more men of this denomination should have appeared, for the Methodist Episcopal church was wracked by controversy over the slavery question, and in New York and New England, abolitionists in their ranks were strong. A survey by Reverend A. A. Phelps in the late 1830's revealed that two-thirds of New England's abolitionists were either Baptists or Methodists. Among the latter, ministers Orange Scott of Springfield, Timothy Merritt of Lynn and Phineas Crandall of Fall River furnished examples of militant and well-known leadership. The rapid organization of Wesleyan Conference antislavery societies swept New England and New York's evangelized expanse including the Troy, Oneida (Utica), Genesee, and Erie conferences. One estimate claimed 50,000 Methodist abolitionists in a church with 300,000 members.[28] Why then, so few signers?

The answer is difficult to furnish inasmuch as Methodist church records are incomplete or simply missing (as I found in Utica and Fall River). However, we might speculate that the large number of unidentified signers conforms to the occupational and property-owning patterns established in Tables 2.1 through 2.3. If they do, and if the missing men were also church members, they probably were Methodists or Baptists. Both churches tended to be more attractive to workingmen and their families than other Protestant denominations. Thus, in Rochester, New York, the Methodist church was "blue collar." And in Fall River, where the Methodist church was third in worker membership behind the Baptist and Christian Union, the Bronson-workingmen's alliance on the ten-hour question pointed to a Baptist working-class congregation.[29] We might infer from these indications that many of the unknown petitioners were artisans and perhaps some laborers who followed the lead of Bronson, Crandall and Scott, as well as Wetmore.

The ratio of artisans to proprietor-manager signers in the churches strengthens our appreciation of the class character of some of the churches and of the class responses to the antislavery petitions. In Table 2.7, Baptist and Methodist skilled petitioners stand in a better than two to one ratio to the entrepreneurs, merchants, and other middle-class men. On the other hand, Presbyterian signers tend to be more middle-class and professional, although a related denomination, the Congregationalists, tended to be like the Baptists, Methodists and Christians. Although the ratios do not dem-

Table 2.7
OCCUPATIONAL STRUCTURE OF PETITIONERS' CHURCHES
(NUMBER AND PERCENT OF PETITIONERS IN EACH DENOMINATION)

Occupational Group	Total (N)	%	Baptist (N)	%	Christian (N)	%	Congregational (N)	%	Methodist (N)	%	Presbyterian (N)	%	Dutch Reformed (N)	%	Quaker (N)	%
Unskilled	9	3.9	3	5.9	2	11.8	1	2.8	1	5.3	1	1.3	–	–	–	–
Semiskilled	4	1.7	–	–	1	5.9	1	2.8	–	–	–	–	1	6.7	–	–
Proprietor-Manager-Official	70	30.4	10	19.6	5	29.0	8	22.0	6	31.6	32	40.0	5	33.3	2	50.0
Skilled	99	43.0	27	52.9	7	41.0	14	38.9	12	63.1	29	36.3	6	40.0	2	50.0
Commerce and Sales	13	5.7	3	5.9	1	5.9	1	2.8	–	–	8	10.0	–	–	–	–
Semiprofessional	1	0.4	–	–	–	–	–	–	–	–	–	–	–	–	–	–
Professional	20	8.7	2	3.9	–	–	7	19.4	–	–	7	8.8	3	20.0	–	–
Farmers	14	6.1	6	11.8	1	5.9	4	11.0	–	–	3	3.8	–	–	–	–
TOTALS	230		51		17		36		19		80		15		4	

SOURCES: See sources cited following Tables 2.1 and 2.6.

onstrate sharp class lines between churches, they do show a connection between artisan culture and religion. They also show that abolitionism was not the exclusive domain of middle-class evangelicals; and that workingmen were not alienated by bosses and nabobs from the struggle against chattel slavery.

The mystery of the unidentified petitioners remains intriguing and important. If, as in many antebellum cities, men in the wage-earning classes tended to display high residential turnover rates, then we might infer a similar pattern among the unidentified antislavery petitioners. Journeymen wage earners were regularly missing from early Philadelphia city directories; propertyless, single and young men were the most transient population of Poughkeepsie, New York; the "lowest economic orders" were among the most unstable residents of Boston; in Rochester during the Finney revival years of the late 1820's fewer than one in six wage earners stayed as long as six years; in Utica, 28 percent of the 1837–38 city directory entries were boarders, suggesting a high rate of residential mobility among men and women in the labor force.[30]

If the unidentified men were not church members, this would conform to the general pattern of male absence from Protestant church membership.[31] If this should be the case, then the artisan and mechanic tendency toward deism and rationalism uncovered by Jentz's study of New York City antislavery petitioners may apply in these four cities as well. Several possibilities are suggested. Some of the unidentified petitioners may have been the heirs of a late eighteenth-century artisan secular radicalism; others may have been members of predominantly working-class churches; both types as well as others may have been embraced by a synthesis of the rationalist craftsman culture and a species of evangelicalism expressing their distinctive class morality.[32]

The artisans who had asserted "natural rights" in the 1830's were inspired by the eighteenth-century Enlightenment. Many also derived strength from democratic rejuvenation of their churches in the Second Great Awakening and its aftermath. Slavery, in any form they chose to define, was abhorrent to them. Thus, the uncertainties of an age of change from workshop to factory and the loss of producer control to capitalists was translated into "wage slavery." At the same time their republican ideals were put to the test when they witnessed the growth and extension of chattel slavery. Many artisans, as the profile here shows, "passed" the test. These middle and lower orders of society were well prepared to oppose slavery and its extension. Their names on these remonstrances were consistent with the struggles of their class against aristocracy and privilege and for democracy in church, state and workplace. In this connection, the profile suggests more complexity to labor-abolitionist hostility than older views of that relationship permit. Supporters of those views have offered the statements of abolitionist and labor leaders, but these should now be reconsidered in the light of rank and file studies.[33]

The profile of antislavery petitioners that emerges from the four cities studied here suggests the character of those who were early advocates of a political response to slavery. Petitioners of Congress on behalf of the slave were native born men, young, ambitious and mobile. Some were entrepreneurs, many were workmen. Included among the former were manufacturers who were shaping a new industrialism; among the latter were both skilled artisans and wage-earning journeymen. The entrepreneurs often also owned substantial real property, but even propertyless laborers could be found among the signers. The owners of real property holdings ranged from those with small family home lots and workshop sites to those owning stores, rental properties and small factories. A few owned very large factories in Fall River, and a small number owned large tracts of town and country lots.[34] All shared a heritage of republicanism and Protestantism.

During the coming decades, economic transformations would widen the crevices of disagreement among signers. Though all agreed that slavery was a danger to free institutions in the late 1830's, economic self-interest, racism and the direction of the antislavery movement prevented the petitioners from evolving automatically into a disciplined antislavery constituency for the Liberty party. Still, many who raised their pens against the slaveholder in the 1830's probably voted against him in the 1840's and ultimately sent their sons to fight against him in the 1860's. James G. Birney, an ex-slaveholder from Kentucky who later ran for president on the Liberty party ticket in 1840 and 1844 described abolitionism's constituency as being in the "warm hearts of our yeomanry, and . . . the artisans and inhabitants of the smaller villages." Another abolitionist, Thomas Wentworth Higginson, meanwhile, recalled it as being in "the factories and shoeshops." The petitions from Utica, Fall River, Rome and Schenectady suggest that both were correct for the 1830's. Artisans, tradesmen and laborers appear to have heeded the advice of early labor spokesmen such as George Henry Evans. In 1831, the same year in which William Lloyd Garrison grandiloquently declared his right to be heard, Evans, although contemptuous of abolitionists, urged all free men to aid the fight to destroy slavery, for the interests of all labor lay in the emancipation of America's black slaves.[35]

NOTES

1. For the history and significance of the petition campaigns I have relied upon Russel B. Nye, *Fettered Freedom, Civil Liberties and the Slavery Controversy, 1830–*

Research for this study was greatly aided by a summer 1978 fellowship awarded by the University Awards Committee/State University of New York Research Foundation. The author wishes to thank Mr. Claude LaBarre of the Computer Center, Potsdam College, for his careful guidance in the application of the SPSS programs; student assistants who helped to transcribe data into computer-usable form; and above all Alan Kraut, Jama Lazerow, Sanford Schram, Robert Schwartz, and Miriam S. Magdol for invaluable criticism and advice; and Arthur L. Johnson for a schedule that allowed time for research and writing.

1860 (East Lansing: Michigan State College Press, 1949), pp. 32–55 and Gilbert H. Barnes, *The Antislavery Impulse, 1830–1844* (New York: Harcourt, Brace and World, reprint edition, 1964; originally published in 1933 by the American Historical Association), pp. 109–289. On the emergence of the Free Soil Party and its constituency see Joseph G. Rayback, *Free Soil, The Election of 1848* (Lexington, Ky.: University Press of Kentucky, 1970), pp. 56–59, 299–300; Richard H. Sewell, *Ballots for Freedom, Anti-slavery Politics in the United States, 1837–1860* (New York: Oxford University Press, 1976). Recent general histories of the antislavery movement are Merton L. Dillon, *The Abolitionists, The Growth of A Dissenting Minority* (DeKalb: Northern Illinois University Press, 1974) and James Brewer Stewart, *Holy Warriors, The Abolitionists and American Slavery* (New York: Hill and Wang, 1976).

2. Barnes, *Antislavery Impulse*, pp. 131–133: Nye, *Fettered Freedom*, p. 48; George A. Stevens, *New York Typographical Union No. 6. Study of a Modern Trade Union and its Predecessors* (Albany: J. B. Lyon, 1913), p. 189.

3. *The Liberator*, April 23, 1837, September 21, 1838; Nye, *Fettered Freedom*, p. 37; Barnes, *Antislavery Impulse*, p. 266; Louis Filler, *The Crusade against Slavery, 1830–1860* (New York: Harper and Row, 1963), p. 155.

4. Providence *Journal*, February 13, 1837; Dillon, *The Abolitionists*, p. 102.

5. Alan M. Kraut, "The Forgotten Reformers, A Profile of Third Party Abolitionists in Antebellum New York" in Lewis Perry and Michael Fellman, eds., *Antislavery Reconsidered: New Perspectives on the Abolitionists* (Baton Rouge: Louisiana State University Press, 1979), pp. 119–145; John B. Jentz, "The Antislavery Constituency in Jacksonian New York City," *Civil War History* 27(June 1981): 101–122. See also: Alan M. Kraut, "The Liberty Men of New York: Political Abolitionism in New York State, 1840–1848" (Ph.D. diss., Cornell University, 1975); Reinhard O. Johnson, "The Liberty Party in New England, 1840–1848: The Forgotten Abolitionists" (Ph.D. diss., Syracuse University, 1976); Edward Magdol, "A Remonstrance Against the Nebraska Bill, 1854: The Case of Ogdensburgh, New York, Antislavery Petitioners," unpublished paper presented at the Organization of American Historians' Annual Meeting, April 13, 1978.

6. David Donald, "Toward a Reconsideration of the Abolitionists," in *Lincoln Reconsidered: Essays on the Civil War Era* (New York: Random House, 1956), pp. 19–36; Gerald Sorin, *New York Abolitionists: A Case Study of Political Radicalism* (Westport, Conn.: Greenwood Press, 1971), pp. 106–109; Leonard L. Richards, *"Gentlemen of Property and Standing" Anti-Abolition Mobs in Jacksonian America* (New York: Oxford University Press, 1970), pp. 131–155; David Walker Howe, *The Unitarian Conscience: Harvard Moral Philosophy, 1805–1861* (Cambridge: Harvard University Press, 1970), p. 289.

7. Betty Fladeland, "Who Were the Abolitionists?" *Journal of Negro History* 43 (April 1964): 99–115; David Brion Davis, ed., *Ante-Bellum Reform* (Harper and Row, 1967), p. 10; Eric Foner, "The Causes of the American Civil War: Recent Interpretations and New Directions," *Civil War History* 20 (September 1974): 208–209; Jentz, "Abolitionist Constituency"; Ronald G. Walters, *Antislavery Appeal, American Abolitionism After 1830* (Baltimore: The Johns Hopkins University Press, 1976), pp. 116, 177; Stewart, *Holy Warriors*, ch. 5; Johnson, "Liberty Party in New England"; Kraut, "Liberty Men of New York."

8. Jentz, "Antislavery Constituency"; Magdol, "A Remonstrance Against the Nebraska Bill, 1854." Jentz and I sampled the vast repository of petitions in the National Archives, which I had begun to explore in 1968 for this purpose. His

profile of New York City artisans and other signers in the 1830's is an important contribution. I used the petitions to build a profile of anti-Nebraska signers in Ogdenburg, N.Y., and one ward of Utica, N.Y. Other scholars, such as Judith Wellman, have made similar examinations of the petition with different propositions to guide them. In my study I linked upstate New York petitioners with city directories, census, tax and church records. This essay, using the same methodology, was assisted by the SPSS (Statistical Package for the Social Sciences) computer programs FREQUENCIES and CROSSTABS.

9. Jacksonian era artisan and mechanic values and beliefs may best be understood in Edward Pessen, *Most Uncommon Jacksonians, The Radical Leaders of the Early Labor Movement* (Albany: State University of New York Press, 1967); Paul Faler, "Workingmen, Mechanics, and Social Change: Lynn, Massachusetts, 1800–1860" (Ph.D. diss., University of Wisconsin, 1971); and Alan Dawley, *Class and Community: The Industrial Revolution in Lynn* (Cambridge: Harvard University Press, 1976).

10. Research was made difficult by incomplete series of data and by such missing sources as poll books and abolition society membership lists in the cities under study. Efforts to link such data often ran into a stony silence in the records.

This is especially true of information about women petitioners whose absence is all the more regrettable because female signers outnumbered males. While their leadership in circulating the petitions and in amassing the signatures for mailing to Washington has been demonstrated by earlier historians, a new generation has undertaken the extremely arduous task of identifying the women signers through petition analysis. Judith Wellman, Ellen Henle, Patricia Heard and Gerda Lerner have shown the family and church networks involved in petition activity and the increasing politicization of women through such abolitionist activity. Judith Wellman, " 'Are We Aliens Because We Are Women?' Female Abolitionists and Abolitionist Petitions and Female Abolitionist in Paris, New York, 1835–1845," paper presented to Berkshire Conference on Women's History, June 1976; Patricia Heard, " 'One Blood All Nations,' Anti-Slavery Petitions in Sandwich [New Hampshire]," *59th Annual Excursion of the Sandwich [N.H.] Historical Society,* August 27, 1978, pp. 26–31; Ellen L. Henle, " 'Forget Not the Matron': Sandwich Women and Antislavery in the Antebellum Years," *59th Annual Excursion of the Sandwich Historical Society,* pp. 32–38; Gerda Lerner, *The Majority Finds its Past* (New York: Oxford University Press, 1979), pp. 112–128.

11. *Friend of Man,* November 3, 1836.

12. These brief descriptive remarks about Utica rely on Richard L. Ehrlich, "The Development of Manufacturing in Selected Counties in the Erie Canal Corridor, 1815–1860" (Ph.D. diss., State University of New York at Buffalo, 1972); Mary P. Ryan, "A Woman's Awakening: Evangelical Religion and the Families of Utica, New York, 1800–1840," *American Quarterly* 30 (Winter 1978): 602–623; Judith Wellman, "The Burned-Over District Revisited, Benevolent Reform and Abolitionism in Mexico, Paris, and Ithaca, New York, 1825–42" (Ph.D. diss., University of Virginia, 1974); Moses Bagg, ed., *Memorial History of Utica* (Syracuse: Mason, 1892); Henry J. Cookingham, *History of Oneida County,* 2 vols. (Chicago: S. J. Clarke Publishing Co., 1912).

13. John L. Myers, "The Beginnings of Anti-Slavery Agencies in New York State, 1833–1836," *New York History* (April 1962): 171.

14. Frederick M. Peck and Henry H. Earl, *Fall River and Its Industries* (Fall

River: B. Earl & Son, 1877); Frank Walcott Hutt, ed., *A History of Bristol County*, 3 vols. (New York and Chicago, Lewis Historical Publishing Co., 1924); Thomas Russell Smith, *Cotton Textile Industry of Fall River, Massachusetts, A Study of Industrial Localization* (New York: King's Crown Press, 1945); John T. Cumbler, *Working Class Community in Industrial America, Work, Leisure and Struggle in Two Industrial Cities, 1880–1930* (Westport, Conn.: Greenwood Press, 1979), pp. 99–104.

15. Edward S. Adams, "Anti-Slavery Activity in Fall River," Fall River *Herald News*, February 17–28, 1939, and in typescript at Fall River Historical Society; *Friend of Man*, June 30, August 25, 1836; Fall River *Mechanic*, September 28, 1844; *The Liberator*, November 23, 1838.

16. Daniel E. Wager, ed., *Our Country and Its People, A Descriptive Work on Oneida County* (Boston: Boston History Co., 1896); Wager, ed., *Our City and Its People, A Descriptive Work on the City of Rome, New York* (Boston: Boston History Co., 1896); Pomeroy Jones, *Annals and Recollections of Oneida County* (Rome: Published by author, 1851); Census of the State of New York for 1835, 1845, 1855; George R. Howell, ed., *History of Albany and Schenectady Counties* (New York: Munsell, 1886).

17. Eight petitions bearing 1,624 names were used, and three issues were supported by the signers: 865 for the abolition of slavery in the District of Columbia; 473 against annexation of Texas; 149 against the gag rule on petitions (sampled only in Fall River). Another category, 137 in Utica's antislavery leadership, completed the sample. Of these the identified signers and leaders were respectively, 351, 173, 38 and 115. The number of identified persons, 677, is 41.7 percent of the beginning sample.

Antislavery petitions sent to the House of Representatives are in Record Group 233, Legislative Records, National Archives. The petitions used in this study are catalogued as follows:

On abolition of slavery in the District of Columbia
Utica, March 21, 1836—HR24A-G22.4
      September 26, 1837—HR25A-H1.8
Rome, (Sept.–Dec.) 1837—HR25A-H1.8
Schenectady, 1838—HR25A-H1.8
Fall River, February 18, 1839—HR25A-H1.8

Against the annexation of Texas
Utica, September 19, 1837—HR25A-H1.8
Fall River, March 12, 1838—HR25A-H1.8

Against the gag rule
Fall River, February 18, 1839—HR25A-H1.7

Utica's leaders' names were gathered from the *Friend of Man*, Utica, N.Y., 1836–1838, and from Leonard L. Richards, *"Gentlemen of Property and Standing"* (New York: Oxford University Press, 1970), pp. 172–173.

18. Nye, *Fettered Freedom*, p. 37; Barnes, *Antislavery Impulse*, p. 137; American Anti-Slavery Society, *Annual Reports*, 1834–1838.

19. Peter Knights, *The Plain People of Boston, 1830–1860: A Study in City Growth* (New York: Oxford University Press, 1971).

20. In addition, some men's occupations were found by utilizing the 1850 census. If a man's occupation was listed in that census and he had been a signer of a petition between March 1836 and April 1839, I calculated his age at the time. If he was eighteen years or older at the time of signing, I assume that, according to early nineteenth-century employment practices, he probably worked at the trade or occupation listed for him in 1850. He could have been apprenticed when fourteen years old. This continuity may not have been true for all. Jama Lazerow, studying the relationships of churches and working classes in antebellum Fall River, suggests the possible weakness of such a retrospective identification. For example, he found some men in 1850—carpenters, blacksmiths, and machinists—who had been mill laborers in the 1830's. In our case, with incomplete mill employee records and uncertain classification of masters and journeymen, we are left with the choice of speculation at best. Use of the 1850 census tends to bias the results toward the persisters and loses sight of the mobile men over a period of from eleven to fourteen years. But it also tends to corroborate city directory occupational designations.

21. Peter Knights used that amount of property ownership to set an upper limit to a "lower middle class" in his study of antebellum Boston wealth and mobility. Rather than risk an unwarranted enlargement of the number of journeymen, I prefer the cautious figure of $500. Knights, *Plain People of Boston,* pp. 78–102.

22. Kraut, "Forgotten Reformers," pp. 129–130. Jentz, "Antislavery Constituency," p. 106.

23. *Friend of Man,* August 25, September 8, 1836.

24. Ibid., August 25, 1836.

25. Reprinted in *The Liberator,* February 4, 1837.

26. Eric Foner, *Free Soil, Free Labor, Free Men: The Ideology of the Republican Party Before the Civil War* (New York: Oxford University Press, 1970).

27. Fall River petitioners' church affiliations were:

Church	(N)	Percentage
Baptist	38	40.0
Christian	18	18.9
Congregational	30	31.6
Methodist	3	3.1
Episcopal	1	1.0
Catholic	1	1.0
Quaker	4	4.2
Total	95	

28. Barnes, *Antislavery Impulse,* pp. 90–91, 241–242; Donald G. Mathews, *Slavery and Methodism, A Chapter in American Morality, 1780–1845* (Princeton: Princeton University Press, 1965), pp. 168, 171; *The Liberator,* March 22, 1839.

29. Paul E. Johnson, *A Shopkeeper's Millenium, Society and Revivals in Rochester, New York, 1815–1837* (New York: Hill and Wang, 1978). A similar pattern emerges in Lynn and Fitchburg, Massachusetts, where Methodist churches were predominantly working class. See Faler, "Workingmen, Mechanics, and Social Change," and Lazerow, personal communication with author.

30. Clyde Griffen, "Workers Divided: The Effect of Craft and Ethnic Difference in Poughkeepsie, New York, 1850–1880"; Stuart Blumin, "Mobility and Change in Ante-Bellum Philadelphia"; and Peter Knights, "Population Turnover, Persistence, and Residential Mobility in Boston, 1830–1860," in Stephan Thernstrom and Richard Sennett, eds., *Nineteenth Century Cities, Essays in the New Urban History* (New Haven: Yale University Press, 1969); Ryan, "A Woman's Awakening," pp. 606–607.

31. Ryan, "A Woman's Awakening," p. 603, details the women's majorities in Utica's revivals from 1814 to 1838. See also Barbara Welter, "The Feminization of American Religion, 1800–1860," in Mary Hartman and Lois W. Banner, eds., *Clio's Consciousness Raised: New Perspectives in the History of Women* (New York: Harper and Row, 1974), pp. 137–157.

32. The roots of artisans' roles in democratizing Protestant churches lay in the American Revolution and its republican ideology between 1790 and 1815. That was a time of "levelling" when, one clergyman feared, religion had come under the supreme control of "tinkers and taylors [sic], weavers, shoemakers and country mechanics of all kinds"—Nathan O. Hatch, "The Christian Movement and the Demand for a Theology of the People," *Journal of American History* 67 (December 1980): 567. Similarly nonconformist English artisans who were predominantly Wesleyan Methodists and Baptists and Congregationalists, displayed exceptionally high participation in the British antislavery movement in 1832–33. Seymour Drescher, "Two Variants of Anti-Slavery: Religious Organization and Social Mobilization in Britain and France, 1780–1870," in Seymour Drescher and Christine Bolt, eds., *Anti-Slavery, Religion and Reform* (Hamden, Conn.: Dawson-Archon, 1980), p. 43.

33. See Joseph Rayback, "The American Workingman and the Antislavery Crusade," *Journal of Economic History* 3 (November 1943): 152–163.

34. Tax lists of Utica 1835 and Fall River 1838; *City Directory, Utica,* 1837–38.

35. Bernard Mandel and other labor historians have adduced evidence of white working class opposition to slavery despite hostility toward abolitionists and blacks. Studies such as this one should lend support to their arguments. Bernard Mandel, *Labor: Free and Slave* (New York: Associated Authors, 1955), pp. 71, 74–75. Philip S. Foner, *A History of the Labor Movement in the United States* (New York: International Publishers, 1947), 1: 266–269. Birney quotation in Stewart, *Holy Warriors*, p. 81. Higginson in *Cheerful Yesterdays,* p. 115. Evans in Mandel, *Labor: Free and Slave,* p. 71.

3

Partisanship and Principles: The Liberty Party in Antebellum Political Culture

Alan M. Kraut

> The political reformer must have a majority with him, else he cannot do anything; he has not carried his point or accomplished his end. But the non-political reformer has accomplished part of his end, if he has convinced one man out of a million; for that one man will work to convince another, and by and by the whole will be convinced. A political reformer must get a majority; a non-political reformer has done something if he has the very smallest minority, if it is a minority of one.[1]
>
> Theodore Parker
> 1856

Almost a decade after the demise of the Liberty Party in 1848, abolitionists continued to debate the merits of their foray into partisan politics. Theodore Parker, never himself a Liberty man, continued to express his frustration with those who defined victory only in counted votes. However, other reformers insisted that abolition politics had been more than an exercise in futility. William Goodell, a veteran Liberty leader, was equally critical of those politicians "accustomed to identify 'success' with the election of their candidates," but unlike Parker, Goodell insisted that even in defeat the Liberty Party had irrevocably altered the nation's political agenda.[2] In 1852, Goodell rhetorically asked, "What would have been the condition of the antislavery cause now, if *all* the voting abolitionists of the country had continued to vote (as all except "Liberty" men did) for the candidates of the old political parties?"[3] The answer that "any intelligent and candid politician" must offer, according to Goodell, was that it would not have "stood on as high ground as it does now." And like many another ex-Liberty man, Goodell continued to wonder, "What would, probably, have been the effect, if the sixty thousand Liberty men who voted for Birney in 1844 had held firmly *that position?*"[4]

Time and mortality have cooled the passions with which Parker and Goodell justified their choices of strategy in the antislavery struggle. Still, the glowing embers of debate emit sufficient energy to fuel an ongoing controversy among historians over the means and ends of American abolitionists. Too frequently that debate has centered upon the success or failure of particular strategies or tactics to arouse popular enthusiasm for reform, or whether abolitionists' behavior revealed the existence among them of a genuinely radical consciousness.[5] True, few historians remain shackled to what David Hackett Fischer has dubbed "the fallacy of false dichotomous questions," and ask, "The Abolitionists: Reformers or Fanatics?"[6] But there remains among scholars, with rare exception, a tendency to isolate the antislavery struggle from the larger social context in which it occurred. The means and ends employed by abolitionists did not evolve in a vacuum, but were the products of larger social, cultural, and political circumstances.

The political efforts to abolish slavery have particularly baffled historians. Their complexity both defies easy labelling and requires students of the antislavery movement to leave the comfortable cul de sac of antebellum reform and enter the busy intersection of partisan politics where parties, candidates, officeholders, voters, and reformers all converged. The Liberty Party, the abolitionist third party launched in 1840 and abandoned by 1848, has sparked considerable disagreement among historians of reform. Some have dismissed the Liberty Party as merely another abortive tactic in the effort to persuade Americans that black slavery was a moral abomination deserving abolition[7]; others, however, have viewed it as more of a surrogate religious denomination formed by those harboring anti-party attitudes even as they sought to achieve moral reform at the polls.[8] To date no study has adequately explained the third party's synthesis of abolitionism and antebellum partisan behavior common to contemporary Whigs and Democrats.[9] Only James Brewer Stewart has concisely articulated the enigma of the Liberty Party with his paradoxical characterization of the third party's politics as "political antipolitics."[10]

This essay examines the Liberty Party against the background of the political culture in which it arose. Studies by this author and others have amply demonstrated that the Liberty Party was a failure at the polls and the victim of clever machinations of Whig and Democratic adversaries.[11] Lee Benson, Ronald P. Formisano, Michael Holt and others have shown that the third party was markedly unsuccessful in substituting slavery for ethnocultural loyalty and local economic considerations as the molders of northern electoral preferences during the 1840's.[12] It remains, though, to explain why the Liberty Party emulated some characteristics of its rivals and not others, why in some ways the Liberty Party was thoroughly modern while in others it resembled pre-modern, traditional associations, founded upon patterns of deference, and how this hybrid quality undermined any possibility of electoral success in the highly competitive second party system.

Two excellent volumes by historians of abolitionism, while contributing substantially to an overall understanding of that reform movement, reflect the confusion among historians over the exact nature of the Liberty Party. In *Ballots for Freedom*, Richard Sewell maintains that the Liberty Party was a political party by design rather than a "religious crusade." He acknowledges that third party appeals often had a religious flavor, the result of the religious conversions experienced by many of the party's leaders earlier in their lives. But, he insists, Liberty men did not view the Bible as their "political textbook." Though largely unsuccessful at vote-getting, they were "intelligent reformer politicians," not "doctrinaire visionaries unfit for the cold world of politics."[13] Ronald F. Walters argues with equal conviction in *The Antislavery Appeal*, however, that the Liberty reformers were politicians in name only and that they adopted the rhetoric and style of partisan politicians only because electioneering was the "great American sport of the day." Abolition politics, he contends, was little more than a propaganda technique, a "gesture of protest against the imperfection in American political life."[14]

But the Liberty men were engaged in more than merely the politics of gesture. And as Lewis Perry has observed, even Sewell's portrait of the Liberty Party suffers from "a narrow perspective on political history." Sewell looks for ways in which abolitionists "transcended the culture in which they operated," but often neglects those ways in which the third party remained bound by the political culture from which it sprang and affected the two party system upon which it had intruded.[15] Despite its dismal electoral returns, the third party had a sustained impact upon antebellum politics. Paul Kleppner and others have noted that by thrusting the slavery issue onto the agenda of national politics, the Liberty Party contributed to the derangement of parties prior to the realignment of the 1850's and the more general political turmoil that prevented the party system from continuing to mediate the escalating sectional strife that ended in civil war. The Liberty Party, according to Kleppner, weakened the attachments of some voters to their old parties and conditioned mass opinion in the North by thrusting anti-southernism into mass politics where it festered until the outbreak of war.[16]

A clique of naive do-gooders who stumbled into significance? Or a coven of disaffected reformers who subverted the political system they had failed to transform? Abandoning old dichotomies and suspending the computation of votes won and lost permits a fresh perspective on the Liberty Party, one taken from both national sightings and state surveys. New York politics has served as an ideal observation post for the latter. The "election fever . . . constantly raging throughout the land" had reached epidemic proportions in New York, wrote French visitor Alexis de Tocqueville.[17] Moreover, New York was the birthplace of the Liberty Party and "for many years an influence on behalf of the slave radiated from the central counties of the state."[18] New York Liberty Party ballots were cast in elections between 1840 and 1847. The party ran candidates in all national, state, and in most local elections in these years. However, in both presidential elections of 1840 and 1844, the third party received its greatest number of votes in New York.[19]

During the early 1830's, the crusade for emancipation had consisted largely of disparate skirmishes fought in New York and elsewhere by individual reformers seeking to build a moral consensus against slavery by proselytizing others in their respective churches, political parties, and communities. Within a few years, some reformers sought greater influence through collective action, forming voluntary societies for the sole purpose of using moral suasion on a large audience. An increasing number of abolitionists had channelled their efforts and enthusiasm into institutional commitments to the American Anti-Slavery Society, established in 1833, and to a wide variety of similar organizations at the state and local levels.

Less than a decade later, it was apparent to some reformers that moral argument alone was insufficient weaponry in the assault upon slavery. They found in partisan politics an alternative to moral suasion. Some reformers such as William Lloyd Garrison pronounced party politics irreparably corrupt, but others believed it possible to adapt partisanship to the purposes of reform.[20] At first, political abolitionists stood at the edge of the partisan arena, but Congress silenced their petitions with gag rules, and politicians too often forgot promises of support made in the heat of campaigns. Frustrated with the reluctance of both Democratic and Whig parties to confront the evils of slavery, some abolitionists chose to enter politics themselves.

The Liberty Party, organized on April 1, 1840, at Albany, New York, evolved out of the realization of some abolitionists that politics was exercising an unparalleled power and influence over individual citizens' imaginations. Tocqueville had noted its influence, observing that, "To take a hand in the regulation of society and to discuss it is his [the Americans'] biggest concern, and, so to speak, the only pleasure an American knows."[21] What the Frenchman saw is confirmed by the turnout figures for the antebellum period. Between 1840 and 1860, voter turnout for all elections in the north was 71.3 percent. Turnout in presidential elections averaged 81.1 percent, with a slightly lower, but still impressive non-presidential election average of 69.9 percent.[22] In New York, always a sure barometer for measuring political enthusiasm, the levels of voter turnout in gubernatorial elections during the years prior to the Liberty Party's formation, 1830–1838, was 77.9 percent.[23] However, between 1840 and 1848, the mean turnout over the five elections for governor in that period was 83.6 percent.[24] Despite variations among state turnouts in the two decades prior to the Civil War, participation in elections was the most enthusiastic in American history, and some abolitionists, sensing the influence of politics, advocated a new departure in the institutional evolution of the antislavery movement—an abolitionist political party.

Traditionally, scholars have defined political parties in America as competing organizations that run candidates for office, advocate particular agendas of government action, and if their candidates are successful, translate their politics into government programs.[25] At the same time, political parties are also the means whereby individual citizens can relate themselves and their values to the larger society. Partisan conflict is thus not merely a contest between institutions but a battle between adherents of very different value systems.[26] Lee Benson and others have described the Democratic and Whig party organizations of the 1840's as coalitions of interests seeking to dominate the government, each claiming to best reflect the values, fears, and aspirations of the majority of voters.[27]

This highly competitive two party system run by professional politicians in the 1840's was markedly different from the deferential, elitist politics of the colonial period or even the transitional period of Federalist-Republican politics that Ronald P. Formisano had called the "deferential-participant phase" of the early Republic. In the latter, parties and partisan competitions had not quite yet become accepted routine.[28] By the late 1830's, the political culture of this new party system was crystallizing. However, dividing the development into "pre-party traditional and post-party modern structures" makes change seem to arrive "abruptly and completely," according to Formisano.[29] Rather, change came slowly, haltingly; tradition persisted, old and new forms were synthesized often making it difficult to perceive the unique and distinctive qualities of "modern" political parties as they evolved.

Like oases for the desert wanderer, precise definitions of "modern" institutions and measurable criteria, universally agreed upon, have often proven to be mirages that vanish when examined too closely. Indeed, modernization, generally, has become "the kind of catchword whose incantation magically resolves the problem by failing to confront it."[30] Still as did other institutions, political organizations in America changed dramatically during the antebellum period. These changes were the result of what Karl W. Deutsch has described as social mobilization, a process by which "major clusters of old social, economic and psychological commitments are eroded or broken and people become available for new patterns of socialization and behavior."[31] Certainly, the movement from deferential-participant politics to competitive party politics, described by Formisano, was the product of social mobilization. However, the aspect of political change most crucial to this transformation was the evolution of the modern political party. According to political scientist Samuel Huntington, a critical aspect of political modernization involves "the differentiation of new political functions and the development of specialized structures to perform those functions."[32] The institutionalization of the political party was therefore an integral part of the larger process of modernization.

Institutionalization is "the process by which organizations and procedures acquire value and stability."[33] Samuel Huntington contends that the level of institutionalization of any political system can be determined by the "adaptability, complexity, autonomy and coherence of its organization and procedures."[34] By autonomy, he means the condition in which an institution serves the needs of an increasing number of social groups and interests, rather than a narrow spectrum of groups having a confined set of concerns. Always, according to Huntington, the differentiation of an institution's sub-units and the differentiation of the political sphere from other societal areas of activity are manifestations of increasingly sophisticated levels of institutionalization.[35]

Applying Huntington's definition of institutionalization to the antebellum party system suggests that party institutionalization did not affect all parties equally or proceed at the same rate in each case. Ronald P. Formisano contends that antebellum parties ought to be viewed along a "traditional-modern axis showing a variety of changing political culture patterns."[36] If one pole of that axis were complete institutionalization and the other pole non-institutionalization, where would the Liberty Party place on that continuum in relation to the two major parties? And what would the third party's place on that axis suggest about the proper place of the Liberty men in antebellum political culture?

Within antebellum political culture, the Democratic and Whig parties experienced very different approaches to the changes, or modernization occurring in the United States. James M. McPherson, has, "at the risk of oversimplification," characterized the Whigs as "the party of modernization" and the Democrats as "the party of tradition."[37] Democrats, he believes, "inherited the Jeffersonian commitments to states rights, limited government, traditional economic arrangements, and religious pluralism," while their Whig adversaries received a legacy of "Federalist belief in nationalism, a strong government, economic innovation, and cultural homogeneity under the auspices of established Protestant denominations."[38] McPherson presents numerous examples in defense of his party profiles. In the area of economic growth, the Whigs wanted to use the federal and state governments to finance development by subsidizing internal improvements and chartering banks. Democrats tended to eschew banks, corporations, and other such economic institutions, fearing that state-legislated economic privilege would endanger equal rights. In the area of public morality, Whigs tended to advocate temperance and public schools, black suffrage and prison reform, while the Democrats were the staunchest opponents of such measures. Whigs generally believed in an "entrepreneurial ethic" that fostered industrialization and urban growth, according to McPherson, while Democrats still steeped in Jeffersonian rhetoric retained an essentially agrarian perspective and were hostile to industry and cities. Both parties advocated expansion, but the Whigs defined it as long-term economic growth and modernization while to the Democrats it meant only a premature territorial acquisition that often involved the brutal suppression of Indian tribes. To Democrats, McPherson explains, new territory was desirable only because it would permit the replication of the institutions already entrenched in the older states.[39]

McPherson's distinctions between Democratic and Whig views of government power and its uses echoes the "positive versus negative liberalism" characterization of party differences advanced earlier by Lee Benson.[40] However, when Whigs and Democrats are compared as to levels of party institutionalization, a role reversal is apparent. It is the Democratic Party that appears modern and the Whig Party that seems pre-modern or traditional in the context of antebellum political culture.

At first glance the parties seem similar. By 1840, both parties had already developed organizational structures to stoke voter enthusiasm and to win votes. At the national level, both parties had central committees to arrange national conventions and raise funds to finance national campaigns. Policies were established and articulated as planks in party platforms at the national conventions, and the candidates for national office were nominated by the delegates present.[41]

Furthermore, each party was organized at the state, county, and local levels. State conventions nominated candidates and passed resolutions dealing with state and local matters, while politicians at these conventions could modify party principles, annunciated in the national platform, to suit local conditions. Committees were appointed to bear the crucial responsibility of mobilizing armies of voters for their respective parties on election day.

Party campaigners made use of every available contemporary technique to appeal to the mass electorate. Many of these techniques took advantage of the recreational role that politics played in the nineteenth-century community. Political parties regularly attracted voters by providing occasions for community recreation and merriment such as barbecues, banquets, and balls.[42] Campaign songs were printed and distributed so that those who gathered to hear speeches might raise their own voices for their party and its candidates.

Party loyalty was fostered by dispensing patronage positions, and an increasing number of professional politicians saw that voters kept faith with their benefactors by voting on election day. Efficiency and coordination at the state and local levels characterized the party system, while loyalty and discipline characterized the partisan constituency.

To assure itself of the maximum amount of voter support, each party routinely sought to absorb and neutralize social dissonance. Divisive issues or personalities could only alienate voters. The party, therefore, carefully avoided controversial issues or rigid intransigence on any subject. Instead, each party pursued sound bargaining positions from which to negotiate compromises with adversaries. Compromise and conciliation, rather than confrontation, were the accepted operating principles of the Democrats and Whigs by 1840.

However, there were significant differences. The Democratic Party of the

1840's nurtured the above mentioned partisan skills to a great degree. Historians have long been impressed by the professional skills of Democratic politicians, especially their organizational ability and their success in mobilizing support at state and local levels as they adapted their electoral techniques to the decentralization of American society. In contrast, the Whig Party has received mixed reviews. Though highly competitive with the Democrats, Whigs often found party organization less congenial than their competitors. This anti-partyism was deeply rooted in the social character of the Whig constituency. Historians generally accept the notion that "Whig anti-partyism drew sustenance from the evangelical, moral reform, benevolent and Christianizing strains lacing Whiggery in many social and geographic sectors."[43] Thus, wherever in the North there tended to be a substantial number of Yankee Protestants and a prevalence of pietism, the Whigs tended toward anti-partyism. This anti-partyism derived from evangelicalism was based upon the concern that organizational loyalty to party would restrict the individual's freedom of conscience so necessary for genuine religious conversion. Partisanship thus elevated disharmony to the level of virtue. In Huntington's terms, the Whigs were refusing to adapt sufficiently to the multiplication of competing interests in the country's electorate that demanded compromise and coalition. From the Whigs' perspective, loyalty to a coalition of interests that supplanted deference to traditional, responsible authority created a vaccuum in responsibility for the public welfare.[44]

The strategies open to the Liberty Party were defined by the keen competition between the two major parties. First, it could try to broaden its appeal, eventually either displacing one of the two major parties, or converting the political arena into a three party system. Or, it could gain concessions to its program from one of the other parties and later coalesce with it. This strategy would be especially successful if the new party could gain just enough votes to hold the balance of power in an election. Finally, the third party could continue its independent existence, getting a small percentage (2 or 3 percent) of the vote, while acting as a perpetual gadfly. The party could use the political podium to inform the public of its program, accepting as unlikely the possibility of immediate social change. The educational value of political debate would compensate for electoral victory.

There never developed among third party men a unanimity as to which of the various available strategies should be adopted. Even after the party was organized, many third party men were still undecided whether or not partisan politics was an appropriate means to moral reform. Their statements on the function of the new party reflect this indecision.

Liberty men such as Dr. Francis J. LeMoyne of Pennsylvania saw the party as a temporary expedient with an "emphatically religious" purpose, and he recommended that tactics be formulated consistent with the party's holy mission.[45] Gerrit Smith and Beriah Green echoed LeMoyne's sentiments when they described Liberty politics as "Bible Politics."[46] Lewis Tappan delayed joining the third party until 1843 precisely because he "feared the danger of getting absorbed in party politics."[47]

Other Liberty men, however, joined with New York's Alvan Stewart to proclaim that the Liberty Party would be permanent and soon competitive with the Democratic and Whig parties.[48] Salmon P. Chase of Ohio sought to hasten the process by advocating that the third party's name be changed from "Liberty" to "True Democrat" in the hope of drawing support from the Democratic ranks in his state.[49] Each Liberty man brought with him into the third party his own recipe for synthesizing moral reform with partisan politics.

Because the Liberty Party in New York, Michigan, and elsewhere in the North preyed disproportionately upon Whig ranks, some historians have dismissed the Liberty Party as merely a mutant of the Whig Party's antislavery wing that had retained many characteristics of the parent, including anti-partyism.[50] However, the Liberty Party occupied its own place on the traditional-modern axis. The Liberty Party demonstrated neither the entrepreneurial, politics-for-politics-sake character of the Democratic Party nor the willingness of many Whigs to pursue political power through compromise and coalition despite anti-party reservations. Liberty men carved for their party a unique niche on the institutionalization continuum between the extremes of party and anti-party. Liberty organizers and candidates clad themselves in the armor and displayed the weaponry of contemporary politicians in the 1840's, but their assumptions about their relationship to the electorate and the ends they prized most were those of a bygone era. Unlike most Whigs, Liberty men could not accept the pluralism of American society and adjust their platform and appeal accordingly. Nor could Liberty men sharply differentiate between religion and politics. Their goal was to synthesize the two. Most of all Liberty men persisted in pursuing power only as a means to a specific end—the abolition of black slavery—even though political power as an end in itself had become the *sine qua non* of partisan politics as practiced by the third party's two major adversaries.

However pre-modern or traditional their political ideas might have been, most Liberty men agreed upon the legitimacy of the American political party system, even as they condemned Democratic and Whig advocacy of slavery's protection by federal law. They did not share the more general anti-institutionalism of many non-political abolitionists. Instead they believed that it was Christians' responsibility not only to condemn evil but to sever their institutional associations with it. The Liberty Party's founding fathers, including abolitionists such as Myron Holley, Gerrit Smith, William Goodell, Alvan Stewart, and Joshua Leavitt sought to remedy the injustice of slavery by acquiring political power through a new, unsullied political institution rather than by renouncing all political institutions. They took pains, therefore, to appropriate the organizational forms and campaign tactics of their opponents, rather than those of their anti-party humanitarian allies in anti-slavery benevolent societies.

Liberty men tailored their style to the expectations of voters in the political culture of the 1840's and did not hesitate to imitate their adversaries in techniques of attracting voters. The popularity of party politics was in no small measure due to its function as a source of amusement.[51] Entertainment opportunities were sparse in antebellum America. In an era long before movies, radio, and television, individuals expected political gatherings to provide entertainment as well as news of public issues. Therefore, politicians in both major parties invested their prowess in creating a pageantry fit for the stage and a competitive ambiance with the flavor of sport. Indeed, wagering on the outcome of elections was as common as betting on a race or prize fight. Picnics, barbecues, mass rallies, parades, debates, and stump speeches all entertained as they informed. Prior to the election of 1840, the Whigs had erected log cabins in every village to dispense hard cider.[52] Enraged that the Whigs had devised such a novel way to practice a time-honored tradition, the Democrats had denounced the cabins as "groggeries." At the same time, however, Democrats hinted that the Whig brew was merely "diluted with whiskey," as compared with the thirst quencher that voters had come to expect at campaign festivities sponsored by the party of Jackson.[53]

Liberty men also sought to mix amusement and politics. In 1843, a New York Democratic newspaper editor described the colorful campaign run by local Liberty men that year:

In truth for weeks before the Election, the county was one immense cauldron of abolitionism—State Conventions, county conventions, town meetings, and District meetings and a touch of the Whig tactics of 1840: we had processions with banners and devices; and the Abolition Conventicles resounded with Abolition sentiment.[54]

While Democrats saw evidence of Whig hoopla in Liberty campaigning, the Whigs likewise claimed that the Democracy was the model for the third party's tactics. Liberty men understood the need to provide liquid refreshment every bit as much as their adversaries. However, since many Liberty men also believed in temperance, the toasts to party unity were often made in pure cold water rather than hard cider.[55]

Because the Liberty men regarded political victory as the means to the abolition of slavery, even festive occasions were slightly muted by the image of brothers bound in chains. On the Fourth of July 1844, some Erie County Liberty men assembled for a mass meeting and picnic:

At ½ past 11 a.m. a procession was formed and marched to a beautiful grove near the Center House, where the exercises consisted of prayer, music, social and instrumental, reading of the Declaration, Oration and Benediction. The weather was delightful and beneath the green canopy of leaves that Nature had hung over him, and accompanied by the music of birds and breeze, the clear tones of the speaker arose, eloquently asserting the God given rights and denouncing the time-sanctioned wrongs of his own injured race, and of universal man.[56]

Some Liberty Party celebrations were as tumultuous as any Whig or Democratic festivity, but more often they reflected the moral reform advocated by the third party and were a synthesis of political rally and church supper. Whatever the tone, the purpose was the same—to enliven politics, and make it palatable to a mass audience.

Of course, no celebration, wild or tame, is complete without music. The Whigs' Log Cabin campaign of 1840 had featured party songs. Roving glee clubs serenaded communities with partisan melodies and party songsters were published. George W. Clark composed many political songs, including one for the Liberty Party and their presidential candidate, James G. Birney:

> We are coming, we are coming!
> Freedom's battle is begun!
> No hand shall furl her banner
>   ere her victory be won!
> Our shields are locked for Liberty,
>   and mercy goes before
> Tyrants tremble in our citadel!
>   Oppression shall be O'er.
> We will vote for Birney! We will
>   vote for Birney!
> We're for Liberty and Birney and
>   for freedom through the land.[57]

Partisan songs were not designed to merely rouse the spirits, but to imprint upon voters' minds the names of candidates and party symbols. Just as the log cabin was an image that Whigs wished voters to recall, so "liberty" and "Birney" were knit into the lyrics that Liberty leaders hoped would be on the lips of voters for days after they heard a campaign melody.

The enthusiasm for politics stirred by parties and songs produced a demand for talented and engaging political speakers. Listening to long political speeches was a favorite pastime of nineteenth-century Americans, one that all parties sought to exploit. The *Liberty Press* of Utica, New York, announced that, "righteous but unpopular reforms must never overlook the instrumentalities in vogue in any age among a people for the circulation of intelligence. . . . In our day, the most popular is that of public lecturing."[58] Liberty speakers mounted the stump to edify and entertain others and, they hoped, to sway votes.

Stumping the state by political candidates was a common practice for those seeking state office. Though few presidential candidates sought to stump all the states where they sought votes, many did schedule speaking tours. Such tours were grueling experiences and often the candidate was vulnerable to adversaries along the way. In the campaign preceding the election of 1844, as Liberty candidates paid the Democrats and Whigs the compliment of imitation, one of the major parties demonstrated its respect for the third party in a slightly different manner—by making it the object of a "dirty trick."

Several days before election day in 1844, a number of northern newspapers published a letter allegedly written by Liberty candidate James G. Birney to J. B. Garland of Saginaw, Michigan. The letter, sworn to by Garland himself, first appeared in the *Genessee County Democrat Extra* of October 21. In the letter, Birney accepted a Democratic county nomination for the Michigan state legislature, professed to be a Democrat, and avowed that if elected, he would not raise the issue of slavery. It was all a skillfully managed fraud.[59]

The letter was republished in Ohio, Massachusetts, Connecticut, Maine, and New York. Birney was on tour travelling westward, across New York State, on October 29, when it appeared in a New York City paper. It had not been published in western New York until after Birney had passed through so that he would not have the opportunity to make a public denial until after he was thoroughly discredited in the eyes of the voters.[60] From the Western Reserve, Birney finally denied authorship of the letter. Only after the election, however, was it revealed as a forgery commissioned by the Whig Central Committee and printed in the office of a Whig paper. Abolitionists believed that the Garland forgery hurt the Liberty Party at the polls in 1844, though they could not estimate its impact.[61]

Speaking tours not only entailed risks but were limited in the number of voters that could be reached. Not so the newspaper. In the antebellum period, newspapers were the single most important source of political information. Financial resources determined size and the range was great, from the eight-page dailies in New York City to the more typical four-page weekly with only one or two of those pages covering news and even that was often derived by "clipping" articles from other papers and republishing them. With the exception of denominational newspapers, almost all antebellum papers were openly partisan, flying one or another party's symbol on the masthead and accepting financial subsidization from that party. Newspapers thrust the party creed and the names of its leaders into readers' homes more regularly than any other vehicle. Editors, who were frequently important members of party hierarchies, themselves, colored the news to suit their party. Their purpose was to hold the committed reader, recover the flagging supporter and convert the dubious.

Though not every third party abolitionist could manage to hear a Liberty Party speaker, he could, for $2.00 a year "payable in advance," receive the *Liberty Press* published by Wesley Bailey in Utica, New York, and edited by James C. Jackson. The *Liberty Press,* which in 1842 succeeded the *Friend of Man* in Utica, and the *Albany Patriot* were the official newspapers of the New York Liberty Party.[62] The *Emancipator,* which had originally belonged to the American Anti-Slavery Society, was taken over by the New York Anti-Slavery Society after the break with the Garrisonians in 1840. In 1842, Joshua Leavitt moved the paper to Boston where it continued to fight for political abolition.[63] In addition, there were many lesser known local Liberty Party newspapers in New York, such as the *Courtland True American* and the *Herkimer Freeman;* in other states, the *Philanthropist* of Ohio, and the *Signal of Liberty* in Michigan spread the abolitionist message.

Liberty newspapers were often short-lived. Because the party won few elections even at the township level, there was no patronage to be bartered for contributions and the Liberty newspapers chronically suffered from financial problems. Party spokesmen blamed the condition on those who were sufficiently sympathetic to the slave to cast Liberty ballots, while continuing their subscriptions to "pro-slavery" papers.[64] Whatever the reason, only contributions by wealthy patrons temporarily staved off the failure of most Liberty newspapers.

The two or three page pamphlets or tracts distributed by Liberty campaigners may have reached more voters than the financially troubled third party newspapers, but the costs of printing and circulation caused tract distribution to be unsystematic and circumscribed, except just prior to elections. Then, Liberty Party presses turned out campaign material comparable to that of the major parties. For example, prior to the election of 1844, copies of Liberty presidential candidate James G. Birney's portrait were made and advertised at one dollar apiece, eight dollars a dozen, or fifty dollars a hundred. As the campaign progressed, over fifty thousand copies of the *Liberty Almanac* were published to publicize Birney's virtues nationally.[65] Newspapers and pamphlets were the new media being used by antebellum politicians to reach members of a dispersed population in a decentralized society. And Liberty men were quick to use them, as well.

Party organization, too, reflected the dispersed population and decentralization of antebellum American society. National parties were a loose coalition of state organizations, each of which jealously protected its powers and prerogatives. Among Whigs and Democrats, national committees sought to give some direction to presidential campaigns and raised and channelled campaign funds to states in special need of assistance. They also issued policy directives but had no means to ensure their acceptance. Party discipline was established at state and local levels largely by a state committee that ran its own campaign and set its own policy guidelines. This lack of centralized party control simultaneously risked factionalism and mutinies even as it allowed politicians to direct their appeals to local concerns, thereby strengthening the bonds between party and voter. Party leaders thus had much independence and bore great responsibility for their party's fate.[66]

Liberty men constructed a conventional organizational structure for their party, one almost exactly like that of the Whigs and Democrats.

State, town, ward, and district committees were formed by Liberty men in all northern states ancillary to a national committee. The national committee had "general care and oversight" of the cause throughout the nation, a mandate that included the same duties performed by the Democratic and Whig central committees—collecting funds, employing campaigners, and arranging conventions.[67] The first Liberty Party national committee consisted of New Yorkers Alvan Stewart, Gerrit Smith, and William Goodell.[68] Less than two years later, though, the triumvirate was replaced with a committee of twelve that reflected greater geographic balance. Prominent abolitionists such as Joshua Leavitt of Massachusetts, Francis J. LeMoyne of Pennsylvania, Salmon P. Chase of Ohio, James H. Collins of Illinois, and Luther G. Stevens of Michigan joined Stewart on the Liberty national committee.[69]

These prominent party leaders and other state delegates met in national conventions to formulate national party platforms and to nominate presidential and vice-presidential candidates. National Liberty conventions were held in 1841, 1843, and 1847. Though the party had entered the campaign of 1840 with only a statement of principles, the Liberty Party quickly conformed to the other parties' style and prepared formal platforms in 1843 and 1847.

Below the national level, Liberty men held state and local conventions to nominate candidates and to perform the other functions of their Whig and Democratic counterparts. Committees were formed to oversee campaign activities. Liberty men were as aware as their adversaries of the importance of grass-roots organization and local elections. Committee leaders reminded campaigners,

It has been found by experiment that county, township, village, city and ward nominations and votes are among the most effectual measures for carrying the discussion of antislavery principles and measures into the minute ramifications of society—the most retiring and remote corners of the community.[70]

What the Liberty men did not say was that the party structure and campaign tactics they used at the grass-roots level emulated those already in use by the Democrats and Whigs.

How could an organization so apparently preoccupied with the paraphernalia of party be practitioners of "political antipolitics?" Even as Liberty men paraded, sang, harangued, and barbecued on behalf of the slave, their basic assumptions about politics and the ends that political endeavors could and should achieve served to subvert their best efforts at self-promotion. The Liberty Party's incomplete political institutionalization, the vestiges of pre-modern or traditional politics woven into its very fabric, limited its possibilities for electoral victory. Compounded by the inherently limited

appeal of slavery's abolition to most northern voters, the third party's vestigial form left it the role of spoiler. Unable to win power themselves, Liberty
men could only snipe at the major parties. The wounds third party men
inflicted, while superficial, were never adequately treated. Left to fester, they
gradually helped undermine the second party system and later contributed
to the political paralysis that failed to arrest secession.

The pre-modern attitude of third party men is best demonstrated by the
absence of "autonomy" and "differentiation", which Samuel Huntington
identifies as essential components of institutionalization.[71] Liberty men rejected autonomy and did not seek to respond to the needs and aspirations
of multiple social groups and interests. Indeed, Liberty men consciously
rejected a pluralistic perspective on American society, arguing that such a
perspective would be divisive and divert attention from the slave's cause.
Liberty men opted to postpone consideration of all issues other than slavery,
rhetorically asking,

What if the *liberty*-party should have its questions?—and suppose they should be
emancipation—abolition—human freedom, instead of the price of cotton? Suppose
"tarrif" [sic].—"Bank."—"Sub-Treasury," and other topics of doubtful disputation
among our wisest and best men, should be left open for future consideration?[72]

In order to assemble large electoral bases, capable of outvoting its opposition, the Democratic Party led the way in the creation of electoral
coalitions including voters of different backgrounds and interests. Through
compromise and consideration, Democratic politicians broadened their party's base by appealing to a broad range of voters, even those whose interests
were in direct conflict with one another. Because perfect agreement upon a
single, rigid political agenda was unlikely among the myriad of America's
economic, religious, ethnic, and sectional factions, professional politicians
pursued the broadest, vaguest program with the possibility of appealing to
the maximum number of voters.

Between 1840 and 1844, the Liberty Party platform was not similarly
expanded to include positions on social and economic issues other than
slavery. Yet Liberty men did seek to follow Gerrit Smith's recommendation
that party documents spell out specifically the broad ramifications of slavery
for the lives of all Americans.[73] The result was an anti-southernism that
focused upon the economic impact of slavery upon the North. The Liberty
Party platform of 1844 mentioned in one resolution the unpaid debts of
slaveholders; a second demanded that the federal government secure the
markets of the world for the produce of "free labor," which clearly would
place southern produce at a disadvantage; and a third demanded that the
federal government refrain from using slave labor on public works in the
slave states. General demands for retrenchment and publicly financed education were included, but not vigorously demanded or discussed at length.[74]

This anti-southernism may have found an audience especially among less affluent artisans, merchants, and laborers who were moved by Liberty appeals that linked the condition of the slave to that of the northern free white worker. In the developing counties of western New York, where the Liberty Party was unusually strong among these occupational groups, there is evidence that the third party sought to demonstrate a link between the interests of southern slaveholders and a northern "aristocracy."[75] Liberty men warned that failure to abolish slavery might enhance the possibility that free white workers would be "reduced . . . to the condition of serfs" by a "system of class legislation" for which southerners and their northern allies would lobby.[76] Never could the parties that oppressed the "poor *black* man," be trusted by "the poor white man," Liberty men insisted.[77] Occasionally Liberty men even referred to themselves as "The Poor Man's Party."[78] Such appeals were as close as Liberty men came to a pluralistic view of the non-slave society.

The Liberty Party's monistic approach was crippling in a society that was becoming increasingly multi-ethnic and celebrating its diversity. The arrival of 4.5 million immigrants between 1840 and 1860 aroused apprehension among many Americans, though many politicians and reformers saw the newcomers as a reservoir of potential support. The Irish were especially attractive to politicians and reformers alike. One and three-quarter million Irishmen arrived in the United States between 1840 and 1860, almost 40 percent of the total immigration.[79] Most were Roman Catholics from the southern provinces, fleeing the potato famine and the oppressiveness of English rule.

The Roman Catholic Church traditionally held that while slavery existed in society as a consequence of original sin, it was not an inherently sinful institution. It did not proscribe slavery and most Irish immigrants were not abolitionists.[80] They feared free blacks as economic rivals for unskilled jobs and preferred that blacks—slave and free—occupy the ground floor of America's economic edifice, rather than themselves.[81] However, Irish Catholic patriot Daniel O'Connell attempted to link his people's struggle against the British for home rule and the slave's plight.[82] In Ireland, O'Connell organized associations to repeal the Act of Union (1800), and in 1840 he issued "An Address From the People of Ireland To Their Countrymen and Countrywomen in the United States"; it was signed by 60,000 Irishmen.[83]

O'Connell described black slavery to his former countrymen as "that foul blot upon the noble institution and fair fame of your adopted country," and entreated them to "take the part of justice, religion and liberty . . . WE CALL UPON YOU TO UNITE WITH THE ABOLITIONISTS." Calling upon Irish immigrants to "treat the colored people as your equals, as brethren," O'Connell urged them to battle slavery at the ballot box as well as with their moral voices.[84]

There is no evidence that Irish immigrants in New York or any other state responded to O'Connell's gesture enthusiastically. And some Liberty men suspected that O'Connell's motive for adopting their cause was less than altruistic. Gerrit Smith wrote a seething reply to an O'Connell request for a donation to American Irish repeal associations in July 1843. Smith fumed, "We cannot connect ourselves with the Repeal associations of this country;—for being principled and impartial lovers of Liberty, we cannot consent to associate for the advancement of her cause with those, who, we know, hate her and who will never even seem to be her friends save when some selfish calculation suggests the expediency or when passion or prejudice impels them in that direction."[85] Neither Democrats nor Whigs hesitated to do what the third party men would not. Both parties ringingly endorsed the repeal cause, even arguing over which of them had been more outspoken in the cause of repeal, in the hope of attracting Irish voters concerned about their native land.[86]

After the Democratic victory in 1844, Liberty men debated more vigorously than ever broadening their party's platform. In 1845, Michigan Liberty men Theodore Foster and Guy Beckley, with the encouragement of James G. Birney, proposed a platform that addressed some major issues of the day. It advocated a lower tariff, reduction of presidential power, a decrease in the size of the armed forces, and thorough judicial reform.[87] Most party leaders rejected the proposals and the plan was dropped, but advocates of a broad platform were only temporarily silenced.[88]

In June 1847, a splinter group of broad-platform advocates led by William Goodell met at Macedon Lock, New York, to form the Liberty League. The Leaguers adopted a platform that proclaimed the Constitution an antislavery document and condemned slavery as "illegal, unconstitutional, and anti-republican." The League approved ultimate disbanding of the armed forces; free trade; direct per capita taxation, including slaves in order to stimulate sentiment for emancipation; and the distribution of public lands "in small parcels, to landless men, for the mere cost of distributing." The League platform condemned secret societies and denounced all monopolies, even that of the federal government in mail delivery.[89] As Liberty men throughout the North considered the League's program and chose sides, the Liberty Party became irreparably factionalized.[90]

Leaguers did not consider themselves out of the Liberty Party, though they maintained a separate organization. They insisted that they merely wished to reform the Liberty Party on the broader principles they advocated. They did, however, nominate Gerrit Smith for the presidency without his knowledge or consent, a month before the National Liberty Party Nominating Convention was scheduled to meet to choose the Party's presidential candidate for 1848. Smith protested at first but then had a change of heart and explained that Liberty Party men need not quit the Party to join the

League but "wherein the latter is superior to the former, 'let us walk by the same rule—let us mind the same thing'—whatever foolish pride or dirty jealousy or any other wicked spirit may counsel to the contrary."[91]

Smith's advice was easier given than taken. When the National Liberty Party Nominating Convention met in Buffalo, October 20–21, 1847, both Liberty Party men and Liberty Leaguers were present. Resolutions calling slavery unconstitutional in the states and widening the platform were both defeated. Moreover, John P. Hale, a former Democrat from New Hampshire, bested Smith for the Party nomination. Those who supported Hale cited not only his commitment to abolitionism but the expediency of nominating an ex-Democrat.[92] Purists raised the question of loyalty, fearing that Hale's apostasy to third partyism was temporary.[93] Mortified Liberty Leaguers called for a second Buffalo convention to meet in June 1848, so that abolitionists could reconsider their decision and perhaps nominate a candidate who professed the principles of a "true Civil Government and a true Liberty Party."[94]

Many Liberty men refused to attend the second convention. Those who did, called themselves the National Liberty Party to distinguish themselves from those who accepted Hale's nomination and the one issue platform. Actually, the convention did little more than appropriate the name "Liberty Party" for the League program, denounce John P. Hale, and nominate Gerrit Smith for the presidency.[95] The Liberty Party had become a scramble of feuding factions, and the cause of the slave was buried beneath a mound of rhetoric.

If the Liberty Party lacked the autonomy of modern, institutionalized parties, it was equally lacking in differentiation, the separation of the political from other societal areas of activity.[96] Tocqueville had observed that although America was without an established church to "exercise influence upon the laws" and the "details of public opinion," religion did direct the "customs of the community and by regulating domestic life, it regulates the state." Religion, he observed, is the "first of their [Americans'] political institutions."[97] The Liberty Party, dedicated to "Bible Politics," sought more than either the Democrats or the Whigs to synthesize religion and politics. Liberty men had repeatedly declared the propagation of moral reform to be the sole justification for partisan political activity. One critic urged Liberty men to behave like other politicians and "strive to separate secular from holy things—'rending to Caesar the things that are Caesar's and to God the things that are God's.' "[98] However, Liberty men claimed to be a different breed of politician. Some, such as Gerrit Smith and Beriah Green, had engaged in the controversial tactic of preaching antislavery politics on the Sabbath. Smith had never in so many words urged worshippers to vote Liberty. Such technicalities, though, did not inhibit non-abolitionists from accusing Smith and others of desecrating the Lord's Day. Beriah Green's ejection from a pulpit in Rochester and similar incidents caused Gerrit Smith to respond to his critics. After apologizing to the "many truly good people, who are not reconciled to the use of the Sabbath," he proceeded to defend his belief that "every man's politics are a part of his religion; and that no man's religion is any better than his politics." If he could only persuade the American people of that proposition, Smith contended, then "there would be a scampering from the Democratic and Whig parties as of rats from a sinking ship."[99] Other Liberty men generally shared Smith's belief and often ended their campaign rhetoric with an appeal directly to the religious convictions of voters. With the humility of the genuinely devout they asked, "Say Christian, will it be 'throwing away' your vote to adopt 'Bible Politics' and vote for righteous law makers? If you pray for righteous rulers, don't vote for unrighteous ones. If you 'remember those in bonds as bound with them,' three hundred and sixty-four days in a year, don't vote yourself a hypocrite on the three-hundreth and sixty-fifth."[100]

The single most anti-political aspect of Liberty Party politics was the unwillingness of Liberty men to treat the acquisition of power through partisan competition and compromise as the proper end of politics. Just as eighteenth-century Americans often defined the proper role of politics as the preservation of a stable social harmony, free of the scramble by competing factions for power, so Liberty men eschewed the pursuit of power for any purpose other than securing slavery's abolition. Liberty journalists entreated their readers, "Let us maintain our integrity, cling firmly to our principles and Heaven will smile upon the first party that this country has ever had whose purpose it is to confer TRUE LIBERTY upon all men."[101] Branding those with views less committed to abolitionism than their one as "unrighteous" or "hypocrites" merely reinforced the third party's public image as one of unyielding self-righteousness in the name of principle.[102] Compromise and conciliation, the linchpins of partisan competition in the antebellum period, were relegated by Liberty men to the moral junk heap of sinfulness. They perceived their party as an extension of a religious anti-institutionalism, called "come-outerism" by contemporaries. Come-outerism required abandoning the world's evil ways and institutions entering into a purified Christian relationship with that world.[103] Moral reform was the vehicle for this new relationship. Thus, Liberty men who had abandoned one of the major parties were renouncing sin by severing their institutional connections with it. In place of these abandoned institutions, they substituted new ones, such as their own party, that would stand erect in an uncompromising moral posture, pursuing power only for the moral purpose to which it could be put.

By August 1848, the Liberty Party had degenerated into squabbling splinter groups when it merged with a coalition of dissident Democrats and antislavery Whigs in the new Free Soil Party.[104] The new party described itself as "a union of freemen for the sake of freedom . . . in common resolve to maintain the rights of free labor against the aggressions of the slave power, and to secure free soil for a free people."[105] Led by New Yorker Henry B. Stanton, the delegation, representing an irreparably factionalized Liberty Party, endorsed the new party and accepted a compromise of candidate for principle. The Liberty men received concessions in the party platform in return for withdrawing Hale's candidacy in favor of Martin Van Buren's nomination. Van Buren had declared in the summer of 1848 that he was not opposed to slavery in the District of Columbia, one of the basic demands of the Liberty Party. He quickly reversed himself, however, when he became convinced that Liberty support for his nomination hinged on the inclusion of that principle in the platform.[106]

The Free Soil platform declared that state law alone was responsible for the preservation of slavery, and therefore, the federal government could not interfere with slavery in the states where it existed. However, to satisfy the Liberty men, the Free Soil platform did provide for the complete separation of the federal government from slavery, which would, in effect, bar the institution from the territories, as well as from the District of Columbia. Some irreconcilable Liberty men accused Stanton of having abandoned Hale for the promise of an attorney-generalship for himself, but most accepted the compromise and agreed with Joshua Leavitt that the Liberty Party was "not dead but translated."[107] Only the small Liberty League clique resisted the Liberty Party's demise by supporting Gerrit Smith for the presidency in 1848.

The Free Soil coalition was not victorious in 1848, though it garnered 10.1 percent of the vote and attracted a broader base of voters than the Liberty Party had in either 1840 or 1844. The Free Soilers could count among their numbers many prominent Liberty men including Salmon P. Chase, Gamaliel Bailey, John P. Hale, and William P. Fessenden. Others who favored a broader platform but deplored coalition with members of other parties, such as William Goodell and Gerrit Smith, refused to become Free Soilers. Liberty men never achieved unanimity on a strategy for victory and that enduring conflict determined the direction that individual Liberty men took after their party's demise.

Examination of the Liberty Party's organizational structure and operation suggests that the third party is worthy of serious study as both a political organization and a vehicle for reform. Liberty men did not belong to a sect in search of converts but consciously chose to adopt the organizational format and strategic approach of a political party pursuing electoral victory. Even the most skeptical Liberty men did not find politics to be irreparably corrupt, just in urgent need of reform. A new party, unsullied by pro-slavery men, seemed preferable to total withdrawal from political participation and more practical than an attempt to bore from within either of the two major parties.

Liberty men never ceased condemning the Democrats and Whigs as the immoral defenders of a heinous and unchristian institution. However, Liberty men were also aware of the intense voter loyalty and partisan discipline that the Democrats and Whigs commanded. The third party's decision to adopt the organizational structure and many of the campaign tactics of the major parties suggests that the Liberty men permitted themselves to be schooled by their adversaries. Anti-party statements uttered by third party abolitionists reflected a hostility to the power and influence of the major parties far more than an ideological uneasiness with the presence of party organization and mass political techniques.

Why then, was the third party so short-lived? The 1840's was an age of partisanship, characterized by a highly competitive two party system. Precisely how to operate successfully within the political culture puzzled third party men. Much of the problem derived from the definition of "successfully." While Democrats and most Whigs defined success as the acquisition of power through electoral victory, Liberty men defined the term to mean progress toward the abolition of slavery. Power was a means to a very specific end but never an end in itself. The moral integrity of the slave's cause must not be auctioned for votes. This definition of success resulted in the incomplete institutionalization of the third party embodied in the colorful label "political antipolitics." On the traditional-modern continuum, the Liberty Party with its vestigial political attitudes placed much closer to the former pole than to the latter. The party's internal tension over the reconciliation of moral reform and political exigency remained unresolved and even escalated between 1840 and 1848.

Broadening the Liberty Party platform and drawing more sharply the distinction between religion and politics may or may not have attracted a wider base of voters. However, the controversy among Liberty men over these issues does reflect the tension that ultimately destroyed the third party. And the major parties were never adverse to greasing the skids by forcing third party men into choices between politics and principles.[108] Ironically, many of those who refused to widen the platform later negotiated a compromise even more deleterious to the third party. They joined the Free Soil coalition in the hope of achieving the third party's goals in exchange for their support of Martin Van Buren in 1848. That hope, too, however, was soon dashed, and the third party's program remained unfulfilled.

As did Liberty man William Goodell, historians can only speculate what the state of antebellum politics would have been "if the sixty thousand Liberty men who voted for Birney in 1844 had held firmly *that* position."[109] Certainly such speculation remains alive among historians who continue to debate the repressibility or irrepressibility of the Civil War. They persist in disagreeing over the role of abolitionists and politicians in exacerbating sectional divisions.[110] Among them, some historians engaged in neo-revisionism, such as Michael Holt, contend that individual decisions of politicians were "important in exacerbating" the sectional conflict. Other scholars, such as Kenneth Stampp, insist that a complex "interplay" of pro-slavery and antislavery forces, not "the irresponsible blunders of northern or southern politicians" created an irrepressible conflict.[111] The Liberty Party is crucial to both views—to the former, because the third party helped crumble the second American party system, served as a "bridge for voters in motion" out of the Whig coalition, and contributed to the political fragmentation that blocked the path to compromise with partisan debris; to the latter, because Liberty Party abolitionists shifted the issue of slavery from the pulpit to the stump, where it would remain a divisive controversy with which northerners and southerners could torment each other until the Civil War.

NOTES

1. Theodore Parker, "The Present Aspect of the Anti-slavery Enterprise," *The Rights of Man,* ed. F. B. Sanborn (Boston: American Unitarian Associates, 1911), p. 397.

2. William Goodell, *Slavery and Anti-slavery* (New York: William Harned, 1852), p. 471.

3. Ibid.

4. Ibid., p. 472.

5. Especially provocative on both of these issues during the 1960's was Aileen Kraditor, *Means and Ends in American Abolitionism, Garrison and His Critics on Strategy and Tactics, 1834–1850* (New York: Pantheon, 1969). Two more recent volumes that deal with the radicalism of abolitionist are Lewis Perry, *Radical Abolitionism: Anarchy and the Government of God in Antislavery Thought* (Ithaca: Cornell University Press, 1973), and Ronald G. Walters, *The Antislavery Appeal, American Abolitionism After 1830* (Baltimore: The Johns Hopkins University Press, 1976). Perry finds the roots of abolitionism radicalism in the thought, especially the religious thought, of reformers. Walters finds the differences among abolitionists less impressive than their similar reaction to cultural tensions produced by rapid social change.

6. David Hackett Fischer, *Historians' Fallacies: Toward a Logic of Historical Thought* (New York: Harper and Row, 1970), pp. 9–10. Among others Fischer refers to Richard O. Curry, ed., *The Abolitionists, Reformers or Fanatics?* (New York: Holt, Rinehart and Winston, 1965).

7. Gilbert Hobbs Barnes, *The Antislavery Impulse, 1830–1844* (New York: Harcourt, Brace and World, 1933), p. 176. Aileen Kraditor, "The Liberty and Free Soil Parties," in Arthur M. Schlesinger, Jr., ed., *History of the U.S. Political Parties* (New York: Chelsea House Publishers, 1973), 1:741 and *Means and Ends in American Abolitionism, Garrison and His Critics on Strategy and Tactics, 1834–1850,* pp. 141–177, passim. Eric Foner, *Free Soil, Free Labor, Free Men: The Ideology of the Republican Party Before the Civil War* (New York: Oxford University Press, 1970), p. 78. Lewis Perry, *Radical Abolitionism: Anarchy and the Government of God in Antislavery Thought,* pp. 170–187, passim.

8. Ronald P. Formisano, "Political Character, Antipartyism and the Second Party System," *American Quarterly,* 21 (Winter 1969): 704–706.

9. Richard H. Sewell, *Ballots for Freedom* (New York: Oxford University Press, 1976) is the most recent and most comprehensive book-length account of the Liberty

Party's history and its significance in the antislavery movement. The only previously published book on the Liberty Party is Theodore Clarke Smith, *The Liberty and Free Soil Parties in the Northwest* (New York: Longmans, Green and Company, 1897). There have also been a few articles published: Julian R. Bretz, "The Economic Background of the Liberty Party," *American Historical Review*, 24 (January 1929): 250–264; R. L. Morrow, "The Liberty Party in Vermont," *New England Quarterly*, 2 (April 1929): 234–248; Joseph G. Rayback, "The Liberty Party Leaders of Ohio: Exponents of Antislavery Coalition," *The Ohio State Archeological and Historical Quarterly*, 57 (April 1948): 165–178; Hugh H. Davis, "The Failure of Political Abolitionism," *Connecticut Review*, 6 (April 1948): 76–86; Aileen Kraditor, "The Liberty and Free Soil Parties," *History of the U.S. Political Parties*, 1: 741–763; John L. Hammond, "Revival Religion and Antislavery Politics," *American Sociological Review*, 39 (April 1974): 175–186; Reinhard O. Johnson, "The Liberty Party in New Hampshire, 1840–1848," *Historical New Hampshire*, 3 (Spring 1978): 123–166, "The Liberty Party in Vermont, 1840–1848: The Forgotten Abolitionist," *Vermont History*, 47 (Fall 1979): 258–275, and "The Liberty Party in Massachusetts, 1840-1848: Antislavery Third Party Politics in the Bay State," *Civil War History*, 28 (September 1982): 237–265; Alan M. Kraut, "The Forgotten Reformers: A Profile of Third Party Abolitionist in Antebellum New York," Lewis Perry and Michael Fellman, eds., *Antislavery Reconsidered, New Perspectives on Abolitionists* (Baton Rouge: Louisiana State University Press, 1979), pp. 119–145 and with Phyllis F. Field, "Politics Versus Principles: The Partisan Response to 'Bible Politics' in New York State," *Civil War History*, 25 (June 1979): 101–118; Lawrence J. Friedman, "The Gerrit Smith Circle: Abolitionism in the Burned-Over District," *Civil War History*, 26 (March 1980): 18–38. Several doctoral dissertations on the Liberty Party include: Margaret Louise Plunkett, "A History of the Liberty Party with Emphasis Upon Its Activities in the Northeastern States" (Ph.D. diss., Cornell University, 1930); John R. Hendricks, "The Liberty Party in New York State, 1838–1848" (Ph.D. diss., Fordham University, 1959); Alan M. Kraut, "The Liberty Men of New York: Political Abolitionism in New York State, 1840–1848" (Ph.D. diss., Cornell University, 1975); Reinhard O. Johnson, "The Liberty Party in New England, 1840–1848: The Forgotten Abolitionists" (Ph.D. diss., Syracuse University, 1976).

10. James Brewer Stewart, *Holy Warriors: The Abolitionists and American Slavery* (New York: Hill and Wang, 1976), p. 97.

11. See especially Kraut and Field, "Politics Versus Principles."

12. Lee Benson, *The Concept of Jacksonian Democracy: New York as a Test Case* (Princeton: Princeton University Press, 1961); Michael Fitzgibbon Holt, *Forging a Majority: The Foundation of the Republican Party in Pittsburgh, 1848–1860* (New Haven: Yale University Press, 1969) and *The Political Crisis of the 1850's* (New York: John Wiley & Sons, 1978); Ronald P. Formisano, *The Birth of Mass Political Parties, Michigan, 1827–1861* (Princeton: Princeton University Press, 1971); Paul Kleppner, *The Third Electoral System, 1853–1892, Parties, Voters and Political Cultures* (Chapel Hill: University of North Carolina Press, 1979).

13. Sewell, *Ballots for Freedom*, p. 82.

14. Walters, *Antislavery Appeal*, p. 16.

15. Lewis Perry, "Review of *Ballots for Freedom*," *Journal of Southern History*, 43 (February 1977): 124–125.

16. Kleppner, *Third Electoral System*, pp. 65–66.

17. Alexis de Tocqueville, *Democracy in America,* ed. Phillips Bradley (New York: Random House, 1957), 1: 258–263. Francis Trollope, *Domestic Manners of the Americans,* ed. Donald Smalley (New York: Alfred A. Knopf, 1949), p. 162.

18. Henry B. Stanton, *Random Recollections* (New York: Harper & Brothers, 1887), p. 65.

19. New York voters contributed almost 40 percent of the national Liberty vote in the presidential election of 1840 (2,790 of a total 7,053 votes), and 25 percent of the national total in 1844 (15,814 votes of a total 62,097). Svend Petersen, *A Statistical History of the American Presidential Elections* (New York: Frederick Ungar Publishing Co., 1963), pp. 24–26. For analysis of the New York Liberty Party vote at the township level, see Kraut, "Liberty Men of New York," pp. 157–208.

20. William Lloyd Garrison, reply to "A Letter on the Political Obligations of Abolitionists" by James G. Birney (Boston: n.p., 1839).

21. Tocqueville, *Democracy in America,* 1: 260.

22. William Gienapp, " 'Politics Seems To Enter Into Everything,' Political Culture In The North, 1840–1860" (unpublished paper presented as part of the Walter Prescott Webb Memorial Lecture Series, University of Texas at Arlington, 1981), pp. 6–8. See also Richard P. McCormick, "New Perspectives on Jacksonian Politics," *American Historical Review,* 65 (January 1960): 292, 296.

23. Calculations based upon data from the *Census of the State of New York for 1865* (Albany: C. Van Benthuysen, 1867), pp. xliii, lxxxii. Also, Richard P. McCormick, *The Second American Party System, Party Formations in the Jacksonian Era* (Chapel Hill: University of North Carolina Press, 1966), passim.

24. Ibid.

25. V. O. Key, Jr., *Southern Politics in State and Nation* (New York: Random House, 1949), pp. 298–311; also Frank J. Sorauf, *Political Parties in the American System* (Boston: Little, Brown and Company, 1964).

26. Richard Hofstadter, *The Paranoid Style in American Politics and Other Essays* (New York: Random House, 1967), p. ix; Murray Edelman, *The Symbolic Uses of Politics* (Urbana: University of Illinois Press, 1964), pp. 166–167; Robert K. Lane, *Political Life, Why and How People Get Involved in Politics* (Glencoe: The Free Press, 1959), pp. 299–300.

27. See note 12.

28. Ronald P. Formisano, "Deferential-Participant Politics: The Early Republic's Political Culture,1789–1840," *American Political Science Review,* 68 (June 1974): 473–487. See also, Formisano, "Federalists and Republicans: Parties, Yes—System, No," Paul Kleppner et al., eds., *The Evolution of American Electoral Systems* (Westport, Conn.: Greenwood Press, 1981), pp. 33–76. Richard Hofstadter, *The Idea of a Party System, The Rise of Legitimate Opposition in the United States, 1789–1840* (Berkeley: University of California Press, 1969), especially pp. 212–271.

29. Ronald P. Formisano, "Toward a Reorientation of Jacksonian Politics: A Review of the Literature, 1959–1975," *Journal of American History,* 63 (June 1976): 53. Historians who have most recently found uses for modernization theory in studying antebellum America have been critical of the methodological problems in utilizing this elusive concept. Eric Foner, "The Causes of the American Civil War: Recent Interpretations and New Directions," *Civil War History,* 20 (September 1974): 201–203; Richard D. Brown, *Modernizations, The Transformation of American Life, 1600–1865* (New York: Hill and Wang, 1976), p. 19; Robert Kelley, *The Cultural Pattern in American Politics, The First Century* (New York: Alfred A.

Knopf, 1979), pp. 20–22. Two excellent critiques of modernization theory are: Dean C. Tipps, "Modernization Theory and the Comparative Study of Societies: A Critical Perspective," *Comparative Study of Society and History,* 15 (1973): 199–226, and Raymond Grew, "Modernization and Its Discontents," *American Behavioral Scientist,* 21 (November/December 1977): 289–312. Nevertheless efforts continue to make modernization measurable. See Allan Schnaiberg, "Measuring Modernism: Theoretical and Empirical Explorations," *American Journal of Sociology,* 76 (September 1970): 399–425.

30. Formisano, "Toward a Reorientation of Jacksonian Politics," p. 65.

31. Karl Deutsch, "Social Mobilization and Political Development," *American Political Science Review,* 55 (September 1961): 494.

32. Samuel P. Huntington, *Political Order in Changing Societies* (New Haven: Yale University Press, 1968), p. 34.

33. Ibid., p. 12. See also, E. Spencer Wellhofer, "Dimensions of Party Development: A Study in Organizational Dynamics," *Journal of Politics,* 34 (February 1972): 153–182, and E. Spencer Wellhofer and Timothy M. Hennessey, "Political Party Development: Institutionalization, Leadership Recruitment and Behavior," *American Journal of Political Science,* 12 (February, 1974): 135–165.

34. Huntington, *Political Order,* pp. 12–24.

35. Ibid.

36. Formisano, "Toward a Reorientation of Jacksonian Politics," p. 54. Modernist theory has frequently bunched elements of political behavior that are separable. In this study the traditional-modern continuum for political institutionalization is being viewed one dimensionally. However, it may eventually be feasible for historians to construct alternative models of party institutionalization that view the process multi-dimensionally. Ideology, social sources of support, voter discipline, temporal stability, and organizational strategy and tactics, are just a few of the dimensions that might be included along continua in such models.

37. James M. McPherson, *Ordeal By Fire, The Civil War and Reconstruction* (New York: Alfred A. Knopf, 1982), pp. 21–22.

38. Ibid.

39. Ibid.

40. Benson, *Concept of Jacksonian Democracy,* pp. 86–109.

41. James S. Chase, *Emergence of the Presidential Nominating Convention, 1789–1832* (Urbana: University of Illinois Press, 1973), pp. 276–292.

42. A good standard account of party procedures and campaign tactics is Roy. F. Nichols, *The Invention of the American Political Parties* (New York: The Macmillan Company, 1967), pp. 328–381. Also, Richard P. McCormick, *The Second American Party System,* pp. 346–356.

43. Ronald P. Formisano, "Political Character, Antipartyism and the Second Party System," p. 685.

44. Ibid, pp. 685–686. Also, Daniel Walker Howe, *The Political Culture of the American Whigs* (Chicago: University of Chicago Press, 1979), pp. 51–54.

45. Dr. Francis Julius LeMoyne to James Gillespie Birney, December 10, 1839, in Dwight L. Dumond, ed., *Letters of James Gillespie Birney, 1831–1857* (Reprinted, Gloucester: Peter Smith, 1966), 1: 511–514.

46. *Madison County Abolitionist,* December 7, 1841. Also Gerrit Smith, "To the Friends of the Slaves in the County of Madison," July 14, 1843, reprinted in *Letters of Gerrit Smith on Preaching Anti-Slavery Politics on Sunday* (n.p., 1943).

47. Lewis Tappan to Elizur Wright, October 9, 1843, Lewis Tappan Papers in the Library of Congress, Washington, D.C.

48. Alvan Stewart to Samuel Webb, November 13, 1841, Alvan Stewart Papers, New-York Historical Society.

49. William Birney to James Birney, November 25, 1844, in Dumond, ed., *Birney Letters*, 2: 886–887.

50. See especially: Formisano, "Political Character, Antipartyism and the Second Party System," p. 704, and *The Birth of Mass Political Parties*, p. 120; Benson, *Concept of Jacksonian Democracy*, pp. 134–135.

51. An excellent discussion of the entertainment function of party politics in antebellum political culture can be found in Gienapp, " 'Politics Seems To Enter Into Everything,' " pp. 23–29. See also Wilcomb Washburn, "The Great Autumnal Madness: Political Symbolism in Mid-Nineteenth Century America," *The Quarterly Journal of Speech*, 49 (December 1963): 417–431; Richard Jensen, "Armies, Admen, and Crusaders: Types of Presidential Elections," *History Teaches*, 2 (1960): 33–50; and Richard P. McCormick, *The Presidential Game, The Origins of American Presidential Politics* (New York: Oxford University Press, 1982), pp. 197–203.

52. McCormick, *The Presidential Game*, pp. 197–198.

53. *Mohawk Courier*, June 18, 1840.

54. *Madison Observer*, November 29, 1843. Similar accounts can be found scattered in newspapers during the early 1840's. *Emancipator*, June 3, August 5, September 23, 1841. *Detroit Advertiser*, December 9, 1941, December 4, 1843.

55. *Buffalo Daily Gazette*, July 10, 1844.

56. Ibid.

57. George Whitefield Clark, *The Liberty Minstrel* (New York: Leavitt and Aldin, 1844). *Liberty Almanacs* also contained such campaign songs.

58. *Liberty Press*, September 19, 1842.

59. Copy of Garland Letter, Dumond, ed., *Birney Letters*, 2: 869.

60. William Birney, *James G. Birney and His Times* (New York, 1890), p. 354.

61. Ibid. Also, Fladeland, *James G. Birney*, p. 245.

62. *Liberty Press*, December 6, 1842.

63. *Emancipator and Free American*, September 14, 1843.

64. *Liberty Press*, September 19, 1842.

65. *Emancipator and Weekly Chronicle*, August 14, 1844.

66. Gienapp, " 'Politics Seems To Enter Into Everything,' " pp. 46–47.

67. "Proceedings and Address of the Liberty National Nominating Convention, May 1841," *Emancipator Extra*, August 25, 1841.

68. Ibid.

69. *Liberty Press*, November 14, 1843.

70. "Proceedings and Address of the Liberty National Nominating Convention, May 1841," *Emancipator Extra*, August 25, 1841.

71. Huntington, *Political Order*, p. 32.

72. "Proceedings and Address of the Liberty National Nominating Convention, May 1841," *Emancipator Extra*, August 25, 1841.

73. Gerrit Smith to President of the Liberty Party, August 8, 1843, Gerrit Smith Papers, Syracuse University.

74. "The National Liberty Convention," *Emancipator and Free American*, September 14, 1843.

75. Kraut, "The Forgotten Reformers," pp. 129–131.

76. *Address read at the New York State Liberty Convention held at Port Byron, on Wednesday and Thursday, July 25 and 26, 1845,* Pamphlet, Olin Library, Cornell University.

77. "The Poor Man's Party," a circular signed "Your Friend," n.p., dated Peterboro, October 17, 1846.

78. Ibid.

79. U.S. Bureau of the Census, *The Statistical History of the United States,* with Introduction by Ben J. Wattenberg (New York: Basic Books, 1976), p. 10.

80. Madeline Hooke Rice, *American Catholic Opinion in the Slavery Controversy* (New York: Columbia University Press, 1944), p. 12. John Tracy Ellis, *American Catholicism,* second edition (Chicago: University of Chicago Press, 1969), pp. 89–90.

81. Most major studies of the Irish experience mention in passing the negative attitude of the Irish immigrant toward the black man and Irish rejection of the antislavery movement: Oscar Handlin, *Boston's Immigrants, A Study in Acculturation* (New York: Atheneum, 1969), pp. 132–133; Florence E. Gibson, *The Attitudes of the New York Irish Toward State and National Affairs* (New York: Columbia University Press, 1951), pp. 52–53; George Potter, *To the Golden Door, The Story of the Irish in Ireland and America* (Boston: Little, Brown and Company, 1960), pp. 371–386; William V. Shannon, *The American Irish* (New York: The Macmillan Company, 1963), pp. 54–56; Earl F. Niehaus, *The Irish in New Orleans* (Baton Rouge: Louisiana State University Press, 1965), pp. 51–54; Joseph M. Hernon, Jr., *Celts, Catholics and Copperheads* (Columbus: Ohio State University Press, 1968), pp. 65–67; Dennis Clark, *The Irish in Philadelphia, Ten Generations of Urban Experience* (Philadelphia: Temple University Press, 1973), pp. 18–19; Lawrence J. McCaffrey, *The Irish Diaspora in America* (Bloomington: Indiana University Press, 1976), pp. 68–69.

82. Ellen M. Oldham, "Irish Support of the Abolitionist Movement," *The Boston Public Library Quarterly,* 10 (October 1958): 75–187; Gilbert Osofsky, "Irish Immigrants and the Dilemmas of Romantic Nationalism," *American Historical Review,* 80 (October 1975): 889–912; Douglas C. Riach, "Daniel O'Connell and American Anti-Slavery," *Irish Historical Studies,* 20 (March 1976): 3–25.

83. *The Irish Patriot* (n.d.), pp. 1–2.

84. Ibid.

85. Gerrit Smith to Daniel O'Connell, July 28, 1843, Gerrit Smith Letters, New York Public Library. See also, Alan M. Kraut, "Irishmen and Abolitionists: The Shaping of Immigrant Attitudes Toward Third Party Abolitionism in Antebellum New York" (unpublished paper presented at the Organization of American Historians Meeting in New Orleans, Louisiana, April 13, 1979).

86. Albany *Argus* quoted by *Freeman's Journal,* July 1, 1843. See speech of Governor William H. Seward in same issue.

87. Theodore Foster to James G. Birney, December 7, 1845, Dumond, ed., *Birney Letters,* 2: 982–984.

88. Printed letter, "Gerrit Smith to the Liberty Party, May 7, 1846," Smith Collection. Lewis Tappan to Birney, March 10, 1846, Dumond, ed., *Birney Letters,* 2: 1029–1030.

89. "Address of the National Nominating Convention, assembled at Macedon Lock, Wayne County in the State of New York, June 8, 9, and 10, 1847," reprinted in *Albany Patriot,* June 23, 1847.

90. Lewis Tappan denied the right of a portion of the Liberty Party to call a separate convention without the consent of the Liberty National Committee. Lewis Tappan to Gerrit Smith, July 23, 30, 1847, Smith Collection. *Cincinnati Herald,* June 2, 1847. (Milwaukee) *American Freeman,* July 14, 21, 1847.

91. *Speech of Gerrit Smith, Made in the National Convention of the Liberty Party at Buffalo, October 31, 1847, on the Character, Scope and Duties of the Liberty Party* (Albany, 1847).

92. "Proceedings of the National Liberty Convention," *National Era,* November 8, 1847.

93. Printed circular, "Gerrit Smith to the Liberty Party of New Hampshire," March 18, 1848, Smith Collection. (Milwaukee) *American Freeman,* November 10, 1847, February 2, 1848.

94. Printed circular, "Gerrit Smith to the Liberty Party of New Hampshire."

95. *Proceedings of the National Liberty Convention held at Buffalo, N.Y., June 14, 15, 1848; including the Resolutions and Addresses Adopted by That Body* (Utica, 1848).

96. Huntington, *Political Order,* p. 32.

97. Tocqueville, *Democracy in America,* 1: 315.

98. *Buffalo Commercial Advertiser,* August 26, 1843. Several studies that suggest the important relationship of politics to religion in the antebellum period are Bertram Wyatt-Brown, "Prelude to Abolitionism: Sabbatarian Politics and the Rise of the Second Party System," *Journal of American History,* 58 (September 1971): 316–341; Kleppner, *Third Electoral System,* passim; John L. Hammond, *The Politics of Benevolence: Revival Religion and American Voting Behavior* (Norwood, N.J.: Ablex Publishing Corporation, 1979). For an examination of the links between politics and religion at the community level, see Paul E. Johnson, *A Shopkeeper's Millenium: Society and Revivals in Rochester, New York, 1815–1837* (New York: Hill and Wang, 1978).

99. *Madison County Abolitionist,* December 7, 1841. Also, Gerrit Smith, "To the Friends of the Slaves in the County of Madison," July 14, 1843, reprinted in *Letters of Gerrit Smith on Preaching Anti-Slavery Politics on Sunday,* located in the Antislavery Collection of Olin Library, Cornell University.

100. *Liberty Tract No. 7,* n.p.

101. *Liberty Press,* November 22, 1842. For the most elegant discussion of eighteenth-century attitudes toward party, see Hofstadter, *Idea of a Party System,* especially chapters 1 and 2.

102. *Liberty Tract No. 7,* n.p.

103. Perry, *Anarchy and the Government of God in Antislavery Thought,* pp. 92–93.

104. *National Era,* August 17, 1848.

105. Ibid.

106. "Free Soil Platform," *National Party Platforms 1840–1872,* comp. Donald Bruce Johnson and Kirk N. Porter (Urbana: University of Illinois Press, 1975), pp. 13–14. Also, Foner, *Free Soil, Free Labor, Free Men,* pp. 124–125.

107. Unsigned letter to John P. Hale, August 19, 1848. Also Joshua Leavitt to Hale, August 22, 1848. Both in John P. Hale Papers, New Hampshire Historical Society Concord, New Hampshire. Richard H. Sewell, *John P. Hale and the Politics of Abolition* (Cambridge, Mass.: Harvard University Press, 1965), pp. 103–104.

108. Kraut and Field, "Politics Versus Principles," passim.

109. Goodell, *Slavery and Anti-Slavery*, p. 472.

110. Eric Foner claims that debates over the inevitability of the Civil War reached a "conceptual impasse" during the 1950's. Eric Foner, "Yes Va., There Was A Civil War," *New York Times*, September 14, 1980. However, Kenneth Stampp demonstrates that the issue continues to surface in contemporary research. Kenneth Stampp, "The Irrepressible Conflict," in Stampp, ed., *The Imperiled Union* (New York: Oxford University Press, 1980), pp. 193–245. Lawrence J. Friedman suggests that the issue continues to arise in the work of those studying abolitionists, though resolution of the reformers' role is as far as ever from settled. Lawrence J. Friedman, " 'Historical Topics Sometimes Run Dry': The State of Abolitionist Studies," *The Historian*, 43 (February 1981); 177–194.

111. Holt, *The Political Crisis of the 1850's*, p. 3, and Stampp, "Irrepressible Conflict," p. 245.

4

Slavery, Race, and the Free Soil Party, 1848–1854

Richard H. Sewell

"An abolitionist is one who is in favor of abolishing slavery, and who works for its abolition," observed Gerrit Smith, the radical reformer and philanthropist, in 1848. "An antislavery person is one who may be but opposed to slavery."[1] Most historians have accepted this distinction and have characterized the Free Soilers of 1848 and 1852 as, at best, antislavery persons. In sharp contrast to the Liberty party that preceded it, "the Free Soil movement . . . made its primary appeal to the self-interest, rather than the spirituality, of whites." Content merely to *quarantine* slavery rather than seek its destruction everywhere, moved as much by race prejudice as by moral aversion to the "peculiar institution," Free Soilers succeeded in democratizing antislavery sentiment only by forsaking genuine abolitionist principles. The nomination of Martin Van Buren, long the quintessential doughface ("the catch-pole of slaveholders," John Quincy Adams had called him), seemed only too characteristic of the new party's cynicism, its willingness to trade "moral purpose for votes."[2]

There is much to be said for such views. Inevitably, once Barnburner Democrats and Conscience Whigs merged with Liberty party idealists, political abolitionism lost some of its radical edge. Open declarations of emancipationist intent were at first set aside, lest "the cry of Abolition" frighten off potential recruits.[3] Liberty denunciations of the Fugitive Slave Act, though reiterated in 1852, were prudently forgotten in 1848. Attacks upon a conspiratorial "Slave Power" became as common as attacks upon slavery itself. Most conspicuously, racial bigotry became more pronounced, and Free Soilers gained the dubious distinction of being "the first major antislavery group to avoid the question of Negro rights in their national platform."[4]

Especially among Democratic Free Soilers, race prejudice bulked large. Noting that "many of the leading Barnburners were among the bitterest opponents of the right of poor Blacks to vote. . . ," Horace Greeley pointedly asked: "Do you think they are more careful of Human Rights in New Mexico than in New York?"[5] Indeed, New York's Barnburners not only freely confessed their aversion to black suffrage (an unthinkable reform, given the natural "antipathy between the two races")[6] but frequently justified slavery restriction as a step essential to the human rights of *white* Americans. "The question is not whether black men are to be made free," shouted one Free Soil Democrat, "but whether we white men are to remain free." Similarly, the *New York Post,* in an editorial entitled, "WHAT SHALL BE DONE FOR THE WHITE MAN," insisted that champions of free soil "put aside the question how long the slave owner is to hold his negroes, and how he is to get rid of them, if at all; and only demand that he shall not take them into the territories to expel the free laborer by the repulsion of their presence."[7]

Free Soil Democrats in other states also displayed a strong attachment to white supremacy. Jacob Brinkerhoff of Ohio, for example, explained his qualified support for his state's discriminatory black code by saying "I have selfishness enough, greatly to prefer the welfare of my own race to that of any other, and vindictiveness enough to wish to leave and keep upon the shoulders of the South the burden of the curse which they have themselves created and courted."[8] Congressman David Wilmot, a Democratic Free Soiler from western Pennsylvania, repeatedly denied that his celebrated Proviso (which would have barred slavery from lands won in the Mexican War) had been drafted out of any softhearted concern for black liberty.

I have no squeamish sensitiveness upon the subject of slavery [Wilmot told the House of Representatives in February 1847], no morbid sympathy for the slave. I plead the cause and the rights of white freemen. I would preserve to free white labor a fair country, a rich inheritance, where the sons of toil, of my own race and own color, can live without the disgrace which association with negro slavery brings upon free labor.[9]

Small wonder that Barnburners often labeled Wilmot's Proviso the "White Man's Resolution."

Whiggish recruits to Free Soil were, as a rule, substantially more liberal on the subject of race than were ex-Democrats. Yet even among such "Conscience Whigs," precious few wholly escaped the racist currents of the day. Boston's Richard Henry Dana, Jr., found it scandalous that black workers on John Brown's Adirondack farm were all called "Mister" and allowed to sup at the family table, showed no qualms about pocketing fees for lectures he gave to segregated lyceum audiences, and confessed that in the event of a slave uprising his duty would be to "my own race." To save but a single white life, said Dana, he would sacrifice a "whole zoo" of lesser breeds.

Horace Mann twice shocked Afro-American conventions by announcing his belief in the intellectual superiority of whites to blacks—a belief privately shared by other Conscience Whigs, among them Henry Wilson and Charles Francis Adams.[10]

As might be expected, radical emancipationists found the Free Soilers wanting when measured against the standard of true abolitionism. The Reverend Samuel Ringgold Ward and other black leaders in New York bitterly attacked Barnburner shortcomings—especially their racist rhetoric, their obstruction of equal suffrage, and their alleged insincerity on abolition in the District of Columbia.[11] White abolitionists, too, took Free Soilers to task for seeking merely to cordon off slavery, for neglecting abolition and racial equality in their anxiety to protect free white labor against a menacing Slave Power. Not only was the Wilmot Proviso a half-measure at best, but, Garrisonians contended, one doomed to failure. All attempts "to restrain slavery by laws and constitutions," declared the Massachusetts Anti-Slavery Society, were "precisely equivalent to damming up the Mississippi with bulrushes." Still worse, enchantment with free soil undercut honest-to-God abolitionism by corrupting consciences and siphoning off support. "Free Soil has done desperately little for us," complained the radical Parker Pillsbury, "but it has dug fearful drains in the treasury that sustains us." Even some Liberty party abolitionists—notably Gerrit Smith, William Goodell, and Lewis Tappan—found the Free Soil creed wanting and retained a rump organization of their own pledged to a war "against slavery itself as well as against its extension."[12]

The critics have a point. Yet even before the mass exodus of Barnburners in 1849 and 1850—and much more thereafter—Free Soilers revealed an attachment to the goal (if not the label) of abolition and a willingness to defend the basic rights of black Americans that calls into question too rigid a dichotomy between "abolitionist" and "antislavery person." Lest one too quickly accept the notion that the Free Soil party represented a drastic shift away from bona fide political abolitionism, it is well to remember that the Liberty party itself had been drifting toward the Free Soil position for years. While publicly proclaiming their devotion to human brotherhood and the overthrow of slavery, most Liberty men, distinguishing between what as abolitionists they found desirable and what as antislavery politicians they found constitutionally possible, sought not immediate emancipation (which, they held, lay beyond the constitutional powers of any party) but "the absolute and unqualified divorce of the general government from slavery." That cardinal principle—reaching beyond the Wilmot Proviso—lay firmly embedded in the Free Soil party's national platforms of 1848 and 1852. The Free Soil creed, reported Sherman Booth, the abolitionist editor of the *American Freeman,* "pledges the new party against the admission of any more Slave States, and to employ the Federal Government not only to limit, localize, and discourage, but to abolish slavery wherever it has Constitutional power to do so." That, he admitted, "is all the Liberty party, as such, ever demanded." Similarly, Owen Lovejoy, brother of the martyred Elijah, assured western abolitionists that "the principles of Liberty are in this movement, undergird and surround it—the immediate object aimed at is one which we cordially approve, and the ultimate object is identical—the extinction of slavery."[13]

Booth and Lovejoy doubtless read greater antislavery aggressiveness into the Free Soil platform than did many of their new associates. Yet while some may have viewed slavery restriction as a basically conservative doctrine—as a way of holding planter oligarchs at bay and keeping the West a white man's country—most Free Soilers looked upon the Wilmot Proviso as a perfectly constitutional but deadly antislavery weapon, an "iron shroud," which, by preventing slavery's spread, would put it on the path to extinction.

Even among former Democrats, the most racist of Free Soilers, the belief was widespread that human bondage, if not a sin, was a national disgrace, "a great moral, social and political evil—a relic of barbarism which must necessarily be swept away in the progress of Christian civilization."[14] Often, to be sure, condemnation centered on slavery's alleged threat to free white labor: its degradation of honest toil, its exhaustion of the soil, its corrosive effect upon manners and morals. Yet Barnburners as well as other Free Soilers also denounced slavery for its fundamental inhumanity, for the wrong done to the slaves themselves. "To buy and sell human beings," remarked Martin Van Buren's son John, "is revolting not only to a freeman and a democrat, but to a philanthropist and a christian." Northern freemen, wrote another Barnburner, ought to resist the spread of an institution "which would fill their public papers with advertisements of men, women and children, for sale as chattels; their market places with wretched human beings in coffles, marked with scourges and making the air vocal with wailing and lamentation."[15]

Outside New York, Free Soilers protested the immorality of bondage in still stronger terms. E. S. Hamlin, a Whiggish convert to Free Soil, judged the antislavery struggle a "far more glorious one than that of our Revolution." For, he explained, "Our father's weapons were *carnal,* ours spiritual: they fought for *their own* liberty; we are fighting for that of *others,* a poor, despised, downtrodden race." In 1852, after most Barnburners had returned to the Democratic fold, the Free Soil national platform damned slavery as "a sin against God and a crime against man, which no human enactment nor usage can make right." Even skeptical Garrisonians conceded that among Massachusetts Free Soilers "the prevailing spirit seemed to be one of opposition to slavery *per se,* and not merely on account of its interference with the rights and prosperity of white men."[16]

Believing slavery a great evil—anything but the "positive good" Southerners now proclaimed it—Free Soilers sought both to check its growth and, in the process, to send it to its grave. "Our mission," E. S. Hamlin bluntly declared, "is to overthrow slavery *in the States,* as well as to keep it out of the territories." Congressman Erastus Culver of New York preached the same message to the National Free Soil Convention of 1848: "Now gentlemen, I say check slavery where it is and then I will show you a man that will go still farther. We have never guarantied [*sic*] that slavery shall rest on that 50 square miles [the District of Columbia] yet.—[No, no, no.] When my constituents sent me to Congress, I told them plainly just what I meant to do. I said as long as there is a loophole through which I can fire on this abominable old institution, I shall fire away. [Good, good, give 'em hell.]"[17]

Free Soilers readily conceded that the North had no right to tamper with the internal affairs of the South. Slavery, nearly all admitted, was a purely local institution, established by state law, and as such was shielded by the Constitution against direct outside assaults. Congress had no better right to abolish slavery in South Carolina than to abolish free schools in Massachusetts. At the same time, most agreed, antislavery advocates had a right and a duty to expose the "moral evil" of slavery and, by denying slaveholders fresh lands and government favor, force the South to implement some plan of emancipation.[18]

Whatever its other attractions, the Wilmot Proviso appealed to most Free Soilers because it offered a perfectly constitutional, if roundabout, road to abolition everywhere. "Let us have a cordon of free territory around slavery and its days are numbered," contended James Wilson of New Hampshire. "Keep it hedged up within the old field and it burns itself out. It cannot live long on old ground. It is too improvident and exhausting a system for that and must seek a new, vigorous virgin soil to sustain it." Not only would the fencing in of slavery devalue Southern lands, but it would make increasingly burdensome and dangerous an ever larger, ever more concentrated slave population. And, of course, slavery restriction would curtail the South's political power and hence its ability to fend off future attacks upon the "peculiar institution." "The Black Hole at Calcutta was not more fatal to its inmates," concluded one Free Soil editor, "than would be a limited area to slavery."[19]

Many Northerners who shared the Free Soilers' desire to hold slavery in check nonetheless argued that the Wilmot Proviso was unnecessary and hence, in Stephen A. Douglas' phrase, "mischievous and wicked." The Almighty Himself, some maintained, had set natural limits beyond which slavery could not take root. "Physical geography," claimed Daniel Webster in his celebrated speech on the Compromise of 1850, had made the question of slavery in the territories acquired from Mexico "a mere abstraction." "The whole controversy," another observer insisted, "related to an imaginary negro in an impossible place." It was a grave mistake, such men argued, to risk sectional discord merely "to reaffirm an ordinance of nature . . . to reenact the will of God." Besides, Mexican law as well as the law of nature had already abolished slavery in the new southwestern territories, making the Wilmot Proviso doubly superfluous.[20]

Free Soilers objected to such reasoning on many counts. To begin with, the proviso offered a golden opportunity to pass moral censure on a barbarous institution. What better way to expose slavery as the plague it was, Free Soilers asked, than to place it under a congressional quarantine? Other formulas for resolving the territorial question—extension of the Missouri compromise line, territorial self-determination, opposition to any new land acquisitions—all dodged or denied slavery's basic immorality. Only the Wilmot Proviso straightforwardly countered the pernicious notion that slavery was a positive good, a blessing to be spread far and wide. Only the proviso reaffirmed the Founding Fathers' determination to treat it as a curse. Indeed, some insisted, slavery's moral reputation bore a direct relation to its vitality. The failure to place a ban on slavery expansion, observed one Barnburner newspaper, was causing "slavery itself . . . to lose its abhorrent features in the eyes of many, and its advocates, emboldened by the timidity of those who entertain different views, claim for it unlimited extension and perpetuity of duration."[21]

As for Webster's thesis that "Slavery, like the cotton-plant, is confined by natural laws to certain parallels of latitude," most Free Soilers rejected it out of hand. Bondage, they pointed out, had at one time or another existed the world over. "Wherever labor is in demand," Wilmot asserted, "wherever there is work to do, there the slave is valuable, and there he will be taken, unless legal barriers are interposed to prevent it." Others, arguing from more moralistic premises, came to the same conclusion. "Slavery," New Hampshire's leading Free Soil newspaper remarked, "is the handmaid of luxury, intemperance, slothfulness and all vice; and wherever these are able to find rest for the soles of their feet, there will slavery go and reign, unless forbidden by the strong arm of government." Without the Ordinance of 1787 the Old Northwest would surely have been lost to slavery.[22]

Mexican law, Free Soilers agreed, presented an equally flimsy barricade to slavery's advance. Whatever the Mexican precedent, Joshua Giddings cautioned the Free Soil National Convention in 1848, only the Wilmot Proviso could keep slavery from being entailed upon the Southwest by force. "Leave the slave-holder to convey his slaves there," Giddings maintained, "let him but once gain a foothold there and by force of superior intelligence and power; by the bowie-knife, the scourge, the whip and the dread instruments of torture, he will establish slavery there unless prevented by law."[23]

The fear that if granted a foothold slavery would be devilishly hard to dislodge from any territory was basic to the Free Soilers' attachment to the Wilmot Proviso. "Just as the twig is bent, so the tree's inclined," they liked to say, and that barely a handful of slaves ever resided in Utah and New Mexico—and fewer still in California—gave little comfort to Free Soil spokesmen. Once accord slavery equal rights with freedom, many argued, and even a relatively small band of planters could overwhelm a vastly larger contingent of nonslaveholders and shape the still malleable institutions of the new West to their own satisfaction. Since, that is, slave labor and free labor were fundamentally incompatible, the introduction of even a few thousand slaves would precipitate an exodus of enterprising freemen, leaving the country to masters, slaves, and poor white hangers-on. "One slaveholder with his gang of negroes," claimed the *New York Post,* "elbows out thousands of free settlers who bring only the implements of their toil and their own hardy families." And, of course, once rooted in the territorial stage, the question facing a new state would no longer be whether to *permit* slavery, but whether to *abolish* it. Given the hegemony of powerful and imperious planters, the answer could scarcely be doubted.[24]

The danger of the Slave Power spreading its domain over the vast Southwest—perhaps down into the Caribbean as well—thus struck Free Soilers as altogether real. Senator John P. Hale of New Hampshire, for one, perceived in 1849 a "great and imminent danger" that slavery would force its way into all lands won from Mexico, California included. "While the interested & venal are lulling us with the syren [sic] song that there is 'no danger' slaves are being carried into those territories, the clanking of whose chains, and the cries of whose agony shall fill the ear of the Most High, calling for vengeance upon us, if through timidity, party spirit or any other cause, we hold our peace, and do not do what we may to prevent so great a wrong."[25] Even if one conceded that New Mexico was ill-suited to the production of staple crops (a concession not all Free Soilers were willing to make),[26] the menace of slavery there remained frightening. Domestic slaves could already be found in Santa Fe, and as Southerners themselves admitted, bondsmen might be profitably employed in mining gold and silver. Free Soil fears mounted after the Compromise of 1850 left the territorial legislatures of Utah and New Mexico free to decide the fate of slavery in those regions. Mexican-Americans were generally hostile to slavery; yet, party leaders like Horace Mann maintained, they were a "feeble, effeminate, unprincipled race," no match for energetic and domineering Southern whites.[27] Territorial Governor William Carr Lane's purchase of two black slaves at Santa Fe in 1852 further alarmed Free Soilers, and seven years later their direful prediction that only positive congressional barriers could keep slavery out of the Southwest seemed confirmed when New Mexico enacted a stringent slave code.[28]

To most Free Soilers, then, the Wilmot Proviso was anything but an idle abstraction. Or, if it were, Charles Francis Adams told delegates to the party's formative convention, then "so was the Magna Charta an abstraction. And so was the declaration of independence an abstraction. . . . So is the idea of right and justice and the truth of God an abstraction. And it is these abstractions that raise mankind above the brutes that perish."[29]

Slavery restriction, though the Free Soilers' primary concern, was far from being the whole of their antislavery program. "To arrest the extension of slavery is the beginning," explained Stephen C. Phillips, Free Soil candidate for governor of Massachusetts in 1848, "—its abolition, the end."[30] Like the Liberty creed earlier, Free Soil platforms in 1848 and 1852 called upon the federal government to "relieve itself from all responsibility for the existence or continuance of slavery" wherever it possessed the constitutional power to act. What such a program of "denationalization" might mean if practiced, Free Soilers spelled out on many occasions. Characteristic was the response of the *Boston Daily Republican* to challenges from two newspapers in neighboring Lowell: one chiding Free Soilers for neglecting the problem of slavery in the states, the other rapping the *Republican* for slighting constitutional safeguards for slavery. To the first complaint the *Republican* (then edited by Henry Wilson, a one-time Conscience Whig) replied with a reminder that the 1848 Free Soil platform made it Congress' duty not merely to limit but to *discourage* slavery by denying it federal support. "There is a *power* in the INFLUENCE of the Federal Government," it added, "which is now almost entirely exerted for slavery. We mean it shall be exerted for freedom." To the charge that it advocated improper intervention in the domestic affairs of Southern states, the *Republican* answered:

We would have the National Government pass an organic law, that should *forever* preserve all the territories to freedom; we would have it abolish slavery and the slave trade in the District of Columbia—forbid the interstate slave trade—repeal the fugitive slave law of 1793 and all other acts that in any way make the people of the free States responsible for the existence of slavery—exercise all its constitutional power to discourage, localize, and destroy slavery—and use its patronage and influence to sustain the friends of emancipation in all lawful, constitutional, and just means, to free the slave States from the wrongs and evils of a system that blasts their prosperity, disgraces the country, and destroys the rights and happiness of three millions of our fellow men. If this is interference with slavery in the States, so be it.[31]

By arresting slavery's growth, by using federal powers to attack it wherever possible, and by placing the moral influence of government firmly on the side of liberty, the nation might at last annihilate its most wicked and reactionary institution. Such, at least, was the Free Soilers' dream.

Just as most Free Soilers looked beyond slavery restriction to the ultimate goal of universal emancipation, so many revealed a commitment to racial equality that, if timid by abolitionist standards, far exceeded that of most contemporaries. Political expediency and pressure from bigots within the party kept Free Soil national platforms silent on the question of Negro rights. Yet individually, and within the Northern states, Free Soilers often took the lead in defending—and extending—the civil rights of black Americans.

Far from seeking to strengthen or extend racial discrimination, Free Soilers frequently went out of their way to debunk conventional stereotypes of black inferiority and to preach the "equality of all men, of every climate, color, and race." None did so more passionately than Wisconsin's Free Soil congressman, Charles Durkee. "Sir," he lectured the House of Representatives in 1850, "you may take from . . . [a man] his wife, his children, and his friends, and put handcuffs on his wrists and fetters on his feet, and brand him as your property . . . yet he is still a *man*—he is still our brother." In the same spirit, the Washington *National Era* explained that Free Soilers were "opposed to the spirit of caste, whether its elemental idea be a difference of color, birth, or condition—because its inevitable tendency is to create or perpetuate inequality of natural rights."[32]

Although conspicuously reticent with regard to social equality, and often patronizing in their relations with blacks, many Free Soilers perceived a grating disparity between the Declaration of Independence and the Bill of Rights, which spoke of natural rights belonging to *all* men, and the web of discriminatory laws and customs that in every corner of the land consigned black Americans to second-class citizenship. As one Ohio Free Soiler caustically observed, " 'All men by nature are free and independent,' don't look well by the side of 'every White male citizen.' "[33] Accordingly, Free Soilers in many states and on many occasions braved taunts of "amalgamationist" and "woolly-head" and joined out-and-out abolitionists in the fight against institutionalized racism. And since at mid-century something like nineteen of twenty Northern Negroes lived in states that banned or severely restricted their right to vote, suffrage reform was an obvious starting point.

Wisconsin witnessed the most nearly successful campaign for color-blind voting requirements. Though the 1850 census showed only 635 blacks, scattered widely about the state, the question of their enfranchisement inevitably surfaced during debates over the state's first constitution. Most Democrats followed the lead of Moses M. Strong, who declared himself "teetotally opposed" to any form of black suffrage. A great many Whigs, however, as well as most Liberty men and Free Soilers, endorsed equal suffrage from the outset. At its annual meeting in 1848, the Wisconsin Liberty Association (virtually all of whose members soon merged with the Free Soil party) resolved that suffrage was an "inalienable right" belonging to all men, that to deny this right to any would be to open the door to disfranchisement for all, and that the principle that had robbed the Negro of one right "only needs scope and opportunity to rob him of *all* rights." Early the next year Wisconsin Free Soilers boldly proclaimed: "We are in favor of equal and impartial suffrage, and are the friends of man and the advocates of human rights the world over." The issue was "one of vital importance," the *Wisconsin Free Democrat* contended. "Practically," the paper admitted, "it would not affect the rights of a hundred voters in this State to exclude colored citizens from the polls." But, it went on, "it would sacrifice the vital principle of Democracy, by making *color,* and not *character*—factitious circumstances, and not manhood, the foundation of political rights." True democracy, it maintained, called for equal rights, human brotherhood, Christianity in government.[34]

As became increasingly clear, such sentiments were too radical for most Wisconsinites. In March 1847, a special referendum on equal suffrage and the right of blacks to hold office showed 7,664 in favor, 14,615 opposed. Significantly, the returns revealed a strong county-by-county correlation between support for black suffrage in 1847 and support for the Free Soil ticket in 1848. Of the ten counties most decidedly in favor of enfranchising blacks, eight ranked among the top ten Van Buren counties in 1848.[35] Defeat of the constitution to which the suffrage referendum was tied gave advocates of black rights another chance. A second state convention, meeting in 1848–49, drafted a constitution that restricted suffrage to white males but empowered the legislature "to admit colored persons to the right of suffrage" after approval by a majority of voters. Accordingly, Wisconsin's first legislature, after meager debate, authorized a plebiscite on equal suffrage at the fall canvass in 1849.[36]

As election day drew near, the Free Soil press beseeched "every true [Free] Democrat . . . to vote for this democratic principle of equal suffrage to all without distinction of color." Warren Chase, the party's gubernatorial nominee, was touted as one who in both constitutional conventions and in the legislature had openly endorsed full political equality for all men. A good many Whig newspapers, notably the *Milwaukee Sentinel and Gazette,* also plumped vigorously for impartial suffrage. Yet even so, apathy was widespread. "There seems to have been very little feeling among the people on this question," the *Southport Telegraph* noted soon after the election. Even Free Soilers, embroiled in a quarrel with old-line Democrats with whom they had hoped to coalesce, gave the matter only fitful attention.[37]

Still, a clear majority of those who cast votes in the 1849 referendum backed black suffrage. Once tallied, the ballots showed 5,265 for, 4,075 against. As before, strongest support came from banner Free Soil counties. In fact, the four counties giving the heaviest vote to Van Buren and Adams in 1848 (excluding Waukesha, which topped all others in support of the 1847 suffrage referendum but mysteriously made no official return in 1849), approved impartial suffrage by a margin of nearly 3–1. On the other hand, the four weakest Free Soil counties reporting returns in 1849, voted better than 5–1 *against* enfranchising Wisconsin blacks.[38]

Owing to a technicality, however, Wisconsin Free Soilers and their allies came up empty-handed. Since, that is, the language authorizing the referendum required approval by "a majority of all votes cast" before black men might gain the ballot, and since nearly 32,000 voted for governor in 1849, the State Board of Canvassers ruled that suffrage extension had failed to win an *adequate* majority. Free Soilers protested this "back-handed blow" and argued that it made no sense to record "no" votes unless the referendum were considered an independent, self-contained issue. The semantic trickery that had misled the Board of Canvassers they found rooted in "the indisposition of tyrants to concede the rights to the people which they have usurped and exercised . . . ." Where so vital a democratic principle was at stake, fumed the *Oshkosh True Democrat,* political liberalism should be given the benefit of doubt. Nothing came of such protests until 1866 when, in the case of *Gillespie* v. *Palmer et al.,* the Supreme Court of Wisconsin belatedly overruled the Board of Canvassers, holding that the simple majority in favor of black suffrage in 1849 had in fact been sufficient. For Wisconsin blacks, justice delayed had indeed been justice denied. But precious little blame fell on Free Soilers.[39]

Neighboring Michigan emphatically rejected black suffrage in 1850, but once again Free Soilers led the doomed fight for reform. At the 1850 state constitutional convention, Free Soilers DeWitt C. Leach and Joseph R. Williams were the only delegates to advocate forcefully the enfranchisement of blacks. And when the convention turned a deaf ear to their pleas but decided to submit black suffrage to a statewide referendum, Free Soilers gave it strong backing. Unhappily for Michigan blacks, third party support was not nearly enough and the measure failed resoundingly.[40]

In Connecticut, too, Free Soilers spearheaded an unsuccessful campaign to restore voting rights taken from Negroes in 1814. Especially active was William H. Burleigh, a pioneer abolitionist and first editor of the Free Soil *Hartford Republican.* When Burleigh relinquished his editorship in 1849, the Hartford Colored Washingtonian Temperance Society saluted his "arduous labors" on behalf of the slave and his advocacy of "the moral, social, and political right of the free colored man." Burleigh's successor at the *Republican,* John D. Baldwin, kept up this struggle. Reporting on a convention of Colored Citizens of Connecticut, Baldwin took the occasion once again to urge restoration of black suffrage. "The man who would deny the common rights of manhood to so much intelligence and moral worth as was represented in that Convention," he proclaimed, "deserves to be pitied for his subserviency to a blind prejudice." Prejudice, however, ran deep in the state that had once made a martyr of Prudence Crandall for daring to open a school for black girls. Despite the efforts of abolitionists and Free Soilers, it took the Fifteenth Amendment to restore voting rights to Connecticut blacks.[41]

In Ohio and Indiana, Free Soilers battled not only against inequalities in the suffrage, but against comprehensive Black Laws designed to buttress white supremacy. Few Northern states more systematically abridged the rights of black citizens than did Ohio. From the earliest days of statehood, Ohio blacks found themselves excluded from militia service and jury duty, barred from testifying in cases involving whites, denied poorhouse relief, banished from public schools, and deprived of the right to vote. Free Negroes from other states were deterred from entering Ohio. And in 1839, the state assembly went so far as to deny blacks the right to petition the legislature "for any purpose whatsoever."[42]

For years Ohio's blacks and white abolitionists, especially on the Western Reserve, had urged repeal of these repressive measures. Liberty men had made repeal a party measure. Early in 1845, a majority of the select committee appointed by the house to consider the question recommended annulment of the Black Laws as a matter of enlightened policy and simple justice. The following year Governor Mordecai Bartley, a Whig, publicly condemned those "laws which unjustly degrade our colored population." Their revocation, he said, was "demanded alike by the spirit of our religion and the philosophy of the age."[43]

Ohio Free Soilers not only echoed such sentiments (denouncing the Black Laws as "legalized injustice") but developed a blueprint for reform. The chief architect was the ambitious yet principled Salmon P. Chase, perhaps Free Soil's most prominent spokesman and theoretician. Finding that his party held the balance of power in both houses of the state legislature in 1849, Chase contrived a plan whereby Democrats agreed to back his election to the United States Senate and abrogation of the Black Laws in exchange for enough Free Soil votes to permit them to organize the house. All worked much as planned. Most Democrats (acting grudgingly, "under the most determined and rigid application of party discipline") as well as many Whigs and all Free Soilers joined in overturning the most flagrant laws of discrimination. Henceforth, blacks might enter Ohio freely, testify in any legal proceeding, and attend common schools. "Ohio," cheered the *National Era*, "has at last done herself the credit of repealing her absurd, inhuman Black Laws."[44]

Even so, racial democracy had by no means arrived. Schools open to black children were, when feasible, to be strictly segregated. Senate amendments, moreover, had cut from the reform bill (drafted by Chase and introduced in the legislature by John F. Morse, a Free Soiler from the Western Reserve) clauses granting blacks the right to serve on juries and to benefit from the poor laws. Ohio's 1802 constitution still barred blacks from voting or holding office. Significantly, Ohio Free Soilers, though acquiescent in such matters as segregated schooling, continued in the years ahead to urge political equality for blacks. All Free Soil delegates to the state constitutional convention of 1850–1851 publicly endorsed political equality, and when the question of black suffrage arose, they backed it to a man. "To attempt to govern men without seeking their consent is usurpation and tyranny, whether in Ohio or in Austria," argued Norton S. Townshend, a Free Soil delegate from Elyria. "Humanity does not depend upon the color of the hair, or eyes, or skin, or where a person may have been born, or what his origin or capacity—the essentials of humanity are independent of all these peculiarities; they may be changed or varied indefinitely, but 'A man is a man for all that.' " Predictably, such arguments made few converts. Yet so long as their party remained in the field, Ohio Free Soilers continued to push for the enfranchisement of *all* men.[45]

Indiana Free Soilers labored nearly as hard and without success to overthrow that state's Black Laws. Like their Ohio cousins, Indiana Negroes faced a battery of discriminatory codes. The constitution of 1816 restricted voting rights and militia duty to white citizens. State statutes banned black testimony in cases to which whites were a party and sternly outlawed interracial marriages. Since 1831, blacks settling in Indiana had been required to post a $500 bond "for their good behavior and self support." And public opinion kept black children from attending the common schools.[46]

Condemnation of such discrimination came primarily from antislavery Whigs like Schuyler Colfax, who favored colonization and opposed black suffrage but blamed the "degradation" of blacks on "the lust and avarice of the white race."[47] Hoosier Free Soilers, owing to a disastrous policy of coalition with the major parties, had by 1850 lost much of whatever moral and political influence they once possessed. Yet especially in the "Burnt District" of the upper Whitewater Valley, Free Soilers enthusiastically joined in the campaign against the "disgraceful" Black Laws. In Centreville, home of Free Soil Congressman George W. Julian, the *Free Territory Sentinel* (later the *Indiana True Democrat*) was especially active. In November 1849, the paper launched a petition drive designed to persuade delegates to the upcoming state constitutional convention of the need for reform. It supported this tactic with a series of hard-hitting editorials, and by the end of January 1850 some 3,000 signatures had been affixed to memorials urging repeal or ameliorization of the Black Laws. While admitting that Indiana Free Soilers stood divided on the question of equal suffrage, the paper's own editorials vigorously insisted that "principles of JUSTICE and RIGHT" demanded an end to discrimination at the polls.[48]

To the dismay of Free Soil liberals, the anti-Black Laws campaign soon backfired. With but a single Free Soil delegate present, the 1850 constitutional convention not only crushed a proposal to enfranchise black males (1 aye, 122 nays), but added a new article 13 that prohibited all Negroes or mulattoes from entering the state and hinted at the removal of blacks already in residence. In a special referendum in 1851, Indiana voters ratified this article by more than five to one, thus seconding the position of William C. Foster, a downstate Democrat, who had assured fellow delegates to the 1850 convention: "We cannot . . . be charged with inhumanity in preventing our state from being overrun with these vermin—for I say they are vermin, and I know it."[49]

Most Indiana Free Soilers seem to have rejected such gross bigotry. At the 1850 convention, Isaac Kinley, the sole Free Soil representative, lambasted article 13 as unconstitutional, unchristian, and unAmerican. "Instead of encouraging the [black] man to rise, you lay heavier burdens upon him, and then insult him because he is degraded," he scolded. "We must watch, that in our efforts to degrade lower and lower the negro race, we do not degrade ourselves." The Free Soil *True Democrat* reproved those who ratified the exclusionary clause for having "voluntarily and *gratuitously* published to the world . . . that they are barbarians." In 1852, the state party's official platform denounced the "notorious 13th article," committed Free Soilers to wage "exterminating warfare" against it, and stoutly proclaimed, "That this is not less the *native land* of the negro than the white man," and that it was "in every way as unjust and impudent" to seek to expel the former as the latter." Such sentiments were remarkable indeed in this, the most racist of free states.[50]

Most Free Soilers confined their campaigns for black rights to the political sphere. Even then, of course, there were many who dissented. At times, however, third party leaders joined Northern blacks and radical abolitionists to combat social discrimination as well. In Massachusetts, for example, such Free Soil spokesmen as Charles Francis Adams, John G. Palfrey, and Henry Wilson had helped to rescind, in 1843, the state's ban on interracial marriages—"a staggering blow . . . to the monster prejudice," William Lloyd Garrison described it. Adams and others also fought successfully for an end to segregated seating on Massachusetts railways. Less availing were efforts to admit blacks to the state's militia and the public schools. None labored harder for these reforms than did Charles Sumner. Together with Henry Wilson, a fellow Conscience Whig turned Free Soiler, Sumner promoted militia reform in the constitutional convention of 1853, and in his celebrated argument in the Roberts Case of 1849 he assailed segregated schools as inherently unequal and hence socially undesirable. Conservative delegates tabled the proposal to integrate the militia, and the Roberts decision upheld school segregation in Boston. Massachusetts Free Soilers continued to plug away, however, and in 1855 had the satisfaction of seeing the state legislature at last outlaw racial or religious discrimination in the public schools.[51]

Not only in Northern statehouses but in Congress itself a small band of Free Soil radicals strove to block discriminatory legislation and to rebut Southern allegations of black inferiority. Salmon Chase in the Senate and Joshua Giddings, Edward Wade, and Alexander DeWitt in the House lobbied to make blacks eligible for homestead grants. Free Soil's only national newspaper, the *Washington National Era,* earnestly endorsed these efforts, calling homestead restriction "barbarous and unreasonable." And Congressman Palfrey of Massachusetts, for one, pointed to the accomplishments of distinguished blacks from Hannibal to Frederick Douglass to show that Negro inferiority stemmed not from "congenital incapacity" but from the burdens and stigma of slavery.[52]

Attitudes toward colonization offer yet another window on the racial attitudes of Free Soilers. Like Liberty men earlier, most Free Soil spokesmen assailed proposals to expatriate black Americans as being both impractical and immoral. Colonization, they claimed, was a "nefarious scheme" designed to intensify racial prejudice and thereby tighten, not loosen, slavery's grip.[53] And if colonization were a pro-slavery movement, some Free Soilers contended, then opposition to colonization might be made an antislavery measure. None advanced this notion more forcefully than did Indiana's George W. Julian, the Free Soil candidate for vice-president in 1852. It was especially important, Julian advised Illinois Negroes, for the black man himself to resist colonization.

He should resolutely demand his rights as a man and a citizen, and thus demonstrate that he *is* a man. . . . The degradation in this country of its free colored people, their expatriation from it, is an essential part of the policy of the slave interest. The presence of such a people is a perpetual danger to that interest, as well as a reproach to the slave holder; and therefore, by firmly and unitedly resolving to remain among us, they can perform an important work in the deliverance of their brother in chains.[54]

Although Martin R. Delany, Henry Highland Garnet, H. Ford Douglass, and other black leaders had lately begun preaching the benefits of emigration, most Afro-Americans applauded Julian's logic and willingly followed his advice.

Some Free Soilers, it must be admitted, believed that ultimately the black man's destiny lay in other climes, that God had intended a separation of the races. Salmon P. Chase, for example, frankly told Frederick Douglass that in his opinion blacks and whites were adapted to different latitudes. Only the coercion of slavery had conjoined the two races in the United States, and after emancipation they might be expected naturally to drift apart. "I have thought it not unlikely," Chase remarked, "that the islands of the West Indies & portions of South America would be peopled from the United States by the Black Race—that, by them, civilization would be carried back into Africa, not under the constraints of any colonization scheme, but of choice & free will."[55]

Although Douglass flatly rejected such advice, insisting that "the black man's constitution as readily adapts itself to one climate as another," other Free Soilers echoed Chase's theme. "While the white population of Europe is colonizing the United States and Canada," Gamaliel Bailey suggested, "why should not the colored population of the United States colonize Mexico and the West Indies?" In that way black emigrants might at last gain the blessings of citizenship and their adopted homelands a welcome infusion of democratic ideas. (The irony of an oppressed people serving as schoolmasters of democracy seems utterly to have eluded Bailey.) Horace Mann was yet another Free Soiler who expressed such notions of "white nationalism," insisting that blacks were best suited to tropical climes. Similarly, Ohio Free

Soilers introduced a plea for repeal of the Black Laws by declaring: "We desire a homogeneous population for our State, and believe that we shall have it whenever slavery shall cease to force the victims of its tyranny into the uncongenial North." Too impatient to await emancipation's homogenizing magic, a few Free Soilers, mainly in Ohio, urged a stop-gap policy of "internal colonization." In 1851, a majority of Free Soilers in the Ohio senate called upon the federal government to set aside a portion of the public lands exclusively for black settlers. The *Cleveland True Democrat,* heavily influenced by Salmon Chase, also recommended the establishment of a separate preserve for American blacks, somewhere "in the southern climate."[56]

Obviously, the Free Soil party was by no means immune from the racist currents of the age. Even among those prepared to defend the basic civil and political rights of black Americans, many flinched at the thought of social mixing between the races. Indeed, to Frederick Douglass even the radical Charles Sumner seemed painfully tentative when it came to recognizing "the entire manhood and social equality of the colored people." When in congressional debate Andrew Johnson asked the high-minded John G. Palfrey how he would like it if his daughter married a black man, Palfrey replied evasively and sought to have the exchange suppressed in Massachusetts—"for my poor daughter's sake," he lamely explained. And though castigated as a "nigger-lover" by his critics, Joshua Giddings betrayed a paternalism toward blacks that, in his biographer's words, left him "unwilling to sponsor unreserved equality for every man in the nation."[57]

Yet if one measures the Free Soilers by the standards of their day rather than our own, what is remarkable is not that they showed signs of racial bias. Even moral suasion abolitionists, not to mention Liberty party men, at times displayed ambivalent feelings concerning racial equality.[58] Rather, what is noteworthy is that members of a broad antislavery coalition, dependent upon majorities to implement their program, time and again braved popular opinion and insisted that as members of the human family blacks were entitled to full rights of citizenship. Some, at least, went further, denouncing the prejudice that sustained Jim Crow. The *National Era,* for example, lampooned the irrationality of Negrophobia by likening it to discrimination against the Cagots, a group of Spanish outcasts who, it was said, differed from their neighbors only in the absence of an ear lobe![59]

A good many Free Soilers, moreover, denied that the degraded status of most Afro-Americans either justified racial discrimination or proved the *innate* inferiority of blacks to whites. "The colored race is an improvable one," Gamaliel Bailey maintained, and if not yet a match for whites, blacks might be expected to narrow the gap once economic and educational opportunities were opened to them. A high rate of poverty and crime among free Negroes, he believed, "only proves that their release from slavery has been too recent and their disabilities are too heavy to allow their easy ascent to the elevation of a people whose fathers have never known the yoke of bondage or the degradation of class legislation." Austin Blair, a Free Soil legislator (and later Republican governor) from Michigan had earlier made much the same point in arguing for black suffrage. "If by our unjust laws we have degraded the man and besotted his intellect," he declared, "it is a refinement of our cruelty to make this the pretext of our continuous oppression." Likewise, Norton Townshend praised the accomplishments of black students at the Collegiate Institution of Lorain in explaining Free Soil objection to Ohio's Black Laws. "Our sympathy, sir, for colored persons does not spring from our ignorance of them," he insisted, "but from the conviction that they, equally with other men, are susceptible of intellectual and moral elevation."[60]

Whatever its shortcomings, therefore, the Free Soil movement clearly represented something more than the selfish interests of Northern whites. For what it is worth, a great many abolitionists, black and white alike, found in the Free Soil party a promising (if flawed) instrument of abolition and racial justice. A few black leaders, it is true, refused any association with a party whose national platforms said nothing of equal rights. Some, like Frederick Douglass, blew hot and cold, now praising the Free Soil party for its sterling antislavery principles and urging support for its candidates, now pointing to the inadequacies of "mere Free Soil" and recommending that black voters back the nearly defunct Liberty party or stay at home. Most Northern blacks, however, gave Free Soil candidates whatever support they could. Flattered that Douglass and Henry Bibb had been invited to address the Free Soil convention in 1848 and that Douglass had been selected as a secretary of the party's national convention four years later and persuaded that despite their defects the Free Soilers had more to offer than did Whigs or Democrats, "the great majority of Negroes" wished the new party well.[61]

Radical white abolitionists took a somewhat more jaundiced view of the Free Soil enterprise. From the very beginning the *National Anti-Slavery Standard* admonished its readers to remember "that the 'Free Soil' party is not an Abolition party in any sense of the word." Too often, the Garrisonians complained, Free Soilers focused on the aggressions of the Slave Power, on slavery's threat to the well-being of Northerners and poor *white* Southerners; too infrequently did they denounce the sinfulness of "manstealing" or preach the need for racial democracy. Opposition to the spread of slavery, said Garrison's disciple Samuel J. May, was "but a small matter—a straining at a gnat, after we had swallowed the camel."[62]

Nearly always, however, abolitionists softened such criticism by coupling it with praise for the motives and goals of the Free Soil movement. However timid and narrow their tactics, the Free Soilers seemed to be taking a long step in the right direction and most antislavery radicals easily accepted James Russell Lowell's advice that it was wiser "to be thankful for what they are than to reproach them with what they are not." The Free Soil party, conceded Edmund Quincy in a *Liberator* editorial, "has sprung from an honest hatred of Slavery, or genuine jealousy of its encroachments, and it is led by men whose purity of purpose and personal honor are above suspicion. Its direction is the same as ours." True, slavery restriction was not immediate emancipation. "But," observed Sidney Howard Gay, "an earnest opposition to the extension of Slavery presupposes a sincere conviction of the wrong of its existence anywhere." Free Soilers would soon discover "that there was no essential difference between extending Slavery in *space* and in *time*."[63].

Although careful to dissociate themselves from Garrisonian heresies like disunionism and nonresistance, a surprising number of Free Soilers reciprocated such cordial respect. Charles Sumner, John G. Palfrey, and other Massachusetts Free Soilers maintained fruitful—if sometimes strained—relations with Bay State abolitionists whose "noble courage, constancy & disinterestedness" they openly applauded. Salmon P. Chase, whose own sister had married such an abolitionist, spoke of the radicals he met at her home as being "fine, upright & worthy" crusaders in a glorious cause. Predicting that the nation was "on the eve of a mighty moral revolution," Congressman Charles Durkee pointed approvingly to the influence of "The sublime truths proclaimed by a Garrison in the streets of Boston, with a halter around his neck."[64] At times, prominent Free Soilers consorted so openly with abolitionist radicals as to alarm their more cautious brethren. In May 1853, after third party politicians had joined William Lloyd Garrison and many of his disciples in hoisting cold-water toasts to John P. Hale, lately Free Democratic candidate for President, Gamaliel Bailey fretted:

I fear our friends are affiliating too much with Garrison. They will get into difficulties consorting with him; they must either quietly bear the responsibility of his views & policy, or be at the pains of constantly disclaiming & protesting. Better let him alone. He works in his way—we, in ours; he has his own concerns, we have ours. And we'll [?] not fight him, but let us not by any kind of association become in the judgement of the Public responsible for him. We have to keep a constant look out to prevent our friends from [slipping] into mere partisanship on one side, or an impractical ultraism on the other.[65]

Impractical ultras the Free Soilers were not. Neither were they mere partisans, sailing always before the breeze of public opinion. They were instead a disparate band of politicians whose positions on slavery and race occupied far higher ground than those taken by either of the major parties. In transmitting so much of the abolitionist Liberty party's creed to the vastly more powerful Republican party, Free Soilers helped to force a sectional confrontation of frightening proportions. None foresaw this more clearly than did William Lloyd Garrison. "I long to see the day when the great issue with the Slave Power, of the immediate dissolution of the Union, will be made by all the free States," he wrote to his wife in July 1848, "for then the conflict will be a short and decisive one, and liberty will triumph. The Free Soil movement inevitably leads to it, and hence I hail it as the beginning of the end." Except that the decision for disunion came not from the North but from the South and that the ensuing conflict was anything but short, it proved a remarkably accurate prophecy.[66]

NOTES

1. *Letter of Gerrit Smith, to the Liberty Party of New Hampshire,* March 18, 1848, p. 2.

2. Ronald G. Walters, *The Antislavery Appeal: American Abolitionism after 1830* (Baltimore, Md.: The Johns Hopkins University Press, 1976), p. 42; James B. Stewart, *Joshua R. Giddings and the Tactics of Radical Politics* (Cleveland: The Press of Case Western Reserve University, 1970), p. 157. See also C. Duncan Rice, *The Rise and Fall of Black Slavery* (New York: Harper & Row, 1975), pp. 348–49; C. Vann Woodward, *American Counterpoint: Slavery and Racism in the North-South Dialogue* (Boston: Little, Brown, 1971), pp. 147–48; Eugene H. Berwanger, *The Frontier Against Slavery: Western Anti-Negro Prejudice and the Slavery Extension Controversy* (Urbana: University of Illinois Press, 1967); Louis Filler, *The Crusade Against Slavery, 1839–1860* (New York: Harper & Bros., 1960), pp. 187, 191; Chaplain W. Morrison, *Democratic Politics and Sectionalism: The Wilmot Proviso Controversy* (Chapel Hill: University of North Carolina Press, 1967), pp. 70–73; Frederick J. Blue, *The Free Soilers: Third Party Politics, 1848–54* (Urbana: University of Illinois Press, 1973), pp. 81, 87, 101–2, 290.

3. Stanley Matthews to Salmon P. Chase, June 12, 1848, Salmon P. Chase Papers, Library of Congress. In 1852, after most Barnburners had returned to the Democratic party, Free Soilers restored to their platform a vehement demand for slavery's abolition.

4. Eric Foner, "Politics and Prejudice: The Free Soil Party and the Negro, 1849–1852," *Journal of Negro History,* 50 (October 1965): 239.

5. Greeley to Joshua Giddings, June 20, 1848, Miscellaneous Manuscripts, New-York Historical Society.

6. Speech of John Van Buren at Hudson, N.Y., April 21, 1848, quoted in *Albany Atlas,* April 28, 1848.

7. O. C. Gardiner, *The Great Issue: or, the Three Presidential Candidates; Being a Brief Historical Sketch of the Free Soil Question in the United States, from the Congresses of 1774 and '87 to the Present Time* (New York: Wm. C. Bryant, 1848), p. 108; *New York Weekly Evening Post,* April 27, 1848.

8. Brinkerhoff to Salmon P. Chase, November 22, 1847, Salmon P. Chase Papers, Pennsylvania Historical Society.

9. *Congressional Globe,* 29 Cong., 2 sess., Appendix, p. 317.

10. Samuel Shapiro, *Richard Henry Dana, Jr., 1815–1882* (East Lansing, Mich.: Michigan State University Press, 1961), pp. 33–34; Foner, "Politics and Prejudice," pp. 246–49.

11. See especially S. R. Ward, *Address to the Four Thousand Colored Voters of the State of New York* (August 16, 1848), quoted in Rochester (N.Y.) *North Star,* September 1, 1848.

12. Boston *Liberator,* February 4, 1848; Pillsbury to William Lloyd Garrison,

January 8, 1849, quoted in ibid., January 12, 1849; Lewis Tappan to Joseph Sturge, November 8, 1848, Lewis Tappan Papers, Library of Congress. James G. Birney, presidential candidate of the Liberty party in 1840 and 1844, refused to support Van Buren in 1848 but voted the Free Soil ticket in 1852 and the Republican in 1856. See Betty Fladeland, *James Gillespie Birney: Slaveholder to Abolitionist* (Ithaca, N.Y.: Cornell University Press, 1955), pp. 265–66, 292.

13. Kirk Porter and Donald Johnson, comps., *National Party Platforms, 1840–1960,* 5th ed. (Urbana: University of Illinois Press, 1973), pp. 13–14, 18–19; Milwaukee *American Freeman,* August 23, 1848; Chicago *Western Citizen,* August 22, 1848. Among the Liberty delegates to the Buffalo Free Soil convention of 1848 who expressed unalloyed pleasure at the new party's platform were Milton Sutliff, one of the founders of the American Anti-Slavery Society in 1833, and Asa Mahan, first president of Oberlin College and an abolitionist of long-standing. See Oliver Dyer, *Phonographic Report of the Proceedings of the National Free Soil Convention at Buffalo, N.Y., August 9th and 10th, 1848* (Buffalo: G. H. Derby, 1848), p. 22.

14. Gardiner, *Great Issue,* p. 119.

15. *Albany Atlas,* April 28, 1848, August 10, 1847.

16. Hamlin to Salmon P. Chase, February 19, 1850, Chase Papers, Pennsylvania Historical Society; Porter and Johnson, *National Party Platforms,* pp. 18–19; *Liberator,* September 15, 1848.

17. Hamlin to Salmon P. Chase, March 11, 1850, Chase Papers, Pennsylvania Historical Society; Dyer, *Phonographic Report,* p. 12. See also Concord, N.H. *Independent Democrat,* February 28, 1850; Montpelier *Green Mountain Freeman,* November 2, 1848; *Boston Daily Republican,* August 9, September 29, 1849; Stephen C. Phillips to Salmon P. Chase, October 19, 1848, Chase Papers, Library of Congress.

18. See especially George W. Julian's speech in the U.S. House of Representatives, May 14, 1850, *Cong. Globe,* 31 Cong., 1 sess., Appendix, p. 574; *National Era,* May 24, 1849; Centreville (Ind.) *Free Territory Sentinel,* August 14, 1848; *Independent Democrat & Freeman,* August 3, 1848. A very few Free Soilers privately expressed a willingness to bend the Constitution so as to make it an antislavery instrument. "I think we should let slaveholders understand that we make war upon the institution of slavery itself wherever it exists," one such advised Salmon P. Chase, "& when we have strength to legislate for its overthrow in the States, I think we shall find Constitutional powers through which to exert that strength." E. S. Hamlin to Chase, April 25, 1850, Chase Papers, Pennsylvania Historical Society.

19. Wilson to Moses A. Cartland, December 11, 1848, Moses A. Cartland Papers, Houghton Library, Harvard University; *National Era,* February 20, 1851. See also *Independent Democrat & Freeman,* October 21, 1847, October 12, 1848; *New York Weekly Evening Post,* June 3, 1847. Congressman Wilmot himself, though at times denying that his proviso in any way threatened slavery in the states, frequently asserted the contrary. "Slavery has within itself the needs of its own dissolution," he said in a speech at Albany, N.Y. in 1847. "Keep it within limits, let it remain where it now is, and in time it will wear itself out." *Albany Atlas,* November 9, 1847.

20. Robert W. Johannsen, *Stephen A. Douglas* (New York: Oxford University Press, 1973), pp. 254–56; *Cong. Globe,* 31 Cong., 1 sess., Appendix, pp. 269–76; Arthur Bestor, "Patent Office Models of the Good Society: Some Relationships Between Social Reform and Westward Expansion," *American Historical Review,*

58 (April 1953): 505–26. Among those who subscribed to the natural limits theory—"the ordinance of the universe," he called it—was Ralph Waldo Emerson: "Wherever a cooler climate, wherever frost—which is good alike for apples and for men—comes in, Slavery cannot subsist." New York *National Anti-Slavery Standard*, August 23, 1849.

21. *Oswego Palladium*, quoted in *Albany Atlas*, August 17, 1847. See also Jacob Brinkerhoff's speech in the U.S. House of Representatives, February 10, 1847, *Cong. Globe*, 29 Cong., 2 sess., pp. 378–79.

22. *National Era*, November 28, 1850; *Cong. Globe*, 31 Cong., 1 sess., Appendix, p. 515; *Independent Democrat*, May 2, 1850. See also Horace Mann to Mrs. Mann, March 10, 1850, Horace Mann Papers, Massachusetts Historical Society; speech of George W. Julian in the U.S. House of Representatives, May 14, 1850, *Cong. Globe*, 31 Cong., 1 sess., Appendix, p. 578.

23. Dyer, *Phonographic Report*, p. 9.

24. *Albany Atlas*, August 11, 1848; Salem (Mass.) *Essex County Freeman*, March 23, 1850; *Speech of Hon. W. Collins, of New York, on the Bill to Establish the Territorial Government of Oregon. Delivered in the House of Representatives, July 28, 1848* (Washington, D.C., 1848), pp. 4, 8–9; *New York Weekly Evening Post*, March 23, 1848.

25. Hale to Moses M. Davis, August 25, 1849, Moses M. Davis Papers, State Historical Society of Wisconsin. See also *Essex County Freeman*, August 11, 1849; *National Era*, July 5, 1849; *Green Mountain Freeman*, November 8, 1849.

26. For example, the *Boston Weekly Commonwealth*, August 16, 1851, insisted that New Mexico possessed land fit for the cultivation of cotton, corn, and wheat.

27. Mann to Mrs. Mann, March 14, 1850, Mann Papers. See also *National Era*, March 14, 1850, February 20, 27, 1851; *Boston Weekly Commonwealth*, August 16, 1851.

28. Holman Hamilton, *Prologue to Conflict: The Crisis and Compromise of 1850* (Lexington: University of Kentucky Press, 1964), p. 175; Harry V. Jaffa, *Crisis of the House Divided: An Interpretation of the Issues in the Lincoln-Douglas Debates* (Garden City, N.Y.: Doubleday, 1959), pp. 390–91. So deep were Free Soil fears of slave power aggressions in the Southwest, in fact, that even after California's admission to the Union as a free state in 1850 party spokesmen warned of maneuvers to carve a slave state from its southern half. See Richard H. Sewell, *Ballots for Freedom: Antislavery Politics in the United States, 1837–1860* (New York: Oxford University Press, 1976), pp. 194–96.

29. Dyer, *Phonographic Report*, p. 7. For Wilmot's own denial that his proviso was a pointless abstraction, see *Albany Atlas*, November 9, 1847.

30. Phillips to Salmon P. Chase, October 19, 1848, Chase Papers, Library of Congress.

31. *Boston Daily Republican*, August 9, September 29, 1849.

32. Henry Wilson et al. to John P. Hale, March 30, 1853, quoted in *Green Mountain Freeman*, April 21, 1853; *Cong. Globe*, 31 Cong., 1 sess., Appendix, p. 741 (June 7, 1850); *National Era*, June 28, 1849.

33. Berwanger, *Frontier Against Slavery*, p. 40.

34. Leslie H. Fishel, Jr., "Wisconsin and Negro Suffrage," *Wisconsin Magazine of History*, 46 (Spring 1963), 180–82; *American Freeman*, February 23, 1848; *Wisconsin Free Democrat*, January 24, April 11, 1849.

35. Milo M. Quaife, ed., *The Attainment of Statehood*, Publications of the State

Historical Society of Wisconsin, Collections, 29 vols., Constitutional Series (Madison, 1928), 4: 191.

36. Fishel, "Wisconsin and Negro Suffrage," pp. 183–84.

37. *Wisconsin Free Democrat*, October 24, November 7, 1849; *Southport Telegraph*, October 19, November 9, 1849.

38. Madison *Wisconsin Democrat*, December 15, 1849. The Wisconsin pattern apparently repeated itself in other Northern states. After an "in depth" study of 668 counties in twelve free states, Tom L. McLaughlin found that receptivity to political rights for blacks were hand-in-hand with support for the Free Soil ticket in 1848. "More than half of the counties that gave above 20 percent of their support for Van Buren also favored Negro equality," he concluded. "Popular Reactions to the Idea of Negro Equality in Twelve Nonslaveholding States, 1846–1869: A Quantitative Analysis," (Ph.D. diss., Washington State University, 1969), pp. v, 84. Even in New York there appeared a positive, though weaker, correlation between support for black suffrage in 1846 and for Van Buren in 1848. See Phyllis F. Field, "The Struggle for Black Suffrage in New York State, 1846–1869," (Ph.D. diss., Cornell University, 1974), pp. 77–79.

39. Fishel, "Wisconsin and Negro Suffrage," pp. 184–96; *Wisconsin Free Democrat*, November 21, December 19, 1849; *Southport Telegraph*, November 23, 1849; *Oshkosh True Democrat*, December 28, 1849.

40. Ronald P. Formisano, *The Birth of Mass Political Parties: Michigan, 1827–1861* (Princeton: Princeton University Press, 1971), pp. 99, 214–15; Formisano, "The Edge of Caste: Colored Suffrage in Michigan, 1827–1861," *Michigan History*, 56 (Spring 1972), 19–41. Formisano notes that Flavius Littlejohn, Whig-Free Soil candidate for governor in 1849, had six years earlier, as a Democratic representative in the Michigan legislature, written a demagogic report condemning black suffrage and stirring fears of race mixing. He also correctly observes that the Free Soil platform of 1849 "wholly ignored racial political equality." Still, as Formisano himself remarks, "Although opposition to non-white voting cut across party lines, a scanning of township returns suggests that 'no' votes came mostly from Democratic strongholds. Similarly, county and township returns (and county-level correlations) either support or do not contradict the commonly accepted proposition that antislavery voters (Liberty and Free Soil) tended to follow abolitionist leaders on this issue and supported equal suffrage." Ibid., p. 30.

41. *Hartford Republican*, September 13, 27, 1849; James T. Adams, "Disfranchisement of Negroes in New England," *American Historical Review*, 30 (April 1925): 545.

42. Leon Litwack, *North of Slavery: The Negro in the Free States, 1790–1860* (Chicago: University of Chicago Press, 1961), pp. 72–74, 93–94, 114; Foner, "Politics and Prejudice," 240; Frederick J. Blue, "The Ohio Free Soilers and the Problems of Factionalism," *Ohio History*, 76 (Winter 1967): 23.

43. *Report of a Majority of the Select Committee* [of the Ohio House of Representatives], *Proposing to Repeal All Laws Creating Distinctions on Account of Color, Commonly Called the Black Laws, January 18, 1845*, Slavery Pamphlets, State Historical Society of Wisconsin; *Documents, Including Messages and Other Communications Made to the Forty-Fourth General Assembly of the State of Ohio*, 10, Pt. I (Columbus, 1931), p. 11; Frank U. Quillin, *The Color Line in Ohio* (Ann Arbor: University of Michigan Press, 1913), p. 36.

44. *National Era*, February 22, 1849; Blue, "Ohio Free Soilers," pp. 20–23; Edgar A. Holt, *Party Politics in Ohio, 1840–1850* (Columbus: F. J. Heer, 1931), p. 400; E. S. Hamlin to Salmon P. Chase, January 18, 19, 20, 30, 1849, Chase Papers, Pennsylvania Historical Society. In his letter to Hamlin of January 20, 1849, Chase spoke of the Black Laws' repeal as "an object dearer to me than any political elevation whatever; and . . . worth more to us as a Party than the election of any man to any office in the gift of the Legislature. It removes out of our path the greatest obstacle to our complete triumph, while it is in itself a great victory of humanity and justice." Doubtless Chase's senatorial hopes burned brighter than he here admitted. Still, his idealism in pressing for revocation of the Black Laws seems altogether genuine—as does that of Hamlin himself, who described for Chase the "fluttering" and "dodging" which attended repeal, and then asked: "Will not the blessings of 20,000 [black] people made happy by our acts fully compensate us for all?" January 30, 1849, Chase Papers, Pennsylvania Historical Society.

45. Foner, "Politics and Prejudice," p. 241; Quillin, *Color Line*, pp. 39–40, 70; *Report of the Debates and Proceedings of the Convention for the Revision of the Constitution of the State of Ohio, 1850–1851* (Columbus: S. Medary, 1851), 2: 550–52.

46. John W. Lyda, *The Negro in the History of Indiana* (Terre Haute; n.p., 1953), pp. 15–17; Litwack, *North of Slavery*, p. 115; Centreville *Free Territory Sentinel*, December 5, 1849, January 30, 1850.

47. *Report of the Debates and Proceedings of the Convention for the Revision of the Constitution of the State of Indiana, 1950,* 2 vols. (Indianapolis: A. H. Brown, 1850), 1: 456–57.

48. *Free Territory Sentinel*, November 28, December 5, 1849; *Indiana True Democrat*, January 30, July 3, 1850.

49. Theodore C. Smith, *The Liberty and Free Soil Parties in the Northwest* (Cambridge, Mass.: Harvard University Press, 1897), pp. 193, 335–36; *Report of the Debates . . . of the Convention for the Revision of the Constitution of . . . Indiana,* 1: 451. Randolph, after Wayne, Free Soil's strongest county, and LaGrange (which also gave substantial backing to Van Buren in 1848) were the only counties to show a majority against the black exclusion clause. Illinois produced a similar pattern. Although a statewide referendum in March 1848 resulted in overwhelming approval for Negro exclusion, most proto-Free Soilers apparently voted in the minority. See John M. Rozett, "Racism and Republican Emergence in Illinois, 1848–1860: A Reevaluation of Republican Negrophobia," *Civil War History*, 22 (June 1976): 109–11.

50. *Report of the Debates . . . of the Convention for the Revision of the Constitution of . . . Indiana, 1850,* 1: 583–86; *Indiana True Democrat*, August 28, 1851.

51. Litwack, *North of Slavery*, pp. 104–10, 143–49; Foner, "Politics and Prejudice," pp. 244–46; David Donald, *Charles Sumner and the Coming of the Civil War* (New York: Alfred A. Knopf, 1960), pp. 180–81; Frank O. Gatell, *John Gorham Palfrey and the New England Conscience* (Cambridge, Mass.: Harvard University Press, 1963), pp. 95–96; Stanley K. Schultz, *The Culture Factory: Boston Public Schools, 1789–1860* (New York: Oxford University Press, 1973), chap. 8; *Boston Weekly Commonwealth*, March 19, July 2, October 1, 1853.

52. *Cong. Globe*, 30 Cong., 1 sess., p. 246, Appendix, pp. 134–35, 33 Cong., 1 sess., pp. 504, 549; *National Era*, March 16, 1854.

53. *Essex County Freeman,* January 21, 1852; *Portland Inquirer,* April 24, 1851; *National Era,* January 23, 30, 1851; *Indiana True Democrat,* May 22, June 5, 1851.

54. Julian to Colored Citizens of Illinois, September 17, 1853, George W. Julian Papers, Indiana State Library.

55. Chase to Douglass, May 4, 1850, Chase Papers, Pennsylvania Historical Society.

56. Douglass to Chase, May 30, 1850, Chase Papers, Library of Congress; *National Era,* February 8, 1849, March 13, 1851; Foner, "Politics and Prejudice," pp. 243, 247–48.

57. Douglass to Sumner, April 24, 1855, Philip S. Foner, ed., *The Life and Writings of Frederick Douglass,* 4 vols. (New York: International Publishers, 1950), 2: 362–63; Gatell, *Palfrey,* pp. 155–56; Stewart, *Giddings,* p. 199.

58. William H. and Jane H. Pease, "Antislavery Ambivalence: Immediatism, Expediency, Race," *American Quarterly,* 16 (Winter 1964): 682–95; Bertram Wyatt-Brown, *Lewis Tappan and the Evangelical War Against Slavery* (Cleveland: Case Western Reserve University Press, 1969), pp. 176–79; Sewell, *Ballots for Freedom,* pp. 99–100.

59. *National Era,* November 9, 1848.

60. *National Era,* April 24, 1851; Formisano, "Edge of Caste," p. 27; *Report of the Debates . . . for the Revision of the Constitution of . . . Ohio, 1850–1851,* 2: 13.

61. Foner, ed., *Writings of Douglass,* 2: 26, 71–77, 206–9, 211–19; Benjamin Quarles, *Black Abolitionists* (New York: Oxford University Press, 1969), pp. 185–87; Foner, "Politics and Prejudice," pp. 251–53; Dyer, *Phonographic Report,* pp. 4, 21, 24.

62. *National Anti-Slavery Standard,* August 10, 1848; May's speech to the Buffalo Free Soil Convention, quoted in Dyer, *Phonographic Report,* pp. 22–23. See also *Liberator,* August 25, September 8, November 17, 1848; Philadelphia *Pennsylvania Freeman,* September 6, 1849.

63. Martin Duberman, *James Russell Lowell* (Boston: Houghton Mifflin, 1966), p. 111; *Liberator,* August 11, 1848; *National Anti-Slavery Standard,* August 17, 1848, February 22, 1849. See also Samuel J. May to Charles Sumner, July 12, 1848, Charles Sumner Papers, Houghton Library, Harvard University; William Lloyd Garrison to Helen Garrison, July 26, 1848, William Lloyd Garrison Papers, Boston Public Library; W.H. Furness, *An Address Delivered before a Meeting of the Members and Friends of the Pennsylvania Anti-Slavery Society during the Annual Fair[,] December 19, 1849* (Philadelphia: Merrihew & Thompson, 1850).

64. Edward L. Pierce, *Memoir and Letters of Charles Sumner,* 4 vols. (Boston: Roberts Brothers, 1877, 1893), 2: 195; 3: 264, 307; Wendell Phillips to Sumner, July 29, 1851 [March 1853?], Sumner Papers; Palfrey to Samuel May, Jr., July 27, 1849 (copy), John G. Palfrey Papers, Houghton Library, Harvard University; Chase to [?], July 10, 1853, Chase Papers, Library of Congress; *Cong. Globe,* 31 Cong., 1 sess., Appendix, pp. 744–45.

65. Bailey to Charles Sumner, May 19, 1853, Sumner Papers. For the Hale testimonial dinner, see Richard H. Sewell, *John P. Hale and the Politics of Abolition* (Cambridge, Mass.: Harvard University Press, 1965), pp. 1–2.

66. July 26, 1848, Garrison Papers.

5

Party Politics and Antislavery Idealism: The Republican Approach to Racial Change in New York, 1855–1860

Phyllis F. Field

From the era of the anti-Masons to that of John Anderson, American voters have shied away from political commitments that have led them outside the two party fold. Consequently, the "success" of third party movements has often been measured not in their electoral totals but in their ability to influence subsequent policy decisions by the major parties. But have attempts to pressure the major parties really worked? Does operating within the traditional two party system result in the neutralization of political activists and the compromise of their principles, or does it give them their only real chance to exercise power and lay the groundwork for the kind of change they desire? Such questions have long intrigued historians, including those who have examined the fate of the antislavery cause in the 1850's. In that decade the Republican Party rose to political ascendancy in the North. But was that party the product of antislavery idealism, the legitimate offspring of the earlier Liberty and Free Soil Parties, as Southern radicals feared, or was it a political bastard, born of political expediency and the ultimate ruination, as Gerrit Smith termed it, of the causes of both freedom and temperance?[1]

Abolitionists themselves were often torn between a moral belief that no man should support a party that compromised an issue of moral principle and their practical realization that some political candidates and programs were much more attractive than others. Nonetheless the Republican Party won many friends among those abolitionists who participated in politics. James McPherson's detailed study of the reactions of most factions within the movement to the 1860 election shows many abolitionists supported Lincoln, while continuing to deplore some aspects of the Republican program.[2] Gerrit Smith, who ran for President on the Radical Abolitionist ticket in 1860, not only believed he would be defeated but also acknowledged from previous experience that even the most enthusiastic campaigning would not persuade former political abolitionists to leave the Republican ranks. He frankly admitted that he expected no more than a dozen votes in any county.[3]

If a number of political abolitionists did seek a home in the Republican Party in the 1850's, it raises the question of the consequences of this move for their program. Did the Republican Party channel abolitionist causes toward ultimate realization or sidetrack them forever in oblivion? As a case study one may analyze the Republican Party's treatment of a single issue dear to the hearts of abolitionists: equal voting rights for black men in the state of New York in the 1850's. In this context one can see the response of an emerging major party to both ideological and institutional pressures placed upon it and begin to understand its behavior with respect to such pressure groups as abolitionists.

Black suffrage was an important issue to abolitionists including those in New York. The same spirit of caste and belief in innate racial differences that fostered slavery also justified the denial of basic rights to free blacks. Since 1821, New York's constitution had demanded that black voters meet a $250 property qualification that was not required of white voters. To abolitionists this provision symbolized the types of attitudes that they were warring against. It served too as a constant reminder of the moral failings of the politicians who had permitted such an official sanction of racial discrimination to enter the fundamental laws of New York. Not surprisingly this provision became the target of organized abolitionist groups beginning in the 1830's.[4]

While the property qualification seemed clearly wrong to abolitionists, for politicians it was not so simple. Even though blacks, if fully enfranchised, would compose only a minute fraction of the electorate and even though the question directly affected only the state of New York, the issue was still politically dangerous.[5] New York had been a slaveholding state as late as 1829; it contained many groups openly hostile to blacks. To showcase the issue was to invite backlash, especially given the highly competitive character of New York politics. American parties were national in scope, too, and the Southern wings of the Whig and Democratic Parties could hardly fail to note or to be concerned about the emergence of sentiment against racial discrimination in such a large and politically important state as New York. In short, racial change could bring political embarrassment both at home and abroad. As a result, the political abolitionists in the Liberty Party were constantly frustrated in their efforts to achieve equal suffrage in the 1840's. In 1846, for instance, on the occasion of the holding of a new constitutional convention, Whig, and to a lesser extent Democratic, convention candidates in areas of Liberty Party strength condemned third partyism and pledged themselves to seek equal suffrage if elected. The convention, however, left the issue to a referendum vote of the people in which, as expected, equal suffrage was crushingly defeated. This provided evidence for politicians to claim that further efforts to achieve the reform were hopelessly impractical.[6]

The Republican Party, however, appeared to be potentially a much more promising vehicle for racial change. It was, first of all, a sectional party with no Southern wing to humor. It was also a *new* party, free to form new commitments on issues. Organized during a period of party realignment when thousands of voters were seeking new political homes, it had to interest and attract voters who were highly dissatisfied with the current state of politics and willing to devote their energies and enthusiasm to building a new political structure. It had to appeal, therefore, to precisely those individuals, like the political abolitionists, who were interested in politics but who had been frustrated in their ability to achieve particular goals in the past. Not all Republicans were seeking the same goals, of course. They could and did put different priorities on curbing Southern power, halting slavery's extension or slavery itself, protecting American institutions from alien/immigrant influence, etc. But they all saw the Republican Party as a useful organization for achieving their goals. And for the Republican Party to grow beyond the scant 31 percent of the vote it had won in its first electoral outing in 1855, it had to articulate and respond to the issues of concern to its constituents.[7]

The popular base of the Republican Party was soon centered in areas more favorable to black suffrage than had been the case with any previous major party. In 1846, the year of the popular referendum on black suffrage, Whig strength had correlated with support for the reform at a low 0.18 while the Democratic vote correlated negatively at -0.43. Republican voting strength between 1855–1860, however, correlated with the reform much more strongly. It ranged from 0.35 in 1855 to 0.65 in 1860 and averaged 0.55 for the period.[8]

Both from the circumstances of the Republican Party's birth and the nature of its constituency, one would expect more enthusiasm among Republicans for black suffrage than had been the case among Whigs. The fact still remained, however, that prejudice and discrimination against blacks had distinguished New York society for generations. Race was still a highly controversial issue, especially since the concentration of racial liberals in Republican ranks meant that Democrats were more united than ever in opposition to the reform. Race was a convenient issue for them to use to try to scare away racial traditionalists from the Republican Party. Thus, the Republicans in New York faced the persistent dilemma of answering the demands of the antislavery elements within their ranks without at the same time jeopardizing their own political future.

Throughout the late 1850's, black rights' groups pressured New York Republicans to act on black suffrage. To amend the constitution qualification for black voters was difficult, requiring the approval of two successive state legislatures elected at different general elections and the subsequent consent of the voters in a referendum.[9] In September 1855, New York blacks formed the New York State Suffrage Association to begin the struggle.[10] This organization met annually through 1860. Unlike previous efforts to influence the legislature to pass a black suffrage amendment, this one relied *not* on amassing vast numbers of signatures on petitions—although as many as nineteen petitions were presented to the 1856 legislature—but on working directly with favorable legislators on appropriate strategy and tactics.[11] Thus, the Association employed a lobbyist, Stephen Myers, who lived in Albany. Myers was heavily involved in politics, even to the point of publishing a Republican campaign paper, *The Voice of Freedom,* in 1858.[12] Likewise, when a general agent of the Association spoke, it was apt to be in a setting designed to attract Republican politicians as an audience, as, for example, when William J. Watkins gave a public address in the Assembly Chamber in 1859.[13]

The Association also tried to show that blacks were an organized voting bloc that could reward their friends. Thus, there was a campaign to enroll as voters those blacks who could already meet the property qualifications.[14] While there was some sentiment among black leaders that blacks should vote *only* for those who supported their rights, open endorsements of the Republican Party were more common. Such blacks identified the Democrats as their "most inveterate enemy" and feared, like Stephen Myers, "If we should vote against the Republican ticket, we should commit suicide so far as the right of franchise is concerned."[15] Clearly many suffrage advocates had dropped the political purism of the past. They were willing to work within the political system with that organization that seemed most likely to advance their cause "regardless," as Henry Highland Garnet put it, "of the unkind things uttered by some of the Republican leaders."[16]

In certain respects the New York Republican Party seemed to respond favorably to the subtle and not-so-subtle pressures from its antislavery elements on the suffrage issue. Between 1856 and 1860, the only three legislatures to consider seriously the issue of the property qualification for blacks and to vote on a constitutional amendment were ones with Republican majorities. In addition, each time equal suffrage came to a vote, it received near unanimous support from Republicans. In the Senate from 89 to 100 percent of Republicans present and voting in the three sessions favored the reform. In the Assembly from 93 to 99 percent did the same.[17] While some American Party members and an occasional Democrat endorsed the reform, Republicans provided the clear margin of victory in all three sessions.[18]

Those few Republicans who opposed equal suffrage did not form an organized faction. Rather they tended to come from the more racially conservative eastern portion of the state, where slavery had once flourished and which had never experienced the evangelical, reformist enthusiasm of the western "Burned-over" district of New York. Some showed strong racial antipathies. Thus, one senator in debate likened propertyless blacks to "cattle" while another assemblyman insisted that blacks were both inferior and degraded beings.[19] Significantly, Republicans who flaunted their opposition to black suffrage were subject to partisan condemnation. When, for example, an Assembly Republican from Saratoga County denounced equal suffrage in a speech, several of his Republican colleagues attacked him, accusing him of being submissive to the wishes of Southern guests at the Saratoga spas.[20]

Republican support for equal suffrage in the legislature, however, was not without its ambiguities. An analysis of legislative speeches on the issue shows that while some Republicans did endorse the reform with the kind of moral enthusiasm that an abolitionist would have expected, others sought expedient reasons to defend it. Thus, on one hand, Samuel Cuyler, a strong opponent of slavery who was convinced that discrimination held blacks back from their rightful opportunity to improve their condition, approached equal suffrage with the zeal of a missionary: "Come, then, legislators, let us rise above the drivelling cant of conservatism and miserable cells of fossil ages, and breathe the better air of a living age, an age of great thoughts and philanthropic deeds."[21] In the speeches of Cuyler's fellow Republicans, however, other rallying cries were heard. Endorsing equal suffrage for blacks was cited at times as a way to express resentment of the South and its pursuit of slavery extension. Thus, the greatest unity on the suffrage issue achieved by Assembly Republicans came in the wake of the announcement of the Supreme Court's Dred Scott decision in 1857. Although the main effect of the decision was to declare the Missouri Compromise unconstitutional, three justices gave the opinion that blacks were not citizens, and Chief Justice Taney himself argued that historically blacks had had no rights that whites were bound to respect.[22] In some Republican speeches the discriminatory property qualification was now portrayed as the product of "slaveholding influence" and "complaisance to our southern brethren," a complaisance that had brought only "indignities and humiliations," such as the Dred Scott decision.[23] To pass equal suffrage was to assert Northern independence from, and contempt for, the South. Practically every debate on the suffrage question in the 1850's contained references to perceived Southern aggression: in 1856 and 1857, the situation in Kansas was brought forward: in 1860, the Fugitive Slave Law.[24] Perhaps the suffrage question even served at times as a surrogate. The 1860 legislature refused to act on a constitutionally doubtful personal liberty law designed to override the federal Fugitive Slave Law but did pass equal suffrage, an "anti-Southern" measure whose constitutionality could not be questioned.

Likewise, some Republicans portrayed equal suffrage as a means of retaliation against Democrats whom they insisted wished to deny blacks the right to vote only because they thought blacks would vote for Republicans.[25]

Others, responding to nativist concerns, argued that blacks were "better qualified to vote than are the mass of ignorant foreigners who have no knowledge of, or regard for the institutions of the country."[26]

The introduction of all these themes was a reminder that equal suffrage was a controversial issue that needed all the extra reinforcement it could get to pass. Indeed some Republicans still had to be cajoled with the reminder that their votes were not *really* in favor of enfranchising all blacks but merely gave the electorate the chance to adopt or reject such a constitutional amendment when it was submitted to them.[27]

For a wide variety of reasons, then, Republicans in New York's legislature backed black suffrage. Most seemed to find it ideologically compatible with their concept of Republicanism, even if their reasons were sometimes other than what an abolitionist might wish. Yet beyond the legislature, the situation was different. Not once before the Civil War did Republicans endorse equal suffrage in their state platform. One, possibly two, attempts were made to quietly abort the amendment process. And, when the constitutional amendment was submitted to the populace, Republican efforts in its behalf were lackluster at best. An ideological leaning toward black rights was not the same as an institutional commitment to it. Like its major party predecessors the Republican Party was distrustful of the race issue and, like them, tried to lessen its impact upon itself.

Republicans were not politically secure in New York in the 1850's. Party alignments changed year by year especially with the rise and fall of the American Party. Not until 1860 did the Republicans win an outright majority in the state entirely on their own, and even then their margin was narrow.[28] Party success demanded party unity and the avoidance of issues that factionalized Republicans or discouraged their party's growth. The Republican unity on black suffrage displayed in the legislature was in a sense misleading, for those Republicans represented primarily areas of established Republican strength, often overwhelming strength. (In 1856 when the Republican Party had two rivals, eight of New York's sixty counties gave the Republicans more than 65 percent of their vote and nine more provided between 60 and 65 percent.) Republican legislators tended to represent northern and western sections of the state, the regions that had showed the least opposition to black rights in the 1846 referendum. Such Republicans might not consider black suffrage a grave risk, but when the issue was *generally* raised throughout the state, the situation was entirely different.

No sooner had Republicans passed the black suffrage amendment for the first time in 1857 than Democrats moved to attack *all* Republicans on the issue. From March through May the leading Democratic journal, the *Albany Argus* blasted black suffrage in a series of long editorials. Political equality for blacks, it claimed, was a new plank in the "Black Republican" platform. Raising the specter of black power, the paper asserted that the Republican aim was "to add ten thousand voters to the ranks of Black Republicans of the State, to assist them in their failing fortunes."[29] The Democratic minority in the legislature echoed this theme. Linking the suffrage amendment to another resolution passed during the session, condemning the Dred Scott decision, and to a bill intended to secure freedom for slaves brought into the state, the Democrats proclaimed in their legislative address that the Republicans had issued:

an invitation to the negro slaves of the South to escape to this State, to be protected here against . . . the reclamation of their owners, if need be, by armed power, and to be incorporated into the mass of voters and into the militia, to enter into the organization of Juries, and to be eligible to all offices and functions of Magistracy, within the State.[30]

With great joy the *Argus* reminded voters that the next Senate and Assembly should be chosen on the suffrage question.[31]

The Democratic attacks did not generate ringing Republican defenses of black suffrage. On the contrary, on September 4, Horace Greeley revealed in the Republican *New York Tribune* that "somebody" in the Republican governor's office had neglected to publish the proposed amendment three months before the general election as required by the state constitution.[32] (The procedure was intended to inform voters of what amendments the next legislature would be considering.) The failure to publish meant that the amendment process would have to be started all over again for equal suffrage to be adopted. Democrats, convinced that the mixup was no accident, expressed the hope in their platform that voters would still "hold them [Republican candidates] to strict accountability" on the issue.[33] Interestingly, when a black convention protested the Republican oversight, Greeley emphatically dissociated the Republican Party from the suffrage cause, claimed that it had no immediate prospects for victory, and argued that it was the Democrats who had suffered a defeat, since they would have to give up the race issue.[34] Defeating Democrats, Greeley implied, was more important than upholding a single principle.

The Republican organization continued to keep its distance from the suffrage issue. Although Governor John A. King did try to explain to the legislature in 1858 how the suffrage resolution had been overlooked and called for its reconsideration and passage (a suggestion not followed since Republicans lacked a majority in the legislature), King's Republican successor, Edwin Morgan, did not mention the reform in his annual message, even though blacks in New York had actively campaigned for him.[35] Suffrage activists were clearly upset, Frederick Douglass questioning whether any progress at all had been made in the struggle. The *National Anti-Slavery Standard*, reviewing Morgan's views on slavery extension, agreed that little could be expected from such a man.[36] Yet other Republicans sent different signals on the party's racial views. Republican legislators continued to support equal suffrage, for instance. One result of the Democrats' efforts to make the issue a partisan one was to make it difficult for Republicans to openly disavow it without embarrassment.

The greatest pressures on the Republican Party as a result of the suffrage issue came in 1860. In that year the legislature repassed the suffrage amendment adopted in the 1859 legislature, thus preparing the way for the amendment's submission to the people in a popular referendum. Yet 1860 was also a presidential election year, the Republicans' great opportunity to win the White House for the first time. Both nationally and in New York the Democrats' strategy was to portray Republicans as extremists who could not be trusted with power. The black suffrage issue fitted conveniently into this campaign strategy. The *Argus* called equal suffrage a "radical" measure and stressed that Republicans wanted a:

government controlled and conducted by an intermixture of races, which shall place the Negro, the Indian, the Feejee [*sic*] Islander, and every other race of men, of whatever grade of civilization alongside of the whites, at the ballot-box, in our municipal and local boards, in the legislative hall, and in the Executive Chair.[37]

The Democratic minority in their legislative address implored voters to "rally to the side of the Democrats, and vote down the proposed amendment, which is intended to recruit the ranks of fanatic abolitionism and sectionalism."[38]

Once again the ideological and institutional needs of the Republican Party were clearly in conflict. The party responded by following the road of compromise, neither abandoning equal suffrage nor supporting it wholeheartedly. Although more Republicans opposed equal suffrage in the crucial 1860 legislature than in prior sessions, Republican strength was more than sufficient for the amendment's approval. Yet following its passage, the only comments of the Republican *Albany Evening Journal* was a brief statement arguing that black suffrage was not really radical because 1,500 blacks in New York already had the right to vote.[39] The "radical" *New York Tribune* made no comment whatever.

Toward the end of the legislative session suffrage activists discovered to their horror that no bill had been introduced to arrange the procedural details for holding the referendum on the proposed constitutional amendment.[40] In 1850 an attempt to amend the constitution had died when such a bill had failed to pass.[41] Although once the lapse was pointed out, a bill was introduced and passed,[42] the whole episode was an unpleasant reminder that some Republicans would apparently have preferred black suffrage to be conveniently forgotten, and it recalled once again the "oversight" in the governor's office in 1857.

Efforts to prevent the suffrage issue from interfering with Republican prospects at the polls characterized the Republican campaign in the fall. Horace Greeley set the tone when he warned Republicans in mid-September that it was a "mistake of Republicans to suppose that they must answer all the slang of their opponents and dispute all their bugaboo stories." Party members need only defend the doctrines in their platform, which made no mention of black suffrage. Discussion of other matters took them away from the "main" issues. What some Republicans chose to endorse *as individuals* was their own affair, not the party's.[43] Greeley himself endorsed equal suffrage as did many other Republican editors, but he insisted that it did not constitute the essence of the Republican cause.[44] If Republicans found the issue a hindrance, they were free to ignore it—as many did.

It was the Democrats who tried to keep the issue alive. "You that are for negro suffrage, will please vote the Republican ticket—you who are not for it will of course go the Democratic ticket. Negro suffrage is a part of Republicanism," urged one newspaper.[45] Democratic preelection parades in Brooklyn and New York featured depictions of Republican leaders embracing black women amid such slogans as "Free love and free niggers will certainly elect Old Abe."[46]

When Republicans did defend equal suffrage, they often tried to make it appear less threatening. Some Democrats too, they urged, believed that blacks should vote. Had not Democratic constitutional conventions enfranchised blacks with $250 freeholds in 1821 and 1846?[47] Besides, the issue was not one of race at all but instead of property qualifications![48] Political equality did not mean social equality either: "Who has contended for the *social* equality of the negro? Who has claimed that he shall be admitted to our houses—shall associate with our wives and our daughters—should sit at our tables and partake of all the comforts of our domestic fireside?"[49] Another paper stressed "there is no danger of his [the black man's] ever attaining positions of distinction in society or government."[50]

Republicans endorsing suffrage often related the issue to other questions (the South, slavery) or groups (Democrats, aliens) upon which they expected greater unanimity. The Democrats, it was asserted, wanted to keep all blacks depressed to please the Southerners who dominated their party.[51] Similarly, how could a qualification to vote be demanded of blacks when it was not required of "the ignorant, foul, priest-ridden Paddy just landed upon the dock at Castle Garden"?[52]

By and large the approach Republican leaders took in 1860 rarely showed voters the genuine indignities and wrongs of racial discrimination or presented the Republican Party as a positive force to end such abuses. The party's strategy served primarily to help Republicans, not blacks. As a result the referendum had little hope for success. In November, it went down to defeat by a vote of 345,791 to 197,889.[53] (Meanwhile Lincoln carried New York with 53.7 percent of the vote.)

Many Republicans, of course, did vote for equal suffrage for blacks. Indeed support for the measure increased almost 9 percent over a similar referendum in 1846. The Republican vote at the township level correlated at a high 0.78 with the vote in favor of the amendment. But the vote totals also show that many Republicans opposed the amendment or failed to vote at all on the measure. Even assuming that none of the votes in favor of the amendment came from Democrats, only a little more than half (54.5 percent) of the Lincoln voters *must* have endorsed the amendment. Likewise, more votes were recorded against the amendment than there were supporters of the Democratic candidates in 1860. Therefore, it seems likely that at least a minimum of 14 percent of all the Republican voters (presumably many more) were actively opposed to further additions to the black electorate.

Evidence also suggests that disproportionate numbers of Republicans avoided the question altogether. Frederick Douglass observed, "While the Democrats at the polls never failed to accompany their state and national tickets with one against the proposed amendment, Republicans—many of them—refused to touch a ticket in favor of the amendment."[54] In the thirteen counties of southeastern New York the support for equal suffrage was 30 percent or more below that for the Republican Party. The vote in favor of equal suffrage correlated 0.53 with the proportion of all voters casting a ballot on the suffrage question. This meant that in areas where black suffrage was accepted there were relatively few abstentions, but where it was generally unpopular the opposite was true. That most of the abstainers were Republicans is indicated by a correlation of -0.72 between the percentage of all voters participating in the referendum and the amount by which the pro-suffrage vote in an area fell short of the Republican vote.[55] Where turnout in the referendum was low, Republicans were not voting on the suffrage question. Such behavior suggests that some Republicans felt cross-pressured. They were racially conservative but disliked taking the partisan "Democratic" position of opposing the amendment.

Analysis shows that the Republicans who dissented from the majority of their party on the suffrage question were more likely to come from the eastern, more heavily Democratic section of the state than from the areas of more recent New England settlement in the North and West. The two regions seemed to have had different political personalities, the area of New England settlement more attuned to pietistic religion, Republicanism, and moral reform in general and the older, eastern region more orthodox, conservative, and suspicious of change and activist reformers. Blacks made up relatively more of the population in areas of Republican opposition to black suffrage and the nativistic American Party was more likely to have flourished there as an alternative to the Republicans and Democrats in the 1850's.[56]

Partisan cues were clearly important for the majority of voters participating in the suffrage referendum in 1860. In working within a major political party, some antislavery reformers had hoped to make use of the discipline and organization that such parties possessed to achieve their goals. The fate of black suffrage in New York highlighted what such reformers could expect as a result of working "within the system."

The political abolitionists who rejected the third party alternative in the 1850's were undoubtedly correct in perceiving the Republicans as potentially far more favorable to their cause than previous major parties. Republican legislators had resurrected the suffrage issue after nearly a decade in which it had been virtually ignored. They had also given the measure solid support.

The Republican association with the prosuffrage cause (even though it never received a formal endorsement) undoubtedly helped to increase public support for it among the Republican rank and file as well. Table 5.1 shows the results of a multiple regression analysis to determine those variables that were most associated with the changes in support for black suffrage in New York townships between the referendums of 1846 and 1860.[57] Clearly partisanship played a major role. There was a general tendency for areas to increase their prosuffrage totals as more Republicans, unlike Whigs earlier, reacted positively to the issue. Meanwhile "reformist" areas where Democrats had abstained or voted in favor of black suffrage in 1846 showed backsliding as the issue became so important for Democratic politicians. Areas moving away from the Democratic Party in the era became more favorable to the reform. Overall, gains for equal suffrage were likely to be centered in townships where Republican strength was increasing, where the Whig and Free Soil Parties had obtained a preponderance of the vote in

Table 5.1

PARTIAL REGRESSION COEFFICIENTS FOR VARIABLES EXPLAINING EQUAL SUFFRAGE VOTING SHIFTS, 1846–1860

Variable	Beta	Coefficient of Variability
Percent Prosuffrage, 1846	−.92	1.25
Change Percent Democratic, 1844–1860	−.29	0.61
Percent New England Born, 1845	.19	1.54
Percent Whig/Free Soil for Governor, 1848	.17	1.70
Area of Pre-1790 Settlement	−.16	0.86
Percent Democrat/Nativist, 1846	−.14	3.55
Percent Black, 1855	−.13	0.61
Percent American for Governor, 1858	−.12	0.98

N = 486

Fraction of Explained Variance 61%

1848, and where New Englanders were an important part of the population. Areas least likely to add to their prosuffrage totals were in the older, eastern section of the state, where the Democratic Party had been well entrenched in 1846, where blacks were numerous, and where the American Party had attracted adherents as late as 1858. While a number of factors were present, clearly party played an important role.

The prosuffrage gains, however, had not even come close to making black suffrage a reality. While this was not necessarily the fault of the Republican Party alone, it does suggest some of the limits of working within a major party. Seemingly the first priority of the Republican Party was to secure its own position by satisfying as many diverse elements within it as possible. A party could not command intensely loyal adherents if it rode roughshod over their beliefs. It was important to offend no one grievously. Therefore, politicians sought conciliatory stands on issues that divided their parties. Some Republicans described black suffrage, for instance, in terms that had little to do with race and instead related the issue to the evils of property qualifications in general or to the fondness of Democrats, Irishmen, and Southerners for racial discrimination. Lost, thus, was the opportunity to communicate effectively the reality of racial bias and why it was wrong.

Party security also demanded "managing" controversial issues. Black suffrage was too important to too many Republican party members for the party simply to abandon it. But black suffrage was also too politically volatile not to be controlled. If the issue promised to hinder Republican prospects in an election, action had to be taken to forestall this "forgetting" about the amendment, as in 1857, or dissociating it from the party officially, as in 1860. For Republicans in 1860 as for Whigs in 1846, the device of a referendum proved in some sense to be useful. It served to show that black suffrage was so unpopular it could not be enacted. The blame for the defeat could be placed on the electorate, not the party.

The issue could, therefore, be laid aside again without incurring the righteous wrath of suffrage supporters. A strong denunciation of the Republicans' suffrage efforts did come from black abolitionist Frederick Douglass: "The negro was stowed away [by Republicans] like some people put out of sight their deformed children when company comes."[58] Yet while white abolitionists condemned belatedly the Republican Party's halfhearted suffrage efforts, nearly all, even those traditionally favoring third parties, saw, as Gerrit Smith put it, "great good" ultimately coming from the election of Lincoln, imperfect as he and other Republicans might be.[59] Perhaps the Republican Party had indeed done all it could be expected to do as a viable political organization in the American two party system. More might be expected from it or a successor major party in the future. Most New York abolitionists had seemingly come to accept the give and take of politics as something they could live with. Whether the Republican Party's efforts were enough given the size and gravity of America's race problem, however, is another and more disturbing question.

NOTES

1. *Principia* (New York), September 15, 1860. One may find an interesting variety of interpretations of the nature of the Republican Party before the Civil War in such works as Richard H. Sewell, *Ballots for Freedom: Antislavery Politics in the United States, 1837–1860* (New York: Oxford University Press, 1976); Eric Foner, *Free Soil, Free Labor, Free Men: The Ideology of the Republican Party Before the Civil War* (New York: Oxford University Press, 1970); Eugene Berwanger, *The Frontier Against Slavery: Western Anti-Negro Prejudice and the Slavery Extension Controversy* (Urbana, Ill.: University of Illinois Press, 1967).

2. James M. McPherson, *The Struggle for Equality: Abolitionists and the Negro in the Civil War and Reconstruction* (Princeton: Princeton University Press, 1964), chap. 1.

3. *Principia,* September 15, 1860.

4. Herman D. Bloch, "The New York Negro's Battle for Political Rights, 1777–1865," *International Review of Social History* 9 (1964):65–80.

5. Blacks made up 1.3 percent of the population in New York in 1860. The proportion of blacks in the populace had been on the decline since 1731.

6. Alan M. Kraut and Phyllis F. Field, "Politics Versus Principles: The Partisan Response to 'Bible Politics' in New York State," *Civil War History* 25 (June 1979):101–18. Black suffrage was voted down by a vote of 224,336 to 85,406.

7. Votes are taken from the *Tribune Almanac.*

8. Correlations are based on county level data. Returns for the referendums are from the *Tribune Almanac for 1870,* p. 53.

9. See Charles Z. Lincoln, *The Constitutional History of New York* (Rochester: Lawyers Cooperative, 1906), 2: chap. 7.

10. Howard Holman Bell, *A Survey of the Negro Convention Movement, 1830–1861* (New York: Arno Press and *The New York Times,* 1969), pp. 185–90.

11. This is based on a count of the petitions listed in the Assembly and Senate journals. No more than five petitions were submitted to any other legislature in this period. At least some whites participated in the prosuffrage activities.

12. Philip S. Foner and George E. Walker, eds., *Proceedings of the Black State Conventions, 1840–1865* (Philadelphia: Temple University Press, 1979), pp. 1–76.

13. Ibid., pp. 89–92.

14. Ibid.; *New York Tribune,* September 12, 1855; *Frederick Douglass' Paper* (Rochester), September 21, October 5, 1855.

15. *National Anti-Slavery Standard* (New York), October 9, 1858.

16. *New York Tribune,* September 24, 1856.

17. New York State Senate, *Journal,* 80th Sess., 1857, pp. 353–54; New York State Assembly, *Journal,* 80th Sess., 1857, pp. 862–64; New York State Assembly, *Journal,* 82nd Sess., 1859, p. 732; New York State Senate, *Journal,* 82nd Sess., 1859, pp. 633, 701; New York State Assembly, *Journal,* 83rd Sess., 1860, p. 332; New York State Senate, *Journal,* 83rd Sess., 1860, p. 468. Party affiliations are taken

from the Albany newspapers, which often listed the members of the legislature on the eve of its opening.

18. In the Senate five American Party members and one Democrat in 1857 backed the amendment. In the Assembly four Americans in 1857 and one Democrat in 1859 supported it.

19. *Albany Argus,* April 10, 1860; see also February 11. No official record of legislative debates was kept. The Albany newspapers printed summaries of debates and occasionally the entire texts of speeches.

20. Ibid., February 11, 1860; *Albany Evening Journal,* February 20, 1860.

21. *Albany Evening Journal,* February 20, 1860.

22. Allan Nevins, *The Emergence of Lincoln* (New York: Charles Scribner's Sons, 1950), 1:91–95.

23. *New York Tribune,* March 28, 1857.

24. *Albany Argus,* March 7, 1857, February 10, 1860.

25. *Albany Evening Journal,* March 23, 1859.

26. *Albany Argus,* February 11, 1860. See also *Albany Evening Journal,* March 7, 1857.

27. *Albany Argus,* March 24, 1859.

28. Republicans won 31.3 percent of the vote in 1856, 46.3 percent in 1856, 40.3 percent in 1857, 46.0 percent in 1858, and 53.7 percent in 1860. In 1859 the American Party endorsed some Democratic candidates. The Republican Secretary of State (not endorsed) won 49.9 percent, the comptroller (endorsed) won 54.8 percent.

29. *Albany Argus,* March 27, 31, April 1, 1857.

30. Ibid., April 24, 1857. To stress the importance of the point, the original quotation was entirely in italics.

31. Ibid., April 1, 1857.

32. *New York Tribune,* September 4, 1857.

33. *Albany Argus,* September 14, 1857.

34. *New York Tribune,* September 26, 1857.

35. New York State Senate, *Documents,* 81st Sess., 1858, No. 3, p. 12.

36. *Douglass' Monthly* (Rochester), March 1859; *National Anti-Slavery Standard,* January 8, 1859.

37. *Albany Argus,* February 12, 1860.

38. Ibid., April 18, 1860.

39. *Albany Evening Journal,* February 13, 1860. Two Republicans in the Senate and five in the Assembly voted against the proposed amendment in 1860.

40. *Weekly Anglo-African* (New York City), April 21, 28, 1860. The paper (March 31) had also reported that Stephen Myers had had to pressure the Republican controlled committee considering the original resolution to report it out.

41. Lincoln, *Constitutional History,* 2:226.

42. New York State Assembly, *Journal,* 83rd Sess., 1860, p. 1263; New York State Senate, *Journal,* 83rd Sess., 1860, p. 737.

43. *New York Tribune,* September 15, 1860.

44. Ibid., September 17, 1860. The *Roman Citizen,* October 17, 1860, was one of the few Republican papers insisting that *all* Republicans should favor the amendment.

45. *Steuben Farmer's Advocate* (Bath), October 31, 1860.

46. *New York Herald,* October 24, 1860; *Brooklyn City News,* November 2, 1860.

47. *Albany Evening Journal,* August 27, September 21, 1860.

48. See, for example, *Albany Evening Journal,* October 26, 1860; *New York Evening Post,* October 19, 1860; *Elmira Weekly Advertiser,* September 8, 1860; *Cortland Republican Banner,* October 24, 1860.

49. *Oneida Weekly Herald,* October 23, 1860.

50. *Buffalo Morning Express,* October 24, 1860.

51. *Suffrage Herald* (Patchogue), November 2, 1860; *Long Islander* (Huntington), November 2, 1860; *Albany Evening Journal,* November 1, 1860.

52. *Independent* (New York) quoted in the *Buffalo Daily Courier,* November 5, 1860.

53. *Tribune Almanac for 1870,* p. 53. Corrections have been made in the returns for Orange, Herkimer, and Chenango as a result of an analysis of the local returns.

54. *Douglass' Monthly,* December 1860.

55. The latter variable was calculated by taking the difference between the Republican and prosuffrage votes and dividing by the Republican vote.

56. Phyllis F. Field, "Republicans and Black Suffrage in New York State: The Grass Roots Response," *Civil War History* 21 (June 1975): 143; Dixon Ryan Fox, *Yankees and Yorkers* (New York: New York University Press, 1940); Whitney R. Cross, *The Burned-Over District* (Ithaca, N.Y.: Cornell University Press, 1951).

57. Listed in the table are those variables that added at least 1 percent to explained variance. Also entered in the regression equation but failing to add 1 percent were average value of dwelling per family and percent nonevangelical communicants. Some variables (percent Irish and German, percent Republican) were excluded because they correlated highly with some of the other independent variables. The referendum data came from 29 counties where local (township) returns were available from the two referenda. Demographic data came from the *Census of the State of New York for 1855* (Albany: C. Van Benthuysen, 1857).

58. *Douglass' Monthly,* December 1860.

59. *National Anti-Slavery Standard,* November 17, 1860, February 2, 1861; Ralph Volney Harlow, *Gerrit Smith: Philanthropist and Reformer* (New York: Henry Holt and Co., 1939), p. 428; *Principia,* November 19, 1860; McPherson, *Struggle for Equality,* chap. 1.

II

THE POLITICS OF ANTISLAVERY VERSUS THE STRENGTH OF POLITICAL PARTISANSHIP

6

"There Are Other Questions Beside That of Slavery Merely": The Democratic Party and Antislavery Politics

Joel H. Silbey

Any attempt either to end slavery in the United States or to prevent its further expansion had to take into account a political system largely dominated by the Democratic Party after 1828. Democrats did not always have their own way, but despite significant opposition from the Whigs and occasional defeats, as in 1840 and 1848, they usually controlled the federal government from Andrew Jackson's day to James Buchanan's. The way that the party's hundreds of thousands of supporters reacted to the rise of political movements against slavery was a major factor in the calculus shaping antislavery fortunes after the 1830's.[1]

While recognizing that the Democrats were generally hostile to the antislavery movement in every form, historians have paid particular attention to those in the party who espoused antislavery extension in the 1840's and then moved into the Republican Party in the 1850's. The role played by the "Democratic Republicans" in the years leading to the Civil War has been especially well told. With the Barnburner revolt in New York and its transformation into the Free Soil movement in 1848 as the starting point, the Hannibal Hamlins, Francis P. Blairs, Preston Kings, James Doolittles and Gideon Welleses have all had their actions recorded in the annals of the antislavery political movement.[2] The reasons for their behavior are clearly marked as well. The "Civil War Synthesis" in American political history assigns a persistent, all encompassing centrality and influence to sectionalism and the slavery-extension issue in antebellum politics.[3] Opposition to the expansion of slavery, Eric Foner writes, became "the central political question of the late 1840's, and the vehicle by which antislavery became, for the first time, a truly mass movement in the North."[4] By the beginning of

1848, another historian has written, sectional antagonisms were heated "to the flash point, and in both major parties sizable free-soil factions stood ready to renounce old allegiances rather than acquiesce in the South's latest demands." Party splits and party collapse followed, all made possible because "traditional issues were fast dropping by the wayside."[5] The Democrats were not immune. "Antislavery sentiment was increasing among their constituents," Aileen Kraditor sums up, and, therefore, they had to take a stand as a matter of political survival.[6]

The focus on the antislavery Democrats is understandable in certain terms: tracing the linear development of American politics toward the emergence of the Republican Party and the sectional confrontations of the 1850's is attractive because it is an important matter. The Civil War did occur when the forces opposing slavery's extension won control of the government. Some Democrats, as recently joined converts to the Republican Party, did play a role in that triumph. But does such emphasis accurately depict the politics of the time or portray the overall posture and behavior of the Democrats in response to those politics? The answer is clearly "no" to both questions. Too much emphasis on the power of the sectional forces in the politics of the period from the 1830's on, distorts the rich complexity of political reactions to the events of the day.[7]

The scholarship of the past twenty years has sensitized us to the amount of hostility in the North to sectionalism and antislavery movements, a hostility that lasted late into the era of sectional conflict.[8] Many antebellum politicians were not especially responsive to the slavery question. Furthermore, sectional fears and tensions remained largely unfocused into the late 1840's because there existed in the United States a set of non-sectional partisan political divisions. As a result, the response of politicians and voters to the rise of antislavery political movements was inconsistent and complex, never exclusively sectional and clear-cut. And nowhere was this complexity more evident than in the Democratic Party's posture toward antislavery politics.

There was antagonism toward independent, antislavery-extension, third party movements among Whigs and later among some Republicans as well. Similarly, many Whigs proved hesitant about changing their accustomed ways in politics. Nevertheless, the core of such hesitating responses to the rise of sectional politics clearly lay with the bulk of the Northern Democrats. The number of Democrats who supported the Liberty Party or became Free Soilers and later joined Republicans on the slavery issue was but a very small part of the whole Northern constituency of the party. The majority—the mainstream of the party in the North—challenged the rise of antislavery and did not join the movement when it did emerge, even when some of the key leaders of their party defected either temporarily or permanently. They remained loyal during the Van Buren defection in 1848 and stayed on after 1854 and the rise of Republicanism. They soldiered on in their party with its antislavery stance despite the loss of friends and power. As a result, the party's vote in the North remained high right through the election of 1860 (see Table 6.1).

Antislavery politics involved different levels of commitment, different intensity, tactics, and even diverse opinions on the legality of slavery's suppression. Mainstream Democrats, for the most part, vigorously resisted all genre of antislavery politics. Democrats marched to a different drummer than the reformers and followed a different political tradition.[9] Throughout the political turmoil of their generation they remained loyal to their old associates and the commitments and traditions of their party.

They never assigned to the antislavery movement a high priority among Democratic issues and concerns. Moreover, Democratic spokesmen attacked antislavery political movements and did their best to ignore, play down, and contain the sectional tensions rising within the country. In so doing, they reflected some of the mainstream political currents of their age. Given their numbers, given what they represented, their advocacy and behavior and the reasons that underlay each, the Democratic posture toward the movement to abolish black slavery is worth tracing, clarifying, defining, and emphasizing. Only then will the antislavery political movement, the Democratic Party, and the larger political culture to which they both belonged be fully understandable.

Rhetorically, the Democrats never left anyone in doubt where they stood. Their intense opposition to antislavery and antislavery political movements, in whatever form and degree, was well and fully articulated. As early as 1835, in their *Address to the People of the United States,* the party's battle cry for the upcoming presidential election, they proclaimed that "it has ever been a fundamental article in the Republican creed," that "Congress has as little right to interfere with the domestic relations of *master and apprentice* in Massachusetts, or *master and servant* in Virginia, as they have to meddle

Table 6.1
DEMOCRATIC VOTE, NORTHERN STATES:
PRESIDENTIAL ELECTIONS, 1840–1860

	No.	Percentage
1840	809,485	47.2
1844	927,333	48.8
1848	810,662	40.0
1852	1,153,556	50.2
1856	1,227,106	41.4
1860	1,488,391*	43.8

* Combined Douglas and Breckinridge totals.

with similar social relations in Great Britain, France, or Spain. . . . No man, nor set of men, can interfere or even wish to interfere, with the reserved rights of the States, embracing their domestic institutions and social relations, and call himself a Democratic Republican, or a friend of the Union." Therefore, the official Democratic organ, the Washington *Globe* succinctly summed up, "the whole democracy of the North . . . are opposed, upon constitutional principles, as well as upon views of sound policy, to any attempt of the abolitionists" to accomplish their purposes.[10]

In every one of their national party platforms between 1844 and 1856 the Democrats repeated the same attacks on abolitionism, branding it a threat to the Union and thus detrimental to "the happiness of the people." During the battles over the question of slavery in the territories in the late forties, a Democratic Northern newspaper lamented that too much of Congress's time had been taken up on the question of slavery. Every act that Congress passed on the slavery question, the paper asserted, "will be a violation of the Constitution, and a usurpation of powers that were never delegated by that instrument." The general government simply had no power to do anything about slavery "without violating the constitution, and he who would sacrifice the constitution deserves to be branded as a traitor."[11]

Such sentiments were cool and reasoned in comparison with the more bitter, hostile expressions of Democratic opposition to antislavery reformers that appeared with increasing frequency. Pamphlets, platforms, and speeches exuded a litany of hostility, condemnation, and abuse persistently from the 1830's onward. Some politicians made distinctions between abolitionism and antislavery-extension. Mainstream Democrats did not. David Potter's remark that the Barnburners "shunned abolitionists as if they were diseased" is descriptive of a broader Democratic reaction as well.[12] Abolitionism was "politico-religious fanaticism." It was the evil work of extremists, of the "Hartford Convention and Nullification factions," a "joint plot" of sectional "disturbers." Abolitionist schemes were "mad and fanatical."[13]

Even as sectional agitation increased in the mid–1840's, the Democratic position remained largely unchanged. The behavior of Democratic dissenters and Wilmot Proviso supporters during the Polk Administration was "factious and unnecessary" and grounds for withdrawing support from them at election time. The Wilmot Proviso itself, a "miserable hobby," had been "introduced out of time, and of place." Representative John Smith Chipman of Michigan believed that the preservation of the Union "was worth a million times more than the pitiful consideration of a handful of degraded Africans."[14] Free Soilers of 1848, even with their Democratic component, were "disunionists . . . a sectional faction." Martin Van Buren was "the leader of a faction of disorganizers" who would not attract Democrats from their integrity to "pander to his treason." Democratic congressman William H. Bissell, argued that the South was misbehaving as well but had been "goaded and harrassed by . . . Northern fanatics until they have become as unreasonable, impracticable, insane and reckless as the most fanatical abolitionist." A circular from Tammany Hall in 1850 referred to "the fanatics and demagogues who are waging an unholy crusade. . . . We sincerely deprecate sectional issues and contests." The Democrats' mission in this situation was to "rebuke fanaticism," reassure the South, and "renew old associations."[15]

Finally, when the Republicans emerged in the mid-1850's, they were, in Democratic eyes, no different from their antislavery Whig antecedents. Republicans embodied the "wild spirit of abolitionism" that destroyed everything. They had "but one common aim—the dissolution of the Union." How could it be otherwise, given the nature of their leadership? "The archfiend of American politics during the last twenty years has been William H. Seward."[16]

Such constantly repeated expressions were more than a grab bag of miscellaneous quotations. There was a steady, repetitious, consistency from first to last, a continuity to the Democratic assaults on all forms of antislavery, no matter what its nature. Abolitionism, antislaveryism, and Republicanism were enemies of the Democracy and of everything for which the party stood. Antislavery advocacy and political activities were inimical to the country and the things that were important in politics. The repeated raising by antislavery leaders of an issue that was superfluous, dangerous, and outside the pale of reasonable concern, could only be laid to a desire to distract voters, fragment parties, and destroy the Union. Antislavery advocates were, therefore, not to be seen as legitimate, but for what they were and to be described in the harshest terms possible.

Rhetoric, of course, is one thing, behavior another. But mainstream Democratic behavior conformed to what Democratic leaders said. Whenever they could, Democrats acted clearly, directly and hostilely toward antislavery efforts. During the presidential election of 1836 they moved briskly against abolitionist petitions and the demands embodied in them. They first issued a pamphlet: "Opinions of Martin Van Buren . . . Upon the Powers and Duties of Congress in Reference to the Abolition of Slavery Either in the Slave Holding States or in the District of Columbia." This was followed by Van Buren's promise to veto any bill of Congress abolishing slavery in the District of Columbia.[17] Governor William Marcy of New York sharply assailed the abolitionists' "pernicious schemes" in his annual address to his state legislature in 1835. Other Northern Democratic state legislatures passed resolutions against abolitionism. Those of the Michigan legislature argued that since "domestic slavery of the southern States," was "a subject exclusively within the control of said States, every interference with the subject by the General Government or any other States is an assumption of power not delegated by the Federal Constitution." Although "the freedom of the press, and the freedom of speech, are sacred and inviolable rights guaranteed to the people" there was also an "obligation to preserve them from abuse." Finally, "the formation of societies, and the acts and proceedings of individuals in the non-slaveholding States, having for their object an interference in the rights of the slaveholder, are in direct violation of the obligations of the compact of our Union and destructive to the tranquility and welfare of the country."[18]

All of these activities reassured those sensitive to the dangers posed by abolitionism and helped reinforce the bonds of the Democratic community. Southern Democrats described Van Buren as bringing with him into the presidential race of 1836 "principles congenial to those of the South." What that meant, specifically, was ideological: "his political creed is republican of the old democratic school." At the same time, other Northern Democrats were commended for their assault on the abolitionists. All of this was of a piece. As the Milledgeville (Georgia) *Federal Union* summed up in 1836, "next to Andrew Jackson, Martin Van Buren is the most powerful enemy of the abolitionists; and the safest president for the South."[19]

In Congress as well, Democratic hostility toward antislavery activity was marked and clearly different from Whig reactions. In the House of Representatives during the Tyler Administration, congressmen voted on a number of resolutions relating to black rights, antislavery petitions, and the slave trade in the District of Columbia. On these issues, Northern Democrats generally voted against the antislavery position in alliance with Southern colleagues from both parties. Northern Whigs, in contrast, did not. Later in the decade, as sectional tensions increased in the aftermath of the Mexican War and the introduction of the Wilmot Proviso, such partisanly defined differences in behavior on these matters continued. Unlike the Northern Whigs, most Northern Democrats resisted committing themselves to the antislavery side of matters whether on the Wilmot Proviso or on similar issues dealing with the expansion of slavery.[20] Some congressional Democrats succumbed to antislavery voting most of the time, many did part of the time, but in general, their position varied from indifference and hostility to antislavery extension activities to lukewarm support of the reformers at certain moments. Their position was echoed by Democratic state legislators and delegates to state party conventions even as tensions and pressures increased. A few of them joined the bulk of the Whigs to create majorities in favor of the Wilmot Proviso in several state legislatures, but most of them remained true to their hostile position.[21]

Finally, the behavior of Democratic voters when faced at the polls with the option of voting for antislavery political parties was consistent from 1840 onward. The total vote for antislavery political parties grew from 7,000 (0.3 percent of the national total) for the Liberty Party in 1840, to 1.8 million (39.8 percent of all votes cast) for the Republicans in 1860. But where did the votes for these parties come from? Or, more pertinently, how many came from Democrats?

There was a clear tendency among voters in the pre-Civil War era to repeatedly vote for their own party and not to defect or drop out of the electoral system. Thomas B. Alexander's study of voter constancy in presidential elections between 1836 and 1860 concludes that about 90 percent of the voters for a party in one election supported that same party in a subsequent contest.[22] His figures suggest that the Democrats were hardly a prime source of antislavery political votes. Observers at the time were certainly quite conscious of the difficulty of luring Democrats away from their party homes. William Gienapp quotes one Republican as complaining about how long it took to wean any Democrat into antislavery politics, no matter what his ideological commitments. "When men have formed the habit of acting together & have got their party into power," he wrote, "its policy will be shaped by the majority of the party and the minority however reluctant will continue to act for a long time & till they are led away from their own purposes rather than seek a new alliance."[23] The voting returns confirmed that persistent pattern.

There were occasional deviations, to be sure. They were small in numbers, and many defectors were off only temporarily. Gienapp cites the behavior of those Democrats who deserted the party in opposition to the Kansas-Nebraska bill in 1854. Many of them "quickly returned to the party fold. Their 1854 bolt represented a one-time protest against party policy. Torn between their party identity and a dislike of national party policy, they eliminated the cross pressure they felt, not by abandoning their party, but by gradually adopting new opinions."[24]

Analysis of Democratic voting behavior supports Alexander's and Gienapp's findings. The Liberty Party attracted few Democrats. Rather, they drew the bulk of their support from Whig constituencies. A Whig complained to Hamilton Fish in 1844 that "every new faction that springs up . . . subtracts largely from our votes while the rascals on the other side escape without even a blemish." The various "isms," including abolitionism, were "the bastard children of the Great Whig party." In the opinion of at least one Democrat each "ism" and its Whig supporters were separated from the Democratic Party by a kind of "unholy alliance."[25] That judgment about numbers has been borne out by a number of close studies of popular voting returns.

Lee Benson points out that in New York State Democratic popular vote percentages remained relatively constant between 1840 and 1844 in towns where the Liberty Party received more that a scattering of the vote, while Whig percentage declines in those towns almost equalled the Liberty percentages. The exception to this general pattern occurred in only one county: Madison—the center of Liberty activity—where Democrats apparently were affected by the pressures there.[26] Benson uses Putnam in Washington County as more representative of the Democratic pattern:

Table 6.2
VOTE IN PUTNAM TOWNSHIP IN WASHINGTON COUNTY, NEW YORK

	Whigs		Democrats		Others	
	(N)	Percentage	(N)	Percentage	(N)	Percentage
1840	113	80.7	27	19.3	—	—
1844	68	50.4	25	18.5	42	31.1
1850	—	79.1	—	20.9	—	—

He quotes, in summary, Horace Greeley's observation in 1844 that "any third party based on convictions of moral duty must naturally draw ten recruits from the Whig ranks to every one taken from the other side."[27]

Even in the much more wide-ranging Free Soil revolt in 1848, led by the greatest Democrat of them all, Martin Van Buren, mainstream Democrats largely shunned the chance to participate in the milder form of antislavery politics. It was during this election that Democrats unleashed a particularly raucous version of what two historians have called their "nigger yell" against blacks, their defenders, and any politics based on changing the situation of the blacks in the country—even when slavery-extension, not abolition, was the issue.[28] The party's call to duty was usually effective. As James Buchanan noted, Pennsylvania Democrats, with few exceptions, were "sound upon the slavery question."[29] Traditional party ties remained very strong in the election of 1848. No more than a small, albeit vigorous, minority of Democrats voted for Free Soil.

The numbers of such voters varied dramatically from Northern state to Northern state. Kevin Sweeney estimates that 83 percent of the Democratic voters in the Massachusetts gubernatorial election in 1847 voted Democratic in 1848; only 17 percent of them voted for the Free Soilers.[30] In the four Midwestern states of Ohio, Indiana, Illinois, and Michigan, Ray Shortridge found that neither the Liberty Party nor the Free Soil Party drew many Democratic votes. In the latter case he concludes that "only an insignificant number of 1844 Democratic voters turned out for the Free Soil Party in 1848 in the Midwest." The major pool of Free Soil voters were either 1844 Whig voters or people who did not vote then.[31] In New Jersey where there was an insignificant antislavery vote (0.1 percent for Liberty in 1844, 0.9 percent for the Free Soilers in 1848), the correlation between the Democratic vote before the rise of the Free Soilers and their vote in the election is so high as to suggest that the number of defectors was very few indeed.[32] Only in New York State, site of the largest Free Soil vote anywhere in 1848, was there a different pattern. Paul Kleppner estimates that 40 percent of the Democratic vote in 1844 went into the Free Soil Party four years later, that is, about 95,000 Democrats of the 237,000 who had voted for Polk. In summary, Michael Holt suggests that the Democrats held about 84 percent of their 1844 presidential vote in 1848 in the Northern states.[33] The total defection figure is distorted by the large defection in New York State—a defection that reflected many more things than commitment to antislavery politics. It is also pertinent to note that the majority of party supporters in New York remained loyal to the Democracy as they did in much larger numbers elsewhere. Finally, and tellingly, most Democratic defectors in New York and elsewhere returned to their traditional party base in time for the election of 1852.[34]

All of which confirms the comment in the *Albany Argus* just after the Free Soil election, that "the great body of the democracy could not be seduced from their true party attachments."[35] The Free Soilers saw the Democrats somewhat less favorably while making the same point. The Democratic Party, a Free Soil pamphlet of 1848 argued, "is so openly and recklessly committed to the slave power, that it seems like a needless work to offer any proofs of its proslavery character."[36] This mainstream Democratic behavior prompted a Virginia Democrat to comment that "all reflecting men . . . must see, and do see, that the association of the Democratic party is now the only hope of the Union. The fidelity of Northern Democrats to the compromises of the Constitution . . . will defeat all the base sectional maneuvers of fanatics and knaves."[37]

But it is the movement of Democrats into the Republican Party that is the crucial indicator of the nature of the Democratic-antislavery political relationship. There have been a number of estimates by historians (based on newspaper and manuscript reports) that suggest that as high as 25 percent of the Northern Republican vote by the election of 1856 was made up of ex-Democrats. These estimates, however, cannot be taken for granted for, as one critic noted, the "judgements may be correct, but they cannot be proved by the manuscript sources" on which they rest.[38] Twenty-five percent of the Republican vote in 1856 is 335,586. Since the Democratic vote in 1852 in the North was just over a million, such a figure suggests that a very high proportion of Democrats, almost 34 percent, became Republicans four years later. However, voting data available does not bear out such an estimate. Two extreme cases suggest the boundaries of the Democratic defection. In 1852, Massachusetts was one of the weakest Democratic states. The party received 44,569 votes there. Dale Baum estimates that, in fact, 25 percent of these 1852 Democratic voters permanently defected to the Republican Party in the mid-1850's, that is about 11,000 votes.[39]

But in the Midwest the pattern was quite different. The rank and file did not come over in large numbers even though the Republican Party's leadership contained a significant number of Democratic politicians. One-quarter of the 1856 Republican vote, just over 350,000, was cast in these four states. It consisted largely of Free Soilers, former Whigs and non-voters in 1852. Only 11 percent of the region's 1852 Democrats (42,563), voted Republican in 1856, and this was the result of a skewed pattern. In Indiana, 4 percent of the Democratic voters of 1852 moved over to the Republicans. In Ohio, the figure was 12 percent; in Illinois, none did. In the least populous state, Michigan, 28 percent of the 1852 Democrats moved over.[40]

These returns suggest that an extraordinarily high Democratic defection took place elsewhere in the North (approximately 282,000 of 670,000 voters, or about 42 percent of the total in the northeast outside of Massachusetts). But close scrutiny of the returns does not bear out such a figure. In the largest state, New York, for example, the Democrats won 262,000 votes in 1852, and just under 196,000 four years later. They lost 25 percent of their total vote. But some close county-by-county and township assessment of this drop suggests that it went in three directions, not only to the emerging Republicans. The bulk of the Democratic defectors went to the Know-Nothings, but others became non-voters, simply sitting out the election. Moreover, by 1860, many of the 1856 defectors had returned to their original party home.[41]

In the midwestern states, post-1856 defections from the Democracy were also relatively small. In the region as a whole, 2 percent (8,900) of the Democratic voters of 1856 switched to the Republicans in 1860 (almost all of these from Indiana where 5 percent [5,900] of the Democratic electorate moved over). These are hardly impressive figures. By 1860, just over 51,000 of the 390,000 voters who had supported the Democratic Party in the early 1850's voted Republican in these states. In short, in the middle western states, the rank and file movement of Democrats into antislavery political coalitions was very limited from 1848 onward.[42]

What is most to the point is that Democratic defectors in the 1850's left behind a majority of the party's rank and file and a significant portion of its Northern leadership as well. As Shortridge concludes in his study of the Middle West, "the voting choices made by the mass electorate seem to have been remarkably stable. Most Democrats apparently resisted the blandishments of the Republican and nativist politicians and continued to support the Democracy."[43] Even without a full study of all of the permutations of voter behavior during the years of antislavery political activity, it is clear that between 80 percent and 90 percent of Democratic voters in the Northern states were habitual and steadfast in their behavior and remained true to their normal party loyalties. Many were periodically concerned with Southern expansionism. But most of them usually eschewed the sectionalist impulse. The importance of the Democrats who defected should not be minimized, regardless of numbers, in shaping the way the Republicans behaved and in helping them to victory. Nor should we minimize how the core and masses of the party reacted to the attractions of antislavery political movements, even in their least revolutionary guise.

The mainstream Democrats' record on antislavery reform is clear. Less plain is the reason for their behavior. Some historians see the origin of the party's stance rooted in a conscious agreement, worked out as early as the

1820's, between leaders in the North and the South to protect slavery, a position necessary to maintain the party organization, win elections, and hold the reins of national power. Because of Southern sensitivity about slavery, Martin Van Buren's principal concern from 1819 onward was "how best to protect Southern security in the Union." The answer was to keep in office a party "responsive to the South because it was dependent on it for election."[44] Slavery, as a moral issue, would be ignored and antislavery forces would be repressed in the North. Neither was difficult because of the indifference of most Northern Democrats to the fate of the slave.

There was more to this position as well. Many Northern Democrats have been seen as ideologically pro-slavery. They believed in what they were doing. As a result, the Democrats, when in power, protected and then helped extend slavery into new areas of the continent. In John Quincy Adams' terms, the "South has the Democratic party in its pocket."[45] That section "was in the saddle of national politics" so long as the Democrats ruled. This was "the central fact of American political history to 1860." The Whig, Zachary Taylor, "was the only president between John Quincy Adams and Abraham Lincoln whose politics was not proslavery."[46]

Historian John McFaul dissents from this position. He believes that the Jacksonians were not "a conscious and active agent of the slave power." Party members, he concedes, engaged in strong anti-antislavery rhetoric and their actions often were useful to slavery's defenders. But he believes that the central core of Democratic concerns were not ideological but politically "expedient." The party leaders were political animals indifferent to moral concerns and to slavery and interested primarily in their own electoral survival. They had to maintain a party containing many different interest groups. They believed in mediating among the different groups and did not make moral distinctions among them. Since Southern slave owners were members of their party, since they were sensitive about antislavery, and since they threatened dire consequences if abolitionist agitation continued, Democratic leaders responded by doing their best to tame that concern. They chose to maintain their organization and preserve the political situation as it was. They acted the way they did because it made political sense, in their view, to do so.[47]

McFaul's corrective emphasis has much to recommend it. The fact that Democratic behavior was pro-slavery in effect does not mean that party members were pro-slavery in intent, an important distinction necessary to understand the nature of their behavior. Nor would they even understand such terms of reference. The Democrats' hatred of abolitionism was deep and enduring. But they were not, in their own minds, any more pro-slavery than pro-Northern in their approach. Their hostility and commitments ran in other channels. They came out of different traditions; they had little comprehension of the central concerns of antislavery advocates. Some nineteenth-century reformers and others involved in politics, as well as many twentieth-century historians, have argued for the centrality of the slavery issue—or at least its importance for much of the antebellum era. Such arguments would have surprised antebellum mainstream Democrats.

There remains more to understand about the relationship of political expediency to the behavior of antebellum Democrats. Too often political expediency has been defined simplistically as the "hunger for spoils." Among party activists, "the hunger for spoils was basic." They were "opportunistic, materialistic" and "ambitious for worldly success."[48] This is direct enough and a common enough historiographic characterization. But it is distorted and leaves out too much. If, by expediency, we mean conscious political calculations to achieve essentially electoral ends only, this does not cover the whole situation affecting party members. The Democratic leaders were political animals, and it was not out of character for them to act for political reasons, particularly to consider tactical necessities. They tried to manage conflict in a way that ensured electoral success. But party calculations and conscious activities to further specific ends stemmed not only from the leaders' rational assessment of the specific costs to the party and to themselves, especially the dangers to their future electoral success of rousing sectional tensions. Their behavior also stemmed from a wider and deeper commitment to the way their political world operated and what was important in it. One consideration was never favored to the exclusion of the other—both interacted with each other.

There was a powerful political culture developing and taking control of the American scene in the late 1830's.[49] Partisan politics played a central role in that scene as part of the process of national integration and as a focus for achieving power. It was an important aspect of the matrix of people's lives. At its center were the two national political parties. As the Liberty Party appeared in the early 1840's, the national parties were defining themselves in sharp, highly differentiated terms from one another. They were reaching out to encompass the entire political world as it then existed. Democrats, as did Whigs, used the party to organize that political world.

Parties did two things extremely well in this political culture. They combined intense emotive loyalties based on deeply rooted family and community norms and tensions growing out of the social differences within the society, with attention to a structure of issue commitments and desires. They organized and agitated for specific policies desired by their members. Both reasons, loyalty and faith, as well as policy and principles, structured political competition in mid-nineteenth century America in wide ranging and crucial ways. Party loyalties ran deep among Americans. Parties were clung to tenaciously and with an intense loyalty almost impossible to shake, for ideological, social, and symbolic reasons.[50]

Americans lived within highly charged, close-knit, partisan networks. An intricate web of interactive institutions, centered in the communities, functioned constantly—and in a most partisan manner. Parties appealed to their communicants in massive, broad ranging, ways, symbolically rooting out devils and threats surrounding them all, emphasizing issues and interests of concern to their component groups. At the local levels, highly partisan newspapers with no commitment to objectivity led the way; vitriolic pamphlets followed along. Even social organizations, volunteer fire companies, for one, were rooted in community norms and often highly partisan. In every community there were frequent nomination and election rallies as well as partisan meetings on New Orleans Day (the anniversary of Jackson's victory over the British), or over a new piece of significant legislation. Few occasions passed without one of these hectic meetings with large attendance.[51]

Party rhetoric and platforms presented by each party gave strong clues to their positions. Parties were not ambiguous about what they stood for. They forthrightly asserted what they believed. More to the point, they stood for different things quite distinct from each other. In the rousing political debates of the period, each party strongly spelled out its advocacy and its conception of what the other side was up to. Political meetings, with their fiery speeches and extensive activities, served as entertainment and as social gatherings for a community. But their main purpose was to reinforce the communal solidarity and partisanship of the group involved. There was intense and constant reinforcement of one's beliefs, the identification of one's enemies and friends. These were polarizing debates that clarified and made coherent what was at stake and why votes should be cast in particular ways. They reinforced existing commitments.[52] The exposure of the average voter to an unbiased version of the other side's viewpoint was minimal.

Elections had important societal functions in this atmosphere. They provided an opportunity for communities to express themselves, their desires, fears and problems, and to affirm their communal commitments. Elections usually were intense experiences: the partisan communications networks offered them as the moral equivalent of war, providing opportunities to reaffirm one's devotion and to smite one's enemies. And as time passed in this atmosphere, Americans developed formidable allegiances to the parties because these institutions expressed their deepest values, beliefs, and preferences. Parties were part of the culture of the groups. An individual's values, ideals, and desires were caught up in them. They were communities of loyalists with shared commitments and emotive memories and symbols.[53]

Democrats were particularly committed to politics as organized and practiced in the middle of the nineteenth century. They intensely accepted and strongly advocated the imperatives of the partisan political culture of their time. It is easy to detect hunkerism, lusting after the spoils of office, and traditionally defined expediency as the pivot of Democratic behavior. There were party hacks, and there was expediency and lusting for office—but within certain boundaries that deserve as much understanding as that of the political opportunism present. As John Van Buren said in a speech in early 1848, there was much at stake in American politics. He had "been brought up to believe" that the fights between Whigs and Democrats "involve some principle." Later, John Dix added, "I consider [the Whigs to be] at an immeasurable distance from us in all that concerns the true interpretation of the Constitution and the proper administration of government."[54]

It is easy to dismiss all of this as cant. But there was more to it than that. Party leaders could not be, nor did they desire to be, exclusively or simply pragmatic in their calculations. Pragmatic expediency was part of their makeup. They constantly had to think through how to build coalitions and how to prevent divisions in their party. But there were boundaries to their expediency. First, Hunkers (those who supposedly thought only about victory at the polls and not principle) were as ideologically committed as anyone else in the party. They, too, were communicants in what one convention delegate referred to as "the Democratic church."[55] They never advocated that the party abandon, or even temporarily suspend, its principles. Rather, they wanted those principles supplemented—not weakened—by careful attention to electoral context and a willingness to shape an appeal in such a way as to improve chances of winning.

Second, boundaries were also set by how the rank and file thought about politics and what they considered to be involved in party battles. The leadership was never alone in shaping party behavior. The Democratic Party, despite factional strife was a robust entity. What gave it its robustness was the extent, depth, and intensity of its mass support and the reasons that underlay that support. Elite perceptions of party differences were absorbed at the mass level, given the partisanship of the atmosphere and of its communication and prevailing social institutions. The constituents' understanding of the electoral necessities in a given situation was not as fully formed as was the Democratic leadership's. But, like their leaders, they had drunk deeply of the imperatives of the partisan political culture dominating their lives.[56] No party leader could ignore for very long, therefore, the things that made their party different from the opposition in the minds of the voters. Everyone operated within defined limits set by the party's traditions, principles and distinctive outlook.[57]

The political debates of the antebellum period were marked by the Democratic focus on so much other than antislavery. The dominant influences shaping partisan discourse and belief found little room for such matters. It was the "old and true measures"—banking, tariffs, foreign affairs, the nature of the federal government's power and responsibilities, that were the everyday concerns of Democrats throughout the period.[58] Antislavery, on the other hand, was part of a quite different world with a different set of priorities from those of mainstream Democrats. Their vision of the way politics operated and what was important in politics confined sectionalism/slavery concerns to the periphery. While always present, these issues did not have the force and influence that many historians have assigned to them. Partisan institutions had been defining and shaping political activity and reactions for a generation, certainly for most of the active lives of antebellum Democrats, while sectional concerns had remained unfocused and largely undefined.

It seems clear, then, that any understanding of Democratic reaction to antislavery politics has to take into account the intense imperatives of the existing partisan political culture as they penetrated among all of the members of the Democratic community, top to bottom. The Democratic leadership thought about slavery and antislavery a great deal. There was a great deal of calculation, for instance, in their response to the slavery issue and to antislavery politics—something that has always been recognized by historians. The leadership, socialized in day to day contacts with sensitive Southerners and having to weigh the balance of forces within the party, often talked about the danger of slavery disputes to current politics, ultimately, to the union. They constantly had to maneuver with the Southerners, to work out agreements, to soothe, and to hold hands—to evaluate prevailing pressures.

It is not clear, however, that such a highly conscious weighing of sensitivities and consequences existed among the rank and file mainstream Democrats. To some of the leaders such as Van Buren, necessity led them into political actions that may be overstressed as representative of rank and file Democrats. The latter—the masses of the party—moved in a world where highly specific, conscious calculations about political affairs were less present and where priorities about issues and politics emerged in a different form. They remained loyally committed to the imperatives of the partisan political culture, partly consciously, partly not, partly principled, partly not, partly expedient, partly not. They shared with the leadership a set of assumptions and interacted with them to preserve a particular vision of the political world. In the mass-defined world, antislavery politics of every variety, from abolitionism to Free Soil, to Republicanism, were vaguely understood foreign ideologies to be ignored, rejected, and repudiated.

All of the elements helping define the Democratic reaction were present when issues connected with sectionalism and slavery erupted in the 1830's. It is not surprising that Democrats treated them as something foreign, something they were not used to and did not understand, since they were not part of their normal political discourse.[59] In Democrats' reactions, therefore, partisan commitments and responses and the particular rhetoric that flowed from them, predominated. As some Virginia Democrats put it in 1839, the old battles over the two principles of government, centralism and localism, were still at the center of the political stage. "All the rest is ephemeral and transitory."[60] Echoes of such aspects of the partisan imperative kept coming up again and again. The New York Democrats, for instance, who later led the Free Soil revolt, at first saw the introduction of the Texas issue as a Southern-inspired plot to win party laurels for a particular faction of the party. They were irritated and resistant but understood the issue in a partisan way. "Calhoun has designedly put slavery in the foreground for mischief," one wrote in late 1844. The "Texas humbug" was being used by the South to defeat Van Buren for the party's nomination. Again and again that theme ran through their private correspondence.[61]

Prominent Democrats reacted by reminding the South that Northerners, too, had their own local questions, demands, needs, and difficulties and that if the South made too much of a fuss then even Northern Democrats would have to strike back against excessive Southern attempts to get their own way. Intra-party strife would be regrettable after such a long time of ignoring local concerns in favor of joint fighting on behalf of common Democratic politics.[62] In short, the problem was seen as entwined with Democratic politics. It was the understandable reaction of a group shaped by partisan norms, not sectional ones.[63]

Another aspect of this partisan reaction concerned such Democratic stalwarts as the two New York congressmen: John Dix and Preston King, who were clearly against admitting Texas as a slave state. They, too, thought about it in party terms when it first arose. They looked to their party leaders for advice and guidelines to action.[64] Again, such is not surprising. Behind their behavior was their sensitivity to what they believed were Whig attempts to use sectional rhetoric against the Polk Administration. They saw efforts under way to thwart them on matters other than sectional ones. The Wilmot Proviso was "stalking horse for factions and ambitious politicians." It was but a link in a chain of measures "designed to give aid and comfort to the enemy." Its supporters "are not governed in their course by a love of the slave or a horror of the extension of the 'area of slavery' but by an inveterate hatred of the administration." Therefore, Democrats should ignore "this pretended question of free soil."[65]

Echoes of the full range of partisan reasons continued to affect Democrats' discourse throughout the late 1840's. When a severe party disruption occurred between 1845 and 1848, centered on differences over slavery extension, the leadership was fully involved on the battle lines. But how much were the masses involved in that disruption or affected by it? Most specifically, how committed were party voters to the factions erupting all around them? The New York leader Silas Wright had one answer in a letter to James K. Polk in 1845. "The democratic party of this State is not a unit . . . ," he wrote.

It is not, however, so much divided as appearances at a distance would indicate, although the division between those who have held prominent places in the party is extensive. It is rather a difference among the officers than the men, the leaders than the members of the party.[66]

This had immediate meaning for the President. Polk's "sound measures . . . will be sustained by the friends of Governor Wright," the New York party leader Azariah Flagg wrote late in 1845, "without regard to the person who may be in his cabinet from this state." This was because "the great mass of the party" supported Polk's program, which contained the old and true measures of the Democratic party. On those he will be supported by both "the friends of Mr. Calhoun & Mr. Wright."[67] Even though the elite split, then, occurred between the New Yorkers and the President, similar sentiments about mass behavior continued to be expressed. "The masses of the party are disposed to get together," despite the splits over slavery extension and the Wilmot Proviso, even though the leaders were so "embittered against each other" as to make that difficult.[68]

"The principles of Free Soil are the only ones at issue in the contest for President," the editor of the *New York Evening Post* argued in October, 1848. It was reassuring to the Free Soil Democrats to repeat that their principles "are fast gaining the ascendency" and that there was "a great revolution in public opinion" under way.[69] Not so, most of the mainstream Democrats replied. A Democratic meeting in Cuyahoga County, Ohio, in 1848, resolved that despite the fact that they were opposed to slavery, "we cannot throw aside party usages or relinquish regular nominations to join any bolting movement founded on this one principle." A Midwestern party newspaper thundered that Democrats "are not Mexicans to break up into factions and follow leaders instead of old principles and social party attachments by which these great principles are carried out." Alfred Burr, the editor of the *Hartford Times,* reminded Gideon Welles that "a large portion of the Democrats of this State do not look upon the [Wilmot] Proviso as a practical or at all important question. They think that Congress should not meddle with Slavery in the territories." Welles had been receiving similar letters for some time and their view of local Democratic attitudes confirmed Burr's estimates. Former Senator John Niles wrote, for example, that although many people attended Free Soil meetings during the campaign of 1848, "a considerable part of them came out of curiosity or some worse motive." Joseph Rayback quotes a New Jersey newspaper as saying that "it is true that Gen. Cass does not advocate the Wilmot Proviso, but he is a democrat. On every cardinal point of the democratic creed he is known to be right and we have no wish to introduce other issues in this election." Another Democrat agreed. "I have so strong a repugnance to see the Whigs . . . elect General Taylor," one wrote, "that I am resolved to give my vote to General Cass." Cass is "with us on all those issues that have divided parties for years past." The correspondent was in favor of Free Soil but not at the expense of the other issues he held dear and sacred.[70]

Such partisan assertions became a familiar, oft-repeated litany. The *Detroit Free Press* argued that while it opposed the extension of slavery, "we opposed the introduction of new issues, and the Proviso is one of them."[71] Even as many Northern Democrats grew restive, irritated, and then, furious, against their Southern colleagues on such matters, their devotion to their common partisan associations continued to be present and potent. They did not believe that the old issues of partisan definition grew obsolete or faded away. These issues remained important. Factiousness and sectional irritation would only allow the Whigs to impose the bank, tariff, and the rest of their odious program. As Silas Burroughs, a New York Democrat, put it at the state convention in 1849, "he did not believe that the great questions of a Bank, a protective tariff, internal improvements by the general government . . . were now settled—that we could dispose of the old platform and make something new." Therefore, another argued, "we can act with democrats, whatever their views in regard to slavery may be, if in other respects sound."[72] Even John Wentworth, leader of the pro-Wilmot Proviso forces among Illinois Democrats, wrote in 1848, "let us Barn Burners strive to lick Taylor first. He must be beaten, & if we have an independent organization in democratic states, he will beat us." And, after the election, Wentworth lamented that "in losing sight of the old issues between the two parties at the elections," those who voted for Free Soil would see too late that they committed an error.[73]

All of this rhetoric and behavior put the issues raised by the antislavery movement into a highly specific perspective. As the *Cleveland Plain Dealer* put it early in 1847, "we have been in the habit of supposing, and still believe, that there are other questions besides that of slavery merely which should enter into the canvass and election of [the] President of this country."[74] "No one," a resolution of the State Convention of Hunker Democrats in New York argued in 1848, "can be regarded as a true democrat who at any time would insist upon the political agitation of a moral abstraction, as of paramount importance, when the direct tendency of such agitation is to create sectional dissensions and divisions between us and our natural allies in upholding and advancing the great doctrines of the democracy." Another New York politician, Samuel Beardsley, saw the party's divisions based on a "wretched and most frivolous" controversy. The party's position in regard to slavery has always been "entire toleration of opinion in regard to it." Let us, therefore, he concluded, "discard now and forever, the idea of dividing on abstractions which have been brought out for the sole purpose of getting up a quarrel between the democracy of the North and South."[75] In short, the important matters of the time united Democrats. Whatever divided them, they argued, was unimportant and unnecessary, only "passing excitements and controversies."[76] Divisive issues had been raised for political reasons, in order to hurt the Democratic community.

The leaders of the Free Soil revolt came to perceive the basic problem they had in dealing with Democrats. The latter saw the political world as unchanging. They wanted no new issues, no new problems, no changes. Mainstream Democrats did not want to expand the boundaries of political discourse. Democrats continued to believe that there was much more distance between themselves and Whigs, later Republicans, than between Northern and Southern blocs within their own party on issues related to sectionalism. Most Democrats, the Free Soilers wearily concluded, were "passion-blinded partisans who resolve to see nothing but through the mist of an unreasonable prejudice." When parties err, honest citizens should leave them and form third parties. Unfortunately, they found that many of the Democrats they counted on were simply not willing to desert.[77]

This reaction, partisan and static as it was, continued well into the 1850's, despite the escalating sectional crisis. The Democratic congressman, William Bissell of Illinois, complained in 1850 that all of the discussion of slavery extension fomented by the original introduction of the Wilmot Proviso was "embarrassing and retarding the proper business of Congress."[78] Differences between the parties "never die out," Horatio Seymour said in 1855, "Today we are discussing the very questions which divided parties at the very formation of our government." Parties continue to differ "with regard to principles of action."[79] Mainstream Democrats clung to and constantly reaffirmed the importance of the old issues and the general nature of political warfare as they had always known them. There was little weakening of this for most of the period during which antislavery politics established itself. The commitment to what one group called the "pure and holy principles" of the Democratic party remained staunch and continuous. Democrats had to continue together to contend for "the *principles* of our faith." In 1856, the pro-Wilmot Proviso Democratic leader of Illinois, "still defined 'Republican' as the 'name generally used to designate a Whig of Know-Nothing and Main Law proclivities.' "[80]

Even given the great sensitivity among Southerners to the antislavery crusade, so frequently and strongly expressed by some political leaders there, and frequently and strongly noticed by historians since, there were Southern Democrats throughout the period from the 1830's onward who also tried to maintain the party structure. Their reasons included seeing the parties as a means of defending slavery. But their arguments also included many of the same things Northerners espoused—most particularly the importance of the party and its stances in their lives. They too, argued in favor of continuing the existing pattern of politics despite the rise of agitation about slavery. "The Wilmot Proviso is paramount to all Party," a South Carolinian wrote in 1847. But neither his correspondent nor many others agreed. As the resolutions of the Democrats of the 6th Congressional District of Georgia said in 1847, after listing all of the traditional policy positions of the party, "that with . . . every member of the Democratic party, it is a cardinal duty always, and under all circumstances, to maintain the doctrines of his political faith above all other considerations, and that we as a party adhere to, and do hereby declare it as a fundamental rule of our action; that the great principles and measures of the democratic party are entitled to our first, and last, and only allegiance."[81] The Northern Democrats could not have said it better.

These ideas, whether emanating from Northern or Southern Democrats, were always powerfully stated, obviously designed to convince and reinforce mass party opinion. But such advocacy could not achieve its political goals unless it resonated with an already existing mind set among partisan loyalists. As Lee Benson has written, it is easy to dismiss partisan rhetoric as not always stemming from the fervent convictions of those who write and speak the chosen words. But "no one can deny," he continued, that such statements reflect the author's "convictions on what the voters want to hear" and were prepared to believe, given their commitment and loyalties.[82] Some mainstream Democrats were hostile to slavery, others were indifferent to it, or had guilt feelings concerning it, or thought it was appropriate as a form of social control or economic endeavor and/or were sensitive to its implications. None of this made it a prime political issue for many of them even into the 1850's and the beginnings of the Republican Party. If slavery was an evil, it was a distant one. If it was a major political issue, it was not theirs. They did not believe that a new political era rooted in North-South differences had emerged in the mid-1840's.[83]

Historians frequently seek to pinpoint the end of one pattern of behavior and the onset of another. The 1840's are usually marked as a transforming period when sectional antislavery forces rose to a new importance to replace what had been. One historian has suggested, in a useful description, that as sectional forces erupted, old political landmarks disappeared. It was, he writes, "as if the entire state [Ohio] had lost its political memory."[84] But, when it came to the mainstream Democrats, this never happened. They did not ignore slavery and antislavery. They were aware of both. They could not keep the issues raised out of their calculations, especially after 1846. Recognizing them to be part of a crosscutting political cleavage incorporating matters of less value and concern to them and yet of some difficulty, they reacted in familiar terms. They lived in another kind of political complex and wanted little to do with what was being said and demanded about slavery. When a Massachusetts mass meeting of anti-Texan advocates argued that Texas "transcends all the bounds of ordinary political topics," the mainstream Democrats did not and could not agree.[85]

This led to a policy of containment and attempts to play down the slavery issue. More to the point, through it all, Democrats constantly looked for ways out, to return to party unity and the party's real commitments. Their position became that one's position on slavery extension should not be a test of fealty to the Democratic Party. You suggest, one wrote Gideon Welles in 1849, that "Democrats & Free Soilers should come together and 'agree to disagree'. That is my doctrine . . . I supported candidates last spring so long as they went with the Democratic party, whether they were Proviso men or not."[86] They should bend over to allay Southern fears and not push except when absolutely necessary. Democrats followed this policy partly out of fear of splitting the party and partly out of impatience with the issue altogether.[87] Thus, they were quick to endorse the compromise measures.

American politics in the pre-Civil War era began by defining where one stood in relation to other groups in the society, in setting priorities as to policy goals, and in building coalitions based on one's stance and commitments. Democrats strongly resisted any transforming of the political outlook, values, assumptions, and practices into something new and different revolving around the slavery-extension issue. It was the Republicans, seeking to wean people to their new coalition, who argued that the political issues of former years were "obsolete." Democrats did not think so.[88] As the editor of the *New York Post* sadly lamented during the Free Soil election, "if the action of the people in the free states was not diverted from their convictions by prejudices, by old and defunct party ties, and by incorrect representations," the Free Soil candidate for the presidency would receive every vote from the Northern states.[89] Perhaps the editor believed party ties to be old and defunct. The mainstream Democrats did not. They did not lose their memory. They continued to react to the political world in their established, traditional ways.

Still, from the early 1840's through the final emergence of the Republican Party in the 1850's, some Northern Democrats did throw off their partisan commitments and join the final version of the antislavery political movement. As noted, their numbers were relatively few in relation to the size of the total party constituency.[90] But a question remains: given all that can be demonstrated about the Democrats and their outlook in the era, why should any of them become part of the antislavery political movement at all? Some historians have ventured reasons that combine a certain amount of sensitivity to sectional-slavery issues with some political expediency as well. Eric Foner, for example, has vigorously reiterated the traditional assessment that antislavery pressures grew strong enough in the North to force some Democrats to go along. The growing sectional anger and rising sentiment against slavery extension among their constituents left them no choice. He also argues that Republican ideals interacted with Democratic conceptions of the free individual in a free society to draw Democrats over.[91]

Such pressures and ideals may have affected some of the Democratic defectors. Still, more remains to be said about those who left to join the ranks of antislavery politics. From the beginning, such Democrats did so for a variety of reasons. In the late forties many of them who joined the Free Soil revolt had other motives besides that of slavery extension in general. The reasons some joined the Republicans may have included antislavery sentiment. But the electoral realignment of the 1850's, with its consequent Democratic disruption and Republican ascendency, was also only partially based on the attractions of antislavery politics. It is worth remembering, for example, how much regional and intra-state variation there was in such defections. In Pennsylvania, Roger Peterson found Democratic movement into Republicanism limited to former New England and New York State residents living in a narrow band of counties close to the New York border. In New York State a similar limited pattern of movement occurred.[92] In Massachusetts, where the Democrats were always in a hopeless political minority, defection toward any movement that might help them gain something from the Whig majority—such as in a Democratic-Free Soil coalition—served as a motivating force. In a state such as New Jersey, however, where powerful competition between the two parties was highly organized and constant and the primary fact of political life, defections were rare.[93] What broke the second party system apart and cost the Democrats a certain number of their supporters and, crucially, their national majority, was a set of local conditions and diverse pressures reflecting the powerful cultural tensions in the society. These were far more important in drawing masses of voters away from the Democratic Party than any direct, single-minded commitment against slavery and its expansion. The Know-Nothing movement played a significant role in these developments. Paul Kleppner's careful quantitative study of the national realignment of the 1850's argues that as a result of the electoral disruption, the emerging Republican Party inherited the old Whig vote, the Free Soilers and a "strong majority" of those who first supported the Know-Nothings. Yankee stock areas, he writes, because of their "congruence of . . . antisouthern and anti-immigrant . . . attitudes produced a reasonably rapid consolidation of voting support against the Democracy, the party of the South *and* of the Catholic and German Lutheran immigrants." In Cincinnati, William Gienapp found Know-Nothingism a crucial factor in detaching many Protestant and Freethinking Germans from their traditional Democratic moorings. In parts of New England, land of a very weak Democracy, Dale Baum argued that Know-Nothingism and Republicanism seemed to have been distinct phenomena not readily united. But elsewhere the two movements eventually melded together.[94]

The electoral disruption had another quality. Rather intriguing national variations and complexities were present in it. The same groups in different situations did not always shift in the same magnitude. Kleppner demonstrates, for example, that there were two different realignments in the North: one in New England, the other among the belt of New England expatriates across New York into the Middle West, the latter a very narrow belt of change, the former a very large shift.[95]

What determined this pattern was the different ways members of demographic groups reacted to the newly emerging political agenda. In most places, Yankee Protestants revolted against the Catholic-immigrant, slavocracy menace. Before the realignment, Yankees had been divided along denominational lines, some in the Democratic Party, others in the Whig. Now they became more politically cohesive. But other groups did not shift in a unitary way, and still others behaved strangely. Know-Nothings detached some Protestant Democrats, including both Yankees and Irish-born Yankees and Irish-born Orangemen. The latter "leaned over backward" to become "ardent nativists," out of their hatred of Catholics. Other Know-Nothing support varied demographically. A very few German Catholics may have voted for them out of their hatred of the Irish hierarchy. But usually German Protestants did not (late in the fifties some became Republicans).[96]

Kleppner's description of one group's behavior illuminates the central reasons and the complexities present that led to a specific political result. Differences in religious outlooks, in sociopolitical contexts, and in historical experiences all explain the variations in Dutch Calvinist voting behavior. New York's Old Dutch were moderately Democratic, and slightly more so where they lived close to Yankees. The Old Dutch had experienced the invasion of the Empire State by "restless" New Englanders and had experienced much Yankee disdain against them. They defended their ethnoreligious identity by voting for the Democrats as the anti-Yankee party. However, the changing context of political behavior in which the Democracy became identified as the Catholic party in the 1850's, cross-pressured them, and began to draw them away. The character of New York's Republican Party resonated with their own restrained pietism and strong anti-Catholicism and led many of the Old Dutch to become anti-Democratic voters.[97]

Hostility to slavery expansion and to Southern power affected some Democrats, but not necessarily all anti-Democrats, either, as Republican leaders quickly learned. The antislavery revolt in the summer of 1854 did not attract every one it might. The Republican coalition reached a certain level of support and then its growth slowed or stopped. The slavery issue, as Robert Imholt has argued, "was not sufficient in [New York State] to submerge antipathies" among the opponents to the Democrats and unite them.[98] The critical task for the Republican leadership, therefore, was to win those still outside their coalition, the Know-Nothings and others who were deemed attractable because they had in common, a strong anti-Democratic commitment and values similar to those held by Republican supporters.

The genius of the Republican leadership was to recognize the extraordinary diversity and heterogeneity of society and to increasingly structure an appeal that could encompass as many varieties of behavior as it did. In the years between 1857 and 1860 this broadening out effort dominated Republican strategy. Opposition to the South was the nexus of the appeal. However, it was not until antislavery politics merged into anti-Southernism and incorporated other things, especially the ethnocultural tensions erupting in many areas of the North, that a major part of the political transformation drawing some Democrats into new political patterns occurred. Republican rhetoric became more anti-Southern and more concerned to promote wide scale affective images of their opponents. They stigmatized the Democrats as the party that used foreign-born Catholics (particularly Irish Catholics) and non-British Protestants, antithetical to native-born Protestant cultural groups, to give government power to arrogant Southern slaveholders. The latter, in turn, bullied Northern freemen and debased the American Republic, in part because contemptible Northern Doughfaces were subservient to them.

As Ronald Formisano has written, "despite extravagant claims . . . the Republican crusade . . . did not pursue the broad interests of humanity. Its passion flowed from the desire of most Northern white Protestants to assert their rights and manhood against the threat of domination by white slavocrats, and to protect their values and status from the threat of disintegration from aliens and Catholics."[99] Republicans successfully tied together different things. As an 1854 editorial from the *Cattaraugus* [N.Y.] *Whig* put it, "Temperance and Freedom are as inseparably connected as Intemperance and Slavery." And, on the other side, "the foreign element is a natural ally of the slave power."[100]

Ex-Democrats contributed to the Republican victory in the nation in 1860. But they, like other Republicans, traveled many diverse paths to the polls that autumn. The results of that victory were stupendous for the nation— culminating in emancipation five years later. Whatever the result, however, one thing is clear: antislavery was so insignificant in the world view of those Democrats who voted Republican in 1860 that it bore little influence upon how they cast their ballots that year. They revolted against what their old party had become on several fronts: not just against slavery though that was a variable for some more than others. Nor should the importance of later events based on the Democratic defeat in 1860 lead to a neglect of the much larger group of mainstream Democrats that the defectors left behind, loyal in their party faith and hostile to antislavery politics, men who continued to represent an older partisan, nonsectional tradition that remained alive.

The Democratic interrelationship with the antislavery political movement was not particularly rewarding for either side. From the 1830's onward, Democrats had been part of the attempts to confront slavery. But, clearly, most of them had always been in opposition to those efforts. Some historians have seen the rise of the antislavery political movement as making the Democrats more aware of slavery and more committed against its extension. But there is little sign that Democrats became more sensitive to the matter on moral grounds, and it is also clear that they tried every device to prevent it from becoming an issue of importance in the Northern states. It is true that for tactical reasons they sometimes spoke in ways that many slave owners found inadequate (an objection that slaveholders had occasionally raised even before this). But these rhetorical flourishes were aberrations, brief and tactical. The mainstream Democrats made it very clear throughout the forties and fifties that they knew who their enemies were.

The evil forces in the society, as they saw it, were the sectional, antislavery extension movements culminating in the Republican Party. They never lost sight of this fact and continued to battle against political sectionalism and political antislavery as long as they could. The whole Democratic style and substance dictated such behavior. In short, although they were Northerners, they never subscribed to free soil, free labor, and free men as articulated by the Republican Party. Their definitions of each of these things differed greatly from the Republican version.

At the same time that Democrats did not lose their souls to the antislavery political movement, they also did not lose many of their faithful in the Northern states as a whole. Those who did desert to the Republican Party were an important force there when joined with the Whigs, Know-Nothings, and committed antislavery groups. But their role and victory in the 1860's should not blind us to the pattern and stance of the mainstream Democrats— and their importance in the period as well. In his Webb prize essay, William Gienapp quotes an English traveler's remark that "unflinching adherence to party is principle with . . . [Americans] and to forsake a party is regarded as an act of the greatest dishonor."[101] Democratic behavior confirmed that. One analyst of the antislavery movement argues that the Free Soil Party "helped to break 'the thraldom of party' and to increase the likelihood of more successful challenges in the future."[102] There is little evidence of that in terms of numbers. The Democrats' main losses in the 1850's were not due to the shaking of the tree by Free Soilers ten years before, although that affected some of them, but rather, as already noted, from the complex of local, ethnocultural, and other issues that led people to break away from the party in search of something more compatible and responsive to their needs. It was in the 1850's, not the 1840's, that a political revolution erupted, one that drew only partially on the antislavery extension conflicts of the decade before.

Finally, each party's position in regard to antislavery and antislavery politics was shaped by the contours of its Northern support as well as of its Southern and by the political memories of all of its constituents as well. The particular social groups making up each party's constituency had specific ways of looking at the world that led to specific political stances. The strong racism of many Democrats is well documented. But there were other things as well. The Democrats originated as, and remained largely, the party of ethnoreligious outsiders and others (including *some* slave owners) fearful of the power of the federal government to shape and regulate behavior and institutions.[103] Democratic rhetoric was filled, from the 1830's onward, with their memories of the abusive power of the government as wielded by their political opponents against particular immigrant social and religious groups, their values, habits, and lifestyles. Images of Puritan interventionism against their religious opponents filled Democratic pamphlets and editorials. At heart, they argued, Republicans, as the Whigs before them, were centralizing, overbearing, Federalist Tories, intent on destroying the liberties of the American people through the extensive intrusion of government power into the personal lives, conduct, and beliefs of individuals and groups within the Union.

The essential "principle of Republicanism," as seen through the Democratic filter, was "to meddle with everything . . . to force their harsh and uncongenial puritanical creed down the throats of other men and compel them to digest it under pains and penalties." Behind laws regulating or prohibiting the sale and consumption of alcoholic beverages, vigorously debated throughout the fifties, or other legislation governing the language of school instruction, which textbooks to use, who could teach, or the sources of financial support for schools, Democrats saw a Republican determination to foster a particular code of behavior and belief on all Americans. This cultural interventionism posed grave threats, in the Democrats' view, to individual freedom in America. Party spokesmen, therefore, railed against "the evils of political meddling with morals, religion, and the rights of distinct communities." They demanded that the government not be allowed to "invade the territory of the Church" on behalf of only one particular point of view within a highly pluralist nation.[104]

All of this stemmed from, and resonated with, the fears, prejudices, values, and memories of the outsider groups that made up the Democratic Party. They feared the uses to which government was to be put on behalf of moral reform. They wanted no part of it, and it led them to look at antislavery movements in a particular way—as an aspect of an engine of oppression directed against certain white people in the society. Much of their behavior followed from that perspective.

Despite their long resistance to the movement, the Democrats lost their electoral majority in the North and in the nation, and then control of the government to forces that ultimately ended slavery in the United States. By then, many of the Democrats who had remained loyal to the party had come to agree that slavery should end.[105] But there is little sign that they were ever delighted by the turn of events.

It was recently said about the Democrats in the 1860's that:

They were, perhaps, wrong-headed. They were certainly not congenial either to their Republican contemporaries or to late-twentieth century tastes. But their ideology was congruent with many of the political and social rhythms of their day. Certainly, the Democrats provided a reference point, a focus, for a significant number of Americans.[106]

This is equally applicable to them in the antebellum period as well. The pre-war Democrats would not have recognized themselves in the company into which some of them had fallen by 1860. However, most retained a good grasp of what they were about and of their feelings toward their Whig, antislavery, and Republican enemies. Despite defeat and the destruction of so much of what they had fought to save, they never lost that grasp, that perspective, and set of commitments, that kept most of them loyal to the Democracy.

NOTES

1. There is no inclusive study of the Democratic Party in these years. A useful overview is Michael F. Holt, "The Democratic Party 1828–1860," in Arthur M. Schlesinger, Jr., *History of U.S. Political Parties* (New York: Chelsea House Publishers, 1973), 1: 497–571.

2. The phrase is Eric Foner's and appears in the best study of this group, *Free Soil, Free Labor, Free Men: The Ideology of the Republican Party Before the Civil War* (New York: Oxford University Press, 1970), chapter 5.

3. Joel H. Silbey, "The Civil War Synthesis in American Political History," *Civil War History* 10 (June, 1964): 130–140.

4. Eric Foner, *Politics and Ideology in the Age of the Civil War* (New York: Oxford University Press, 1980), p. 72.

5. Richard Sewell, *Ballots for Freedom: Antislavery Politics in the United States, 1837–1860* (New York: Oxford University Press, 1976), pp. 138, 84.

6. Aileen Kraditor, "The Liberty and Free Soil Parties," in Schlesinger, ed., *History of U.S. Political Parties*, 1: 753.

7. Silbey, "Civil War Synthesis."

8. George Fredrickson, *The Black Image in the White Mind: The Debate on Afro-American Character and Destiny, 1817–1914* (New York: Harper & Row, 1971); Eugene Berwanger, *The Frontier Against Slavery: Western Anti-Negro Prejudice and the Slavery Extension Controversy* (Urbana: University of Illinois Press, 1967); C. Vann Woodward, "The Antislavery Myth," *American Scholar* 31 (Summer, 1962): 312–328; Joel H. Silbey, *The Shrine of Party: Congressional Voting Behavior, 1841–1852* (Pittsburgh: University of Pittsburgh Press, 1967).

9. Joel H. Silbey, *A Respectable Minority: The Democratic Party in the Civil War Era, 1860–1868* (New York: W. W. Norton and Co., Inc. 1977).

10. The *Address* is reprinted in Joel H. Silbey, "The Election of 1836," in Arthur M. Schlesinger, Jr., ed., *History of American Presidential Elections, 1789–1968* (New York: Chelsea House Publishers, 1971), 1: 623; *Washington Globe*, May 18, 1835.

11. Mount Vernon (Ohio) *Democratic Banner*, February 13, 1849, in Athens (Ga.) *Southern Banner*, March 1, 1849; *Detroit Free Press*, March 17, August 23, 1849; Springfield *Illinois State Register*, December 8, 1848. The party's national platforms are reprinted in Kirk H. Porter and Donald Bruce Johnson, *National Party Platforms 1840–1964*, 3rd ed. (Urbana: University of Illinois Press, 1965).

12. David M. Potter, *The Impending Crisis, 1848–1861* (New York: Harper & Row, 1976), p. 79.

13. "Sketches of the Lives of Franklin Pierce and William R. King. . . ." (Washington, D.C., 1852), pp. 8, 9; *Washington Globe*, October 14, 1835, May 28, 1836.

14. D. L. Gregg to Sidney Breese, February 15, 1848, Sidney Breese Papers, Illinois State Historical Society; *Congressional Globe*, 29th Cong., 2nd sess., Appendix, pp. 159, 322; *Detroit Free Press*, December 31, 1847.

15. *Albany Argus,* November 1, 2, 1848; Springfield *Illinois State Register,* July 14, 1848; William Bissell to William Martin, February 5, 1850, Miscellaneous Papers, Illinois State Historical Library; Circular dated May 7, 1850, in William L. Marcy papers, Library of Congress; Nahum Capen to William L. Marcy, May 23, 1851, Marcy Papers.

16. *Illinois State Register,* October 4, 1859; *Fremont-His Supporters and Their Record* (Washington, D.C. [1856]), p. 12; *Remarks on the Majority and Minority Reports of the Select Committee on Secret Societies of the House of Delegates of Maryland* (New York, 1856), p. 28.

17. Silas Wright to Thomas Ritchie, May 10, 1835, Martin Van Buren Papers, Library of Congress.

18. Charles Z. Lincoln, ed., *Messages from the Governors* (Albany: J. B. Lyon Company, 1909), 3: 573, 582n, 589; Silbey, "Election of 1836," in Schlesinger, Jr., ed., *History of Elections,* 1: 590.
In related matters as well the Democrats remained consistent. As early as 1837, Democrats in the New York State legislature rejected decisively with their votes pro-black suffrage resolutions. At the 1846, Constitutional convention in that state they took the lead in resisting efforts to extend voting rights to blacks. Alan M. Kraut and Phyllis F. Field, "Politics Versus Principles: The Partisan Response to 'Bible Politics' in New York State," *Civil War History* 25 (June, 1979): 101–118.

19. "Address of the Democratic Members of The Legislature to The People of Virginia," ([Richmond, 1836]), pp. 7, 10; *Federal Union,* October 3, 1836; Gideon Pillow to Martin Van Buren, March 2, 1836, Van Buren Papers.

20. Silbey, *Shrine of Party,* passim.

21. Chaplain Morrison, *Democratic Politics and Sectionalism: The Wilmot Proviso Controversy* (Chapel Hill: University of North Carolina Press, 1967), pp. 22ff. Ernest Muller, "Preston King: A Political Biography" (Ph.D. diss., Columbia University, 1957), p. 420.

22. Thomas B. Alexander, "The Dimensions of Voter Partisan Constancy in Presidential Elections From 1840 to 1860" (Paper presented as part of the Walter Prescott Webb Memorial Lecture Series, University of Texas at Arlington, 1981).

23. William Gienapp, " 'Politics Seems To Enter Into Everything': Political Culture In The North, 1840–1860" (Paper prepared as part of the Walter Prescott Webb Memorial Lecture Series, University of Texas at Arlington, 1981), p. 49.

24. Gienapp, " 'Politics Seems To Enter . . .' " p. 51.

25. Jonathan Nathan to Fish, January 3, 1844, Hamilton Fish Papers, New-York Historical Society; Azariah C. Flagg to "Dear Sir," October 14, 1844, Azariah C. Flagg Papers, New York Public Library.

26. Lee Benson, *The Concept of Jacksonian Democracy: New York as a Test Case* (Princeton: Princeton University Press, 1961), p. 208n. See also, Alan M. Kraut, "The Liberty Men of New York: Political Abolitionism in New York State, 1840–1848" (Ph.D. diss., Cornell University, 1975); Ronald P. Formisano, *The Birth of Mass Political Parties: Michigan, 1827–1861* (Princeton: Princeton University Press, 1971), pp. 120–121.

27. *New York Tribune,* November 23, 1844.

28. Kraut and Field, "Politics Versus Principles," p. 110.

29. James Buchanan to William L. Marcy, November 21, 1850, Marcy Papers.

See also, Joseph Rayback, *Free Soil: The Election of 1848* (Lexington: University of Kentucky Press, 1971); and Frederick Blue, *The Free Soilers: Third Party Politics, 1848–1854* (Urbana: University of Illinois Press, 1973).

30. Kevin Sweeney, "Rum, Romanism, Representative, and Reform: Coalition Politics in Massachusetts, 1847–1853," *Civil War History* 22 (June, 1976): 116–137.

31. Ray M. Shortridge, "Voting For Minor Parties in the Antebellum Midwest," *Indiana Magazine of History* 74 (June, 1978): 130.

These four states cast approximately one-third of the popular vote in the Northern states between 1840 and 1848.

32. Philip C. Davis, "The Persistence of Partisan Alignment: Leaders and Votes in New Jersey, 1840–1860" (Ph.D. diss., Washington University, 1978).

33. Paul Kleppner, *The Third Electoral System, 1853–1892, Parties, Voters and Political Cultures* (Chapel Hill: University of North Carolina Press, 1979), p. 65; Michael Holt, *The Political Crisis of the 1850s* (New York: John Wiley & Sons, 1978), p. 65.

34. As Thomas P. Alexander has written, "the voters rode out the stormy national controversies from 1848 through the compromise of 1850 and were still able to regroup for the 1852 presidential election very nearly in the party pattern of the elections preceding the sectional storm, those of 1840 and 1844. This is striking evidence of the power of party labels to direct the response of all but a small proportion of voters. The deviations of 1848 were substantial, principally because of Van Buren's name and the comfort it gave to Democratically aligned voters aroused to cast a protest vote on either ideological or party factional grounds. Alexander, "Dimensions of Voters Partisan Constancy," p. 38.

35. *Argus*, November 28, 1848.

36. *Cass and Taylor: Is Either Worthy of a Freeman's Suffrage?* (n.p., 1848, p. 1.

37. John Y. Mason to Lewis Cass, September 25, 1848, Lewis Cass Papers, William E. Clements Library, University of Michigan.

38. Foner, *Free Soil, Free Labor, Free Men*, p. 165; Sewell, *Ballots for Freedom*, p. 263; David Donald, review of Sewell, *Journal of American History* 64 (December, 1977): 798.

39. Dale Baum, "Know-Nothingism and The Republican Majority in Massachusetts: The Political Realignment of the 1850's," *Journal of American History* 64 (March, 1978): 959–986.

The estimates were computed by means of an ecological regression formula. See J. Morgan Kousser, "Ecological Regression and The Analysis of Past Politics," *Journal of Interdisciplinary History* 4 (Autumn, 1973): 237–262.

40. Ray M. Shortridge, "The Voter Realignment in the Midwest During the 1850s," *American Politics Quarterly* 4 (April, 1976): 193–222.

41. This material is drawn from a project on New York State voting patterns under way by Lee Benson and myself.

42. Shortridge, "Voter Realignment in the Midwest."

43. Ibid., p. 219.

44. Richard H. Brown, "The Missouri Crisis, Slavery, and the Politics of Jacksonianism," *South Atlantic Quarterly*, 65 (Winter, 1966): 70–71.

45. Leonard Richards, "The Jacksonians and Slavery," in Lewis Perry and Michael Fellman, eds., *Antislavery Reconsidered: New Perspectives on the Abolitionists* (Baton Rouge: Louisiana State University Press, 1979), pp. 99–118.

46. Brown, "Missouri Crisis," p. 55; Daniel Walker Howe, *The Political Culture of the American Whigs* (Chicago: University of Chicago Press, 1979), p. 147.

47. John McFaul, "Expediency vs. Morality: Jacksonian Politics and Slavery," *Journal of American History* 62 (June, 1975): 24–39. The quotation is on page 25.

48. Sewell, *Ballots for Freedom*, p. 227; Edward Pessen, "How Different from Each Other Were the Antebellum North and South?" *American Historical Review* 85 (December, 1980): 1139.

49. Much of the material on political culture that follows stems from two papers: Lee Benson and Joel H. Silbey, "The American Voter, 1854–1860 and 1948–1984" (presented at the Annual Meeting of the Organization of American Historians, 1978); and, by the same, "American Political Eras, 1788–1984" (Presented at the Annual Meeting of the Social Science History Association, 1978).

50. See, Silbey, *A Respectable Minority*, chapter 1, "A Party of Habits, Prejudices and Traditions."

51. See, for example, the description in Richard S. Alcorn, "Leadership and Stability in Mid-Nineteenth Century America: A Case Study of an Illinois Town," *Journal of American History* 61 (December, 1974): 693; Gienapp, " 'Politics Seems To Enter Into Everything,' " passim.

52. The election pamphlets and "Addresses to the People," issued by each party throughout the period from the 1830's onward reflected these characteristics repeatedly. The question of what was at stake was clearly spelled out and the relationship of that to community norms and fears heavily stressed. See, as examples of such, Richard Rush, *To the Democratic Citizens of Pennsylvania* (n.p., 1844), and *Addresses and Resolutions of the Democratic State Convention of New York . . . January 26, 1848* (n.p. [1848]).

53. See Silbey, *Respectable Minority*, pp. 7–11.

54. *The Utica Convention: Voice of New York* (Albany, 1848), p. 21; *Speech of Hon. John A. Dix, of New York, at the Mass Meeting . . . Newburgh . . . 26th July, 1852* (n.p. [1852]), p. 1.

55. *Official Proceedings of the National Democratic Convention, Held in Cincinnati, June 2–6, 1856* (Cincinnati, 1856), p. 22.

56. See Silas Wright to James K. Polk, July 21, 1845, in Ransom Gillett, *The Life and Times of Silas Wright* (Albany: Argus Company, 1874), 2: 1648.

57. As Giovanni Sartori has written: "To be sure, party members are not altruists, and the existence of parties by no means eliminates selfish and unscrupulous motivations. The power-seeking drives of politicians remain constant. What varies is the processing and the constraints that are brought to bear on such drives. Even if the party politician is motivated by crude self-interest, his behavior must depart— if the constraints of the system are operative—from the motivation. The difference is, then, that parties are instrumental to collective benefits, to an end that is not merely the private benefit of the contestants." Giovanni Sartori, *Parties and Party Systems: A Framework for Analysis* (New York: Cambridge University Press, 1976), p. 25.

58. This comes through in both the correspondence and newspaper editorials

written by mainstream Democratic sources. See, for example, Columbus *Ohio States-man* in Richmond *Enquirer,* July 1, 1848; Washington *Union,* April 11, 1848.

59. *Address of Democratic Members to People of Virginia,* p. 14. John Niven describes one Connecticut politician of the time as "a fierce partisan, a Democrat who worshipped at the shrine of organization. Principle and party were so fused in his mind that it was difficult for him to grasp new issues if they seemed to threaten the Democracy." Niven, *Gideon Welles: Lincoln's Secretary of the Navy* (New York: Oxford University Press, 1973), p. 225.

60. *Proceedings of the Republican Convention* [of Virginia] ([Richmond, 1839]), p. 10.

61. Preston King to Azariah C. Flagg, December 21, 1844; Michael Hoffman to Flagg, October 19, 1844, Flagg Papers.

62. Silas Wright to Benjamin Butler, May 15, 1844, Benjamin Butler Papers, New York Public Library; Azariah C. Flagg to Orville Hungerford, May 9, 1844, Flagg Papers.

63. See Silas Wright to Azariah C. Flagg, January 23, 1844; Michael Hoffman to Flagg, October 19, 1844; Preston King to Flagg, December 21, 1844; John A. Dix to Flagg, March 3, 1845, Flagg Papers. Silas Wright to Benjamin Butler, May 20, 24, 1844, Butler Papers. See also, John Niven's discussion of Gideon Welles' reaction to these events in Niven, *Welles,* pp. 202, 220–221.

64. John A. Dix to Azariah C. Flagg, January 20, 26, 1845; Orville Robinson to Flagg, January 28, 1845, Flagg Papers.

65. *Illinois State Register,* April 2, 1847.

66. Wright to Polk, July 21, 1845, in Gillett, *Life of Wright,* 2: 1648.

67. Azariah C. Flagg to John Lawrence, October 27, 1845, Flagg Papers.

68. Quoted in Walter Feree, "The New York Democracy: Division and Re-Union, 1847–1852" (Ph.D. diss., University of Pennsylvania, 1953), p. 246. See also Edwin Croswell to Horatio Seymour, October 22, 1849, Horatio Seymour Papers, New-York Historical Society.

69. *New York Evening Post,* October 14, 1848; New York *The Barnburner,* July 29, August 26, 1848.

70. Cleveland *Plain Dealer,* September 18, 1848; Columbus *Ohio Statesman,* in Richmond *Enquirer,* July 1, 1848; Alfred E. Burr to Gideon Welles, September 9, 1849, John M. Niles to Welles, September 17, 1846, October 28, 1848; William Pettit to Welles, October 28, 1848, Welles Papers. Rayback, *Free Soil,* p. 232.

71. *Detroit Free Press,* December 31, 1847.

72. *Proceedings of The Democratic and Free Conventions Held At Rome on the 15th, 16th and 17th Days of August, 1849* (Rome, 1849), pp. 12, 14.

73. John Wentworth to E. S. Kimberly, June 27, 1848, E. S. Kimberly Papers, Chicago Historical Society. *Chicago Democrat,* December 22, 1848. See also, *Milwaukee Weekly Wisconsin,* June 28, 1848; *Ohio Statesman,* September 14, 1848; Cleveland *Plain Dealer,* June 12, September 18, 1848.

74. *Plain Dealer,* March 30, 1847.

75. *Address and Resolutions of The Democratic State Convention, . . . Syracuse, 1848* (Syracuse, 1848), p. 7; *Proceedings . . . Rome . . . 1849,* pp. 18, 21, 38.

76. *Plain Dealer,* September 10, 1846; *Proceedings of the Democratic National Convention Held at Baltimore, June 1–5, 1852* (Washington, D.C., 1852), p. 61.

77. *"One Idea"* (n.p., [1848]), p. 3. *Barnburner,* July 29, 1848.

78. William Bissell to William Martin, March 5, 1850, Miscellaneous Papers, Illinois State Historical Society. See also, *Plain Dealer,* September 18, 1848; William Pettit to Gideon Welles, October 28, 1848, Welles Papers.

79. *Speech of Hon. Horatio Seymour, Delivered at Tammany Hall, . . . Sept. 28, 1855* (n.p., [1855]), p. 9.

80. *Address and Resolves of The Democratic Members of the Massachusetts Legislature of 1838. . . .* (n.p., [1838]), p. 2; *Speeches Delivered at Tammany Hall, New York City, Sept. 2, 1852. . . .* (n.p., [1852]), p. 7; Don E. Fehrenbacher, *Chicago Giant: A Biography of "Long John" Wentworth* (Madison: University of Wisconsin Press, 1957), p. 139.

81. Isaac Holmes to Howell Cobb, August 21, 1847, in Ulrich B. Phillips, ed., "The Correspondence of Robert Toombs, Alexander Holmes Stephens and Howell Cobb," *Annual Report of The American Historical Association for 1911* (Washington, D.C.: American Historical Association, 1913), p. 88; *Washington Union,* June 17, 1847.

82. Lee Benson, *Merchants, Farmers and Railroads* (Cambridge: Harvard University Press, 1955), p. 138.

83. Nor do I believe that this lack of preoccupation with slavery related issues made the Democrats' concerns and behavior "artificial." See Richard P. McCormick, *The Second American Party System* (Chapel Hill: University of North Carolina Press, 1966), p. 353.

84. Stephen Maizlish, "The Triumph of Sectionalism: The Transformation of Politics in The Antebellum North, Ohio, 1844–1860" (Ph.D. diss., University of California, Berkeley, 1978), p. 224.

85. *An Appeal To The People of Massachusetts on The Texas Question* (Boston, 1844), p. 4.

86. Alfred E. Burr to Welles, August 9, 1849, Welles Papers.

87. John W. Lawrence to Azariah C. Flagg, October 23, 1845; John A. Dix to Flagg, March 5, 1847, Flagg Papers.

88. *Address of the Republican State Committee to the Electors of Rhode Island* (Providence, 1857), p. 1.

89. *Evening Post,* October 16, 1848.

90. See above, second section.

91. Foner, *Politics and Ideology,* especially chapters 1–3.

92. Roger Peterson, "Reactions to a Heterogeneous Society: Voting Behavior in Pennsylvania, 1848–1860" (Ph. D. diss., University of Pittsburgh, 1973); Kleppner, *Third Electoral System,* chapter 3.

93. Baum, "Political Realignment of the 1850s," Davis, "Persistence of Partisan Alignment," pp. 91ff.

94. Kleppner, *Third Electoral System,* p. 57; William E. Gienapp, "The Transformation of Cincinnati Politics, 1852–1860" (seminar paper, Yale University, 1969); Thomas Kremm, "Cleveland and The First Lincoln Election: The Ethnic Response to Nativism," *Journal of Interdisciplinary History* 8 (Summer, 1977): 69–86.

95. Kleppner, *Third Electoral System,* chapters 3, 21.

96. Robert Ernst, *Immigrant Life in New York City, 1825–1863* (New York: King's Crown Press, 1949), p. 168; Peterson, "Reactions to a Heterogeneous Society," p. 34.

97. Kleppner, *Third Electoral System,* p. 168.

98. Robert Imholt, "Beyond Slavery: The Transformation of Issues in the Politics of New York, 1852–1860" (Ph.D. diss., University of Kentucky, 1974).

99. Formisano, *Birth of Mass Parties,* p. 266.

100. The clipping is in the Daniel Ullman Papers, New-York Historical Society; Corning (N.Y.) *Weekly Journal,* October 29, 1857.

101. Gienapp, " 'Politics Seems To Enter . . .' " p. 46.

102. Sewell, *Ballots for Freedom,* p. 169.

103. Robert Kelley, *The Cultural Pattern in American Politics: The First Century* (New York: Alfred A. Knopf, 1979).

104. *New York Herald,* September 21, 1860; Thomas M. Cook and Thomas W. Knox, *Public Record of Horatio Seymour* (New York: I. W. England, 1868), p. 21; C. L. Vallandigham, *The Record of the Hon. C. L. Vallandigham on Abolition, the Union and the Civil War* (Columbus, Ohio: Walter & Co., 1863), p. 13.

105. Silbey, *Respectable Minority,* chapter 8.

106. Ibid., p. 245.

III

SOCIETY AND THE POLITICS OF ANTISLAVERY

7

Vote As You Pray and Pray As You Vote: Church-Oriented Abolitionism and Antislavery Politics

John R. McKivigan

The election of Abby Kelley to the business committee of the American Anti-Slavery Society (AASS) in May 1840 marked the first time a woman had been chosen to hold office in that body or in any national reform organization. This action signaled that the AASS had fallen under the control of the followers of veteran antislavery editor William Lloyd Garrison. Consequently, abolitionists who disapproved of the highly perfectionist views of the "Garrisonians" on women's rights, religion, politics, and other controversial issues seceded from the AASS. For most non-Garrisonian abolitionists, the old AASS produced two legitimate successors, the American and Foreign Anti-Slavery Society (AFASS) and the Liberty party. The AFASS was created to permit non-Garrisonian abolitionists to maintain the antislavery movement's traditional moral suasion strategy in church circles. The Liberty party was launched to allow the advancement of the immediate emancipation program through partisan politics. The founding of both vehicles attested to the intention of non-Garrisonian abolitionists to pursue antislavery agitation in both the religious and political spheres. The present essay will briefly examine the various tactics that the political and church-oriented wings of the non-Garrisonian abolition movement developed to assist each other in the 1840's and will illustrate important elements of this cooperation that persisted until the Civil War.

The modern abolition campaign in the United States emerged during the 1830's as a by-product of the upsurge of revivalism popularly known as the Second Great Awakening. The original abolitionist principles and objectives revealed a deep impress of evangelical tenets. Revivalistic assumptions led many churchmen to regard social problems, such as slavery, as the products of personal sin. These religiously inspired abolitionists contended that slaveholding was a sin that required repentance in the form of immediate emancipation. They demanded that the churches testify to slavery's inherent sinfulness by barring slave owners from their communion and fellowship. Opponents of slavery believed that the denominations could coerce slaveholders to manumit their slaves by threats of church discipline. As evidence that churches could survive and prosper without the support of slave owners, the abolitionists pointed to the example of traditionally antislavery denominations, such as the Quakers and Freewill Baptists. Abolitionists also recognized that slavery received moral support from racial prejudice and lobbied the churches to overturn their many discriminatory practices against blacks. Throughout the 1830's, the AASS employed a variety of moral suasion tactics aimed at converting the churches into agencies to eradicate human bondage.[1]

The rejection of the immediate emancipation and anti-racial discrimination program by nearly every major American religious body in the 1830's forced abolitionists to reconsider their church-oriented strategy. Many followed the lead of Garrison and abandoned the churches as hopelessly corrupted by slavery. These Garrisonians also adopted pacifistic or "nonresistant" political practices and counseled northerners to withhold their sanction from the proslavery Constitution by refusing to vote. According to conventional historiography, many non-Garrisonian abolitionists shared their rivals' hostile attitude toward churches but not toward the government and consequently shifted their energies from religious to political antislavery reform. When the federal government failed to respond to their petitioning or lobbying, these politically minded abolitionists began in the late 1830's to advocate the formation of an independent antislavery party. A final group of abolitionists, preferring neither the Garrisonian nor the political course, retained faith in eventually converting the churches. After the climactic 1840 annual meeting of the AASS, the political and church-oriented abolitionists abandoned the society to the Garrisonians.[2] Despite their different emphases, the political and religious wings of non-Garrisonian abolitionism soon learned to cooperate productively.

The post-1840 activities of church-oriented abolitionists have not been as intensively studied as that of their political or Garrisonian counterparts. In addition to the AFASS, non-Garrisonian abolitionists founded the American Wesleyan Anti-Slavery Society, the American Baptist Anti-Slavery Convention, and a number of other denominational antislavery organizations to better conduct their agitation in those churches. Similarly, religious abolitionists created new interdenominational bodies such as the American Missionary Association and the American Reform Tract and Book Society to protest the toleration shown slavery by the established religious benevolent organizations. This proliferation of new religious abolitionist institutions ultimately weakened the AFASS through competition for the funds and labor of abolitionists still committed to antislavery church reform. As a substitute for strong national organization, church-oriented abolitionists adopted the practice of sponsoring regional, interdenominational "Christian Anti-Slavery Conventions" to coordinate their religious abolitionist activities.

The most important religious abolitionist institutions of the 1840's and 1850's were the antislavery "come-outer" congregations and sects. After years of unsuccessful effort to reform the churches, many zealous abolitionists resolved to heed the Biblical injunction to "Come out from her, my people, that ye receive not of her plagues."[3] These come-outers regarded separation from a contaminated religious body not only as a means of protecting one's own soul but also as a forceful testimony against the churches' toleration of slaveholding.

Unlike the Garrisonians who frequently abandoned all types of organized religion, non-Garrisonian come-outer sects formed a variety of new religious institutions upon abolitionist principles. In upstate New York and western New England, abolitionist come-outers gathered into more than forty interdenominational "Union Churches" based upon a shared commitment to refuse fellowship to slaveholders and all other types of unrepentant sinners. Most religious abolitionists were not prepared to follow the Union Churches in abandoning all old familiar sectarian forms. Instead, they launched new come-outer sects that retained distinctive denominational dogma and policy, shorn only of proslavery and anti-black components. The most influential of the come-outer sects were the Wesleyan Methodist Connection, the Free Presbyterian Church, the Franckean Evangelical Lutheran Synod, and the American Baptist Free Mission Society. Although the come-outers never approached the size of their parent bodies, the threat of additional secessions eventually helped persuade the larger bodies to adopt a stronger antislavery position.[4] Together with the traditionally antislavery churches such as the Quakers and Freewill Baptists, the come-outer sects formed one of the largest potential blocs of voters for the abolition cause.

In the early 1840's, there was considerable reluctance among church-oriented abolitionists to give public support to the fledgling Liberty party.

Table 7.1
ESTIMATED MEMBERSHIP IN COME-OUTER AND TRADITIONALLY ANTISLAVERY RELIGIOUS BODIES IN 1850

Wesleyan Methodist Connection	20,000
American Baptist Free Mission Society	10,000
Free Presbyterian Church	3,000
Franckean Evangelical Lutheran Synod	3,500
Independent ("Union") Congregations	1,000
Society of Friends	90,000
Freewill Baptists	55,000

Many abolitionist churchmen shared the antebellum religious community's mistrust of politics as sordid and compromising. Lewis Tappan, the leading figure in the AFASS leadership, feared that involvement in "independent nominations" would "lead abolitionists away from the moral and religious aspects of the cause" and taint the abolitionist movement in the eyes of high-minded churchmen who frowned upon political scheming.[5] Religious abolitionists also were sensitive to the Garrisonians' charge that the Liberty party was founded as an attempt to protect the churches from potential disruptions by diverting antislavery reform into politics.[6]

Another reason for the reluctance to support the Liberty party was the strong allegiance of many church-oriented abolitionists to the Whig party. The same evangelical trends that had awakened many churchmen to abolitionism in the 1830's had also drawn them into politics on the Whig side. Through its requirements of continuous proof of conversion, evangelical theology inclined its adherents toward both religious and political efforts to eliminate sin. Compared to the laissez-faire ideology of the antebellum Democrats, the Whigs' moralistic rhetoric and occasional support of sabbatarian and prohibition measures was highly attractive to evangelical voters. Even on issues of slavery and racial discrimination, northern Whig politicians often took positions that won the sympathy of pro-abolition evangelicals. The Liberty party challenged the Whig claim on evangelical voters and sparked heated disputes. Rather than risk offending churchmen with strong partisan loyalties, the AFASS and other religious abolitionist groups maintained a policy of strict political neutrality in the early 1840's.[7]

The Liberty party attempted to win the active support of antislavery churchmen by advancing a program that retained much of the abolitionist movement's traditional emphasis on the moral and ethical aspects of the slavery question. Although some political abolitionists made efforts to introduce economic considerations into their party's arguments against slavery, the Liberty platform in the 1840 and 1844 presidential elections differed little from those of the old antislavery societies. The abolitionist political party condemned not only slaveholding but also the nation's pervasive racial prejudice as an affront against God's laws. It called for the immediate abolition of slavery wherever constitutionally possible and for the repeal of all racially discriminatory legislation as a religious as well as a political duty. By characterizing slavery as "a great question of public morality,"[8] Liberty party spokesmen hoped to win the votes of churchmen who believed politics should be conducted according to Christian principles.

After pointing out the moral implications of slavery-related political issues, the Liberty men denounced those who still refused to vote for the new antislavery party. In their battles with the Garrisonians, the political abolitionists charged that nonresistant principles conflicted with what the 1844 Liberty platform described as "the moral and religious duty" to vote for antislavery candidates. The third party spokesmen also censured the Garrisonian policy of advising those abolitionists who persisted in voting to support the candidate of the major parties who had the strongest antislavery stance.[9] Liberty men complained that this practice was based on the unacceptable "axiom, that politics, of necessity, must be impure—that they must be conducted on principles of mere expediency and that moral principle, for the time being must be laid aside."[10]

The Liberty party also attacked antislavery churchmen who continued to vote for the Whigs and Democrats. Political abolitionists asserted that both of the major parties were subservient to slave interests and hence unfit for the support of antislavery Christians. Liberty men denounced the practice of voting for the less objectionable Whig or Democratic candidate as an immoral "least-of-two-devils-doctrine."[11] Congregational minister Jonathan Blanchard reported being one of many veteran abolitionists forced to "run a regular gauntlet" of moral condemnations from Liberty party champions for "the sin of voting for [Whig William H.] Harrison" in 1840.[12] To capture and hold the loyalties of pro-abolition churchmen, third party advocates developed the argument that ethically consistent Christians must "vote as they pray"; in other words, those opposed to holding fellowship with slaveholders in their churches should likewise refuse to vote for candidates and parties that took no stand against slavery. An Indiana Liberty party newspaper summarized this argument with the admonition: "Vote as you pray. You must do it, or be recreant to your country, recreant to your religion, recreant to your God."[13]

In addition to defining the moral responsibilities of voters in relation to slavery, the Liberty party encouraged the churches to undertake antislavery reform. Liberty party conventions regularly endorsed the view that slavery was inherently sinful. Occasionally these meetings also recommended that the churches cease all religious fellowship with slaveholders. In 1842, the nominating convention of the New York Liberty party called on church members to renounce the "sin of patronizing pro-slavery preachers."[14] Liberty party newspapers also acted as forums for the public discussion of purely church-related abolitionist questions such as the morality of slaveholding, the propriety of sharing religious fellowship with slave masters, and the necessity for secession from denominations sanctioning slavery. The third party press, in particular, provided invaluable publicity to the antislavery movements in the Methodist and Baptist churches, where denominational editors habitually censored news of abolitionist activities. Although most Liberty party editors refrained from endorsing the controversial practice of come-outerism, they applauded the ability of the new abolitionist sects to "goad" the old denominations toward stronger antislavery positions.[15]

Liberty party leaders did not merely express support for the principles of abolitionism in church affairs. James G. Birney, the party's presidential nominee in 1840 and 1844, wrote *The American Churches: The Bulwark of Slavery,* an uncompromising denunciation of the churches' failure to enforce their discipline against slave owning. Liberty party politicians such as Presbyterian Birney, Methodist Samuel Lewis of Ohio, Unitarian John Pierpont of Massachusetts, Congregationalist Owen Lovejoy of Illinois, Presbyterian Alvan Stewart of New York, and Congregationalist Samuel Fessenden of Maine were also prominent campaigners for antislavery reform in their denominations. In 1845 and 1846, Liberty men sponsored a series of regional conventions where thousands of delegates and spectators heard both religious and political antislavery questions discussed. For example, the "Great Convention of the Friends of Freedom in the Eastern and Middle States," held in Boston in October 1845, adopted a series of resolutions that condemned slave owners as "men-stealers" who "ought to be so regarded and treated in the instructions of religious teachers and in the administration and discipline of Christian churches."[16] The Liberty party's efforts to remake the churches into pro-abolition vehicles set an important precedent for later antislavery political organizations.

The Liberty party's moralistic propaganda and program and its endorsement of antislavery reform in the churches gradually overcame the hesitation of most religious abolitionists to publicly support the new party. Although the AFASS constitution condemned Garrisonian nonresistance and proclaimed the moral obligation of antislavery voting, the society initially refused to ally itself with the Liberty party. In 1841, church-oriented abolitionists, such as Lewis Tappan, had successfully resisted an attempt by a pro-Liberty party faction led by Birney, Henry B. Stanton, and Joshua Leavitt to take over active management of the AFASS. Under the influence of William Jay, Amos Phelps, and other abolitionists who conscientiously supported both religious and political antislavery activities the position of Tappan and the AFASS toward the Liberty party slowly changed. In 1842, the society's periodical, *The American and Foreign Anti-Slavery Reporter,* began giving favorable coverage to Liberty party activities. Immediately preceding the 1844 election, the *Reporter* praised the high antislavery principles of Birney and the Liberty party, but stopped short of an outright endorsement. At its annual meeting in May 1845, the AFASS overcame its final qualms and called upon abolitionists to "secede from the political parties, Whig and Democratic, to which they may belong, and unite their efforts with the Liberty party for the overthrow of slavery and the restoration of the principles of liberty."[17] While the AFASS continued to concentrate the bulk of its limited propaganda resources on antislavery church reform, support for the Liberty party and its candidates became a regular part of the society's program.

Another source of support by church-oriented abolitionists for the Liberty party came from the "Christian" or "religious" antislavery conventions held in New York and New England in the 1840's. These gatherings usually restricted their attendance to ministers and church members in order to bar potentially disruptive Garrisonians. Although discussion of religious antislavery questions generally received first priority, the Christian Anti-Slavery Conventions also possessed an important political dimension. Most of the New York gatherings limited themselves to a general statement that voting should be governed by moral antislavery principles; however, some openly endorsed the Liberty party. For example, a convention in Hamilton, New York, resolved that:

those who admit the sinfulness of slavery . . . and yet vote for oppression, or for those who are connected with proslavery parties, are guilty of most gross inconsistency; and are undeserving the name Christian patriots, and unworthy to be recognized as the true friends of downtrodden humanity.[18]

In Maine, Connecticut, and Vermont, the Christian Anti-Slavery Conventions functioned as adjuncts to the Liberty party movement, with religious and political gatherings scheduled to reinforce each other's attendance. In Massachusetts, several religious antislavery conventions were held to voice the northern churches' opposition to the Mexican War and especially to any territorial acquisitions from the conflict.[19]

Antislavery politics also played an important role in the operations of the religious come-outer bodies. Many of the new Union Churches made antislavery voting a requirement for membership. Gerrit Smith, William Goodell, and Beriah Green, the most prominent figures in the Union Church movement, were all leaders in the New York Liberty party. Goodell, the major propagandist for this movement, stressed the need for abolitionists to behave consistently in their religious and political lives by abandoning old slavery-tainted affiliations to join the Union Churches and the Liberty party. Only a few Union Church members, such as the Reverend Luther Myrick of Cazenovia, New York, balked at this linkage, adopting instead the Garrisonian political position of nonresistance. Garrison's newspaper, the *Liberator,* applauded Myrick and assailed Goodell and Smith for attempting to transform the new congregations into religious auxiliaries for the third party movement.[20]

The come-outer sects also committed themselves to political action against slavery. Although a Garrisonian minority existed in several of these bodies, come-outer sect officers and editors generally opposed the politics of nonresistance and disunion. In fact, the leaders of the come-outer sects were among the foremost proponents of the non-Garrisonian argument that antislavery Christians had a religious duty to use all means—moral amd political—to abolish slavery. The Free Presbyterian Church made it a disciplinable offense for sect members to vote for any candidate "guilty of the crimes of slave-holding, dueling, or other scandalous offences against the law of God."[21] The conventions and newspapers of the Free Presbyterians, Wesleyans, and Free Mission Baptists all counseled voting for antislavery candidates as a moral obligation. As a result of this prompting, come-outer sect members took an active interest in Liberty party affairs. Third party leaders, however, often complained of a "dictorial [*sic*] spirit" among come-outer sect members that caused the latter to work toward nominating only those men who shared their advanced religious views.[22] The issues of support for come-outerism by political antislavery groups would manifest more serious divisive aspects within a few years.

The exact amount of electoral support that the church-oriented abolitionist bodies were able to supply the Liberty party is difficult to ascertain. In recent years, American political historians have developed sophisticated quantitative techniques to measure the voting behavior of various religious, social, and economic groups. For the early period of antislavery politics, however, data sufficiently accurate to undertake such research methods is almost impossible to locate. In the case of religious abolitionist institutions, the relatively small size and the geographical dispersion of the membership renders efforts to discern their voting patterns through statistical analyses virtually impossible.

Fortunately some insight into the political practices of abolitionist religious groups can be gained from recent historical research into the antebellum voting preferences of the larger denominations. Although their evidence is fragmentary, these studies have shown that antislavery voters tended to belong to the most evangelical elements of the Methodist, Baptist, Congregational, and New School Presbyterian churches. Historians explain this relationship as a product of the value structure of evangelicals. As noted above, elements in evangelical theology encouraged the "saved" to strive to reform not only their own moral behavior but that of the entire nation. Nonevangelical denominations, in contrast, placed greater emphasis on other requirements for salvation and therefore disapproved of the evangelical's attempt to regulate personal behavior. The Democrat's laissez-faire ideology and the Whig's moralistic program and rhetoric roughly represented the nonevangelical versus evangelical split in nineteenth-century politics before the rise of the slavery question. By thrusting a new ethically defined issue into politics, the Liberty party challenged the Whig hold on the evangelical vote. Once convinced of the evil nature of slavery, these morally inclined voters would be tempted to support the Liberty party. The support for Liberty party presidential candidate Birney, 7,000 votes (0.29%) in 1840, and 62,000 votes (2.31%) in 1844, however, showed that the single issue of slavery was not yet strong enough to sway most evangelicals away from the Whigs.[23]

Impressionistic evidence indicates that the Liberty party did well among one group of evangelical antebellum churchmen, the church-oriented abolitionists. The gradual but steady movement of the AFASS into the Liberty party camp already has been documented. With the exception of reports of a small nonvoting Garrisonian faction among the Wesleyans and in some Union Churches, the antebellum press contains few notices of members of the highly evangelical religious groups supporting other than the Liberty party. This compares particularly well with the abolitionist press' frequent denunciations of the continuing allegiance of the older nonevangelical anti-slavery churches, the Quakers and Freewill Baptists, to the Whig and Democratic parties respectively. Public support for the Liberty party was also quite prominent among western Congregationalists especially those who had severed fraternal relations with the Presbyterians during the 1840's in protest of Presbyterian conservatism on antislavery as well as on theological issues. Among the northern religious and benevolent bodies, the church-oriented abolitionist groups were alone in their public endorsements of the Liberty party. By the mid–1840's, an informal alliance had been created between the forces of political and religious abolitionism.[24]

Fundamental disagreements over how to build upon the Liberty party's limited success in the mid-1840's eventually destroyed the unity of the political abolition movement. A faction led by Salmon P. Chase, Gamaliel Bailey, and Henry B. Stanton advocated electoral cooperation with moderate antislavery groups in the major parties. The Mexican War and the subsequent opposition of many northerners to the admission of slavery into western territories provided a ready issue for the construction of an anti-extensionist coalition in the election of 1848. In a complicated series of intra-party battles, the pro-coalition forces outmaneuvered all opponents and merged the Liberty party with anti-extensionist Whigs and Democrats, creating the new Free Soil party. Unlike the Liberty party, the Free Soilers gave no endorsements for immediate abolition or equal rights for blacks. In fact, many Free Soilers held strong negrophobic sentiments and supported anti-extensionism as a means to keep black labor—free or slave—from the territories.[25] What the Free Soil party offered in lieu of the Liberty party's high standards was the chance to vastly expand antislavery influence, albeit of a limited nature, on the political system.

Not all Liberty men could accept the compromised antislavery position of the new party. As early as 1845, Birney, Goodell, and Gerrit Smith had proposed to broaden the Liberty party platform into a program of universal reform. Calling themselves the Liberty League, this faction also advanced the theory that the Constitution did not sanction slavery and that therefore Congress had the power to abolish slavery everywhere in the Union. Although the Liberty League failed to capture control of the Liberty party or to block the Free Soil merger, they vowed to continue to work for their undiluted abolitionist program. In 1848, the Liberty League ran Smith for president in opposition to the Free Soil and major party candidates. Despite its lack of electoral success, the Liberty League continued to function under a variety of names until the Civil War.[26]

The Free Soilers and Liberty League members may be compared as representatives of contrasting approaches to antislavery politics. The Liberty

Leaguers presented a host of philosophical, legal, and historical arguments to support their cardinal tenet that slavery was unconstitutional, but the capstone of their case was the contention that

slavery is so evidently contrary to the paramount law of nature, to justice, to fundamental morality, and the law of God, that it never was, and never can be legalized; and that no legislature nor monarch possesses the power to make it legal.[27]

Because they defined slaveholding as both sinful and illegal, the Liberty Leaguers could tolerate no compromise on any political question touching slavery. Thus the Liberty League charged the Free Soil movement with sanctioning the sin of slaveholding on the grounds that the anti-extension platform recognized slavery's right to remain undisturbed in the South.

The Free Soilers, however, found several ways to defend anti-extensionism as a morally responsible policy. They pointed out that the Liberty League's view of slavery as unconstitutional conflicted with the generally accepted belief that the federal government could not abolish slavery where it already existed. Free Soilers also observed that Americans commonly believed their country had a divine mission to Christianize the world. The spread of slavery to the West jeopardized this mission by threatening to pervert the Christian character of the nation. Free Soilers therefore maintained that their program to arrest the expansion of slavery served an important moral purpose, not merely the selfish interests of the North. Although the Free Soilers took no official position on the rights of blacks, many party members and newspapers exhorted their fellow citizens to abjure racially discriminatory practices. For reasons such as these, George Julian, the anti-extensionists' candidate for vice-president in 1852, defended his party's platform because it "embodies . . . the unfashionable political virtue of recognizing the distinction between right and wrong, and the government of the world by a Providence."[28] Such pronouncements reveal a loftier motivation for the political behavior of many Free Soilers than just the desire to keep the West an exclusive preserve for free, white labor.

Although both the Liberty League and the Free Soil party claimed to take a highly ethical approach to political issues, the Free Soilers trailed their rivals' in the old Liberty party's other role; that of encouraging reform in the northern churches. The high point of Free Soil action in this regard was a resolution passed by their 1852 national convention declaring "that slavery is a sin against God and a crime against man, which no human enactment nor usage can make right."[29] Unlike the original political abolitionists, the Free Soilers refrained from stating that Christians should deny fellowship to slaveholders. In their personal church relations, most leading Free Soilers remained in denominations that tolerated slavery. Although Free Soil newspapers frequently reported on church affairs, their editors hesitated to endorse either the expulsion of slaveholders from religious fellowship or the secession of antislavery Christians from proslavery denominations as a moral duty.[30]

The Liberty Leaguers campaigned far more actively against church complicity with slavery than the Free Soilers. In their political platforms and convention resolutions, the Liberty Leaguers gave clear, unqualified endorsements to the doctrines of slavery's inherent sinfulness and of the Christian's obligation not to remain in communion with slaveholders. Liberty League periodicals, edited by Goodell and others, regularly condemned the toleration of slavery by the churches and benevolent societies. Liberty Leaguers placed the major blame for the proslavery tone of the nation's politics on the churches and warned:

That so long as the Church and ministry stumble at the problem, whether or not "the sum of all villanies" is *malum in se*—it is not strange that graceless politicians should stumble at the problem whether the temple of the Holy Ghost can be legislated into a commodity of lawful merchandise.[31]

Like the old Liberty party, the Liberty League viewed the antislavery agitation of both religious and political institutions as one inseparable movement.

The only dissension in Liberty League ranks over questions of proper antislavery church relations concerned the practice of come-outerism. The Liberty Leaguers condemned the Garrisonian variant of come-outerism as an evasion of moral responsibility. Although the Liberty League's newspapers publicized the activities of the come-outer sects, they did not endorse the establishment of new antislavery denominations. In their private lives, many leading Liberty Leaguers were exponents of the nondenominational "Union" form of come-outer congregation. Goodell, in particular, publicly feuded with the leaders of the come-outer sects over their "sectarianism."[32]

Significant changes had taken place in the shape of the church-oriented abolitionist movement by the time of the Liberty League-Free Soil party rivalry. After about a decade as an important religious force, the Union Church movement faded with the decline of revivalistic enthusiasm and the growth of moderate antislavery sentiment in the established denominations during the 1840's. The growth of the come-outer sects slowed following the secession of southerners from the Baptist and Methodist denominations. By the late 1840's, the AFASS lacked the financial resources to sustain a lecturing cadre or a newspaper and so limited its propaganda efforts to printing occasional pamphlets and circulars.

While some church-oriented abolitionist institutions were weakening, others were growing and new ones were being created. The Christian Anti-Slavery Convention movement continued with meetings in Cincinnati in 1850 and in Chicago in 1851 that approached the scale of national gatherings of abolitionist churchmen. In 1846, two abolitionist-sponsored conventions for "Bible Missions" led to the founding of the American Missionary Association. In addition to an overseas department, the new mission society supported over a hundred antislavery ministers preaching throughout the North and in several southern states. In 1851, a Cincinnati convention of church-oriented abolitionists launched the American Reform Tract and Book Society (ARTBS) to protest the refusal by established religious publication associations to publish a single word of condemnation of slavery. Within a few years, the Cincinnati body was circulating over 100 tracts on both religious and political antislavery topics as well as its own newspaper, the *Christian Press*.[33]

It is revealing to compare the political support the Free Soilers attracted among church-oriented abolitionist groups with that drawn by the Liberty Leaguers. The results of the presidential elections of 1848 and 1852 in which the two parties competed, tell much of the story. The 1848 Free Soil ticket of Martin Van Buren and Charles Francis Adams received 290,000 votes, compared to only 2,500 votes for the Liberty Leaguers, largely concentrated in Gerrit Smith's home state of New York. Four years later, the anti-extension party's totals dropped to 156,000. But Goodell, the Liberty League's presidential nominee, collected so few ballots that no state reported them.[34] Two important facts can be deduced from these election results: first, the small size of the Liberty League vote indicates that most abolitionist churchmen chose the more moderate antislavery political position; and second, the Free Soilers had attracted considerable support from northerners who had never backed the abolitionist position in religion or politics.

Impressionistic evidence tends to confirm these conclusions. In May 1848, the AFASS endorsed John P. Hale, the candidate originally chosen by the Liberty party but took no stand on the eventual Free Soil nominee, Van Buren. Although the American Missionary Association regularly passed resolutions encouraging its supporters to vote against slavery, it never officially endorsed a particular candidate. As individuals, the officers of both the AFASS and the American Missionary Association divided their support between the moderate and radical antislavery parties. This ambivalence so angered Gerrit Smith and many Liberty Leaguers that they halted their financial contributions. In a public letter to the American Missionary Association, Smith declared "that for the officers of a religious body to vote for anti-abolitionists . . . whose sentiments and characteristics unfit them to administer righteous Civil Government, is to furnish a sufficient ground for the withdrawal of patronage from such body."[35]

Evidence of a preference for the Free Soilers over the Liberty Leaguers was also present in the activities of midwestern religious abolitionists. Prominent Free Soil politicians, George Julian and Stephen C. Stevens of Indiana and Samuel Lewis of Ohio, played leading roles at the Christian Anti-Slavery Conventions in the early 1850's. These meetings condemned the major party politicians for their role in the passage of the Fugitive Slave Act of 1850 and helped popularize the "Higher Law" argument against its enforcement.

Although delegates to the conventions criticized the low moral tone of the Free Soil program, they still voiced no support for the Liberty League. The Cincinnati-based ARTBS's *Christian Press*, under the editorship of the Reverend Charles B. Boynton, applauded the Liberty League's contention that slavery was unconstitutional but nevertheless endorsed the Free Soilers.[36]

Although Goodell believed that most of the Liberty League's support came from voters who had quit proslavery churches, even in those come-outer groups many preferred the Free Soilers. Smith's and Goodell's strong advocacy of the interdenominational "Union Church" movement had alienated many of the churchmen struggling to create the various come-outer sects. Although the come-outer denominations' press generally acknowledged the Liberty League's superior principles, the majority of come-outer sect editors endorsed the Free Soilers as the only realistic hope for political abolition. A Free Mission Baptist periodical praised the "moral effect" of the Free Soilers' anti-extension platform and predicted that if slavery were to "be inhibited from entering upon ground where it is not . . . its existence in the slave states will soon cease, as though taken away 'without hands.' "[37] The traditionally antislavery denominations, the Quakers and Freewill Baptists, generally abandoned their allegiance to the old major parties only to shift support to the Free Soilers. This lack of backing for the Liberty League among even the most militantly abolitionist churches, underscored the general lack of enthusiasm for radical antislavery politics in the northern religious community.

While the Liberty League had difficulty establishing a base of support among abolitionist church groups, the Free Soilers made important gains among members of the major Protestant denominations. Although unwilling to accept the abolitionist position that slaveholders were sinners who must be expelled from Christian communion, a growing number of northern antislavery moderates acknowledged that slavery was an undesirable moral evil that should be peacefully extinguished. Many of these churchmen found in the Free Soil party an acceptable outlet for their cautious antislavery sentiment. A large portion of the northern religious press endorsed the moral character of the anti-extension program. The Free Soilers attracted many nationally prominent, moderate antislavery ministers such as Henry Ward Beecher, Leonard Bacon, and Theodore Parker, who had never voted for the Liberty party.[38] These moderate antislavery Christians became a valuable bloc in the Free Soil ranks, and their influence helps to explain why the new party so readily dropped the Liberty party's endorsement of abolitionist religious practices.

The trend toward political activism by moderate antislavery churchmen greatly intensified during the troubled events of the 1850's. Historians have long noted the repercussions on northern public opinion of such incidents as the Fugitive Slave Law, the Kansas-Nebraska Act, "Bloody Kansas," and the Dred Scott decision. For example, thousands of northern clergymen who had never acted against slavery in church affairs preached sermons or signed memorials against these proslavery government measures and policies. The volume of these protests led Democrats such as Senator Stephen A. Douglas of Illinois to charge that abolitionists and their political allies had induced northern ministers "to desecrate the pulpit, and prostitute the sacred desk to the miserable and corrupting influence of party politics."[39] In contrast, abolitionists and antislavery politicians hailed these activities as an indication that the northern churches were "waking up at last to a sense of their duty."[40]

As increasing numbers of northerners became alarmed at what they perceived as aggressive acts of the "Slave Power," the fortune of antislavery political parties rose. In the same years, the rise of nativism as a salient question among many voters weakened traditional party allegiances. The greatest casualty of the divisive political issues of the 1850's was the Whig party. No longer able to satisfy either sectional or nativist militants, the Whig party performed poorly in the 1852 election and disintegrated amidst the turmoil accompanying the Kansas-Nebraska Act. At the same time, passage of this controversial bill strengthened the popularity of anti-extensionism among northerners. In 1854, the Free Soilers merged with recent converts to anti-extensionism from the Whigs and Democrats to form the Republican party. The new party attracted a broad range of voters, including many who were more concerned with economic development and freedom from competition with black labor than with ending slavery. The presence of these conservative and racist elements worried antislavery churchmen that the new party might abandon all consideration for the moral aspects of the slavery question.[41]

The Republicans' positions on the ethical duties of antislavery northerners relieved the fears of all the most uncompromising abolitionists. The new party's leadership included a large "radical" faction, including Joshua Giddings, George Julian, Henry Wilson, Charles Sumner, and Salmon Chase, who acknowledged the immorality and inhumanity of slavery. Republican spokesmen advocated anti-extensionism not just as a means to confine slavery, but as an unquestionably Constitutional program to hasten the extinction of the institution. Republicans extolled the ethical merits of an absolute ban on slavery's growth that affixed an unequivocal stigma on the system. While seldom challenging the pervasive racial prejudice, Republican rhetoric nevertheless was superior to the demagoguery practiced by their northern Democratic opponents.[42]

In addition to agitating political issues in a moral context, a number of prominent Republicans actively worked for antislavery reform in the northern churches. Rather than risk offending moderate antislavery churchmen, the Republican party avoided official comment upon ecclesiastical affairs in its platforms. Most Republican leaders belonged to denominations that still included slaveholders and took no part in abolitionist efforts to end that practice. There were significant exceptions, however, particularly among Republicans who had been active in earlier third party ventures. Giddings, Julian, and Wilson all attended interdenominational antislavery gatherings and endorsed their work in both the religious and political spheres. In public lectures, Chase declared that the political toleration for slavery would end as soon as "every Christian Church [resolved] to stand up in the sacred majesty of a solemn testimony against slavery; to free themselves from all connection with the evil and to utter a calm, deliberative voice to the world."[43] The Republicans' most valuable assistance to abolitionist churchmen came from party newspapers such as Gamaliel Bailey's *National Era,* which gave publicity to the activities of religious antislavery movements, often shut out of the denominational press.

A hardcore of political abolitionists opposed the Republicans' diluted antislavery program. In 1855, the Liberty League reorganized itself as the American Abolition Society and absorbed the American and Foreign Anti-Slavery Society. This event marked a formal reconciliation between the Smith-Goodell faction and the coterie of New York City religious abolitionists, including Lewis Tappan and William Jay, who had managed the AFASS and still directed the American Missionary Association. The American Abolition Society denounced slavery as "sinful, illegal, and unconstitutional" and acknowledged "the duty of Christians to hold no church relations that involve religious fellowship or ecclesiastical connection with slaveholders."[44]

In addition to conducting a limited propaganda effort, the American Abolition Society ran its own political nominees under the banner of the Radical Abolitionist party. The Radical Abolitionists used Gerrit Smith's presidential candidacies in 1856 and 1860 primarily to assail the moral deficiencies of the Republicans' anti-extension program. While the Republicans conceded that the Constitution tolerated slavery where it already existed, Goodell declared that the Bible did not allow northerners "to recognize any such States' rights as the sovereign right to make merchandize of men's souls."[45] Republicans responded to such criticism by accusing the Smith-Goodell group of "moral dilettantism" in refusing to "come down from their perch on platforms which embraced all the moralities, to work on one which only said to slavery 'not another foot of territory.' "[46] The *National Era* protested that "a political party is not a philanthropic association" and therefore could never define slaveholding as a sin or justify unconstitutional measures to satisfy the dictates of individual consciences.[47]

Although church-oriented abolitionists frequently echoed Radical Abolitionist criticism of the Republicans' weak stands on the moral questions of emancipation and racial equality, more and more of them in the late 1850's decided to support the moderate antislavery party. Even leaders of the come-outer sects, who preached that religious principle must govern a

Christian's voting, endorsed the Republicans' limited antislavery position. Frequently these groups conceded that they were "discouraged with the diluted notions of the anti-slavery-for-white-men-party."[48] Nevertheless, many come-outer churchmen believed that they could elevate the Republican program by cooperating with the advanced antislavery element of the party. For example, veteran Free Mission Baptist William H. Brisbane pledged to "get into harness" for Salmon Chase's campaign for the presidential nomination in 1860 because his election would be "no half way victory" for antislavery principles but "the result of a direct and understood issue."[49] Events in the 1850's convinced many in the antislavery sects that the Democrats must be driven from control of the federal government at all costs. These considerations led church-oriented abolitionists to believe that they faithfully served the antislavery cause by helping to elect Republicans. The editor of a Free Presbyterian journal aptly expressed that sentiment:

All great enterprises, especially those which are moral in their character and aim, reach success through a slow and painful process. . . . The election of Lincoln we well know is not the equivalent to the abolition of slavery but it will be a long step toward that result.[50]

The other surviving religious abolitionist institutions either endorsed the Republicans or adopted a position of neutrality. Despite the reconciliation between Gerrit Smith and the leaders of the American Missionary Association, the antislavery benevolent organization continued to refuse to endorse candidates. The ARTBS's publications praised the Radical Abolitionists' interpretation of slavery as unconstitutional but, nevertheless, supported Republican candidates. When a new abolitionist organization, the Church Anti-Slavery Society, was founded in the late 1850's by the Reverend George B. Cheever, the political loyalties of its members were too divided for the organization to endorse either the Republicans or the Radical Abolitionists. The drift of Union Church members toward the Republican party led to Gerrit Smith's adoption of increasingly heterodox views on the Bible and church organization and to Goodell's complaint that those bodies had been "seduced into political compromises fatal to their purity."[51]

Often the church-oriented abolitionists' criticism of the Republicans was aimed at encouraging the new party to take a less diluted antislavery position. A new series of Christian Anti-Slavery Conventions in Columbus, Ohio, and in Chicago in 1859, stated profound disappointment that Republican platforms and candidates emphasized economic and sectional rather than normal arguments against slavery. These interdenominational meetings, especially, warned Republicans "against the adoption of compromising platforms, and the nomination of candidates whose only recommendation is their 'availability.' "[52] Giddings, a leading Republican radical, attended the Columbus convention and implored the churchmen to bring pressure upon the temporizers in his party. The more cautious Chase also applauded these meetings but privately advised antislavery clergymen "not to go too far" by insisting that the Republicans violate the Constitution "in order to satisfy the demands of moral principle."[53] Despite the Christian Anti-Slavery Conventions' criticism of the Republicans, few delegates at the meetings announced their readiness to defect to another political party.

Church-oriented abolitionists also acted individually to urge Republicans not to compromise the ultimate goals of emancipation and racial equality. They corresponded with Republican leaders, counselling them about the moral obligations of the slavery question. Sermons and religious newspaper articles discussed the duty of voting for antislavery candidates. Abolitionist churchmen who were aligned with the Republicans rallied behind those party leaders perceived to be most vehemently antislavery. Giddings and Julian were the usual favorites of abolitionists pursuing this tactic. After tireless courting, Chase also attracted the backing of several prominent abolitionist ministers in his unsuccessful attempt to capture the 1860 Republican presidential nomination.[54]

The results of the 1856 and 1860 elections reveal that nearly all church-oriented abolitionists had joined the Republican fold. Although losing in 1856, the Republican presidential candidate John C. Fremont carried all but five northern states. Four years later, Republican Abraham Lincoln was elected by a minority of the popular vote but with an outright majority in every Free State except California, Oregon, and New Jersey. The success of the Republicans was paralleled by the final collapse of the Radical Abolitionist party. In 1856, the Radical Abolitionist ticket received at most a few thousand votes. When Gerrit Smith began advocating a "Religion of Reason" in 1860, the Radical Abolitionist party fell apart. Rather than support a man of suspected orthodoxy, many Radical Abolitionists including Goodell sat out the election. Only a few die-hards like Lewis Tappan, Frederick Douglass, and George Cheever voted for Smith.[55]

An important element in the Republican victory was the unprecedented degree of public support they received from moderate antislavery Christians. Among northern churchmen, former Free Soilers enrolled in the new party. Many northern clergymen and editors of religious periodicals actively campaigned for the Republicans, just as they had earlier spoken out against the Fugitive Slave Law and the spread of slavery into the territories. In addition, the Republicans recruited many first-time antislavery voters from among influential churchmen such as Francis Wayland, Gardiner Spring, Leonidas L. Hamline, and Dudley A. Tyng. Often, but not exclusively, former Whigs, these men expressed alarm at the growing power of slavery in national affairs. While many other factors also contributed to the Republican victory, the growing willingness of northern churchmen to act against slavery played a salient role in placing Lincoln in the White House.[56]

In a development largely unforeseen by religious abolitionists, the growth of moderate antislavery political sentiments among northern churchmen helped encourage some northern denominations to strengthen their testimony against slavery. Although stopping short of declaring slaveholding inherently sinful and a disciplinable offense, many denominations made significant advances toward the abolitionist ground of denying Christian fellowship to slave owners. This trend was strongest among the most evangelical of northern churches. For example, the combined pressure of abolitionists outside the denominations and antislavery moderates within them induced southerners to secede from the New School Presbyterian and Methodist Episcopal Churches in 1857 and 1860.[57] Most Congregational state associations ended fraternal relations with denominations that still welcomed slaveholders. The officers of the major interdenominational missionary societies made similar concessions to the intensifying antislavery opinions of their predominantly Congregational and New School Presbyterian contributors. Among northern Baptists in the same years, benevolent societies greatly curtailed their dealings with slaveholders. Only within old-line Calvinist denominations, such as the Old School Presbyterians, and liturgical faiths, such as the Lutherans and Roman Catholics, did little antislavery reform occur before the Civil War. Significantly, quantitative studies have revealed that support for the Republicans was much lower among those churches than among their evangelical counterparts.[58]

This essay has briefly described the intimate relationship between religious and political antislavery activities in the 1840's and 1850's. Before 1848, the two movements exchanged endorsements and exhorted their members to vote as they prayed and to pray as they voted—that is, in bodies separated from the corrupting fellowship of slaveholders or their northern apologists. When the Liberty party disintegrated in the late 1840's, the Liberty League-Radical Abolitionist faction maintained the policy of pursuing both goals. With the exception of a relatively small handful, however, even abolitionists committed to extreme measures to separate the churches from slavery preferred a more pragmatic approach in politics. The parties that pursued this limited antislavery political program, the Free Soilers and Republicans, also gave important assistance to efforts to strengthen the northern churches' testimony against slavery. Although both parties remained officially neutral toward abolitionist agitation in the churches, some of their leaders participated actively in the campaign to expel slaveholders from all religious bodies.

NOTES

1. David B. Davis, "The Emergence of Immediatism in British and American Antislavery Thought, *Mississippi Valley Historical Review,* 49 (September, 1962):

224; Anne C. Loveland, "Evangelism and 'Immediate Emancipation' in American Antislavery Thought," *Journal of Southern History*, 32 (May, 1966): 181–83, 187; Thomas Drake, *Quakers and Slavery in America* (New Haven: Yale University Press, 1950), pp. 167–200; Norman A. Baxter, *History of the Freewill Baptists: A Study in New England Separatism* (Rochester, N.Y.: American Baptist Historical Society, 1957), pp. 99–101.

2. Aileen S. Kraditor, *Means and Ends in American Abolitionism: Garrison and His Critics on Strategy and Tactics, 1834–1860* (New York: Pantheon Books, 1969), pp. 7–30, 119–22; Richard H. Sewell, *Ballots for Freedom: Antislavery Politics in the United States, 1837–1860* (New York: Oxford University Press, 1976), pp. 6–15, 20–23, 43–44; James B. Stewart, *Holy Warriors: The Abolitionists and American Slavery* (New York: Hill and Wang, 1976), pp. 81–83, 107–8; Merton L. Dillon, *The Abolitionists: The Growth of a Dissenting Minority* (De Kalb, Ill.: Northern Illinois University Press, 1974), pp. 121, 127–28.

3. Rev. 18:4; *Christian Investigator*, 3 (March, 1843), 12; John G. Fee, *Non-Fellowship with Slaveholders: The Duty of Christians* (New York: John A. Gray, 1851), pp. 37–38.

4. I have described the history of these antislavery congregations and sects at greater length in "The Antislavery 'Comeouter' Sects: A Neglected Dimension of the Abolitionist Movement," *Civil War History*, 26 (June, 1980): 142–60. I have based my estimate of membership in antislavery religious bodies upon the following sources: *British and Foreign Anti-Slavery Reporter*, new ser., 6 (June, 1858), pp. 128–31; Carleton Mabee, *Black Freedom: The Nonviolent Abolitionists from 1830 Through the Civil War* (London: Macmillan Co., 1970), p. 230; Douglas C. Stange, *Radicalism for Humanity: A Study of Lutheran Abolitionism* (St. Louis, Mo.: Oliver Slave, Limited, 1970), p. 31.

5. Lewis Tappan to William Jay, September 9, 1843, Lewis Tappan Papers, Manuscript Division, Library of Congress (hereinafter cited as L. Tappan Papers); also Boston *Emancipator and Free American*, May 20, December 16, 1841; Lawrence J. Friedman, "Confidence and Pertinacity in Evangelical Abolitionism: Lewis Tappan's Circle," *American Quarterly*, 31 (Spring 1979): 101–6.

6. American Anti-Slavery Society, *American Anti-Slavery Almanac for 1847* (Boston: The Society, 1847).

7. Ronald P. Formisano, *The Birth of Mass Political Parties: Michigan, 1827–1861* (Princeton, N.J.: Princeton University Press, 1971), pp. 104, 120, 164, 178; Lee Benson, *The Concept of Jacksonian Democracy: New York as a Test Case* (Princeton, N.J.: Princeton University Press, 1961), pp. 209–13; Richard Jensen, *The Winning of the Midwest: Social and Political Conflict, 1888–1896* (Chicago: University of Chicago Press, 1971), pp. 58–59; John L. Hammond, *The Politics of Benevolence: Revival Religion and American Voting Behavior* (Norwood, N.J.: Ablex Publishing Corporation, 1979), pp. 189–94; John M. McFaul, "Expediency vs. Morality, Jacksonian Politics and Slavery," *Journal of American History*, 57 (June, 1975): 38.

8. *Anti-Slavery Lecturer*, 1 (December, 1839), quoted in M. Leon Perkal, "William Goodell: A Life of Reform" (Ph.D. diss., The City University of New York, 1972), pp. 121–22; also Hartford (Ct.) *Christian Freeman*, November 13, 1845; Stewart, *Holy Warriors*, pp. 97, 104–5; Dillon, *The Abolitionists*, pp. 141–44; Sewell, *Ballots for Freedom*, pp. 81–82, 95–96.

9. Donald Bruce, comp., *National Party Platforms,* 2 vols. (Urbana: University of Illinois Press, 1978), 1: 256–57; Kraditor, *Means and Ends,* pp. 167–68.

10. William Goodell, *Slavery and Anti-Slavery: A History of the Great Struggle in Both Hemispheres; with a View of the Slavery Question in the United States* (New York: William Harned, 1852), p. 523; also William L. Garrison to James S. Yerrington, May 7, 1844, in Walter H. Merrill, ed., *No Union With Slaveholders, 1841–1849,* vol. 3 of *The Letters of William Lloyd Garrison,* 6 vols., ed. Walter H. Merrill and Louis Ruchames (Cambridge: The Belknap Press of Harvard University Press, 1971–81), pp. 256–57.

11. Hartford (Ct.) *Christian Freeman,* January 9, 1845; Goodell, *Slavery and Anti-Slavery,* pp. 472–73; Joseph G. Rayback, *Free Soil: The Election of 1848* (Lexington: University Press of Kentucky, 1970), p. 102; Stewart, *Holy Warriors,* pp. 99–100.

12. Jonathan Blanchard to Henry Cowles, August 4, 1840, Henry Cowles Papers, Oberlin College Library (hereinafter cited as Cowles Papers); also Gerrit Smith to John Rankin, n.d., in Cincinnati *Herald and Philanthropist,* August 28, 1840, January 6, 1841; Boston *Liberator,* July 17, 1840.

13. Indiana *Democrat and Freeman,* quoted in New Concord (Oh.) *Clarion of Freedom,* March 24, 1848; also *American and Foreign Anti-Slavery Reporter,* November 1, 1842; Chicago *Western Citizen,* October 24, 1844; Ann Arbor (Mich.) *Signal of Liberty,* July 3, 1847.

14. Boston *Emancipator and Free American,* February 10, 1842; also Boston *Weekly Chronotype,* March 25, 1847; Chicago *Western Citizen,* February 1, 1844; Goodell, *Slavery and Anti-Slavery,* pp. 188–98.

15. Chicago *Western Citizen,* November 2, 1843, also October 31, November 7, 1844; Utica *Liberty Press,* June 14, August 16, 1845, November 19, 1846; Utica *Friend of Man,* April 20, 1841; Hallowell (Me.) *Liberty Standard,* July 26, September 15, 1841, June 8, November 16, December 21, 1842, May 17, June 14, 1843, June 20, 1844; Hartford (Ct.) *Charter Oak,* n.d., in Boston *Emancipator and Free American,* December 7, 1841; Ann Arbor (Mich.) *Signal of Liberty,* December 29, 1841, January 19, June 27, November 7, 1842, November 13, 1848; New Concord (Oh.) *Clarion of Freedom,* March 24, 1848.

16. *Proceedings of the Great Convention of the Friends of Freedom in the Eastern and Middle States, Held in Boston, Oct. 1, 2, & 3, 1845* (Lowell, Mass.: Pillsbury and Knapp, 1845), pp. 5–6; also Utica *Friend of Man,* July 20, August 24, 1841; Hartford (Ct.) *Christian Freeman,* October 23, 1845; Chicago *Western Citizen,* June 30, 1846; William G. Lewis, *Biography of Samuel Lewis* (Cincinnati: Methodist Book Concern, 1857), pp. 306–7; Betty Fladeland, *James G. Birney: Slaveholder to Abolitionist* (Ithaca, N.Y.: Cornell University Press, 1955), pp. 202–3, 256–57; Edward Magdol, *Owen Lovejoy: Abolitionist in Congress* (New Brunswick, N.J.: Rutgers University Press, 1967), pp. 60–65, 69–89; Austin Willey, *The History of the Antislavery Cause in the State Nation* (Portland, Me.: Brown Thurston and Hoyt, Fogg & Donham, 1886), pp. 158–59, 224–26, 267.

17. *American and Foreign Anti-Slavery Reporter,* 2 (September, 1841): 31–32, 2 (June, 1842): n.p., 2 (September, 1842), 6–7, 2 (November, 1844): n.p., 2 (July, 1845): 46; American and Foreign Anti-Slavery Society, *Annual Report for 1848* (New York: The Society, 1848), pp. 10–15; Friedman, "Lewis Tappan's Circle," pp. 101–5.

18. Utica *Liberty Press,* July 19, 1845; also Boston *Emancipator and Free American,* February 17, 1842; *Christian Investigator,* 5 (August, 1845): 255; 6 (April, 1846): 315–16.

19. Boston *Emancipator and Free American,* January 25, 1844, January 21, February 11, March 4, May 13, 20, June 3, August 26, 1846, February 17, 1847; Boston *Liberator,* March 6, April 3, 1846; Boston *Weekly Chronotype,* May 26, 1846; *The Declaration and Pledge Against Slavery, Adopted by the Religious Anti-Slavery Convention, Held at Marlboro Chapel, Boston, February 26, 1846* (Boston: Devereaux & Seaman, 1846).

20. Boston *Liberator,* July 31, October 16, 1840; *Christian Investigator,* 6 (March, 1846): 306; Lewis Perry, *Radical Abolitionism: Anarchism and the Government of God in Antislavery Thought* (Ithaca, N.Y.: Cornell University Press, 1973), p. 65; Sewell, *Ballots for Freedom,* p. 76.

21. Quoted in Washington *National Era,* June 21, 1849; also American and Foreign Anti-Slavery Society, *Annual Report for 1850* (New York: The Society, 1850), pp. 43–44, 64–65; Andrew Ritchie, *The Soldier, The Battle, and the Victory: Being a Brief Account of the Work of Reverend John Rankin in the Anti-Slavery Cause* (Cincinnati: Western Tract and Book Society, 1868), pp. 92–94.

22. Samuel Lewis to Salmon P. Chase, December 27, 1845, Salmon P. Chase Papers, Historical Society of Pennsylvania (hereinafter cited as Chase Papers); New Castle (Pa.) *Free Church Portfolio,* January 19, June 28, 1860; New York *True Wesleyan,* February 3, May 11, August 3, September 7, November 2, 1844; *Christian Investigator,* 5 (June, 1845): 288; Free Presbyterian Church, *The Life and Writings of Reverend Joseph Gordon* (Cincinnati: Free Presbyterian Board, 1860), pp. 203–5; Luther Lee, *Autobiography of the Reverend Luther Lee* (New York: Phillips and Hunt, 1882), p. 281; American and Foreign Anti-Slavery Society, *Annual Report for 1850,* pp. 64–65; American Baptist Free Mission Society, *Fourteenth Annual Report . . . 1857* (Utica, N.Y.: The Society, 1857), p. 7; Sewell, *Ballots for Freedom,* p. 67; Formisano, *Michigan,* pp. 45–51; Reinhard O. Johnson, "The Liberty Party in Vermont, 1840–1848: The Forgotten Abolitionists," *Vermont History,* 47 (Fall, 1979): 269.

23. Formisano, *Michigan,* pp. 120, 192; Hammond, *Politics of Benevolence,* pp. 88–91; Gerald Sorin, *The New York Abolitionists: A Case Study of Political Radicalism* (Westport, Conn.: Greenwood Press, 1971), pp. 106–17; Michael F. Holt, *The Political Crisis of the 1850s* (New York: John Wiley & Sons, 1978), pp. 34, 120–25.

24. New York *National Anti-Slavery Standard,* October 27, 1842, March 23, 1843; *American and Foreign Anti-Slavery Reporter,* 2 (March, 1843): 142–43; Boston *Liberator,* November 17, 1843; Walter Edgerton, *A History of the Separation in the Indiana Yearly Meeting of Friends* (Cincinnati: A. Pugh, 1856), p. 205; Drake, *Quakers and Slavery,* pp. 144–47, 164–65; Baxter, *History of the Freewill Baptists,* pp. 98–100; Matthew Spinka, ed., *A History of Illinois Congregational and Christian Churches* (Chicago: Christian Conference of Illinois, 1944), pp. 152–53; Clayton S. Ellsworth, "Oberlin and the Anti-Slavery Movement up to the Civil War" (Ph.D. diss., Cornell University, 1930), pp. 107–8; Goodell, *Slavery and Anti-Slavery,* pp. 196–98, 551–52.

25. Frederick J. Blue, *The Free Soilers: Third Party Politics, 1848–54* (Urbana: University of Illinois Press, 1974), pp. 8–9; Kraditor, *Means and Ends,* pp. 153–

54, 182, 190–91; Sewell, *Ballots for Freedom*, pp. 117–21, 131–69; Stewart, *Holy Warriors*, pp. 119–20.

26. Goodell, *Slavery and Anti-Slavery*, p. 475; Bertram Wyatt-Brown, *Lewis Tappan and the Evangelical War Against Slavery* (Cleveland: Press of Case Western Reserve University, 1969), pp. 332–34; Blue, *Free Soilers*, pp. 2, 103, 233–34, 243–47.

27. Goodell, *Slavery and Anti-Slavery*, pp. 571–72; also Gerrit Smith, Circular, "The Liberty Party," November 28, 1850, American Missionary Association Manuscripts, The Amistad Research Center, Dillard University (hereinafter cited as A.M.A. Manuscripts); Bryan (Oh.) *Political Abolitionist*, September 10, 1857; *Radical Abolitionist*, 2 (January, 1857): 56; Edward Van Horn to Gamaliel Bailey, December 13, 1848, in Washington *National Era*, January 25, 1849.

28. George Julian to F. W. Bird et al., April 29, 1863, Joshua Reed Giddings–George Washington Julian Papers, Manuscript Division, Library of Congress; Eric Foner, *Free Soil, Free Labor, Free Men: The Ideology of the Republican Party Before the Civil War* (New York: Oxford University Press, 1970), pp. 109–15; Grace J. Clarke, *George W. Julian* (Indianapolis: Indiana Historical Commission, 1923), pp. 433–34; Dillon, *The Abolitionists*, pp. 165, 168.

29. Bruce, *National Party Platforms*, 1: 18.

30. Washington *National Era*, May 31, 1849, January 10, February 7, April 25, May 23, September 26, October 31, November 11, 1850, September 2, 1852; Boston *Liberator*, November 14, 1851; New Salem (Oh.) *Anti-Slavery Bugle*, April 26, August 16, 1851; New Concord (Oh.) *Clarion of Freedom*, March 24, 1848; Boston *Weekly Chronotype*, December 30, 1848; Rochester *North Star*, June 2, 1848, June 9, 1849; Lewis, Samuel Lewis, pp. 317–18, 371–72, 423–24; Clarke, *George W. Julian*, pp. 317–18; Martin Duberman, *Charles Francis Adams* (Boston: Houghton Mifflin and Company, 1961), pp. 105–6.

31. *American Jubilee*, 1 (December, 1854): 63; also *Christian Investigator*, 6 (December, 1846): 382–83; William Goodell, *American Slavery A Formidable Obstacle to the Conversion of the World* (New York: American and Foreign Anti-Slavery Society, 1854), pp. 17–18; Goodell, *Slavery and Anti-Slavery*, p. 545.

32. Utica *True Wesleyan*, July 6, 1850; *Radical Abolitionist*, 1 (October, 1855): 18–19; Bryan (Oh.) *Political Abolitionist*, December 18, 1856; Ralph V. Harlow, *Gerrit Smith: Philanthropist and Reformer* (New York: Henry Holt and Company, 1939), pp. 196–97.

33. McKivigan, "Antislavery 'Comeouter' Sects," pp. 145–55; John R. McKivigan, "The Christian Anti-Slavery Convention Movement of the Old Northwest," *The Old Northwest: A Journal of Regional Life and Letters*, 5 (Winter, 1979–80): 352–55; Clifton H. Johnson, "The American Missionary Association, 1846–1861: A Study of Christian Abolitionism" (Ph.D. diss., University of North Carolina, 1958), pp. 81–89, 450–53.

34. Sewell, *Ballots for Freedom*, pp. 167–69, 249–51; Perkal, "William Goodell," pp. 236–38.

35. Gerrit Smith to Lewis Tappan, December 28, 1848, also Stephen S. Sheldon to Lewis Tappan, December 29, 1848, Ovid Miner to George Whipple, March 5, 1848, A.M.A. Manuscripts; American and Foreign Anti-Slavery Society, *Annual Report for 1848*, pp. 7, 10–15; Harlow, *Gerrit Smith*, p. 216; Johnson, "American Missionary Association," pp. 210–19.

36. Washington *National Era,* July 31, August 7, 14, 1851, January 20, 1853; New York *Evangelist,* August 14, 1851; Oberlin (Oh.) *Oberlin Evangelist,* August 27, 1851; *American Missionary,* 6 (August, 1851): 76; Cincinnati *Christian Press,* December 10, 24, 1852; Charles B. Boynton to Henry Cowles, January 8, 1853, Cowles Papers; *Minutes of the Christian Anti-Slavery Convention Assembled April 17th–20th, 1850 at Cincinnati, Ohio* (Cincinnati: Franklin Book and Job Room, 1850); *Minutes of the Christian Anti-Slavery Convention Held July 3rd, 4th, and 5th, 1851 at Chicago, Illinois* (Chicago: Western Citizen, 1851).

37. Utica *Christian Contributor,* August 16, 1848, also September 13, 20, 1848; Boston *Emancipator and Free American,* February 8, 1848; *Non-Slaveholder,* 3 (October, 1848): 220; New York *True Wesleyan,* July 8, 1850, October 4, 1858; Syracuse *The Wesleyan,* April 7, 1853; Albany (Oh.) *Free Presbyterian,* September 7, 1853; Hamilton (N.Y.) *Christian Reformer,* July 28, 1847; *American Jubilee,* 1 (October, 1854): 48; William Goodell to W. M. Stewart, October 6, 1857, American Abolition Society Records, Oberlin College Library (hereinafter cited as A.A.S. Papers); Goodell, *Slavery and Anti-Slavery,* p. 543; Formisano, *Michigan,* pp. 150–51.

38. Auburn (N.Y.) *Northern Advocate,* August 19, 1846, March 17, 1847; Cincinnati *Western Christian Advocates,* December 10, 1846, February 22, 1847; Cincinnati *Watchman of the Valley,* February 25, 1847, August 29, 1848, November 2, 1848; Boston *Zion's Herald,* March 3, 10, 1847, July 12, 1848; Rochester *North Star,* July 21, 1848; Washington *National Era,* August 17, November 2, 1848; Chicago *Watchman of the Prairies,* August 29, 1848; Boston *Congregationalist,* January 23, October 1, 1852; John W. Chadwick, *Theodore Parker: Preacher and Reformer* (Boston: Houghton Mifflin and Company, 1900), p. 248; Ellsworth, "Oberlin," pp. 113–14.

39. Quoted in Ronald D. Rietveld, "The Moral Issue of Slavery in American Politics, 1854–1860" (Ph.D. diss., University of Illinois, 1967), p. 43; also Stanley W. Campbell, *The Slave Catchers: Enforcement of the Fugitive Slave Law, 1850–1860* (Chapel Hill: University of North Carolina Press, 1968), pp. 31, 85; Sewell, *Ballots for Freedom,* pp. 236–39, 254–65, 279–81, 295; Hammond, *Politics of Benevolence,* pp. 121–29.

40. Boston *Liberator,* n.d., quoted in W. P. Garrison and F. J. Garrison, *William Lloyd Garrison, 1805–1879,* 4 vols. (New York: Century Co., 1885–1889), p. 404; Boston *Liberator,* March 17, 31, April 21, 1854; Joshua R. Giddings, *History of the Rebellion: Its Authors and Causes* (New York: Follett, Foster, & Co., 1864), pp. 367–70; Lewis Tappan to Jonathan Blanchard, December 6, 1854, L. Tappan Papers; Richard H. Watkins, Jr., "The Baptists of the North and Slavery, 1856–1860," *Foundations,* 13 (October–December, 1970): 319–28.

41. Foner, *Free Soil,* pp. 11–39; Sewell, *Ballots for Freedom,* pp. 254, 265–79, 292–95; Holt, *Political Crisis of the 1850's,* pp. 119–30, 146–57.

42. Sewell, *Ballots for Freedom,* pp. 292, 295–96, 306, 308, 343; Foner, *Free Soil,* pp. 110–13; Dillon, *The Abolitionists,* pp. 239–40; Stewart, *Holy Warriors,* pp. 174–76; Victor B. Howard, "The 1865 Election in Ohio: Moral Issues in Politics," *Ohio History,* 80 (Winter, 1971): 28, 31; Rietveld, "Moral Issue of Slavery," p. 2.

43. Salmon P. Chase, "Lectures on Slavery," undated, Chase Papers; also Washington *National Era,* May 20, 1858, October 6, December 1, 1859; *Facts for the People,* 1 (August, 1855): 60–61; Salmon P. Chase to George B. Cheever, November

29, 1858, Chase Papers; Henry Wilson, *History of the Rise and Fall of the Slave Power in America,* 3 vols. (Boston: James R. Osgood, 1877), 3: 559–60, 720–21; James B. Stewart, *Joshua Giddings and the Tactics of Radical Politics, 1725–1864* (Cleveland: Press of Case Western Reserve University, 1969), pp. 208–11, 252–53; Foner, *Free Soil,* pp. 78–79, 109–10.

44. "Constitution of the American Abolition Society, Adopted at Boston, October 1855," A.A.S. Papers and *Radical Abolitionist,* 1 (December, 1855): 35, also 1 (August, 1855): 5–6, 3 (May, 1858): 76–77, 4 (October, 1858): 19; *American Jubilee,* 1 (April, 1855): 89; Washington *National Era,* October 18, November 1, 1855; Goodell, *Slavery and Anti- Slavery,* p. 475; Wyatt-Brown, *Lewis Tappan,* pp. 332–34; Blue, *Free Soilers,* pp. 2, 103, 233–34, 243–47; M. Leon Perkal, "American Abolition Society: A Viable Alternative to the Republican Party," *Journal of Negro History,* 65 (Winter, 1980): 58–60, 66.

45. *Radical Abolitionist,* 3 (August, 1857): 2; also *American Jubilee,* 1 (March, 1854): 14, 1 (September, 1854): 37, 2 (June, 1855): 11; William Goodell to Joseph Plumb, August 23, 1856, A.A.S. Papers; Perkal, "American Abolition Society," pp. 59–60.

46. Jane Grey Swisshelm, *Half a Century* (Chicago: Jansen, McClurg, & Company, 1880), pp. 199–200.

47. May 20, 1858.

48. Syracuse *The Wesleyan,* n.d., quoted in *Radical Abolitionist,* 1 (June 1856): 83–84; also Utica *American Baptist,* October 23, 1856, October 30, 1860; *Radical Abolitionist,* 2 (October, 1856): 24; American Baptist Free Mission Society, *Fifteenth Annual Report . . . 1858* (Utica, N.Y.: The Society, 1858), p. 8.

49. William H. Brisbane to Salmon P. Chase, June 22, 1859, Chase Papers.

50. New Castle (Pa.) *Free Church Portfolio,* October 11, 1860; Utica *American Baptist,* July 3, 1856, September 18, 25, October 2, 1860; Washington *National Era,* August 7, 1856; *Freewill Baptist Quarterly,* 2 (July, 1854): 350–52; Syracuse *The Wesleyan,* December 22, 1853, March 11, 1857; Bryan (Oh.) *Political Abolitionist,* January 15, 1857; James M. McPherson, *The Struggle for Equality: Abolitionists and the Civil War and Reconstruction* (Princeton, N.J.: Princeton University Press, 1964), pp. 22–23; Stewart, *Holy Warriors,* p. 171; Howard, "Moral Issues in Politics," p. 29; Watkins, "Baptists of the North," p. 323.

51. William Goodell to W. M. Stewart, October 6, 1857, A.A.S. Papers; also *American Missionary Magazine,* 3 (December, 1859): 271–72; New York *National Principia,* December 31, 1859, June 2, 23, November 3, 1860; American Reform Tract and Book Society, *Duty of Voting for Righteous Men for Office* (Cincinnati: The Society, n.d.), pp. 7–8; Harlow, *Gerrit Smith,* pp. 385–89; Johnson, "American Missionary Association," pp. 209–15.

52. Resolution of the Northwestern Christian Anti-Slavery Convention Quoted in Oberlin (Oh.) *Oberlin Evangelist,* November 9, 1859; also Ohio State Christian Anti-Slavery Convention, *Proceedings* (Columbus, Ohio: n.p., 1859), pp. 10–11.

53. Salmon P. Chase to James Monroe, October 15, 1859, James Monroe Papers, Oberlin College Library; also Ohio State Christian Anti-Slavery Convention, *Proceedings,* pp. 10–11; Dillon, *The Abolitionists,* pp. 199–202; McKivigan, "Christian Anti-Slavery Convention Movement," pp. 358–60.

54. Syracuse *The Wesleyan,* December 22, 1853; *Freewill Baptist Quarterly,* 2 (July, 1854): 350–51; Yellow Springs (Oh.) *Free Presbyterian,* December 13, 1854;

Facts for the People, 1 (July, 1855): 18; Gilbert Haven, *National Sermons: Sermons, Speeches, and Letters on Slavery and its War* (Boston: Lee and Shepard, 1868), pp. 111–12; Armory Battles to Isreal Washburn, February 8, 1854, in Galliard Hunt, *Isreal, Elihu and Cadwallader Washburn: A Chapter in American Biography* (New York: The Macmillan Company, 1925), pp. 62–64; Charles D. Cleveland to Gamaliel Bailey, n.d., in Washington *National Era,* January 18, 1855; William H. Brisbane to Salmon P. Chase, June 22, 1859, Chase Papers.

55. Washington *National Era,* July 24, December 11, 1856; New York *National Principia,* September 29, October 6, 27, November 3, 1860; New York *American Baptist,* October 2, 1860; *Radical Abolitionist,* 2 (March, 1857): 66; Ellsworth, "Oberlin," pp. 123–24; Perkal, "William Goodell," pp. 292–97; Perkal, "American Abolition Society," pp. 60–61.

56. New York *Independent,* May 24, 1860; Haven, *National Sermons,* pp. 111–12, 120–21, 199; Francis Wayland to "Reverend Nott," January 4, 1859, Francis Wayland Papers, Brown University Library; Oliver Johnson to Theodore Parker, August 15, 1856, Theodore Parker Papers, Manuscript Division, Library of Congress; Robert C. Albrecht, *Theodore Parker* (New York: Twayne Publishers, Inc., 1971), p. 119; Gardiner Spring, *Personal Reminiscences of the Life and Times of Gardiner Spring* (New York: Charles Scribner, 1866), p. 186; Paul Kleppner, *The Cross of Culture: A Social Analysis of Mid-Western Politics, 1850–1900* (New York: The Free Press, 1970), pp. 104–5; Foner, *Free Soil,* p. 109; L. Wesley Norton, "The Methodist Episcopal Church in Michigan and the Politics of Slavery, 1850–1860," *Michigan History,* 48 (September, 1964); 209–13; Howard, "Moral Issues in Politics," pp. 29–30, 35–36, 44.

57. Approximately four thousand slaveholders had remained in the Methodist Episcopal Church, following the secession of most southern members in 1844. Emory S. Bucke, ed., *The History of American Methodism,* 3 vols. (New York: Abingdon Press, 1965), 2: 196–202, 209–14; Andrew E. Murray, *Presbyterians and the Negro—A History* (Philadelphia: Presbyterian Historical Society, 1966), pp. 112–18; Milton B. Powell, "The Abolitionist Controversy in the Methodist Episcopal Church, 1840–1864" (Ph.D. diss., University of Iowa, 1963), pp. 210, 216–19, 226–27, 231–32; Victor B. Howard, "The Anti-Slavery Movement in the Presbyterian Church, 1835–1861" (Ph.D. diss., Ohio State University, 1961), pp. 127–29, 181–92, 219–33.

58. Murray, *Presbyterians and the Negro,* pp. 106–12; Donnell R. Harris, "The Gradual Separation of Southern and Northern Baptists, 1845–1907," *Foundations,* 8 (April, 1964): 130–32, 136–39; Robert Fortenbaugh, "American Lutheran Synods and Slavery, 1830–1860," *Journal of Religion,* 13 (January, 1933): 73–76, 86–91; Cuthbert E. Allen, "The Slavery Question in Catholic Newspapers, 1850–1865," *American Catholic Historical Society Records,* 26 (1936): 129–37; Robert C. Senior, "New England Congregationalists and the Anti-Slavery Movement, 1830–1860" (Ph.D. diss., Yale University, 1954), pp. 66–67, 96–98, 209–13, 255–301, 389–98, 405–10; Kleppner, *Cross of Culture,* pp. 104–05; Hammond, *Politics of Benevolence,* pp. 189–94.

8

The Social Origins of Women's Antislavery Politics in Western New York

Nancy Hewitt

Northern women dedicated to the black slave's emancipation frequently organized themselves into associations for the promotion and management of antislavery fairs in the decades prior to the Civil War. These colorful markets, which were held periodically in communities throughout New England and Western New York, offered for sale goods both domestic and foreign produced by friends of the slave. The purpose was to raise money for the pursuit of slavery's abolition and to provide a means for females, themselves the victims of political disfranchisement and social discrimination, to participate in the struggle for reform. Indeed, the fairs organized by local women's antislavery sewing circles and ladies' antislavery societies were perhaps the only tactic that all abolitionists regarded as appropriate for female activists. Yet even the style and conduct of these fairs often reflected the profound division among female abolitionists over the tactics and strategies proper for women to pursue in the slave's cause. Always the clash was between those female reformers who advocated moral suasion, which allowed for the equal participation of men and women in the cause, and those who advocated an electoral solution that limited women to an auxiliary role in the cause.

Historians have amply testified to the significance of women's efforts in both the moral suasion and political wings of the antislavery movement. Gerda Lerner describes them as "an integral aspect of the antislavery movement," though their "peculiar relationship to political power" demanded that they employ innovative methods of political "pressure and persuasion."[1] However, no historian has explained the divisions among female reformers— why some chose to pursue reform through electoral politics despite their "peculiar relationship" to the political system, while others sought to develop new forms of "pressure and persuasion."[2]

Western New York is an ideal location in which to examine this division. The region has long attracted the attention of leading scholars of antebellum politics and reform. It was at once both a cauldron of abolitionism and the center of the first formal woman's rights movement in America. In his classic work on the region, *The Burned-Over District,* Whitney Cross claims that it is women who "should dominate a history" of the area's "enthusiastic movements."[3] Thus, a profile of the social characteristics of female abolitionists, a portrait of individual female reformers and their families, and an analysis of the tactics popular among women abolitionists in a single Western New York community, Rochester, can offer valuable insights into the complex relationship of women to abolitionist politics. This arsenal of evidence cannot explain for certain why any individual chose one avenue of reform and not another. However, it does suggest how distinctions in the social and economic backgrounds of female reformers shaped the approach they adopted toward achieving change for the slave and themselves.

The issue of women's role in abolitionism was directly confronted at the May 1840 meeting of the American Anti-Slavery Society (AASS). Abby Kelley, a Quaker abolitionist, was elected to the Executive Committee that year. Her victory climaxed a series of clashes within the Society and led directly to its division. The division was rooted in three major issues: churches' support of slavery, political action, and the role of women. Those who remained within the AASS criticized churches' collaboration with slaveholders, advocated moral suasion as the primary means of social change, and supported the full and equal participation of women in the antislavery cause.[4] Those who abandoned the AASS emphasized, instead, the continued potential for both churches and political parties to increase antislavery sentiment and the inappropriateness of women's direct efforts in either arena.[5]

There were advocates of each position in Western New York. The first men's antislavery societies of Rochester and Monroe County, established in 1833 and 1834, respectively, supported William Lloyd Garrison's doctrine of immediate emancipation. A black and a white women's antislavery society, founded in 1834 and 1835, respectively, declared themselves auxiliaries to the Garrison-led AASS.[6] In 1837, some of Rochester's male antislavery leaders joined in the call for a state-wide society that would question political candidates on their antislavery stands. Three years later, several Rochesterians were involved in the founding of the Liberty Party and the advocacy of third party politics as the best antislavery strategy. Simultaneously, Garrisonian support among men and women was growing in Rochester, evidenced by the petition campaigns of 1837 and 1842, by participation in the AASS annual meetings, by coverage of local antislavery activities in *The Liberator,* and by the tours of AASS agents in Western New York.[7]

One such agent, Abby Kelley, toured the region in 1840 and 1842 and helped organize the Western New York Anti-Slavery Society. The founding meeting brought together local advocates of both moral suasion and political abolitionism. At the first annual meeting the following December, the advocates of the two positions resolved to work together. We "repudiate with indignation," they claimed,

every sectarian, political, or other test, that may be attempted to be forced upon us as abolitionists; but though we may be of every form of religious and political opinions, Christian and Infidel, war men and peace men, voters and non-resistants, we unite for mutual co-operation to effect the one great object of converting the entire public to abolitionism.[8]

Yet the breach between Rochester's moral suasion and political abolitionists ran far deeper than resolutions could heal. Abolitionism was an ideology that spoke as clearly to abolitionists' own social and economic concerns as to those of the slave. Rochester's antislavery men and women came from different social and economic situations and their abolitionism—both its ideological underpinnings and its expressions in action—continued to reflect those differences.

Moreover, women reformers faced a special obstacle in the 1830s and 1840s that did not affect their male counterparts. New definitions of womanhood, emerging during the first third of the nineteenth century, were constricting women's public role. The evangelical revivals of that era, led in Rochester by Charles Grandison Finney, had initially encouraged women's antislavery activism as an extension of her piety. However, when abolitionists launched an attack on both churches that condoned slavery and those that remained silent on the issue, Finney and other evangelicals began to curb their support of some reform efforts. Specifically, many evangelicals charged that it was unseemly for women to play a public role in reform and that such behavior could only erode the Christian home, which was women's responsibility to preserve.

At the World Anti-Slavery Convention in London in 1840, one of Rochester's leading antislavery ministers, the Baptist Elon Galusha, assured his English counterparts that amongst his exceedingly numerous constituency in America the "ladies took no part in the business of societies" though he admitted that "a very small minority of the abolitionists . . . had allowed the innovation."[9] Reverend Galusha was right in large part; most women chose to retreat into the domestic sphere or at least to shift their efforts into more socially acceptable church and charitable activities. Yet some pursued innovative roles in abolitionism with the support of male co-workers, and many of those who temporarily submitted to social pressure and retreated in the 1830s reemerged as active abolitionists in the 1850s.

The differences among abolitionist women—in their nativity, family background, religious affiliation, work experience, and economic status—were determining factors in the approach they adopted toward reform. Analysis of these differences among Rochester female reformers unearths the roots of female abolitionism in that hothouse of reform. By the 1830s, the village of Rochester was a burgeoning commercial center, the hub of an increasingly specialized agricultural hinterland, and one of the nation's fastest growing cities as well as a hotbed of religious and reform enthusiasms. With the opening of the Erie Canal in 1822, the city became a depot for goods, for people, and for social and political movements as they traveled between eastern urban centers and frontier communities. Rochester's demographic and institutional development was accordingly diversified and dynamic. During the 1830s and 1840s, Quakers, free blacks, and Irish and German immigrants joined New England Yankees and Maryland aristocrats on the community's radiating paths of settlement. Simultaneously, village councils, schools, almshouses, and voluntary associations joined family and church at the loci of community governance. Improvements in transportation and communication and increases in population proceeded apace as did residential segregation and class and ethnic stratification.

These changes nurtured a large and vital community of social activists in Rochester and its hinterlands. From tract to temperance societies, benevolent institutions to woman's rights conventions, moral crusades to political campaigns, Rochesterians carved a profusion of pathways to social change in the first half of the nineteenth century. Women were prominent, often dominant, on these paths. Within the first decade of settlement, the wives of Rochester's religious, political, and business leaders had formed a missionary society, a charity school, and a Female Charitable Society. These activities were well supported by their male kin and by the ministers of Rochester's leading churches: First Presbyterian and St. Luke's Episcopal.[10]

In the winter of 1834, a local antislavery paper, the *Rights of Man,* noted that "many benevolent ladies of Rochester, in years that are past, justly won the applause of the philanthropist and Christian, in their exertions on behalf of the oppressed and suffering *Greeks.*" Yet, noting that "the colored females in this village" had recently formed the first female antislavery society in Western New York, the editor wondered if there were "not motives quite as strong and patriotic to urge" benevolent ladies "onward in behalf of *their own* oppressed and suffering American sisters and brethren?"[11] Regrettably, no further notice exists of the black women who introduced their sex into antislavery activity in Rochester. Their example, however, was followed by white women who formed the Rochester Female Anti-Slavery Society (RFASS) the next year.

Many of the women who led the RFASS in 1835 had been active previously in benevolent enterprises and a substantial majority had husbands or fathers who were active abolitionists. Yet these women were not, generally, members of the city's first families but rather of its most dynamic economic sector of shopkeepers and artisans.[12] Indeed, the RFASS was refused the support of Mrs. Jonathan Child—the daughter of the city's founder, wife of its first mayor, sister-in-law of St. Luke's minister, and officer of the Charitable Society. She replied to their call for assistance by asserting that "combined public effort or co-operation" on the part of females could not be "exerted with propriety" on this subject.[13] Unlike Mrs. Child, who was a Maryland-born Episcopalian aristocrat, Rochester's first female abolitionists were New Englanders or Eastern New Yorkers of middling economic circumstances and Presbyterian or Baptist faith. Several played prominent roles in the Finney-led revivals of 1830–31 and in 1835 turned their evangelical enthusiasm to "immediate emancipation" as the only proper response to slavery, which was "a gross violation of the law of God."[14]

They obtained hundreds of their sisters' signatures on antislavery petitions circulated in Rochester and the surrounding county. The 600 female signatures collected in January 1837 and the 900 gathered the following September are the fullest testimony to the cause's appeal among Western New York women.[15] Yet in the midst of national antislavery debates over women's role in abolitionism, the RFASS disappeared, and no new autonomous female antislavery society was formed for thirteen years.[16] In the interim, men's political antislavery societies flourished as did a joint men's and women's society formed by a new group of local residents.

The signatures of Yankee, evangelical, middle-class women were augmented on the 1837 petitions by those of Hicksite Quaker women from rural New England and downstate New York. The number of these Quakers increased in Rochester from the late 1830s as did their visibility in antislavery circles. After 1840, the AASS concentrated its organizing efforts on this group, sending Quaker Abby Kelley into Western New York. Her labors were complemented by those of male AASS agents and of Lucretia Mott. Mott, a Philadelphia Quaker, provided a prominent voice for abolitionist and feminist concerns within Quaker meetings while Kelley translated that voice into worldly antislavery activity. These two women served as soul-stirring models for their religious sisters in Western New York.

In 1842 the activities of these antislavery and Quaker agents culminated in the founding of the Western New York Anti-Slavery Society (WNYASS). The founding meeting, held at the Washington Street Presbyterian Church, was presided over by Samuel D. Porter, a long-time abolitionist, a Liberty Party member, and the husband of an RFASS founder.[17] A few Yankee, evangelical men joined Porter in the WNYASS, but the vast majority of his co-workers were Hicksite Quaker men and women.[18] Women claimed an equal role in the Society from the beginning: Abby Kelley served on the 1842 resolutions committee while local women served as vice-presidents and members of the Executive Committee that first year. Between 1842 and

1850, women served as officers of the WNYASS, circulated petitions, formed sewing circles, and managed fund-raising fairs throughout Western New York.[19]

A comparison of samples of RFASS and WNYASS members (see Table 8.1) suggests a similarity in the extensiveness of their connections to male abolitionists.[20] The husbands of RFASS and WNYASS women filled an equally wide range of occupations though the latter retained stronger ties to agrarian pursuits while the former more often ventured into commercial enterprises. In religion and in their attachment to other reform causes, they differed more substantially. RFASS members were evangelicals, predominantly Presbyterians, many of whom entered public activism through the benevolent concerns of the local Charitable Society. Women of the WNYASS were predominantly Hicksite Quakers whose abolitionism was less an extension of charitable concerns than an entree to feminist politics.

In the 1840s, as RFASS members retreated from abolitionist to charitable circles, WNYASS women extended their critique of racial and sexual oppression. By 1848, many WNYASS members had become dissatisfied with Hicksite stands on slavery and woman's rights and founded a new Quaker meeting. This association, the Yearly Meeting of Congregational Friends, adopted a "Basis of Religious Association" that established "an order of independent congregations" characterized by "perfect liberty of conscience" and "the equality of women."[22] In the same year, these Quaker women joined Lucretia Mott and Elizabeth Cady Stanton at the Seneca Falls Woman's Rights Convention and resolved,

That being invested by the Creator with the same capabilities, and the same consciousness of responsibility for their exercise, it is demonstrably the right and duty of woman, equally with man, to promote every righteous cause by every righteous means . . . in private and in public, by writing and by speaking, by any instrumentalities to be used, and in any assemblies proper to be held.[23]

A second woman's rights convention, publicized through the pages of Frederick Douglass' *North Star,* was held in Rochester in August 1848.

While a small group of Rochester women were carrying on the work of moral suasion in increasingly feminist tones, male antislavery leaders were pursuing two distinct paths to abolitionism. Quaker artisans, shopkeepers, and farmers joined their female kin in the WNYASS and followed Garrisonian precepts of immediatism, moral suasion, and come-outerism. They were joined by a few Presbyterian and Unitarian merchants and professionals, but these men more often focused their attention on third party politics.[24] Indeed, some of the latter group had triple affiliations, as WNYASS members, Liberty Party supporters, and antislavery Whigs. Multiple affiliations were not uncommon because many reformers viewed a vote for the Liberty Party more as an act of conscience than a choice of temporal lead-

Table 8.1
COLLECTIVE BIOGRAPHICAL DATA ON MEMBERS OF THE RFASS
AND THE WNYASS[21]

	RLASS (1842)	N 35	WNYASS (1851)	N 39
	N	Percentage	N	Percentage
Husband's affiliations				
Abolition	15	62.5	23	65.7
Non-Abolition*	9	37.5	12	34.3
Nativity:				
New England	7	29.2	4	11.4
New York	4	16.7	14	40.0
Other/Unknown	13	54.2	2	51.4
		100.0		100.0
Women's affiliations:				
Benevolent Society	13	54.2	2	5.7
Woman's Rights	0	0	18	51.4
Non-Affiliation	11	45.8	15	42.9
	24	100.0	35	100.0
Religious affiliations:				
First Presbyterian	4	16.7	1	2.9
Reformed Presbyterian	6	25.0	3	8.6
Baptist	3	12.5	0	0
Methodist	0	0	0	0
Episcopal	2	8.3	0	0
Unitarian	0	0	2	5.7
Quaker Orthodox	2	8.3	2	5.7
Quaker Hicksite-Congregational	1	4.2	23	65.7
Reform Presbyterian	0	0	2	5.7
Quaker Hicksite-Unitarian	0	0	2	5.7
Unknown	6	25.0	0	0
	24	100.0		100.0
Father/Husband occupation:				
Merchant-Manufacturer	3	12.5	4	11.4
Professional	1	4.2	3	8.6
Artisan	5	20.8	5	14.3
Shopkeeper	6	25.0	5	14.3
Farmer	2	8.3	7	20.0
Other/Unknown	7	29.2	11	31.4
	24	100.0		100.0

* Three of the nine non-abolitionists belonged to other reform movements.

ership. Liberty Party leader, Samuel D. Porter, for instance, claimed that it was not electoral victory that Liberty Party men sought with their "appeal to the Ballot Box" but the *moral effect of numbers.*"[25]

Porter was one of several men who increased their third party political efforts during the 1840s, while their female kin retreated from the antislavery cause. In 1851, some of these women were wooed back to public action by Julia Griffiths, Frederick Douglass' editorial assistant at the *North Star*. For the first time since 1837, Quaker and evangelical women joined forces in the public pronouncement of their antislavery sentiments: the occasion was the visit of Julia Griffith's countryman, the British abolitionist George Thompson.

By 1851, debates over third party politics and moral suasion had almost wholly rent national antislavery ranks. Yet within Rochester, Thompson's international stature, the opposition of the local press, and the passage of the Fugitive Slave Act caused abolitionists to close ranks.[26] The massive and varied group of abolitionists that gathered to hear Thompson at Rochester's Corinthian Hall in January of 1851 encouraged local women to invite him back to the city for a grand Anti-Slavery Festival in April. The committee of ladies managing the Festival included two former RFASS members, ten members of the WNYASS, Julia Griffiths, and eleven women who appeared in public antislavery ranks for the first time. In addition, the Committee included four members of the Union Anti-Slavery Sewing Society, a local association of black women who held fairs in support of Douglass' *North Star*.[27]

The collective efforts in behalf of the Thompson Anti-Slavery Festival resulted in financial success, yet the Festival was the culmination, not the initiation, of women's unity in the antislavery cause. In the months that followed, white female abolitionists broke into two opposing camps. Their black co-workers, momentarily visible as their efforts converged with those of their white peers, once again faded from public record.[28] In June of 1851, Douglass helped to crystallize local divisions when he announced his conversion to political abolitionism and the merger of the *North Star* with the *Liberty Party Paper*.

While many local moral suasionists, male and female, withdrew their support from Douglass' new venture, political abolitionists applauded his decision. By 1851, the Liberty Party was all but defunct, most of its members having joined the Free Soilers in 1848. Still, several of Rochester's most important Liberty Party leaders, including Porter, were reluctant to accept the more limited antislavery stand of the new party. They were pleased to have such a prominent figure as Douglass advocate in print what they considered their more principled version of third party politics. Others, already having accepted Free Soil doctrines, believed that it would only be a matter of time before Douglass, too, moved from political abolitionism to political non-extension.[29]

Applause did not always translate into subscriptions, however; and at least temporarily, the support of political abolitionists did not offset the loss of moral suasionists' subscriptions. Thus, Julia Griffiths wrote to Liberty Party leader Gerrit Smith that Douglass' "change on the Constitution has thinned our Subscription list considerably." In response, Griffiths continued, she was "forming an Anti-Slavery sewing circle," which, she trusted, would be "influential, permanent, & efficient."[30] She regretted that "bigotry precludes many of the *old* friends from joining" the new Rochester Ladies' Anti-Slavery Sewing Society (RLASS).[31]

During 1851, Rochester's white antislavery women followed male reformers' example and divided themselves into opposing camps. One, formed by WNYASS members, continued to criticize churches' collaboration with slaveholders, advocated moral suasion, and asserted women's right to full and equal participation in antislavery agitation. The other, the Rochester Ladies' Anti-Slavery Society (RLASS), consisted of former RFASS members and newcomers of similar backgrounds. They advocated continued faith in established religion and electoral politics and the establishment of a separate women's society to aid antislavery men seeking political leadership. Douglass exacerbated this division, and implicitly acknowledged the importance of women's support, when he suggested that those women who failed to follow his lead into political abolitionism had abandoned the cause entirely.

In a letter to Mrs. Samuel D. Porter, the first president of the RLASS, Douglass claimed that he looked to the new Society "for important services to the antislavery cause in Rochester. . . . At present, you have the field to yourselves," he continued "and it is meet that you should occupy it."[32] He was quickly reprimanded by Sarah Hallowell, a WNYASS member since 1842, who wrote, "For years (as we need not remind you,) we have labored earnestly and trustingly to get up Annual Fairs, as a means of aiding our cause." She acknowledged that the WNYASS women had recently changed their "modus operandi . . . devoting the principle part of our proceeds to the Boston Bazaar." Yet how could it be otherwise, for the Boston group, led by Garrison, Kelley, and other moral suasionists continued to accept women as equal partners in antislavery agitation. Douglass was asking women who had worked as his equals to suddenly abandon that place and its attendant feminist implications for a separate and subordinate role. While refusing this change in their work, Hallowell assured Douglass that they never thought of "a final cessation of our associated efforts for the *slave*."[33]

Here, then, local antislavery women confronted both long-term divisions within antislavery ranks and emerging debates over women's public role. Yet, whether they were moral suasionists or political abolitionists, women shared exclusion from electoral politics and inclusion in a culturally imposed female subordination. Thus, for women, involvement in antislavery activity necessitated reconciling their own desire for political equality with one of two conflicting tactical approaches to abolitionism.

Both groups made their voices heard in support of the slave. Among moral suasionists, women were given a voice and a vote in abolitionist strategies on principle. Even among political abolitionists, however, women's contributions to the cause, especially as fundraisers, allowed them to participate in the shaping of antislavery policies. Both groups of antislavery women were distinguished from their non-activist sisters in Rochester by their participation, in whatever capacity, in the public, and highly politicized, debates on slavery. Yet in the shaping of a new public and political role for women, their differences were more important than their similarities.

Comparing samples of WNYASS women with those who belonged to the RLASS, clear distinctions emerge (see Table 8.2).[34] WNYASS women were much more likely than their RLASS counterparts to emerge from the agricultural regions of downstate or Western New York. While their husbands pursued a variety of occupations, farming remained the primary occupation for the largest number even after removal to Rochester. For this and other reasons, the families of many WNYASS women lived on the fringes of the city or in nearby towns, limiting their access to the city's central institutions but placing them closer to centers of radical Quakerism in Waterloo and other central New York communities. RLASS women emerged primarily from those areas of greater New England already affected by commercial and industrial expansion. Their husbands were five times as likely to be merchants or manufacturers as farmers. Their families lived near the center of the city, over one-quarter resided in the elite Third Ward; and they worshipped in nearby Presbyterian or Unitarian churches. Finally, RLASS women, like their RFASS predecessors, combined abolition with charitable ventures while WNYASS women continued to extend their abolitionist efforts into battles for women's civil, religious, and political equality.

Differences between female advocates of moral suasion (WNYASS) and political abolition (RLASS) in husband's occupation, religion, community life, and reform affiliation are suggestive (despite the small sample size) and invite speculation. In each area of difference it appears that the experience of Quaker moral suasionists was defined by a democratic diffusion of power and authority and the relative equality of men and women; that of Yankee political abolitionists by hierarchies of power and authority that gradually institutionalized the subordination of women. When Quaker and Yankee women met in Rochester, the latter were subordinate within families bound to the city's central economic and political institutions, while the former were relatively equal within families distant from those same centers.[36]

Political abolitionists emerged from New England villages already penetrated by commercial capitalism.[37] In Rochester, such families' successes rested on the expansion of commerce and industry and the attendant separation of employer and employee, work and home, and men's and women's spheres. Thus, the process that increasingly relegated women to the domestic sphere, also moved their families toward the locus of economic power. Moral

Table 8.2
COLLECTIVE BIOGRAPHICAL DATA ON MEMBERS OF THE WNYASS
AND THE RLASS[35]

	WNYASS (1842)	N 35	RLASS (1851)	N 39
	N	Percentage	N	Percentage
Husband's affiliations				
Abolition	23	65.7	18	46.1
Non-Abolition*	12	34.3	21	53.9
Nativity:				
New England	4	11.4	8	20.9
Eastern New York	2	5.7	9	23.1
Western New York and Long Island	12	34.3	2	5.1
Great Britain	1	2.9	5	12.8
Other/Unknown	16	45.7	15	38.5
		100.0		100.0
Women's affiliations:				
Benevolent Society	2	5.7	15	38.5
Women's Society	18	51.4	0	0
No Affiliations	15	42.9	15	61.5
		100.0		100.0
Religious affiliations:				
First Presbyterian	1	2.9	2	5.1
Reform Presbyterian	3	8.6	9	23.1
Baptist	0	0	1	2.6
Methodist	0	0	2	5.1
Episcopal	0	0	0	0
Unitarian	2	5.7	6	16.4
Quaker Orthodox	2	5.7	1	2.6
Quaker Hicksite-Congregational	23	65.7	1	2.6
Reform Presbyterian-Unitarian	2	5.7	5	12.8
Quaker Hicksite-Unitarian	2	5.7	0	0
Unknown	0	0	12	30.7
		100.0		100.0
Residence:				
Third Ward	3	8.6	11	28.2
Other City Wards	19	54.3	23	59.0
Surrounding towns	9	25.7	0	0
Unknown	4	11.4	5	12.8
		100.0		100.0

* Five non-abolitionist husbands belonged to reform movements other than abolitionism.

Table 8.2 *Continued*

	WNYASS (1842)	N 35	RLASS (1851)	N 39
	N	Percentage	N	Percentage
Father/Husband occupation:				
Merchant/Manufacturer	4	11.4	10	25.6
Professional	3	8.6	4	10.3
Artisan	5	14.3	3	7.7
Shopkeeper	5	14.3	5	12.8
Farmer	7	20.0	2	5.1
Other/Unknown	11	31.4	15	38.5
		100.0		100.0

suasionist women from Quaker farming villages had long labored side-by-side with the men of their family and community. Differences between the particular tasks performed did not diminish the productive character of women's labor. The separation of work and home and the relegation of women to the latter increased as some men moved to shopkeeping and manufacturing in Rochester, but Quaker social and family circles continued to be dominated by agrarian lifeways, which necessitated the cooperation of household members on a seasonal and cyclical basis.[38]

In community life as well as in labor, Quaker women shared public responsibilities with men that clearly differentiated them from their Yankee counterparts. Nineteenth-century Quaker farming communities, whether in Western Massachusetts or on Long Island, maintained informal networks of social control and community welfare that had begun to break down in Yankee villages by the end of the eighteenth century. Quakers cared for the orphaned, old, destitute, and widowed in the midst of dense, kin-connected communities extended through generations of in-marrying neighbors.[39] At the same time that such networks allowed for female economic dependence, the shared labors of agrarian life and women's autonomy in Quaker meeting fostered female independence. Moreover, as in early New England farming communities, the informal character of many social institutions and the importance of face-to-face interactions in community governance enhanced women's public roles and integrated them more fully into economic, social, and political relations.

By the early nineteenth century, the New England villages from which political abolitionists emerged were ordered communities whose hierarchies of status and authority were based on length of residence, wealth, and religious affiliation. New England villages were hardly heterogeneous in twentieth-century terms, but stratification within them was increasingly visible and increasingly a cause of concern. Religious and political leaders voiced even greater concern that geographic mobility, immigration, and economic change would burst the bonds of well-ordered communities and subvert the power of traditional authorities. The establishment of asylums to house deviant and disruptive individuals, the attempts to inculcate social control through religion and education, and the idealization of women as the agents of piety, purity, and order within the home were all employed to sustain the established order.[40] Women were not yet seen as frail vessels. In fact, some memory of Revolutionary foremothers and the tenets of religious revivalism reinforced women's right to a public voice. However, their power was increasingly muted and manifested as feminine influence rather than direct action.

When Yankee women moved to Rochester, they encountered familiar forms whose elaboration and extension heightened their own subordination but also their families' power. Quaker women sought to reestablish the cooperative communities from which they came: they did so on the margins, figuratively and literally, of the city. A primary institutional expression of these divergent relations to local power and community life was the meeting-house. Both the Quaker meeting-house and the major evangelical churches were built at the center of the city in the early years of settlement. The frame building that housed the Hicksite Quakers was overwhelmed, however, by the stone edifices of nearby St. Luke's Episcopal Church and First Presbyterian Church and the more distant spires of the Bethel Free, Baptist, and Methodist churches. Moreover, while evangelical women worshipped in these central churches among fellow Rochesterians, Quakers held their most important sessions outside the city limits. Quarterly and Yearly meetings were held in central New York farming communities while the headquarters of the Congregational Friends was established at Waterloo, some fifty miles east of Rochester, to encourage friends to gather "from various parts of the moral vineyard."[41] Religious meetings held within Rochester, including those of spiritualists, were frequently held in the homes of participants, moving from place to place with a fluidity that mirrored their institutional forms.

While the revivalistic tenets of the Second Great Awakening diffused the hierarchies of eighteenth-century New England church forms, evangelical churches retained the sex segregation of these earlier assemblies. Increased lay participation was accompanied by the elevation of the male minister's personal power while the elevation of woman to a pious and pure pedestal separated her further from the offices of religious authority. Even within evangelical societies that followed congregational forms, women's religious experience was mediated by male ministers, elders, and heads of households.[42] Quakers considered the Inner Light, residing in the individual, as the source of religious truth. This emphasis on unmediated spiritual revelation along with women's right to an equal voice in religious affairs made the Quaker meeting one of the most democratic institutions in nineteenth-century America. Even though these Quaker principles did not always translate into full sexual equality, they provided the surest religious foundation for such equality. Congregational Friends increased the emphasis on the "progressive unfoldings of Divine Light" and on *equality of rights* irrespective of sex" while spiritualist doctrines accepted by some members of the group proclaimed the further diffusion of religious authority and the complete reliance on unmediated revelation through mediums of either sex.[43] Thus, Quakers, emphasizing the Inner Light, gazed outward from Rochester for inspiration and fellowship; evangelicals, more dependent on external authority, established themselves as the city's moral center.

The religious experiences of Quaker women were consonant with their experiences of labor and community life in terms of women's autonomy and equality, the diffusion of authority, and the unmediated character of economic, political, and social relations. Quaker women's political experience was intertwined with labor, religion, and community life in ways that may have been replicated in the nineteenth century only in utopian communities. Nineteenth-century Quakers, like their British forebears, curtailed the state's authority over them by refusing to participate in either military or political battles through individual involvement or financial support. Within local communities, governance of many matters lay with the meeting and women maintained a strong voice there. Decisions were made by the will of the meeting rather than by ballot, and local meetings were relatively autonomous.[44] Thus, democratic decision-making forms, autonomous women's authority, decentralized political power, and dissent from state policies through direct action or the denial of legitimacy defined local moral suasionists' previous political experience.

Political abolitionists sought to mobilize Constitutional principles and republican federalism in the cause of abolition. While working on the fringes of the two party system, political abolitionists accepted the validity of state forms and electoral politics. Federalism linked local antislavery efforts into a national antislavery movement while republicanism linked natural rights with natural order.[45] The meaning of these terms differed among political abolitionists according to gender. Woman's disfranchisement and her "natural" subordination to man relegated her to an auxiliary role in political abolitionism. Yet her location within a hierarchically organized movement that sought state power and asserted natural rights gave her an indirect access to primary political institutions. In the early years of third party politics, when local Liberty Party leaders sought to combine politics and moral suasion, the moral influence of women might have had freest reign. Then, however, concern over the propriety of women's public activism restricted antislavery efforts among Yankee, evangelical, middle-class women. The emergence of this group as auxiliary workers in the cause during the 1850s coincided with a shift of emphasis among male abolitionists from local and state to national electoral campaigns and from the *"moral effect of numbers"* to their office-winning potential.[46] Women's greatest labors, then, were undertaken when they were furthest removed structurally from positions of political influence. The acceptance of existing political institutions and women's structural removal from electoral participation shaped a limited and local role for this second group of abolitionist women. Through fund raising, women could support local advocates of political abolitionism, such as Frederick Douglass, without directly participating in public political action.

Moral suasion abolitionism was grounded in agrarian labor patterns, informal networks of social control and community welfare, decentralized and democratic religious and political associations, and the rejection of state and church authority.[47] Marginality in relation to Rochester's centers of social, economic, and political power reinforced both moral suasionists' bonds with rural communities and their distance from institutionalized authority. Few political abolitionists actually inhabited local centers of political power either, but they were tied to them through kinship and through their gradual movement into local centers of economic power. Should their attempts to reshape national party politics succeed, it was plausible that they might also then attain more influential local political positions. The world they inhabited and in which they sought greater influence was an increasingly urbane one, characterized by commercial and industrial economic relations, institutional forms of social control and community welfare, and hierarchical structures of church and state authority.

As noted above, women inhabited these different environments while sharing certain political and cultural restrictions. Yet the degree to which supposedly universal definitions of woman's nature and woman's role impinged on particular women varied by class, occupation, residence, and religious affiliation.[48] The separation of men's and women's spheres accompanied commercialization and industrialization while the ideological supports for such a separation were articulated through a rapidly expanding popular literature—magazines, novels, advice books—circulated among urban, middle-class women. The tenets of piety, purity, domesticity, and submissiveness proclaimed in this literature were reinforced by the preachings of evangelical ministers.[49] Thus, both the relegation of women to a private and subordinate role and the ideological justification for that change was central to the experience of political abolitionist women. It was less clearly related to the personal experiences of moral suasionists.[50] It seems likely that the marginality of the latter to dominant social institutions and cultural formations facilitated women's full participation in labors that challenged both the institution of slavery and the restriction of women's role.[51] However, the more influential and direct relationship of political abolitionist women to those same institutions and formations through husband and family might have limited their willingness to demand a fuller role in the antislavery cause and reinforced acquiescence to their inferior political status.

The distinctions in the social fabric of female moral suasionists' lives and that of their adversaries, the political abolitionists, can be detected by examining the Porters and the Posts, two prominent antislavery families in Rochester.[52] At least eight Porter women and five Post women were involved in local antislavery activity, the former in the RFASS and the RLASS and the latter in the WNYASS. A comparison of their social and economic backgrounds and experiences with the forms of their antislavery activity will provide case studies of the general patterns described above.

Susan Porter, a member of the RFASS and first president of the RLASS, was born Susan Farley in Waldoboro, Maine, in 1812. Her future husband, Samuel D. Porter, a native New Englander, had moved to Rochester in 1827 to clerk in his brother-in-law Everard Peck's bookstore. In 1831, Samuel accepted the tenets of Finneyite evangelicalism and joined the First Presbyterian Church while increasing his involvement in local reform activities. In 1835, Susan married Samuel, moved to Rochester, and joined him at First Presbyterian. The Porters' antislavery, temperance, and moral reform activities convinced them of the need for an evangelical congregation devoted to reform, and in 1836, they joined in the founding of the Bethel Free Presbyterian Church. They changed church membership again, in 1845 and 1855, each time staying within the Presbyterian fold but choosing to worship in a congregation filled with fellow reformers.[53]

As the Porters increased their activities in evangelical and reform circles, Samuel was also improving his economic status. His success in land speculation combined with his kin connections to the commercially successful Peck family solidified the Porters' economic and social standing though the advocacy of antislavery kept Samuel from winning local political power.[54] The expanding Porter family moved into the city's select Third Ward and, with the Pecks, gathered their kin around them, including Susan's sisters, Laura and Martha (the latter having become Everard's second wife), and Samuel's father, stepmother, and three unmarried sisters. The extended family worked together in local commercial and professional enterprises and in various reform associations and worshipped together at the Washington Street Presbyterian Church or the First Unitarian Church.[55]

Everard Peck was the most successful of the family members. Having moved to Rochester in its early years of settlement, he opened a bookstore, served as one of the village's first trustees, invested in milling and manufacturing enterprises, and played a leading role in tract, missionary, Bible, temperance, and early antislavery societies. By the 1840s, he was a comfortably established village patriarch with ties to First Presbyterian Church and Whig politics. Everard's first wife, a founder of the Charitable Society, died in 1831; his second wife, Martha, joined her sister Susan in founding the local Orphan Asylum in 1837 and in the RLASS. Susan was married to the most upwardly mobile of the family members. The move from clerk to commercial capitalist and from the First to the Third Ward marked Samuel

Porter as one of the new breed of boom town successes. Yet the Porters' continued commitment to evangelical perfectionism and antislavery distinguished them from those who combined upward mobility in the newly competitive commercial world with concern only for self-aggrandizement and social control.

Samuel's own kin may have influenced his perspective on these matters. His father was continually on the verge of economic collapse, being frequently saved from that fate by the labors of his wife and four daughters. Yet Samuel's father, stepmother, and sisters devoted as much time to the antislavery cause as did the more successful branches of the family. Their principled devotion to the cause despite their tenuous economic position likely reminded Samuel of his own good fortune, and the uses to which it should be put. At the same time, laboring for abolition in tandem with the more successful Porters and Pecks may have provided the less successful family members with a sense of stability and inclusion in the city's best circles that their own economic circumstances did not warrant.

The men and women of these families worked for the same causes in sex-segregated religious and reform associations. Susan Porter joined the Charitable Society and the RFASS in 1835, helped found the Orphan Asylum in 1837, labored in women's temperance and moral reform societies during the 1840s, and joined the Home for Friendless Women at its founding in 1849, and the RLASS in 1851. Samuel Porter combined business with activity in Rochester's first men's antislavery society, in the Young Men's Moral Reform Society, the WNYASS, the Liberty Party, and the Industrial School. He also taught Sunday School, worked for temperance, and served on the all-male Boards of Trustees of the Orphan Asylum and the Home for Friendless Women.

When Frederick Douglass announced his conversion to political abolitionism in 1851, Samuel Porter was one of his first and strongest supporters. When Julia Griffiths sought allies for her new Ladies' Anti-Slavery Society, she called immediately on Susan Porter and her kinswomen. Susan and her sisters were joined by Samuel's female relatives, by neighbors, and by fellow communicants from Presbyterian and Unitarian congregations.[56] This close-knit network of kin, neighbors, and co-religionists from leading commercial and professional families aided fugitive slaves and free blacks and supported Douglass's paper and third party political efforts over the next fifteen years.

The Posts traveled a significantly different path to and through antislavery activism. Isaac and Amy Post were born into Long Island Quaker farming communities in 1800 and 1802, respectively. Isaac moved to a central New York Quaker community in the 1820s in search of better farmland, and Amy joined him there upon their marriage in 1828. Sarah Kirby soon journeyed from Long Island to aid her sister Amy in the care of her home and children; and the entire entourage moved on to Rochester in 1836. When Isaac gave up farming for butchering and then shopkeeping, Amy increased her activities in temperance and abolition campaigns. She was joined in this work by her sister Sarah, her daughter Mary, her aunt Phebe Willis, and her cousin Ann Willetts. Amy combined public activism with the rearing of five children in a household continually expanded by relatives, boarders, and free black and Irish servants. The Posts hosted local abolition, women's rights, and spiritualist circles as well as fugitive slaves and itinerant lecturers throughout the pre-Civil War period.

The Posts retained strong ties to the Quaker communities of Long Island and central New York. Many of their friends and fellow activists followed similar paths to Western New York and created a new Quaker community, knit together by associated religious and reform efforts and by intermarriage.[57] Quaker families from Rochester and the surrounding farming communities met at the Yearly Meeting of Congregational Friends in Waterloo, New York, to discuss religion, slavery, temperance, education, Indian rights, capital punishment, communitarian settlements, labor reform, and women's rights. Back in Rochester, these same men and women joined in the establishment of spiritualist circles, manual labor schools, and anti-tobacco campaigns while the women worked separately to organize women's rights conventions, a working women's protective union, and antislavery fairs.

The Posts and their co-workers rarely found acceptance in the city's centers of economic and political power. Most established themselves as shopkeepers, artisans, or farmers in the early 1830s. Many, including the Posts, fell on hard times at least once in the next decade; several changed occupations several times without ever improving their economic status; and a few joined in the California Gold Rush or other westward movements in search of a better living. At best, moral suasionists entered the lower rungs of Rochester's middling classes, but they did not have the ties to local centers of business and politics of similarly situated political abolitionist families. While marginal to Rochester's dominant political and commercial sectors, moral suasionists sought to challenge and penetrate the social conscience and thereby shape the political and economic power of those sectors. Female supporters of political abolitionists were indirectly linked to that sector through their male kin. Female moral suasionists had no such indirect ties; their influence would only be felt, they believed, if they announced their radical doctrines in bold and public voices. Yet because their ideas were likely to be rejected by local leaders, even had they been voiced by men, these women often turned to family, friends, and fellow reformers in Western New York and throughout the Northeast and Old Northwest to sustain their antislavery efforts.

The language and tactics of moral suasionist and political abolitionist women clearly reflect their contrasting social backgrounds, gender relations, and ideological perspectives on abolitionism. Moral suasionist women called on "all who have hearts to feel" to "come forward in the work of banishing slavery from our land" and to "be a 'light unto the world.' "[58] Political abolitionist women stated in equally "plain terms, the course they design[ed] to pursue": our "object shall be to raise funds for Anti-Slavery purposes."[59] Light to the world versus financier to the cause, direct action versus influence and support: these two opposing groups self-consciously and publically articulated their positions on women's proper role in abolitionism. The antislavery fair mentioned in the beginning of this essay is an especially useful vane for detecting differences among antislavery women. Though fairs were universally popular in female abolitionist circles, the style and arrangement of fairs reflected the markedly different backgrounds and values of their organizers.

The Rochester Anti-Slavery Sewing Circle was a democratically organized association of WNYASS women devoted to the work of managing antislavery fairs. The term circle reflected the egalitarian structure of the association. Announcements of fairs appeared with the names of all Sewing Circle members unadorned by titles of office. A secretary and president were selected periodically for the fulfillment of particular duties relating to a fair or convention, but even these offices were defined by a task to be performed rather than a position to be filled. While most activities relating to WNYASS fairs took place in Rochester, fair committees included women from surrounding towns; and in several of these towns, women also formed independent sewing circles. One impetus for the formation of these circles was the desire of WNYASS women to reach the largest number of potential antislavery converts. In the winter of 1848, the WNYASS sponsored fairs in at least fourteen villages. The following November, the Fair Committee announced that the antislavery "friends in Western New York have opened a store for the benefit of the cause in eleven villages in the vicinity of Rochester."[60]

Women advocates of political abolitionism in Rochester organized their fairs through the Rochester Ladies' Anti-Slavery Society, an association exclusively for women. Members generally belonged to no other antislavery society.[61] This Society was hierarchically organized; the nineteen original members elected ten officers from among themselves to run the association. Published reports and announcements were accompanied by lists of the officers in rank order. All officers and members of the RLASS were Rochester residents, and all fairs managed by them were held in the city. This centralization was encouraged by the RLASS's concern with raising funds and by members' centrality to Rochester's social and economic institutions. A few women from surrounding towns did provide goods for the fairs, but the most substantial extra-local contributions came from England, Ireland, and Scotland. Aid from these areas could be accepted without impinging on the centralization of RLASS efforts.

The sale of articles from Britain aided the RLASS in attracting a new class of local citizens to the cause. The RLASS felt "amply repaid" for its labors at the March, 1852 Anti-Slavery Fair because a "class of Rochester citizens were reached" by Douglass' antislavery appeal "who had, in all probability, never heard it before."[62] The particular class attracted is suggested by the Society's prolonged praise of the Fair's "most saleable" items: "finely wrought baby linen, the exquisite seaweed baskets, the drawings, the collection of Irish shells, and the beautiful embroidery."[63] In following years, they accompanied the sale of foreign goods "of surpassing beauty, richness, and elegance" with "eloquent and energetic" addresses by male abolitionists and "brilliant performances" on the "Piano Forte."[64] The dramatic difference from WNYASS fairs is indicated by the latter's 1847 appeal for articles "both useful and ornamental," including "eggs, butter, cheese, cream, turkeys, hams, dried beef, pickles, and fruit" and other goods "of small as well as large value."[65] The WNYASS women hoped that no one would "feel too poor, nor any too rich, to enlist in this holy cause" and asked for " the aid of men and women . . . the old and the young, the farmer, the mechanic, and the merchant."[66]

The desire of the RLASS to raise funds and of the WNYASS to raise moral sentiments was also reflected in their different concerns with social etiquette. Both groups stepped beyond the bounds of the dominant definition of women's proper sphere, but they presented their transgressions to the public in distinctly different manners. WNYASS women uniformly utilized their own first and last names in published reports and pronouncements without titles of marital status. They identified themselves repeatedly with "our sisters, crushed, abused, and bleeding under the lash" and believed that the "social mingling" of blacks and whites at antislavery fairs had "the effect to Kill prejudice."[67] WNYASS extended this mingling to social affairs and traveling though it "caused great dissatisfaction in the Rochester community."[68] As Mary Robbins Post wrote to her sister-in-law Amy, "we rejoice in the commotion for it gives signs of vitality."[69]

Such commotion interfered, however, with the RLASS's plan to obtain funds "devoted to the diffusion of Anti-Slavery Sentiments by means of the Press and Lecturer; to the relief of the suffering Fugitive, and for such other Anti-Slavery objects as may present themselves."[70] RLASS fairs raised five times as much money as those of the WNYASS. This pecuniary success was certainly tied in part to the RLASS's connections to leading families, connections nurtured by RLASS leaders' attention to social propriety whenever possible.[71] Thus, RLASS women generally published reports and announcements under their married names. They did socialize with black abolitionists and Julia Griffiths boarded with the Douglass family despite rumors of improprieties. Yet these women never openly advocated the social mingling of the races nor do they appear to have encouraged it at their fairs or elsewhere. Nowhere in print did RLASS women refer to enslaved women as their sisters. Indeed, reports of the RLASS agent working among ex-slaves in Virginia indicate a paternalistic rather than a sisterly posture toward the "enslaved race": "The Freed people are not all thrifty, neither have they all the ability to improve their condition. Such we must assist and endeavor to elevate in the social scale. Instruction and encouragement will do much for them."[72] RLASS women far surpassed most of their contemporaries in their attitudes toward race relations; yet to appeal to those contemporaries for funds, they had to walk a fine line between social commitment and social etiquette, aid to blacks and distance from them.

Differences between RLASS and WNYASS women in organization, appeals, and tactics were reflections of differences in their access to material resources as well as in the social bases of their activism. For instance, the "*Eating together* of 'Colored with White' " was a form of antislavery statement available to WNYASS women when fairs "came very short of realizing in a pecuniary point of view" the funds necessary for press and lecture campaigns.[73] The RLASS was not only considerably more successful than the WNYASS in raising funds at fairs but also drew upon greater familial economic resources. Thus, these women could mobilize the press and could bring key political and religious figures, such as Horace Greeley and Reverend Henry Ward Beecher, to Rochester to lecture. They were also able to fund fugitives' trips to Canada and to send food, clothing, and other goods to free blacks in Virginia. Moral suasionist women, in more limited economic circumstances, found it easier to offer a sustained antislavery commentary through their personal lifestyle than through the funding of antislavery projects. They ate sugar made from Massachusetts-grown rather than slave-produced beets, wore woolen rather than cotton clothing, sealed letters with antislavery wafers, and socialized in mixed racial company.[74]

Differences in access to material resources and in social bases had more than local import: they were translated into distinct political ideologies that linked local female abolitionism into national antislavery movements. Moral suasionists believed "that when the ear of the American people can be gained, the downfall of slavery in this republic is certain."[75] The goal of moral suasionists was to create a popular discourse on issues of national consequence and to articulate alternative social and political formations that would guarantee the broadest human freedoms. The concern with agitating the public mind allowed for the full participation of those—women, the poor, blacks—outside institutionalized forms of power. In turn, people structurally removed from such loci of power were likely to bring alternative visions of social order and social value to movements for social change.[76] These activists did not so much seek to gain power as to make the powerful responsive to a popular voice that itself advocated the broadest and most thoroughly democratic principles of governance.

For political abolitionists, it was "the National Constitution . . . adopted by the people of the United States" that would "secure . . . the blessings of Liberty."[77] To gain access to existing institutions, political abolitionists needed abundant material resources and popular support, but they could offer those structurally removed from political participation little in exchange for their efforts. Yet female members of Rochester's leading middle-class sector were willing to accept their own subordination in supporting the antislavery tactics of their male allies. For these women, the indirect benefits of male economic and political successes converged with the preachings of evangelical ministers and the teachings of popular literature: they were willing to sustain basic institutions that had rewarded their families well in the past if those institutions would guarantee fundamental human rights to blacks.

Moral suasionists sought to expose the contradictions posed by slavery in a democratic nation; political abolitionists sought to institutionalize a Constitutional resolution to those contradictions. Almost by definition, then, it was political abolitionists who claimed the final victory as the authors of a political emancipation. Yet moral suasionists had long asserted that "political action is only calculated to hold what moral suasion gains."[78] Moreover, as advocates of an unpopular cause, both moral suasion and political abolitionists began their campaigns by seeking to arouse the public in their own communities. As James Russell Lowell so eloquently wrote of antislavery agitators, "The public follows them step by step, occupying the positions they have successfully fortified and quitted, and it is necessary that they should keep in advance in order that people may not be shocked by waking up and finding themselves Abolitionists."[79]

Male political abolitionists increasingly distanced themselves both from agitation and from their local base as they perceived the possibilities of a national electoral victory: they invested their labors in emancipation by law. In supporting their male kin, RLASS women accepted the continued domination of politics by white males though they hoped that the religious and moral principles advocated by antislavery males would make politics more responsive to all. Moral suasionists gradually lost their dominance within the antislavery movement, rejecting participation in an electoral solution. Their continued strength lay in grass-roots organizing and the recruitment of the disfranchised and disaffected. Thus, moral suasion and political abolitionists continued to challenge each other as they challenged the larger society. Advocates, respectively, of agitation and reform, their efforts often overlapped. They could coexist, but the distinctive social bases that underlay their efforts nullified their 1843 call for "mutual co-operation" in the cause of abolition.[80]

Historian Gerda Lerner has claimed that women had a "peculiar relationship to political power" because of their history of disfranchisement. "Disfranchised groups in a democracy," she notes, "can hope to influence those holding political power by persuasion, by educational activities, and by exerting pressure in various forms."[81] Both groups of women abolitionists in Rochester employed pressure, education, and persuasion; both developed and refined grass-roots organizing and fund raising techniques—most notably in the form of petition campaigns and antislavery fairs—that extended the power of the disfranchised. However, the differences in their social and economic bases led them to direct that new-found power to different ends.

Political abolitionist women sought to make common cause with male voters by providing local educational and economic support. Their goal was to influence the content rather than the structure of a political system in which their male kin and neighbors seemed to be gaining power. Moral suasionist women sought alliances with the disfranchised and with white males who rejected existing political structures. Abolitionism was only one crusade through which they hoped to redefine political, indeed all power relations and to assure racial and sexual equality in the nation at large. Each group of female abolitionists expanded the human and financial resources of particular branches of the antislavery movement. Each also extended women's role in politics. RLASS women did so by demanding an auxiliary role in electoral campaigns focusing on antislavery issues; WNYASS women by working to reshape the structure of nineteenth-century politics by introducing methods of pressure and persuasion directly accessible to the disfranchised.

NOTES

1. Gerda Lerner, "The Political Activities of Antislavery Women," in Gerda Lerner, ed., *The Majority Finds Its Past: Placing Women in History* (New York: Oxford University Press, 1979), pp. 128, 114.

2. Female abolitionists are generally treated in biographical form or in works on Garrisonian abolitionism. The best material in this genre can be found in Blanche Glassman Hersh, *The Slavery of Sex: Feminist-Abolitionists in America* (Urbana: University of Illinois Press, 1978). See also, Ronald Walters, *Anti-Slavery Appeal* (Baltimore: Johns Hopkins University Press, 1976) and Lewis Perry, *Radical Abolitionism: Anarchy and the Government of God in Anti-Slavery Thought* (Ithaca: Cornell University Press, 1973). Virtually nothing on women appears in the extensive literature on political abolitionism that has been published in the past decade.

3. Whitney Cross, *The Burned-Over District: The Social and Intellectual History of Enthusiastic Religion in Western New York, 1800–1850* (Ithaca: Cornell University Press, 1950), p. 84. This study focuses on Rochester which was the center of Western New York's antislavery activity. It was the home of the Western New York Anti-Slavery Society and the *North Star* and a center of Liberty Party and women's antislavery leadership.

4. For a detailed discussion of the division of the American Anti-Slavery Society, see Aileen Kraditor, *Means and Ends in American Abolitionism: Garrison and His Critics on Tactics and Strategy, 1835–1850* (New York: Pantheon Books, 1969).

5. The attitudes of evangelical leaders to this division varied somewhat. Evangelical men seem to have predominated among those who left the Society though some, especially Free Will Baptists and Wesleyan Methodists, remained with Garrison. Among women, very few remained both evangelicals and Garrisonians. This pattern was clearly true for Rochester's evangelical Presbyterian congregations. The

records of the Free Will Baptists and Wesleyan Methodists are missing for this period, but ministers for other Baptist and Methodist churches as well as those of Presbyterian churches appear tied to political abolitionism as do the Unitarian ministers, Frederick Holland and William Henry Channing.

6. The existence of a black women's antislavery society was noted in *The Liberator*, March 8, 1834. A manuscript copy of the constitution of the first white women's antislavery society is available in the Samuel Drummond Porter Family Papers, University of Rochester, Rochester, New York.

7. See, especially, the reports of AASS agents in *The Liberator*, March 27 and April 10, 1840; January 29 and March 12, 1841; and August 5 and 12, September 2 and 30, 1842.

8. *The Liberator*, January 5, 1844.

9. *The Liberator*, July 24, 1840. Elon Galusha's wife was a directress of the RFASS in 1835 and reappears as a member of the RLASS in 1853. During the 1840s, she was active in the Female Charitable and the Female Moral Reform societies.

10. On developments in Rochester and Western New York, see Cross, *Burned-Over District;* Lee Benson, *The Concept of Jacksonian Democracy, New York as a Test Case* (Princeton: Princeton University Press, 1961); Blake McKelvey, *Rochester, the Water-Power City, 1812–1854* (Cambridge: Harvard University Press, 1945); Paul Johnson, *A Shopkeeper's Millenium: Society and Revivals in Rochester, New York, 1815–1854* (New York: Hill and Wang, 1978); and James McElroy, "Social Control and Romantic Reform in Antebellum America: The Case of Rochester, New York," *New York History* 58 (January 1977): 17–46. The Erie Canal was opened as far as Rochester in 1822 which initiated a population and economic boom.

11. Quoted in *The Liberator*, March 8, 1834.

12. See Table 8.1, p. 211.

13. Mrs. Jonathan Child to Mrs. Sarah D. Fish, May 14, 1835, Fish Family Papers, University of Rochester, Rochester, New York. Mrs. Fish, the one Hicksite Quaker known to have joined the RFASS, became a leader in the WNYASS in the 1840s.

14. RFASS, Constitution, Ms., [1835], Porter Family Papers.

15. Petitions HR25A-Hl.8 (January 30, 1837) and LC Box #83 (September 19, 1837), National Archives, Washington, D.C. I wish to thank Judith Wellman and Paul Johnson for copies of antislavery petitions sent to Congress from Rochester and Monroe County.

16. The exact cause of the demise of the RFASS is unclear. I would speculate that it was related to the national debates over women's proper role in abolitionism, which converged with a decline in revivalism and an increase in evangelical ministers' disapproval of female public activism. No autonomous white women's antislavery society reappears until the RLASS in 1851; no information on a black women's antislavery society appears in this period except for the notice of two antislavery fairs held by the Union Sewing Society in 1848 and 1850. Whether this is an autonomous women's society is uncertain. See the *North Star,* July 21, 1848, and December 5, 1850.

17. Washington Street Presbyterian Church housed several antislavery meetings during the 1830s and 1840s, many arranged by church members such as Samuel D. Porter. However, as Quakers and women became more prominent in local antislavery circles, these churches began to refuse the use of their rooms for such assemblies.

Moreover, arrangement committees composed of Quakers tended to select civic rather than religious sites for their meetings.

18. The convergence of evangelical political abolitionists and Quaker moral suasionists in the WNYASS and the dominance of the latter can be traced through the proceedings of annual meetings printed in *The Liberator* between 1843 and 1850.

19. Proceedings of the founding meeting are printed in *The Liberator,* January 6, 1843. See also March 24, 1843, January 5, 1844, February 28, 1845, July 24, 1846 as well as frequent reports in the *North Star.*

20. The sample size for each organization is relatively small because I only utilized information on women who were significantly involved in each organization's activity—serving as officers, managing antislavery fairs, and publishing their names in the press as members of the organization. I have tried to balance the size of the sample by collecting a wide range of data on each individual and by using only those statistics in my analysis where a distinct difference is visible. Moreover, the argument regarding the differences among these three groups of women are reinforced by materials from a study of women's activism in Rochester over a fifty year period that examines women in over a dozen reform organizations and movements. See, Nancy A. Hewitt, "Women's Activism and Social Change: The Case of Rochester, New York, 1822–1872" (Ph.D. diss., University of Pennsylvania, 1981).

21. The absence of Free Will Baptist and Wesleyan Methodist records could only increase the evangelical cast of the RFASS since there are no unknown religious affiliations among WNYASS women. Reform Presbyterian includes all those in Presbyterian churches swept or created by Finney's revivals of 1830–31 and who took stronger antislavery stands as a result. First Presbyterian Church was affected by Finney's revivals, but most Finney converts from that church left it in 1836 to found the Bethel Free Church so I have listed membership in First Presbyterian separately. Three of the Reform Presbyterians joined the WNYASS; two of these left the Presbyterian church in 1842 and the third did so in 1845. In Table 8.1, the total number of activist husbands is smaller than the sum of abolition and other reform husbands because several men were active in more than one cause.

22. *Proceedings of the Yearly Meeting of Congregational Friends, held at Waterloo, N.Y., from the 3rd to the 5th of the Sixth month, inclusive, 1850, with an appendix* (Auburn, N.Y.: Henry Oliphant, 1850), pp. 48–49.

23. *Report of the Woman's Rights Convention, Held at Seneca Falls, N.Y., July 19th and 20th, 1848* (Rochester: John Dick, North Star Office, 1848).

24. The ministers of the Second, Third, Bethel, and Washington Street Presbyterian, the Second Baptist, the Congregational, and the Unitarian churches favored political abolitionism in the 1840s, though there is evidence that a few of them also attended annual meetings of the WNYASS. They did not, however, serve as officers of the WNYASS or speak on its lecture circuit. The absence of some Baptist and Methodist records for Rochester creates more serious gaps in the tracing of local antislavery men than women since women are frequently identified by religious affiliation in a number of other sources, most notably the records of the Rochester Female Charitable Society, University of Rochester, Rochester, New York.

25. Samuel Drummond Porter to Gerrit Smith, March 14, 1845, Gerrit Smith Papers, Syracuse University, Syracuse, New York.

26. The proceedings of the meeting at which Thompson spoke are printed in the *North Star* January 23, 1851. See *The Liberator,* March 28, 1851, for a report on

"a series of abusive and insulting tirades against Mr. Thompson" in the (Rochester) *Daily Advertiser*. The Fugitive Slave Act was of particular concern to abolitionists in areas such as Rochester through which many fugitive slaves passed on their way to Canada.

27. On the Ladies' Committee, see the *North Star,* April 24, 1851. On the Union Anti-Slavery Sewing Society, see n.16.

28. No reference was made in notices about the Thompson Festival to the co-operation of black and white women. Black women's presence on the committee was determined by matching the names and addresses of committee members with city directories which listed blacks and whites separately.

29. See Samuel D. Porter to Gerrit Smith, March 14, 1845 and Frederick Douglass to Gerrit Smith, February 13, 1852, Gerrit Smith Papers. On Douglass' willingness to vote for Fremont in 1856 on grounds of expediency, see Frederick Douglass to Gerrit Smith, August 13, 1856, Gerrit Smith Papers.

30. Julia Griffiths to Samuel D. Porter, [1852], Porter Family Papers; Julia Griffiths to Gerrit Smith, February 2, [1852], Gerrit Smith Papers.

31. Julia Griffiths to Gerrit Smith, August 26, [1852], Gerrit Smith Papers.

32. Frederick Douglass to Mrs. Samuel D. Porter, in "Circular, the First Report of the Rochester Ladies' Anti-Slavery Sewing Society," 1852, Porter Family Papers. This letter was also published in *Frederick Douglass' Paper,* April 7, 1852.

33. Sarah Hallowell to Frederick Douglass, in *Frederick Douglass' Paper,* April 22, 1852.

34. On sample size, see n.20.

35. On definitions of religious affiliation and missing records, see n.21. Eastern New York nativity could be distinguished from Western New York and Long Island nativity on the 1855 New York State Census. Eastern New York communities tended to follow the patterns of commercial New England villages while Western New York and Long Island communities remained strongholds of agrarianism in the early decades of the nineteenth century.

36. As noted above, political abolitionists were not generally members of the city's elite families, but they were linked to them by kinship, residence, religious affiliation, and business and professional partnerships.

37. I use the term "commercial capitalism" to refer to the development of market mechanisms and wage labor systems that initiated economic and social changes in New England villages prior to the emergence of fully developed industrial capitalism.

38. Non-Quaker women who were moral suasionists tended to come from similar occupational and economic groups as their Quaker co-workers. Professional status among husbands of WNYASS members meant careers as professional reformers—editors, agents, or lecturers—while among RLASS families, it meant careers in medicine, law, or the ministry. For a provocative analysis of the relations between modes of production, access to community and kin resources, and women's roles in society, see Karen Sacks, *Sisters and Wives: The Past and Future of Sexual Equality* (Westport, Conn.: Greenwood Press, 1979).

39. On Quakers' community and kin-related welfare systems, see Robert J. Doherty, *The Hicksite Separation: A Sociological Analysis of Religious Schism in Early Nineteenth Century America* (New Brunswick, N.J.: Rutgers University Press, 1967). Doherty explicitly distinguishes between a traditional agrarian Quaker set of social relations and beliefs, held by those who became Hicksite, and a more urbane and commercial set of relations and beliefs held by those who became Orthodox Quakers

in Philadelphia. This same division occurs in Rochester, and only the Hicksites continue a strong antislavery position. See also Rufus M. Jones, *Later Periods of Quakerism*, 2 vols. (1921; rpt., Westport, Conn.: Greenwood Press, 1970). The minutes of the Milton Monthly Meeting, the Rochester Monthly Meeting, the Farmington Quarterly Meeting, and the Genesee Yearly Meeting (all Hicksite Meetings the last two of which contained the Rochester Monthly Meeting) provide numerous primary examples. All are housed at the Haviland Records Room, New York City.

40. See David Rothman, *The Discovery of the Asylum: Social Order and Disorder in the New Republic* (Boston: Little, Brown & Co., 1971); Michael Katz, *The Irony of Early School Reform: Educational Reform in Mid-Nineteenth Century Massachusetts* (Cambridge: Harvard University Press, 1968); Barbara Welter, "The Cult of True Womanhood, 1820–1860," *American Quarterly* 18 (Summer 1966): 151–64, 171–74; and Gerda Lerner, "The Lady and the Mill Girl: Changes in the Status of Women in the Age of Jackson," in Lerner, ed., *The Majority Finds Its Past*, pp. 15–30. For a particularly cogent primary source on the new religious definitions of women's role, see the Pastoral Letter of the Congregational Clergy of Massachusetts, in *The Liberator*, August 11, 1837.

41. *Proceedings of the Yearly Meeting of Congregational Friends . . . 1850*, p. 6.

42. Important changes did occur in evangelical churches, including an increase in lay participation and a diffusion of authority to local congregations, as a result of the Second Great Awakening. The point here is that the relative improvements thus made in women's position still placed them in considerably more subordinate positions than those of their Hicksite and Congregational sisters.

43. *Proceedings of the Yearly Meeting of Congregational Friends . . . 1850*, pp. 45, 15. Spiritualist doctrines, accepted by many Congregational, Friends, including the Posts, were highly anti-authoritarian and democratic. On spiritualism in Rochester, see Franklin W. Clark, "The Rochester Rappers," Ms., Rochester Public Library, Rochester, New York, and Adelbert Cronise, "The Beginnings of Modern Spiritualism In and Near Rochester," *Rochester Historical Society Publications 5* (1943): 1–22.

44. Quarterly and Yearly Meetings and Meetings of Ministers and Elders did not have considerable authority within certain sectors of the Society of Friends. The Hicksite and Orthodox Friends divided, in part over this issue, in 1828 with the Hicksites seeking to maintain greater autonomy of and democracy within local meetings. A second split in 1848–49 between Hicksite and Congregational Friends found the Congregational Friends taking the more autonomous and democratic position.

45. The multivalence of terms such as federalism and republicanism is crucial for social activists who seek to employ American political traditions as vehicles for social change. For a discussion of this issue and its relation to religious revivalism, see Harry S. Stout, "Religion, Communications, and the Ideological Origins of the American Revolution," *William and Mary Quarterly* 34 (October 1977): 538–41.

46. Samuel D. Porter to Gerrit Smith, March 14, 1845, Gerrit Smith Papers. See also, Isaac Post to Amy Post, 1850, Isaac and Amy Post Papers, University of Rochester, Rochester, New York.

47. While Quaker moral suasionists conformed to many existing political and religious forms, their willingness to reject or defy state mandates meant that for them institutional legitimacy rested not on natural authority but on popular will.

48. Race is also a crucial issue here, but available sources do not speak to this concern among Rochester's antislavery women.

49. The best description of this ideology and its emergence remains Barbara Welter's "The Cult of True Womanhood, 1820–1860," *American Quarterly* 18 (1966): 151–74.

50. Little direct information is available on the reading habits of Rochester's abolitionist women, so assumptions about the cultural milieu of which they were a part must be based on general patterns for this period. We do know that evangelical sermons would have stressed certain themes that were relatively untouched in Congregational Quaker meetings. We also know that the Post women were familiar with the feminist writings of Mary Wollstonecroft and Margaret Fuller, writings that were never mentioned in the family and personal papers of political abolitionist women.

51. While not all female moral suasionists were Quakers, most were. Of the seven who began as Presbyterians and played leading roles in the WNYASS, five left the church or were excommunicated from it. While we cannot be sure of the relationship of their leaving the church to their antislavery activity, we can be sure that these women did not accept the tenets of evangelical religion as fully as their Presbyterian sisters who worked in the RLASS and maintained their church membership.

52. The Porter and Post families were chosen because of the extensiveness of their involvement in local antislavery societies and the availability of family papers.

53. Other antislavery congregations founded in this period were the Free Will Baptist Church (1845) and the Wesleyan Methodist Church (1843). The First Unitarian Society was founded as an antislavery congregation under the leadership of Liberty Party founder Myron Holley in 1840. For an explicit statement of the Porter's change of church membership as a response to church's stands on antislavery, see Samuel D. Porter to the Pastor and Session of the Washington Street Presbyterian Church, September 29, 1845, Porter Family Papers.

54. Here I am referring to local political power only in the limited sense of city officers and local leadership in one of the two major political parties.

55. The Unitarian congregation brought several antislavery leaders to Rochester in the 1840s and 1850s. Some moral suasionist Quakers also attended Unitarian meetings during the tenure of antislavery ministers such as Frederick Holland and William Henry Channing, though they also retained their membership in the Congregational Friends. Samuel Porter's father and his family had joined the Unitarian Church in Philadelphia where it was a stronghold of abolitionism. They retained that affiliation in Rochester rather than joining the other Porters at Washington Street Presbyterian Church.

56. Though we cannot be sure of the religious affiliations of all RLASS members, the early officers were almost exclusively Presbyterians or Unitarians.

57. For example, the Post's daughter, Mary, married a Hicksite Quaker from Pennsylvania while Sarah married another Pennsylvania Quaker and, upon his death, a Quaker neighbor from Long Island.

58. "Address to the Anti-Slavery Women of Western New York," (Rochester) *Daily Democrat*, April 4, 1848. This address was reprinted numerous times in the *North Star*.

59. "Circular, The First Report of the Rochester Ladies' Anti-Slavery Sewing Society," 1852.

60. *North Star,* November 16, 1849.

61. The RLASS, while supportive of male political antislavery efforts, was not formally auxiliary to any other society. Two or three members of the RLASS did serve as officers in the New York State Anti-Slavery Society in the early 1850s, but they appear to have been token rather than active members in the predominantly male society.

62. "Circular, the First Report of the Rochester Ladies' Anti-Slavery Sewing Society," 1852.

63. Ibid.

64. *Frederick Douglass' Paper,* December 30, 1853.

65. *North Star,* December 3, 1847.

66. "Address to the Anti-Slavery Women of Western New York."

67. *North Star,* January 14, 1848; William C. Nell to Amy Post, July 3, 1850, Post Family Papers. Nell is here quoting from a letter that was sent to him by Amy Post.

68. Mary Robbins Post to Isaac and Amy Post, [1849], Post Family Papers.

69. Mary Robbins Post to Isaac and Amy Post, [1848], Post Family Papers. The writer is here referring to commotion within Hicksite Quaker meetings over abolitionism, but such sentiments occur repeatedly in the correspondence of moral suasionists. See also Anti-Slavery Fair Report, [1850], Ts., Post Family Papers.

70. "Circular, the First Report of the Rochester Ladies' Anti-Slavery Sewing Society," 1852.

71. For further evidence of the RLASS's concern with such connections, see Julia Griffiths to Gerrit Smith, May 3, 1852 and October 26, 1852, Gerrit Smith Papers.

72. Rochester Ladies' Anti-Slavery Society, *Thirteenth Annual Report* (Rochester: Rochester Democrat Steam Printing House, 1864).

73. William C. Nell to Amy Post, July 3, 1850, and Amy Post to Frederick Douglass, February 2, 1850, Post Family Papers.

74. Walters, *Anti-Slavery Appeal,* notes the importance of such badges of loyalty in strengthening commitments of abolitionists. The Post Family Papers and the *North Star* provide numerous examples of these moral suasionist life-styles. This is not to say that economic support and life-style politics are exclusive of each other but simply to recognize that moral suasionists' limited economic resources encouraged their adoption of political expressions not dependent on access to funds.

75. *North Star,* January 7, 1848.

76. Anthropologist Victor Turner has focused on the role of marginal and liminal figures in defining alternative vision of social and moral order. See particularly his *Forest of Symbols: Aspects of Ndembu Ritual* (Ithaca: Cornell University Press, 1967) and *Dramas, Fields, and Metaphors: Symbolic Action in Human Society* (Ithaca: Cornell University Press, 1974), chaps. 1, 6, 7.

77. "Circular, the First Report of the Rochester Ladies' Anti-Slavery Sewing Society," 1852.

78. Isaac Post to Amy Post, May 5, 1844, Post Family Papers.

79. Quoted in Howard Zinn, "Abolitionists, Freedom Riders, and the Tactics of Agitation," in Martin Duberman, ed., *Anti-Slavery Vanguard: New Essays on the Abolitionists* (Princeton: Princeton University Press, 1965), p. 432.

80. See n.8.

81. Lerner, "The Political Activities of Antislavery Women," p. 114.

9

"Pious Fellowship" and Modernity: A Psychosocial Interpretation

Lawrence J. Friedman

In 1956 David Donald published an essay on first generation immediatist abolitionists that evoked one of the most heated controversies the American historical profession has experienced. The essay characterized immediatism as "the anguished protest of an aggrieved class against a world they never made." For Donald, immediatists were representatives of an old Northern rural mercantile ruling elite who were being displaced by a new urbanized and sophisticated manufacturing and commercial elite. They embraced immediatism as an emotional protest against their loss of status more than out of fundamental concerns for black bondsmen in the South. Thus, their antislavery appeal was largely a quest for the restoration of social status and personal power. The quest was irrationally clothed within an appeal for Negro freedom.[1]

Unlike Avery Craven, Hazel Wolf, Arthur Lloyd, and other historians of the 1930's, 1940's, and early 1950's who had advanced somewhat similar characterizations, Donald made an effort at systematic proof. He advanced a clear hypothesis—that status loss provoked an almost fanatical involvement in immediatism—and he attempted to sustain that hypothesis by analyzing the social and leadership characteristics of 106 first generation immediatist leaders. Thus, unlike his predecessors, he gave methodology oriented historians like Robert Skotheim and Robert Doherty something that they could evaluate. They charged that Donald failed to identify his abolitionist leaders or to detail the relationship of leaders to rank-and-file. In addition, they claimed that status loss did not necessarily have to lead to embrace of immediatism and that Donald could only prove this hypothesis if he demonstrated, through a non-abolitionist control group, that declining status was the key independent variable in the embrace of immediatism.[2]

During the 1960's and early 1970's, the unfavorable response to Donald and his predecessors continued. In time, an altogether new characterization of the immediatists emerged. The group of historians who forged this characterization came to be called "neoabolitionists." Martin Duberman was identified as their major "spokesman." He was sustained by Gerald Sorin, Louis Ruchames, Fawn Brodie, James Stewart, and others. By the early 1970's it was clear that the "neoabolitionist" interpretation had gained hegemony over the Donald thesis among academic historians. Whereas Donald had charged that the abolitionists had been displaced from the leadership positions of their fathers by new national elites and that in "anguish" they had embraced immediatism, the "neoabolitionists" placed immediatists in the forefront of the basic institutional changes within antebellum America. Not at all displaced much less frustrated, they embraced immediatism out of a natural and healthy moral commitment to eradicate the horrors of slavery and to promote civil rights.[3]

The major difference between the Donald thesis and the "neoabolitionist" characterization was therefore over the "location" of immediatists in antebellum social processes—whether they lagged behind or promoted the basic institutional changes of the period. More specifically, the difference concerned the degree to which immediatists partook in the modernization of antebellum society. These were decades when sundry modernization processes became irreversibly established in the nation, particularly in the Northern states, and they largely dictated who ruled and who was "displaced." New and relatively efficient national and regional institutions of production and distribution were established, ranging from heavy industries and railroads to government bureaucracies and regimented prison systems. Those at or near their helm exerted shaping influences upon the society-at-large and evidenced what social psychologists call "modern personalities." They sought out new experiences, ideas, and friendships in diverse and distant locations over which the new institutions held sway. Whereas those less involved with these institutions ("traditionalists") tended to stick to their own local communities where they passively accepted locally rooted dogmas and social hierarchies, "modernists" who took the lead in the new and complex antebellum institutions of production and distribution transcended their communities. They energetically absorbed new information, prized efficacious deployment of time and resources, craved long-term planning in both their personal and their more public activities, and sought to cooperate with other "modernists" in achieving calculable long-range goals. Because they prized cooperation and efficiency, these antebellum "modernists" could not have been Donald's obsessive moralists. They were more moderate and tolerant in their behavior. In order to achieve calculable ends, they empathized with and worked alongside others who differed from them. Moreover, since "modernists" were in the forefront of social and economic change, they could not have been Donald's displaced and alienated elite. Nor did they look nostalgically and romantically to an earlier day when their fathers had dominated society. Rather, most antebellum "modernists" probably influenced the course of events more than their fathers had.[4]

What, then, was the political and social "location" of most first generation immediatists? Were they Donald's displaced ruling elite or were they "modernists" in the forefront of the basic institutional changes that antebellum society was experiencing? We shall suggest that they felt like Donald's displaced elites, but, as "neoabolitionist" historians have asserted, their social characteristics and values were those of "modernists." Their self-images as "pious Christian fellows" and their convictions that they were failing in their religious mission to uplift their immoral and hostile countrymen made them feel like an "aggrieved class" protesting in "a world they never made." This was true whether they were Garrisonians who deployed person to person moral suasion, church-centered Tappanites, or political abolitionists who resorted to antislavery third parties and elections. And yet, as we shall also assert, they had patently "modern" social characteristics and values—again regardless of their moral suasion, church, or political antislavery proclivities. Consequently, Donald and the "neoabolitionists" would seem to have overreacted in assaulting each other's interpretations, while historians generally would appear to have overstressed distinctions between Garrisonians, Tappanites, and political abolitionists.

The "neoabolitionist" assumption that first generation immediatists were "modernists" in the forefront of major antebellum institutional change finds strong confirmation in their work experiences. Whether Garrisonians, Tappanites, or political abolitionists, historians have rather conclusively demonstrated that they tended to be moderately prosperous and rather innovative artisans, tradesmen, and manufacturers whose daily work lives were generally tied to the new Northern urban industrial and manufacturing economy rather than to the locally based and declining mercantile economy or to traditional household industry. Consider, for example, those who resided in New York State where scholarship on the social characteristics of abolitionists is the most advanced. According to this scholarship, immediatist leaders were generally well educated, moderately prosperous, and resided in urban centers where they pursued the most influential and innovative occupations that were available. This was true regardless of their proclivity toward moral suasion, church activism, or third party politics. In Rochester, it was assuredly the case with immediatists-at-large, not simply leaders. Roughly 75 percent were professionals, proprietors, clerks, and skilled laborers, and most in these jobs were deeply involved in the processes that were turning the city into a major manufacturing center. Those who changed occupations generally shifted from blue-collar to white-collar jobs and moved upward within the white-collar ranks toward more highly esteemed callings. In New York City artisans and shopkeepers tied to the new industrial and manufacturing economy constituted a majority of those who signed petitions during the early 1830's for the destruction of slavery in the District of Columbia. It is also well to note that the upstate townships that sent most antislavery petitions to Congress during the late 1830's were comparatively well established and prosperous rural communities. Proportionately more people in these townships worked in manufacturing and industry related trade than in townships that did not send petitions. Indeed, Paris township—a center of Garrisonian, Tappanite, and political abolitionist activity in the upstate area—had a considerably higher percentage of people working in commercial, manufacturing, and professional fields linked to emerging industrial and commercial patterns than most other upstate rural townships of comparable size.[5]

Although scholarship on work characteristics of first generation immediatists in cities and towns outside of New York is not as extensive, it tends to follow the pattern of the Empire State. Moreover, as scholars accumulate data on the social characteristics of individual immediatists in all sections of the North, they are finding additional corroboration of the "neoabolitionist" claim that immediatists labored in callings linked to the most rapidly modernizing areas of the regional economy. Finally, the nature of this labor did not correlate, in any consistent way, with the immediatist's proclivities toward Garrisonian, Tappanite, or political abolitionist allegiances.[6]

With these types of work experiences, it is no surprise that first generation immediatists displayed "modernist" attitudes. They frequently lauded the latest technological innovations and industrial achievements. "Hurrah for the Atlantic cable!" Garrison cheered in 1858. "I bless the invention of Telegraphs," echoed his Boston Clique colleague Ellis Gray Loring. Central New York Liberty party immediatist Abishai Scofield was fascinated with the sewing machine, studied it extensively, and predicted that "there are yet great improvements to be made." Whittier, another Liberty party supporter, characterized the transformation of Lowell into a heavy manufacturing town as "a miracle, neither more or less."[7] Often immediatists proposed innovations of a patently "modernist" character. Lysander Spooner offered, for example, a new and more efficient national "system of paper currency," Samuel Sewall proposed a national debt collection system to give creditors better legal protection against out of state debtors, Roberts Vaux suggested dividing Pennsylvania into public school districts in the interests of organizational efficiency, and F. Julius LeMoyne recommended mass importations of Spanish sheep to enhance national wool production. Indeed, this patently "modernistic" perspective with its stress on innovation, technology, manufacturing, efficiency, and trans-community communication was very basic to most first generation immediatist criticisms of the Southern slave system. For them, the "peculiar institution" seemed antithetical to "modernist" values. It discouraged innovative agricultural techniques, it retarded industrial growth, and it destroyed "ingenuity and enterprise."[8]

Thoroughly "modernist" in their everyday work lives and in many of their attitudes, it is not surprising that first generation immediatists structured their abolitionist activities along lines that tended to reflect "modernist" values. Whether Garrisonians, Tappanites, or political abolitionists, they did this in two basic ways. First, they bypassed the traditional families that had run local Northern communities for generations and took their message directly to the constituents of those communities.[9] Second, they contoured their diverse antislavery efforts to reflect centralization, efficiency, and planning. The purpose of the annual meeting of the American Anti-Slavery Society was to adopt broad policies for affiliated state organizations. But the AASS Executive Committee became the organizational power center when the annual meeting was not in session. It provided central direction and coordination of policies that were to be implemented on the state and local level, thereby precluding costly duplications. The national Agency Committee was also crucial in creating central direction and efficiency. This committee saw to it that AASS agents were appointed, paid, trained, and dispersed throughout the North to spread the immediatist message and to implement national organizational policies. By the late 1830's a number of jurisdictional squabbles erupted between AASS state affiliates on the one hand and the national Executive and Agency Committees on the other. When political and Tappanite abolitionists broke off cooperation with the Garrisonians in 1840 and left the AASS, the state affiliates filled the power gap; they came to bypass the national committees as power centers. Nonetheless, most state antislavery organizations, whether Garrisonian, Tappanite, or political abolitionist, went on to stress centralized direction over their own local affiliates in the name of efficiency.[10]

Beyond these similarities, however, it was apparent by the early 1840's that Garrisonians and political abolitionists differed in the way they channeled "modernist" abolitionist activities. Garrisonians proved to be somewhat more adept at deploying the new antebellum mass communications industry that was directed at a new national consumer market. On a considerably larger scale than those political abolitionists who interrogated major party candidates and went on to organize the Liberty party, they availed themselves of reduced postal rates, the steam press, cheap modes of paper production, the mass production of print, and free sample copies of publications to induce regular subscriptions. With these avenues and techniques, the Garrisonians produced and distributed an almost endless flow of low cost newspapers, pamphlets, and circulars throughout the country. To be sure, Liberty party political abolitionists had learned about many of these new mass communication strategies when they associated with Garrisonians in the 1830's and often deployed them in their party ventures of the 1840's. However, unlike Garrisonians, they tended to confine their printed distributions to surrounding towns and countryside. More fundamentally, they prized mass communications less than the modern techniques of political party organization. Like those Democrats and Whigs who helped to forge the second party system, Liberty party abolitionists availed themselves of a highly rationalized and centralized organizational structure. State, town, ward, and district committees were subordinated to a national Liberty committee that exercised "general care and oversight" of all party funds, campaigns, and conventions. Moreover, like their more innovative Democratic and Whig rivals, Liberty men proved most skilled at deploying new mass political "advertisement" techniques to attract voters. They drafted popular platform planks, sought out attractive candidates, invoked appealing emotional slogans, and sometimes skirted divisive issues. If Garrisonians showed their countrymen precisely what could be done with the revolution in printing technology, political abolitionists demonstrated what was to be done with the most innovative organizational and tactical features of the second party system.[11]

The fact that first generation immediatists of all varieties worked in "modernist" callings where they evidenced "modernist" attitudes and went on to structure their antislavery ventures along "modernist" lines involving innovative techniques plus centralization, coordination, and efficiency seems to provide overwhelming support for the characterization of "neoabolitionist" historians. Their assumption that immediatists were in the forefront of antebellum (especially Northern) modernization currents appears undeniable. How, then, can there be any validity in David Donald's claim that these same immediatists were "aggrieved" and displaced local elites who offered "anguished protest" to defy "a world they never made?"

The Donald thesis can be rescued if it is modified to concede the obvious fact the immediatists were modernizers and not socially displaced remnants of a bygone era. Overhauled in this way, the thesis comes to concern immediatists' sensibilities rather than their actual social standings—that they felt themselves "aggrieved" and estranged and were inwardly compelled to issue "anguished protest" against the ills about them. This modification of the thesis can readily be sustained when we consider the cravings by first generation immediatists for both personal piety and the cordial fellowship of missionary reformers—cravings that were not always shared by other antebellum "modernists." The quest for pious missionary fellowship gave them sensibilities that made them cry out in "anguish" against a society that owing to its moral insensitivities did not seem to be of their own making despite their "modernist" propensities.

One clear sign that immediatists, as "pious fellows," often had different sensibilities than most other "modernists" was in their zealous qualities (i.e., their piety). Effective coordination of specialized efforts requires participants in "modernist" institutional activity to have moderate temperaments; they must be capable of reaching their fellow workers. Otherwise, abrasive conflict results, coordination dissipates, and efficiency is impaired. Not even "neoabolitionist" historians have attributed moderate temperaments to most

first generation immediatists. Rather, even these historians have acknowledged that they had strong millenarian goals and imagined themselves God's
agents assigned to uplift immoral peoples and sinful practices with unyielding
missionary zeal. There was to be no moderating of God's demands. The
Lord's missionary had, of necessity, to be zealous.

Because antebellum Northern "modernists" did much to shape the institutional developments about them, very few that historians have studied
felt estranged from those developments. First generation immediatists were
exceptions, and this points to a second personality characteristic that singled
them out. Succinctly put, a great many of them felt distant from the society
about them or, as Donald would put it, they felt displaced. This was predictable in view of the massive hostility that they faced in the early years
of the immediatist crusade, from verbal chastisement to social ostracism
and mob assaults, combined with the continuing willingness of their fellow
Northerners to temporize with slaveholding and other "sins." Reacting to
these adversities, many immediatists withdrew into the sanctuary of small
informal intimacy clusters like the Boston Clique, the circle of central New
York Liberty men that gathered about Gerrit Smith's Peterboro estate, and
Lewis Tappan's intimacy cluster of New York City-Oberlin evangelical
associates. As they embraced immediatism and sought sanctuary in these
sorts of small intimacy groups of the truly pious or, as Charles Follen called
them, "worlds in ourselves and in each other," they felt increasingly estranged from their evangelical missionary colleagues. This was because their
colleagues in temperance, Bible distribution, and other benevolent reform
enterprises vacillated on the slavery issue and rarely came to their defense.[12]

This broad sense of estrangement seemed to provide a third and even
more important distinction between immediatists as devout missionaries
and other Northern "modernists." Because they felt decidedly at odds with
the world about them, they frequently juxtaposed the regrettable conditions
of the present against nostalgic romanticizations of the past when society
seemed simpler and less immoral. This represented their most decided revolt
against modernity. Romantic exaltation of a simpler, pre-modern existence
was no random or occasional occurrence. The researcher regularly uncovers
such references. Although, for example, first generation immediatists tended
to reside in urban areas, they persistently exalted the pristine virtues of
country Calvinism—the world of their fathers. This was particularly true
of Liberty party supporters like Lewis and Arthur Tappan and Joshua Leavitt
and of Garrisonians like Henry Wright and Oliver Johnson. One also detects
this romanticization of a more traditional society when James Mott, successful Philadelphia merchant, urged Friends to "return to the simple doctrine of Quakerism, as believed in and inculcated by George Fox" and retain
their old "peculiarity of dress, and address." Despite the financial success
of his complex and increasingly troublesome merchant trade, Mott exalted
the happy farmer free of debt who "does not know how to write his name!

A person thus situated knows little of the anxiety attendant upon a mercantile life. . . . I say let those who have been brought up in the country, stay there." Similarly, Edmund Quincy blamed the depression of 1857 upon the emerging corporation-centered manufacturing system, which was "false and hollow" and had overproduced. Hopefully, Quincy added, the depression would sweep away corporations and return businesses to the individual or small partner proprietorships that had been dominant during his younger years. Lydia Maria Child and Angelina Grimké romanticized "ancient nations" and societies where people lived "spontaneously good, knew truth by intuition, lived in perfect equality, and had no need of laws, or labour." In time, unfortunately, Christianity and "Civilization" came increasingly to require "entire suppression of the instincts and affections." True instinctive religious piety was thereby destroyed, people were enslaved, and misery had come to characterize modern social existence.[13]

The frequency of such immediatist exaltations of mythic pre-modern conditions, their unmistakable sense of estrangement from the rapidly modernizing society about them, and their patently immoderate conduct all go to demonstrate, then, that abolitionists as pious missionaries, differed fundamentally from many other Northern "modernists." Although they were active in antebellum modernizing processes and built antislavery organizations along "modernist" lines, their experiences as devoted missionaries afforded them experiences that most other "modernists" did not share. These experiences were the basis for certain unique personality features. Thus, it is important to qualify the contention of "neoabolitionist" historians that immediatists were "modernizers." There is a good measure of truth in Donald's assertion that immediatists felt distant from, distinct, and aggrieved by "the world" about them. That "world" had rejected their pious plea for immediate emancipation, it continued to temporize with liquor consumption and other "sins," and it had encouraged mobsters who had assaulted their persons and their property. Therefore, if we treat the Donald thesis as an explanation for immediatist subjective sensibilities, it becomes quite compatible with the "neoabolitionist" finding that they were "modernists." Although decidedly "modernist," immediatists had a pious missionary zeal that tended to make them depart from their "modernist" contemporaries in a number of important essentials. As devout evangelical reformers, they were "modernists" with a difference. That difference counted for much.

First generation immediatists were not simply pious missionary reformers. They were "pious fellows" and desperately sought to convert and gregariously embrace others. Rapport with other Northerners with broadly similar goals was crucial to them. Between the late 1830's, when the fiercest forms of anti-abolitionist hostility receded in the North, and the end of the Civil War, when abolitionists were exalted as heroes, this rapport was gradually effected. Our present task is to suggest how it came about. This is a crucial question, for it probes a fundamental transformation in immediatist social psychology—how they became more gregarious and perhaps somewhat less devout in their general sensibilities.

George Fredrickson's important 1965 book, *The Inner Civil War,* moves us a long way toward an answer. Much of the book concerns what Fredrickson calls antebellum "prophets of progress," who were first generation immediatists (Garrisonian, Tappanite, and political). In the course of the Civil War, Fredrickson demonstrates, these "prophets" came, more and more, to champion greater efficiencies and energy in the conduct of the federal war effort. In order to conquer the Confederacy quickly and expeditiously, they championed reforms within federal bureaucracies and the Union Army in the direction of greater centralization and planning. These reforms would allow Northern troops to inflict the greatest damage on the Confederate enemy at the lowest cost. For immediatists as "prophets of perfection," centralized deployment of information, men, and materials came increasingly to assume priority over individual liberties, black emancipation, and even over life itself.

Fredrickson's study obviously underscores the "modernist" values of immediatists; they wanted a federal war effort conducted through centralized planning and coordination with stress on efficiency. But *The Inner Civil War* also reveals that first generation immediatists, while pious missionaries, generally found much less intolerable "sinfulness" within dominant Northern institutions and values than they had in earlier decades. By the December 1863 meeting of the American Anti-Slavery Society, most political abolitionists, Tappanites, and even Garrisonians were supportive (if in different degrees) of the Lincoln Administration and the Union Army. This revealed, of course, that they had found a significant measure of accord with their fellow Northerners in their dedication to Union victory. Consequently, they tended to feel less estranged than they had in the past; they appeared considerably more moderate and reasonable to their fellow Northerners as they spoke at pro-war rallies and supported established power. Simply put, immediatists had become more flexible and convivial. In their willingness to support other pro-war Northerners like Lincoln and Grant who, to their minds, were temporizers and at least modestly lacking in moral virtue, they were somewhat less the zealous and devout reformers of earlier days.

Essentially, then, *The Inner Civil War* characterizes the wartime organizational experience as central to the increasing emphasis that immediatists placed on strong fellowship with other Northerners. Common interest in an efficient federal military effort is found to have induced immediatists to embrace other "modernist" Northerners. As such, Fredrickson makes little of antebellum roots of this immediatist emphasis on convivial fellowship at the expense of pious missionary devotedness. This is unfortunate, for the basis for immediatists' wartime embrace of less than pious fellow Northerners is to be found within the broad structural changes of antebellum Northern society.

In an 1857 letter to Samuel Sewall, Maria Chapman strongly hinted at the results of these changing Northern structural conditions:

The Mercantile pillars of N. England Churches are not now speculating in Alabama lands, as in 1835, but in Northwestern lands:—& so the clergy have received permission to sign remonstrances, & preach Kansas sermons, & are excused from the necessity of hunting abolitionists as heretics.

Chapman was essentially alluding to the diversification of the Northern industrial economy and the effects of that diversification on the social relationships between immediatists and other Northerners. In the 1830's most Northern manufacturers and their merchant-financier backers were heavily dependent on Southern cotton as a basic staple for production. Indeed, that cotton was the basic source for foreign investment capital, it paid as an export for the major share of American imports, and it supported the structure of national credit. The cotton staple was so important to Northern economic activity that even wealthy abolitionist merchants in Boston, New York City, and Cincinnati engaged in heavy trade with the South. Gradually, however, a substantial number of Northern manufacturers began to move beyond production of cotton goods. Many entered into flour milling, boot and shoe production, plus lumber, leather, and other manufactured produce to meet the demands of the increasingly populous West. This shift was particularly evident in the developing iron industry of Pennsylvania and New Jersey. By 1860 cotton ranked second among Northern manufactures, but Northern industrialists now produced a very wide variety of non-cotton based goods. Consequently, it became possible for a significant portion of highly innovative, rapidly modernizing entrepreneurs in Northern society to make substantial profits without dependence upon Southern cotton and therefore without patronizing the "peculiar institution." Others who had depended on free labor came to feel that because slave labor lowered production costs, it placed their products at a competitive disadvantage. The point is that diverse sorts of Northern entrepreneurs tended to become increasingly receptive to the "Conscience" Whig, Free Democrat, Free Soil, and Republican party condemnations of the Southern "Slave Power," particularly when these condemnations were coupled with support for rapid industrialization, national markets and banking institutions, public education, and moral reform. The very diversification of the Northern economy, which cemented non-abolitionists to antislavery parties that embraced modernizing values and institutions, was a diversification that pleased immediatists like Maria Chapman. It allowed immediatists to identify the forces and values of modernization more closely with their pious mission to free the slaves. At the same time, it gave them a real sense of fellowship with more moderate antislavery Northerners who, like themselves, embraced "modernist" values and work experiences as antithetical to the values and conditions of Southern slaveholding society. These antislavery Northerners sent Lincoln to the White House and like-minded representatives to Congress in political campaigns against the Southern "slavocracy" and in behalf of free soil, free labor, and free men. When the Civil War erupted, immediatists were naturally prone to champion the war effort that their new "friends" directed. After all, the immediatist as a convivial but devout missionary had always craved new social contacts while the Republicans and their president were genuinely opposed to the "immoral" Southern planter class. By reaching out, embracing, and supporting them, immediatists might make the Republicans even more moral. They might enlist them in their own particularly devout and uncompromising mission against the "peculiar institution." Should this occur, there would indeed be a holy war against slavery. "Pious fellowship" would triumph.[14]

This is, of course, but a suggestive corrective of Fredrickson's explanation for the general immediatist endorsement of the Lincoln Administration and the federal war effort. But it is certain that the endorsement had antebellum roots. Moreover, it was inextricably linked to the immediatist's long-standing craving for fellowship and his persistent "modernist" proclivities. The important point, for present purposes, is that the diversification of the Northern economy and the endorsement by many non-abolitionist Northern "modernists" of anti-"Slave Power," Free Soil, Free Democrat, "Conscience" Whig, and Republican parties had a discernible effect upon immediatist social psychology. With "friends" to embrace, they became more gregarious. Because those "friends" temporized with emancipation and did not always endorse other moral reforms, immediatists had to hold back a bit on their missionary zeal—their devotedness—if they were to retain their "friendships." They had to become less zealous in their insistence on moral virtue, and as a trade-off, they came to feel less estranged from the Northern society about them. Succinctly put, as immediatists became more gregarious and somewhat less uncompromisingly devout, they became less distinguishable from other antislavery Northern "modernists."

In sum, then, we have suggested two basic points. First, the Donald thesis on status displacement is eminently compatible with the "neoabolitionist" characterization of immediatists as "modernists." First generation immediatists were "modernists," but highly unusual experiences as champions of an unpopular cause provoked "anguished protest . . . against a world" that they perceived "they never made." Second, what distinguished our immediatists from other Northern "modernists" was a social psychology that we have characterized as "pious fellowship." As time transpired, their gregarious (fellowship) qualities increased out of proportion to their missionary zeal or piety. They therefore underwent fundamental, if subtle, transformation, with the change characterizing Garrisonians, Tappanites, and political abolitionists.

The extensive and systematic accumulation of data that is required to conclusively demonstrate these two basic points necessarily fall beyond the scope of this exploratory essay. It is the sort of long-term research project that could form the entire agenda for the 1980's in abolitionist studies. But a biographical sketch of Elizur Wright, Jr., one of the most important first generation immediatists, can help to concretize our basic points. Wright would never have approved of being singled out for this purpose. He prized his privacy. Moreover, he regarded himself as a "renegade" within the abolitionist crusade and quite different from his immediatist colleagues.[15] Indeed, Wright was a "renegade" in one important sense. His gregarious embrace of moderately antislavery Northern "modernists" coincided, quite atypically, with his withdrawal from the fellowship of old abolitionist colleagues. However, because of their strong senses of selfhood and their markedly idiosyncratic qualities, most first generation immediatists were "renegades" in one way or another. Few neatly illustrated our two basic points in all of their essentials. It is instructive to study Elizur Wright not because he was "typical" or "representative" but because his reform career clearly illustrates our notion of "pious fellowship" and how this quality was subtly modified by modernity and the diversification of the Northern economy. Moreover, although both immediatists and historians have regarded Wright as a political abolitionist, closer examination reveals that his differences with Garrisonians and Tappanites were hardly more significant than his differences with other political abolitionists. Hence, the Wright example vividly illustrates our claim that the traditional Garrisonian-Tappanite-political abolitionist distinction obscures at least as much as it clarifies.

Wright became an immediatist in 1832. Before his conversion, however, he had embraced modernist values. Although his father, a Talmadge, Ohio, deacon, had reared the boy on unreconstructed Calvinist dogmas, stressing human incapacities, he also cultivated in young Elizur a craving for more secular intellectual pursuits, particularly science and mathematics.[16] At Yale, exposure to Nathaniel W. Taylor and his New Haven theology helped to bridge this apparent gap between religious orthodoxy on the one hand and relatively secular scientific and mathematical concerns on the other. There Wright learned that the two were entirely compatible; he could chart his own fate with the assistance of secular knowledge under God's broad moral supervision.[17] Then, as an American Tract Society agent in the West, he became irrevocably committed to a life of reform—to active and "practical" devotion through efficient and systematic organizational effort.[18]

Wright's two salient interests—science and mathematics and moral reform—were effectively reconciled when he accepted a teaching post at Western Reserve College in 1832. There he taught the latest mathematical concepts, and together with college chaplain Beriah Green and President Charles Storrs, he also became an abolitionist. Experiencing conversion to imme-diatist doctrine together, the three felt deep bonds of personal fellowship as they took up the pious, if highly unpopular, cause and attempted to spread their newly discovered moral truth throughout Northeastern Ohio. Young Wright emerged as their spokesman. He penned several articles for the *Hudson Observer and Telegraph* that fully articulated the perspective that had turned all three away from colonization and toward immediatism. Like the black bondsman in the South, Wright suggested, there were pious missionaries in the North who felt trapped or enslaved by the moral blindness of American society, by its restraining rules, and by its constraining social expectations. Just as the slaveholder and the colonizationist kept the black bondsman in shackles, the combination of the orthodox churches and the parochialism of Western Reserve College seemed to keep him and his two friends in shackles. Therefore, like the black bondsman, moral reformers were required to strike out for their own freedom. They were to assume devout and active roles against the "peculiar institution" and were never to compromise their moral commitments. If they feared the "taint" of the less than devout, they could gather strength and renewed moral commitment by withdrawing among themselves. Then they were to strike out again, urging their "fellow men to think and do that which is right."[19]

Although Wright, Green, and Storrs thrived on mutual association in their new immediatist missionary endeavor, they engendered massive hostility from the pro-colonization trustees, faculty, and students of their college, and they found Northwestern Ohio generally too "stagnant" for a sound moral harvest. Green moved on to become president of the Oneida Institute in upstate New York while Storrs, quite ill, set out for Braintree, Massa-chusetts. Wright had always been attracted by the more vigorous intellectual and missionary activity of the urban Northeast. Consequently, he was over-joyed when Arthur Tappan offered him $500 annually as Tappan's anti-slavery secretary in New York City.

Shortly after Wright arrived in New York City late in 1833, he went with Tappan to the founding meeting of the American Anti-Slavery Society in Philadelphia. At this gathering, he was elected the organization's first sec-retary for domestic correspondence. As such, he was the chief administrator of the first national immediatist organization. Wright ran its national head-quarters in New York City between 1834 and 1839 and handled most of the official correspondence. Moreover, he was chiefly responsible for fund raising ventures and for directing the activities of AASS agents in the field.[20]

As AASS secretary for domestic correspondence, Wright was heavily ori-ented toward the "modernist" values of practicality and efficiency. He was very judicious with his time, noting that "my minutes are too deeply mort-gaged." Time seemed scarce because Wright constantly tried to improvise procedures to extend the influence and efficiency of the Anti-Slavery Society.

For one, he struggled to centralize power in the national Executive Committee and particularly in its New York office; this would avoid costly duplication of efforts by state affiliates. Wright also sought to improve the efficiency of AASS agents in the field by drawing them together periodically to exchange data and techniques for peddling Society doctrine. But however efficiently the AASS was run and however tight the control on costs, the organization needed vast funds if it was to turn the nation against slavery. Consequently, Wright introduced a scheme under which local and state societies met regular financial pledges to the national society. In turn, the affiliate societies were to secure pledges of regular donations from antislavery sympathizers in their vicinities. In this way, the AASS could operate with predictable long-range funding sources assured through grass-roots pledges. This commitment to an efficient, well-coordinated, and increasingly active national abolitionist organization was at the heart of Wright's objections, by the late 1830's, to the Garrisonians. They were not necessarily wrong in tacking new reform issues on to the crusade against black bondage. For Wright, the problem with these "extraneous" issues had nothing to do with their intrinsic merits. Rather, these issues fostered discord among immediatists and caused many outsiders to resist the antislavery appeal. Consequently, Garrisonian endorsement of a multi-issue platform threatened to make the AASS considerably less efficient.[21]

Wright's practical, efficiency minded orientation administering AASS operations reinforced an increasingly secular general perspective. He came to regard church services as a "fog-land" and ceased to belong to any congregation.[22] Predictably, this evoked strains in his relationship with Arthur and Lewis Tappan and other church-centered evangelical immediatists. These strains intensified and set Wright's personal relationship with the Tappanites beyond repair when, in 1839, he had become one of the earliest and most vigorous champions of an antislavery third party. It was not the advocacy of a third party *per se,* but the mode of Wright's advocacy that antagonized the Tappanites. Much more than Myron Holley, Joshua Leavitt, or most other early champions of this new Liberty party, Wright saw it as a way "to advance the cause of rational and practical abolitionism." Neither the old Garrisonian tactic of moral suasion nor the Tappanite appeal to church members for antislavery converts was succeeding. Therefore, a third party, which concerned itself not with "self-righteousness" but with garnering more and more Northerners to support antislavery postures and candidates, was needed. Considerations of efficiency and power, much more than abstract moral or theological principles, accounted for Wright's turn, by 1839, away from the AASS and toward the Liberty party. Although he did not understand it at the time, he was actually beginning to seek out ways to mesh the abolitionist appeal within the second American party system. Understandably, he resigned as the AASS secretary for domestic correspondence.[23]

The departure from the New York office of the AASS was troublesome for Wright. He looked forward to the Society's annual meetings: "There is nothing like seeing each other, all together in one great family, once a year, *face to face*." More generally, he found New York's cosmopolitanism and diversity most stimulating and frequently noted how exhilarating it was to work with other immediatists in the New York office that served as the nerve center of national immediatist organizational activity. There, "pious fellows"—men like Arthur Tappan, Abraham L. Cox, John Rankin, Henry B. Stanton, and William Green, Jr.—could gather when repulsed by "proslavery" outsiders. Much like Maria Weston Chapman's house in Boston and Gerrit Smith's Peterboro estate, the New York office served as a sanctuary where immediatists could rest, enjoy each others' company, and gather new energy to convert the nation's sinners. It had been a more robust version of the immediatist sanctuary of the devout that Wright had enjoyed on the Western Reserve with Beriah Green and Charles Storrs.[24]

Wright left the New York office of the AASS, then, a preeminent "modernist" as well as a "pious fellow." He exhibited traits consistent with the "neoabolitionist" interpretive perspective while, at the same time, he met David Donald's characterization of the immediatist as the aggrieved outsider protesting the immoralities of "the world." The problem was that Wright's intense "modernist" quest for efficiency and practicality seemed to reduce his cravings for gregarious rapport with other immediatists. Although he was surely more interested in finding a place for abolitionism within the emerging Jacksonian party system than most Tappanites or Garrisonians, he was, more basically, drifting from these former AASS associates owing to the higher priority that he placed on central administrative efficiency and practical results. This by-product of Wright's extreme "modernist" bent was also evident during his brief one year stint as business manager, corresponding secretary, and general director of the anti-Garrisonian Massachusetts Abolition Society and as the editor of its *Massachusetts Abolitionist* newspaper. Although he represented the center of anti-Garrisonian immediatist activity in the Boston area, the practical efficiency-minded way in which he tackled his new duties and the vehemency with which he advocated a "practical" brand of third party abolitionism lost him the support of many other immediatists in the area. In the spring of 1840, he left his duties with the Massachusetts Abolition Society with no close circle of intimates. Moreover, by Wright's own admission, his stridency in the name of "practical" third party immediatism had reduced the subscriber list of the *Massachusetts Abolitionist* by half.[25]

During the early 1840's, as the Liberty party organized and accelerated its activities, Wright remained in Boston. Off of the payroll of an immediatist organization for the first time since 1833, he tried to cope with a house full of children and an empty bank account. "E. W. Jr & his family are poor & miserably off," Lewis Tappan reported to Theodore Weld in 1844. "They have thrown themselves out of all their social relations & the children are growing up non-descripts." In an effort to support those "non-descripts," Wright translated LaFontaine's fables for a publishing house, but the profits were meager. Finally, in 1846, he established an immediatist and general reform newspaper, *The Chronotype*. By working night and day as publisher and editor, he managed to feed his family. In the late 1840's, however, he had begun to establish a reputation as a consultant to life insurance companies in England and America, finally setting his finances in good order.[26]

Because money problems during most of the 1840's and his new life insurance activities made Wright a somewhat less active immediatist than he had been during the 1830's, historians have generally deemphasized his antislavery activities after 1840. But they were substantial. Consistent with his intense desire to link immediatism to the second party system, he vigorously championed the Massachusetts Liberty party in the early 1840's, defended William Goodell's Liberty League later in the decade, and subsequently became an avid supporter of the Free Soil movement in New England. Moreover, his *Chronotype* became a major organ for political abolitionism in the Bay State. In 1854, he could write, much as he had in 1834, that "the only interest of my life—to the world or to myself—attaches to my humble efforts as an agitator against human slavery." And yet, though Wright continued to view immediatism as his most important activity, the nature of his antislavery career differed significantly from what it had been in the 1830's. Having left behind the close daily contacts of the AASS national office in New York, he lacked similar supportive ties in Boston. His one year stint with the *Massachusetts Abolitionist* exacerbated matters. Boston Garrisonians snubbed him throughout the 1840's as an "impudent varlet," while Boston Tappanites Amos Phelps and Joshua Leavitt would have little to do with their former schoolmate from Yale. On top of all this, Wright found little social support from political abolitionist co-workers in the Massachusetts Liberty party. There was no central office that like the AASS office in New York seemed to serve as a sanctuary for pious reformers like himself. Moreover, key Bay State Liberty party figures like Samuel Sewall and George Bradburn did not regard him as a true colleague. Beriah Green and Gerrit Smith, two Liberty party leaders from upstate New York, urged Wright to come to join them. But he would not leave Boston for the Burned-Over District where he could receive their social support on a daily basis. Clearly, Wright had shunned the fellowship of like-minded pious missionaries for a more isolated immediatist existence, and this was not simply because diverse immediatists had ostracized him. He did not seem to crave convivial contacts with first generation immediatists of any sort—not even with those who, like "Brother Green," shared his desire to fuse abolitionism with the second party system.[27]

The change going on within Wright after he left the *Massachusetts Abolitionist* was broadly similar to the change that many other abolitionists found themselves experiencing. Wright, as "modernist" and "pious fellow" was undergoing the transformation that was starting to make him, like many of his colleagues, somewhat less devout in the sense that he was starting to embrace more than the immediatist "world in ourselves." At the time, as we shall see, he was becoming more gregarious in terms of his willingness to work with Free Soilers and sundry other Northern antislavery "modernists" who lacked the immediatist's missionary zeal to root out the "peculiar institution." But Wright's new gregariousness—his turn to other Northern "modernists" differed from that of most of his old immediatist colleagues in the sense that the beginning of his embrace of new friends coincided with declining enthusiasm for certain of his former abolitionist associates—for Liberty men of the 1840's as well as for the Garrisonians and Tappanites with whom he had cooperated in the New York office of the AASS during the 1830's. What were the forces behind Wright's somewhat unique transformation?

When he administered the national office of the American Anti-Slavery Society, Wright's "modernist" proclivities were quite apparent. The same proclivities were evident in the 1840's and 1850's. But because Wright seldom associated with immediatist organizational activity in these later decades, this quality was less often linked to abolitionism. Rather, Wright's "modernist" bent was more often detectable in his inventions—a mechanical knitting machine, an improved water closet, and a machine to manufacture durable spikes. It was particularly evident in his recommendations as an expert consultant for American and English life insurance companies. Unaided by tables or calculating machines, he could instantly determine the specific policy premium rates that would assure a company adequate liquidity to pay all claims while garnering sufficient investment capital for long-range profits. The persistence of Wright's modernism was also detectable in his never ending enthusiasm for the many exciting technical innovations of the day from P. P. Stewart's new Troy cooking stove to a new and rapid railroad line running from Albany to Schenectady. He had become quite certain that the free North was the only part of the country that encouraged such innovations—that the South's "backward" slave system inhibited the exploratory spirit. Like many of his immediatist colleagues, this perception prompted Wright, during the 1840's and 1850's, to acknowledge that he had a great deal in common with other Northern "modernists"—that his inventions and innovations, like their own, were products of the more "wholesome" Northern economic and moral climate where commerce and industrialization were moving at a much brisker pace than they were in the slave states. Indeed, Wright slowly refined his perspective even further. The most innovative Northern men of trade, manufacture, and invention seemed to him to be those least dependent on the Southern cotton staple. They exchanged goods and services with the West rather than with the slaveholding South. Consequently, like many other immediatists, Wright could understand why these exceedingly energetic fellow "modernists" were becoming increasingly hostile to the Southern "Slave Power." Their hostility seemed comparable to that of his old immediatist colleagues.[28]

During the late 1840's, Wright became very close with a specific group of these non-immediatist Northern antislavery "modernists"—Francis Bird, John Andrew, Henry Wilson, William S. Robinson, George Stearns, Franklin Sanborn, Charles Sumner, and Samuel Gridley Howe. Most were active Massachusetts "Conscience" Whigs. All embraced the new Free Soil movement and went on, during the early 1850's, to organize the Bay State Republican party. Regular readers of Wright's *Chronotype,* they valued it as the most useful reform newspaper in Boston and donated thousands of dollars to keep it afloat. They also admired Wright's technical knowledge of life insurance, urged him to draft bills to reform this new industry in Massachusetts, and sometimes steered his bills through the state legislature. Finally, as a token of their respect for Wright, they invited him to join their Saturday afternoon dining group—the Bird Club—for camaraderie and good cheer among pious Boston area non-immediatist Free Soilers. Socially isolated but lacking any desire to return to his old immediatist colleagues, Wright jumped at the opportunity.[29]

The men of the Bird Club—perhaps forty beyond the inner circle that extended membership to Wright—were non-immediatist antislavery activists who shared certain social characteristics and economic interests. A few were descendants of the old Bay State merchant aristocracy and they were at least modestly apprehensive of being eclipsed by powerful cotton manufacturers who had secured control of the Massachusetts Whig party. With the diversification of the state's industrial economy during the 1840's and 1850's, other Club members had been able to garner substantial profits through rapidly modernizing enterprises like paper manufacturing and boot and shoe production. Like Wright, however, most Club participants served as financial and legal advisors to those who ran these modern enterprises or as editors who received their patronage. Because most who attended the Saturday afternoon sessions therefore supported themselves through "modernist" tasks that were independent of the slave states' cotton staple, they felt few compunctions about embracing non-immediatist antislavery politics. "Conscience" Whiggery often came first, followed by Free Soil, and finally the radical wing of the new Republican party.[30]

After Wright became the first immediatist to join the Bird Club, it is difficult to determine just what transpired. Neither the former AASS administrator nor the group's more moderate antislavery members wrote very much about one another despite Wright's presence at nearly every Bird Club dinner from the late 1840's until at least the mid-1860's. When Francis Bird romantically reminisced on the early years of the Club's existence, for example, he mentioned all of the initial members except Wright. When "Warrington" (William S. Robinson) published his *Pen Portraits,* he provided full, loving sketches of all non-immediatist Bird Club associates but only a sentence concerning Wright: "Elizur is a successful man of business, and the same hard-headed and perfectly honest, non-mystical old radical as ever." Similarly, James Stone made much of John Brown's participation in a Club dinner in May of 1859, remarking how those in attendance were thrilled by the event. But Stone failed to note that Brown came because of his schoolboy friendship with Wright. Stone, moreover, neglected to report the considerable discourse at the dinner between the two. So, too, Wright had very little to say about the Bird Club's dinner discussions. Privately, he noted that the smoking at the conclusion of every regular Club meal was unpleasant and had been rare in immediatist circles. But he also acknowledged that he liked and respected Sumner, Wilson, Andrew, and the other Club members, and this made regular Saturday attendance worthwhile. Wright, however, confided to Nathaniel P. Banks that after about a dozen years of meals, he had not received a word of comment—positive or negative—from a Club colleague concerning any of his many essays on slavery and other vital reform issues. Members seemed interested in him as an efficient "modernist" and a highly innovative life insurance reformer but not as an abolitionist or a general missionary for pious causes.[31]

Quite unlike his crucial position in the immediatist agitation at Western Reserve College and in the New York office of the American Anti-Slavery Society, then, Wright's role in the more moderately antislavery Bird Club was not central, dynamic, or even memorable. This was most clearly illustrated by a series of events that transpired between the fall of 1850 and the spring of 1852. Although Wright had great plans for his *Chronotype* as a newspaper that might unite diverse reformers in behalf of the mission to the slaves and other devout causes, he discovered that most of his Bird Club supporters wanted an organ that devoted itself to the activities of the Massachusetts Free Soil party. Consequently, Wright "felt obliged to merge my own independent paper in the new Free Soil paper," hoping that the new Boston publication that came of the merger "will soon revert to my entire control." But the inner leadership circle within the Bird Club had no such intentions. At the instigation of Samuel Gridley Howe and with the support of other key figures in the Club, a committee was formed that bought up *The Chronotype* and two other Boston antislavery newspapers. With the resources of all three publications, the committee established *The Commonwealth*. Wright was initially employed and salaried at $30 a week to be a minor sub-editor of sorts for *The Commonwealth*. According to Howe, he was to do office work and collect news stories but also "to have a bit in his mouth and say nothing editorially that the *Chief* does not approve." The "Chief" was to be John Gorham Palfrey, the prudent and learned former "Conscience" Whig. Although Wright realized that the Bird Club did not want him to "speak quite so irreverently and saucily" in their *Commonwealth* as he had in his *Chronotype,* he openly refused to "unsay" any of his old immediatist feelings on the printed page. This proved to be Wright's undoing. Howe concluded that Wright's "immoderate" tone was damaging the chances of Club associate Charles Sumner to win a seat in the United States Senate. Wright's ties to the Bird Club and to its new publication seemed to be turning mildly antislavery men against Sumner. Consequently, Howe soon determined to "put an end to the present embarrassing condition of things" by effectively removing Wright from his lowly sub-editor status. Francis Bird became political editor and took charge of antislavery and other reform causes. Palfrey became contributing editor and wrote on topics that Bird did not cover. Wright held the title of "general editor" but was not to draft editorials. Rather, because of his mathematical and managerial skills, he was ordered only to direct *Commonwealth* financial affairs. Finally, in May of 1852, the sole immediatist on *The Commonwealth* staff was entirely removed because he had proven to be wholly unreliable as a Free Soil journalist. His modest share in the ownership of the publication was to be paid off. As an aside to spare him further humiliation, Bird Club associates told Wright that he might want to contribute occasionally to their newspaper.[32]

The most striking question in all of Wright's antislavery career is why he continued to attend Bird Club dinners after this humiliating *Commonwealth* experience in the spring of 1852. As an immediatist and "modernist" who was repudiated by more moderate Free Soil "modernists" of the Club for his "saucy" tone, it is curious why he never sought to reembrace his old and equally outspoken abolitionist colleagues. If he could no longer work with Garrisonians or Tappanites, why did he not at least restore cooperation with old political immediatist colleagues like Gerrit Smith and Beriah Green— abolitionists who were also strongly desirous of deploying the modern techniques of the second party system to secure Negro freedom? In short, what sort of transformation had Wright experienced that caused him to remain an isolated and minimally respected immediatist in a group of more moderate Free Soil antislavery colleagues who went on to organize and control the Massachusetts Republican party?

Wright remained among those Bird Club Free Soilers (soon radical Republicans) who had cast him out of their *Commonwealth* because, even with his "immoderate" personal and political style, he had become more like them than like his old immediatist colleagues. Gradually, in the course of the late 1840's and early 1850's, one could detect a very significant decline in his saint-like missionary zeal to stamp out slavery and to institute other far-reaching moral reforms. He seemed to be devaluating personal piety much more rapidly than most other first generation immediatists. In brief, Wright was lowering his expectations and was willing to settle for realizable improvements, however slight, over the great hopes of 1830's immediatism or the dreams of Liberty men of the early 1840's. Rather than attempting to rebuild totally the moral fabric of society, by 1848, he was acknowledging that there was greater "importance" in "mending it up so that it will do for the present." To the consternation of many of his former immediatist colleagues, Wright insisted that the Free Soilers (and eventually the Republicans) offered some "mending" improvements, however slight. By 1860, he confessed to a surprised Beriah Green that their old Liberty party efforts had been exercises in "shamming" and that fundamental moral reform "is not possible & never will be." Although he still retained the old dream of the immediatist mission to free the slaves and to purify national morals in other particulars, and though he sometimes espoused this dream in typically "immoderate" immediatist tones, "I no longer write expecting to convince anybody—only to let off steam." Pious missionary endeavor had become a self-confessed effort at personal therapy. New "wisdom" of the world's ways compelled Wright to support the compromised "mending" efforts of his more moderate Bird Club colleagues even as these colleagues demonstrated their distrust of his "saucy" style.[33]

Before the guns of Sumter, then, Elizur Wright had completed a very basic transformation. In an important sense, it approximated that of several of his other early immediatist colleagues. His "modernist" proclivities had caused him to look to a variety of Northern "modernist" Free Soilers for camaraderie and social support—particularly to Francis Bird, Henry Wilson, John Andrew, and other dining colleagues at the Bird Club. Like many of his old immediatist colleagues, including most Garrisonians, he had therefore become less discriminating in the Northerners with whom he kept company; they did not have to be impeccable reformers on the slavery question or on other moral issues. Moreover, as Wright came to value personal piety less, the enormous importance that he had always attached to practicality and efficiency caused him to place considerably more value in effective if only marginally devout antislavery associates than in most of his former immediatist colleagues. He seemed to prize these new and powerful Free Soil associates over more uncompromising immediatists even if Free Soilers trusted him less than old colleagues like "Brother Green."

Because Wright remained within the Bird Club even though its members had excluded him from their *Commonwealth* and because he refused to reembrace his former abolitionist colleagues, few were surprised when he, like others in the Club, voted for Lincoln in the 1860 presidential election. The Republican from Illinois had a chance to win the presidency and his party was not dependent upon electoral support from the slave states. Because Lincoln and his party had no vested interest in the "peculiar institution," some good might come of Republican rule. A Republican administration might "mend" the nation's moral fabric, although there was no possibility of a wholesale moral revolution. "In regard to the ordinary working of the government machinery," Wright wrote, "there will doubtless be a great and valuable gain by the introduction of the honest, thrifty methods of the Free States" over the coarser and less efficient methods of a party dominated by the "Slave Power." This was "gain" enough.[34]

If Elizur Wright was relatively inconsequential to his Bird Club associates, especially after the spring of 1852, he was even more irrelevant to the new Lincoln Administration. To be sure, he barraged antislavery moderates within the Administration with suggestions to make the federal war effort more efficient. Reviewing these suggestions, one recalls the chief AASS administrator of the 1830's who struggled to maximize resources and thereby establish an efficient national antislavery organization. The life insurance reformer also comes to mind, crusading to make this new business enterprise serve the public safely, efficiently, and responsibly. The difference was that Wright did not formulate, much less administer, federal government policy during the war years. Treasury Secretary Salmon P. Chase, a former Liberty party colleague, represented his only real contact in Lincoln's Administration. Judging from Chase's wartime diary, he spent little time thinking about Wright or Wright's proposed reforms. Like most other immediatists during the war period, but unlike several of his Bird Club associates, Wright was an outsider to the new Republican Administration. Only on rare occasions was he consulted by the federal government for technical matters of statistical record keeping. He was still too much the pious and "saucy" missionary and too little the pragmatic politician to be allowed to write in the Bird Club newspaper, much less to participate within the circles where national policies were formulated and executed. Convivial as Wright had become with antislavery moderates, he retained certain features of the outspoken and devout missionary and remained distant from power.

In his latter years, then, although Wright had ceased to regard himself as an immediatist, neither the Bird Club nor the Lincoln Administration trusted him more than they trusted most other "old" abolitionists. In this sense, he was in the same boat as his former colleagues, whether Garrisonians, Tappanites, or Liberty party abolitionists. There were few Salmon Chases and Gamaliel Baileys among this first generation of immediatists—abolitionists who had been able to shed much of their pious missionary garb and to become effective power brokers within the Free Soil movement and the new Republican party. Though old first generation immediatists, like most Free Soilers and radical Republicans, had decidedly "modernist" values and though many "old" abolitionists had come to share with Wright the desire to work within moderate antislavery channels, even adamant antislavery Free Soilers turned Republican like Bird and Wilson often held most of them at arms' length. This was because immediatists generally retained a level of moral intensity that was often antithetical to even the mildest power broker machinations inherent in the American political process. This left them no alternative but to register, in David Donald's words, "the anguished protest of an aggrieved class against a world they never made." That was their only real option in the 1850's and the 1860's just as it had been their only possible course of conduct in the 1830's and the 1840's.

NOTES

1. David Donald, "Toward a Reconsideration of the Abolitionists" in *Lincoln Reconsidered: Essays on the Civil War Era* (New York: Alfred A. Knopf, 1956), ch. 2.

2. Robert A. Skotheim, "A Note on Historical Method: David Donald's 'Toward a Reconsideration of the Abolitionists,' " *Journal of Southern History,* 25 (August 1959): 356–65; Robert W. Doherty, "Status Anxiety and American Reforms: Some Alternatives," *American Quarterly,* 19 (Summer 1967): 329–37.

3. Martin Duberman, ed., *The Antislavery Vanguard: New Essays on the Abolitionists* (Princeton: Princeton University Press, 1965) presents many of the "neo-abolitionist" essays. See also Duberman, "The Abolitionists and Psychology," *Journal of Negro History,* 47 (July 1962): 183–91; Louis Ruchames, "William Lloyd Garrison and the Negro Franchise," *Journal of Negro History,* 50 (January 1965): 37–49; Gerald Sorin, *The New York Abolitionists: A Case Study of Political Radicalism* (Westport, Conn.: Greenwood Press, 1971); James Brewer Stewart, *Holy Warriors: The Abolitionists and American Slavery* (New York: Hill and Wang, 1976).

4. The antebellum American modernization process is best described in Richard D. Brown, *Modernization: The Transformation of American Life 1600–1865* (New York: Hill and Wang, 1976), chs. 5–7. By far the most comprehensive delineation of the characteristics of the "modern personality" is found within Alex Inkeles and David Smith, *Becoming Modern: Individual Change in Six Developing Countries* (Cambridge: Harvard University Press, 1974), particularly pp. 19–25, 230–35, 268.

5. Sorin, *New York Abolitionists,* thoroughly explored the "modernist" work experiences of immediatist leaders in the state. The work experiences of Rochester immediatists is examined in James L. McElroy, "Social Reform in the Burned-Over District: Rochester, New York as a Test Case, 1830–1854" (Ph.D. diss., State University of New York at Binghamton, 1974), pp. 168–71. John Barkley Jentz, "Artisans, Evangelicals, and the City: A Social History of Abolitionist and Labor Reform in Jacksonian New York" (Ph.D. diss., City University of New York, 1977), p. 202 treats the signers of early 1830's antislavery petitions in New York City. Judith Wellman, " 'Are We Aliens Because We Are Women?': Female Abolitionist Petitions in Upstate New York," paper presented at the National Archives Conference, Washington, D.C., April 1976, p. 9. Wellman, "To the 'Fathers and Rulers of Our Country': Abolitionist Petitions and Female Abolitionists in Paris, New York, 1835–45," paper presented at the Berkshire Conference on Women's History, June 1976, pp. 7–8.

6. See, e.g., Gerald Sorin, "The Historical Theory of Political Radicalism: Michigan Abolitionist Leaders as a Test Case" (M.A. thesis, Wayne State University, 1964); Theodore M. Hammett, "Two Mobs of Jacksonian Boston: Ideology and Interest," *Journal of American History,* 62 (March, 1976): 862; Leonard L. Richards, *"Gentlemen of Property and Standing": Anti-Abolition Mobs in Jacksonian America* (New York: Oxford University Press, 1970), p. 140 and ch. 5.

7. Louis Ruchames, ed., *The Letters of William Lloyd Garrison* (Cambridge: Belknap Press, 1975), 4: 545 (Garrison); Ellis Gray Loring to Louisa Loring, May 12, 1858, Loring Family Papers, Schlesinger Library, Radcliffe; Abishai Scofield to Seibleir Scofield, November 9, 1870, Abishai Scofield MSS., Burton Historical Col-

lection, Detroit Public Library; John G. Whittier, *The Stranger in Lowell* (Boston: Waite Peirce and Company, 1845), p. 11.

8. Lysander Spooner to Albert Gallatin, July 20, 1840, Lysander Spooner Papers, New-York Historical Society; Samuel E. Sewall to Daniel Webster, January 4, 1846, Samuel E. Sewall Letterbook, Massachusetts Historical Society; Roberts Vaux to the Senate and House of Representatives of Pennsylvania, October 1830, Roberts Vaux Papers, Historical Society of Pennsylvania; Margaret C. McCulloch, *Fearless Advocate of the Right: The Life of Francis Julius LeMoyne, M.D.* (Boston: Christopher Publishing House, 1941), p. 218. For immediatists' "modernist" critiques of the Southern slave system, see Lydia Maria Child, *An Appeal in Favor of that Class of Americans Called Africans* (Boston, 1833), pp. 112, 118–19; John Rankin, *Letters on American Slavery* (Boston: Isaac Knapp, 1838), p. 64; Wendell Phillips Garrison and Francis Jackson Garrison, *William Lloyd Garrison 1805–1879* (New York: The Century Company, 1885–89), 2: 234–36; *The Freeman* (Rochester), August 7, 1839; *Complete Works of John Greenleaf Whittier* (New York: Sully and Kleinteich, 1889–94), 7:45.

9. Richards, *"Gentlemen of Property,"* p. 169; Gerald Sorin, *Abolitionism: A New Perspective* (New York: Praeger Publishers, 1972); Lynn L. Marshall, "The Strange Stillbirth of the Whig Party," *Journal of American History, 55* (December 1968): 466.

10. John Myers, "The Agency System of the Anti-Slavery Movement, 1832–1837, and Its Antecedents in Other Benevolent and Reform Societies" (Ph.D. diss., University of Michigan, 1960), pp. 357–61; Gilbert H. Barnes and Dwight L. Dumond, eds., *Letters of Theodore Dwight Weld, Angelina Grimké Weld, and Sarah Grimké* (New York, London: Appleton-Century Company, 1934), 1: 459–60; Roman Joseph Zorn, "The New England Anti-Slavery Society: Pioneer Abolition Organization," *Journal of Negro History, 43* (July 1957): 175–76; Lewis Tappan to Gerrit Smith, October 13, 1836, Gerrit Smith Papers, Syracuse.

11. Richards, *"Gentlemen of Property,"* pp. 72–73; Steward, *Holy Warriors,* pp. 68–69; Bertram Wyatt-Brown, "Stanley Elkins' *Slavery:* The Antislavery Interpretation Reexamined," *American Quarterly, 25* (May 1973): 154–76; Jentz, "Artisans, Evangelicals, and the City," p. 196; Alan M. Kraut, "The Politics of Reform: An Institutional Approach to Third Party Abolitionism," Southern Historical Assoc., November 1976 (unpublished paper).

12. See, e.g., my case studies of three abolitionist intimacy circles: "Garrisonian Abolitionism and the Boston Clique: A Psychosocial Inquiry," *The Psychohistory Review, 7* (Fall 1978): 6–19; "Confidence and Pertinacity in Evangelical Abolitionism: Lewis Tappan's Immediate Circle," *American Quarterly, 31* (Spring 1979): 81–106; "The Gerrit Smith Circle: Abolitionism in the Burned-Over District," *Civil War History, 26* (March 1980): 18–38.

13. Anna Davis Hallowell, ed., *James and Lucretia Mott: Life and Letters* (Boston: Houghton Mifflin and Company, 1884), pp. 68, 200; Robert W. Tolf, "Edmund Quincy: Aristocrat Abolitionist" (Ph.D. diss., University of Rochester, 1957), pp. 371–72 quotes Quincy; Lydia Maria Child, *The Progress of Religious Ideas, Through Successive Ages* (New York: C. S. Francis & Company, 1855), 2: 164–65, 1: 256; Angelina Grimké in Barnes and Dumond, eds., *Weld-Grimké Letters,* 2: 782–83.

14. Maria Weston Chapman to Samuel E. Sewall, August 9, 1857, Robie-Sewall Papers, Massachusetts Historical Society. Richards, *"Gentlemen of Property,"* p. 55 lists several wealthy abolitionist merchants trading with the South. Barrington Moore,

Jr., *Social Origins of Dictatorship and Democracy: Lord and Peasant in the Making of the Modern World* (Boston: Beacon Press, 1967), especially pp. 116, 124, affords an excellent discussion of the gradual diversification of the antebellum Northern manufacturing economy and its consequences. Eric Foner, *Free Soil, Free Labor, Free Men: The Ideology of the Republican Party Before the Civil War* (New York: Oxford University Press, 1970) is the best available analysis of the "modernist" and antislavery values of "Conscience" Whigs, Free Democrats, Free Soilers, and Republicans.

15. Elizur Wright, Jr., *A Curiosity of Law: or, A Respondent in the Supreme Judicial Court as a Judge in the General Court: and What Possibly Came of It* (Boston: Elizur Wright, Jr., 1866), p. 16.

16. David Charles French, "The Conversion of an American Radical: Elizur Wright, Jr., and the Abolitionist Movement" (Ph.D. diss., Case Western Reserve University, 1970), pp. 19–33 on the fascinating motives for the Wright family moving to Talmadge. Elizur Wright, Sr. to Elizur Wright, Jr., October 22, 1822, August 4, November 1, 1823, October 21, 1824, March 16, 1827, November 20, 1829, Elizur Wright, Jr., Papers, Western Reserve Historical Society.

17. French, "Conversion of an American Radical," pp. 37, 58–60 on Wright's student days at Yale. Elizur Wright, Sr., to Elizur Wright, Jr., April 21, 1827, Elizur Wright, Jr. Papers, Western Reserve Historical Society.

18. For discussion of Wright as a Tract Society agent, see Lawrence B. Goodheart and Richard Curry, eds., " 'A Plea for the West': Elizur Wright, Jr. and the American Tract Society in Western Pennsylvania, 1828–1829," *Pennsylvania History*, 44 (July 1977): 254; French, "Conversion of an American Radical," pp. 87–97; Jane and William Pease, *Bound with Them in Chains: A Biographical History of the Antislavery Movement* (Westport, Conn.: Greenwood Press, 1972), pp. 219–20.

19. *Observer & Telegraph* (Hudson, Ohio), July 12, August 18, September 6, 13, November 8, 1832. See also Elizur Wright, Jr., *The Sin of Slavery and Its Remedy* (New York, 1833), p. 7 and Wright, Jr., *A Lecture on Tobacco, delivered in the Chapel of the Western Reserve College, Judson, Ohio, May 29, 1832* (Cleveland, 1832), p. 13.

20. For Wright's function as AASS secretary for domestic correspondence, see Pease and Pease, *Bound with Them*, pp. 224–25; Barnes and Dumond, eds., *Weld-Grimké Letters*, 1:95 n.1.

21. Dwight L. Dumond, ed., *Letters of James Gillespie Birney* (New York: D. Appleton-Century Company, 1938), 1:204 on Wright's "heavily mortgaged" time. In the *Massachusetts Abolitionist* (Boston), May 30, 1839 Wright makes his fullest case for AASS centralization in the name of efficiency. Dumond, ed., *Letters of Birney*, 1: 364–65 on gatherings of AASS agents. Barnes and Dumond, eds., *Weld-Grimké Letters*, 1: 203–4 on a national system to secure AASS donations. Elizur Wright, Jr., to Amos A. Phelps, September 5, 1837, Elizur Wright, Jr., Papers, Library of Congress (L.C.) on objections to the Garrisonians.

22. For the drift away from orthodoxy, see, e.g., Elizur Wright, Jr., to Amos A. Phelps, January 13, 1835, Wright, Jr., Papers, L.C.; Wright, Jr., "Slavery and Its Ecclesiastical Defenders," *Quarterly Anti-Slavery Magazine*, 1 (July 1836): 371–72; Wright, Jr., in *The Emancipator* (N.Y.), May 5, 1835, August 24, 1837. Elizur Wright, Jr., to Beriah Green, December 15, 1838, and to Mr. and Mrs. Elizur Wright, Sr., December 5, 1839, both in Wright, Jr., Papers, L.C.

23. Elizur Wright, Jr., to Beriah Green, October 10, 1839, Elizur Wright, Jr.,

Typescripts, Boston Public Library (B.P.L.); *Massachusetts Abolitionist* (Boston), October 17, December 12, 1839, May 7, 1840; Pease and Pease, *Bound with Them,* pp. 234–35.

24. Barnes and Dumond, eds., *Weld-Grimké Papers,* 1: 291 quotes Wright on the annual AASS meeting. French, "Conversion of an American Radical," particularly pp. 192–93, 206, provides a cogent discussion of the AASS office in New York as Wright's sanctuary.

25. Elizur Wright, Jr., to Beriah Green, October 10, 1839, Wright, Jr., Typescripts, B.P.L.; Wright to Gerrit Smith, March 20, 1840, Gerrit Smith Papers, Syracuse.

26. Lewis Tappan to Theodore Weld, July 17, 1844, Lewis Tappan Papers, L.C.; Elizur Wright, Jr., to James G. Birney, November 9, 1842, James G. Birney Collection, Clements Library; Wright, Jr., to Gerrit Smith, March 20, 1840, Gerrit Smith Papers, Syracuse; Wright, *Curiosity of Law,* p. 20; Philip G. and Elizabeth Q. Wright, *Elizur Wright: The Father of Life Insurance* (Chicago: University of Chicago Press, 1937), p. 177.

27. Reinhard O. Johnson, "The Liberty Party in New England, 1840–48: The Forgotten Abolitionists" (Ph.D. diss., Syracuse University, 1976), ch. 2 provides the most comprehensive coverage of Wright's activities in the Massachusetts Liberty party. Other data on Wright's Liberty and Free Soil efforts is provided in P. and E. Wright, *Elizur Wright,* pp. 183–85 and *The Chronotype* (Boston), 1846–50. Elizur Wright, Jr., to Charles Scribner, May 19, 1854, Elizur Wright, Jr., Typescript, B.P.L. describing antislavery as his "only interest."

28. Wright discusses his inventions in his letters to Susan Wright, August 3, 1843, to A. L. Whittley, November 5, 1855, and to "Mr. Hanford," June 17, 1857, all in Elizur Wright, Jr., Typescript, B.P.L. P. and E. Wright, *Elizur Wright,* pp. 200, 210, 230–36, 278 on Wright's insurance ventures. Wright, Jr., to Beriah Green, October 10, 1843, on the Troy cooking stove and Wright, Jr., to Susan Wright, August 3, 1843, on the railroad from Albany to Schenectady (both in Wright, Jr., Typescripts, B.P.L.). For examples of Wright's increasing sense of identity with Northern "modernists" who had no commercial ties with the cotton states, see Wright, Jr., ed., *Perforations in the 'Latter-Day Pamphlets,' by One of the 'Eighteen Millions of Bores'* (Boston: Phillips, Sampson, and Company, 1850), pp. 47–48; *Massachusetts Abolitionist* (Boston), January 9, 1840; Wright, Jr., *An Eye Opener for the Wide Awakes* (Boston: Thayer & Eldridge, 1860), p. 58.

29. P. and E. Wright, *Elizur Wright,* pp. 200, 278; Frank Preston Stearns, *Cambridge Sketches* (reprint, Freeport, N.Y.: Books for Libraries Press, 1968), pp. 166, 295–96, 301.

30. Richard H. Abbott, "Massachusetts: Maintaining Hegemony" in *Radical Republicans in the North: State Politics during Reconstruction,* James C. Mohr, ed. (Baltimore: Johns Hopkins University Press, 1976), pp. 2–17; Foner, *Free Soil,* p. 243, and information dispersed throughout Kinley Brauer, *Cotton versus Conscience: Massachusetts Whig Politics and Southwestern Expansion, 1843–1848* (Lexington: University of Kentucky Press, 1967).

31. *Francis William Bird, A Biographical Sketch, by his Children* (Boston: Norwood Press, 1897), p. 34; *"Warrington" Pen Portraits: A Collection of Personal and Political Reminiscences from 1848 to 1876, from the Writings of William S. Robinson* (Boston: Mrs. W. S. Robinson, 1877), p. 497; James W. Stone to Charles Sumner, March 23, 1859, Sumner Papers, Houghton Library; P. and E. Wright,

Elizur Wright, pp. 278–79; Elizur Wright to Charles Sumner, January 19, August 11, 1860, Sumner Papers, Houghton Library; Elizur Wright to Nathaniel P. Banks, n.d. [January 3, 1861], Wright Papers L.C.

32. Elizur Wright to Dr. Gregory, February 10, 1851, B.P.L.; Laura E. Richards, ed., *Letters and Journals of Samuel Gridley Howe* (Boston: Dana Estes & Company, 1909), 2: 331 reports on Wright's contemplated "bit in his mouth" sub-editorial role on *The Commonwealth.* Wright in *The Chronotype,* January 1, 1851, characterizing his contemplated role in *The Commonwealth.* Richards, ed., *Howe,* 2: 340–41 quotes Howe in February 1851 on Wright's damage to Sumner. Harold Schwartz, *Samuel Gridley Howe, Social Reformer 1801–1876* (Cambridge: Harvard University Press, 1956); Elizur Wright to "Brother and Sister," July 23, 1851, Elizur Wright transcripts, B.P.L.; Samuel E. Sewall to Elizur Wright, May 13, 1852, Wright Papers, L.C.

33. *The Chronotype* (Boston), May 2, 1846; Pease and Pease, *Bound with Them,* p. 241; Elizur Wright, Jr., to Beriah Green, October 8, November 3, 1860, Elizur Wright, Jr., Papers, L.C.

34. Wright, Jr., *An Eye Opener,* p. 51.

Bibliography

Neither antebellum politics nor the antislavery movement have wanted for bibliographies during the past decade. As prodigious as the scholarship has been in both areas, the historians and the professional collators of reference aids have more than kept the pace. However, as abolitionist activities are increasingly returned to the broader context of antebellum society, it will be necessary to create bibliographies that reflect the intersection of abolitionism with all else taking place in America during the pre-Civil War decades.

The following bibliography is intentionally less comprehensive than those in many other recently published volumes. There is little need yet to duplicate the still excellent general bibliography of abolitionism crafted by James Brewer Stewart in *Holy Warriors* (1976). Instead, the purpose of the following bibliography is to suggest those sources dealing with the influence of abolitionism upon antebellum politics and the efforts of abolitionists to use politics as a vehicle for social change. Special care has been taken to include the many fresh, innovative studies that have appeared during the past two decades.

BOOKS

Abbot, Richard H. *Cobbler in Congress: The Life of Henry Wilson, 1812–1875.* Lexington: University Press of Kentucky, 1972.

Abzug, Robert H. *Passionate Liberator: Theodore Dwight Weld and the Dilemma of Reform.* New York: Oxford University Press, 1980.

Alexander, Thomas B. *Sectional Stress and Party Strength: A Computer Analysis of Roll-Call Voting Patterns in the United States House of Representatives, 1836–1860.* Nashville: Vanderbilt University Press, 1967.

Barnes, Gilbert Hobbs. *The Antislavery Impulse, 1830–1844.* New York: Harcourt, Brace and World, 1933.

Benson, Lee. *The Concept of Jacksonian Democracy: New York as a Test Case.* Princeton: Princeton University Press, 1961.

Berger, Mark L. *The Revolution in New York Party Systems. 1840–1860.* Port Washington, N.Y.: Kennikat Press, 1973.

Berwanger, Eugene. *The Frontier Against Slavery: Western Anti-Negro Prejudice and the Slavery Extension Controversy.* Urbana: University of Illinois Press, 1967.

Birney, William. *James G. Birney and His Times.* New York: D. Appleton and Company, 1890.

Blue, Frederick J. *The Free Soilers: Third Party Politics, 1848–54.* Urbana: University of Illinois Press, 1974.

Bolt, Christine, and Drescher, Seymour. *Anti-Slavery, Religion and Reform.* London: Dawson; Hamden, Conn.: Archon, 1980.

Bracey, John H., Jr., Meier, August, and Rudwick, Elliott, eds. *Blacks in the Abolitionist Movement.* Belmont, Calif.: Wadsworth Publishing Company, Inc., 1948.

Brauer, Kinley J. *Cotton Versus Conscience: Massachusetts Politics and Southwestern Expansion, 1843–1860.* Lexington: University of Kentucky Press, 1967.

Brock, William R. *Parties and Political Conscience: American Dilemmas, 1840–1850.* Millwood, N.Y.: KTO Press, 1979.

Bronner, Edwin B. *Thomas Earle as a Reformer.* Philadelphia: Press of International Printing Company, 1948.

Brown, Richard D. *Modernization: The Transformation of American Life, 1600–1865.* New York: Hill and Wang, 1976.

Cave, Alfred A. *An American Conservative in the Age of Jackson: The Political and Social Thought of Calvin Colton.* Fort Worth: Texas Christian University Press, 1969.

Chambers, William Nisbet, and Burnham, Walter Dean. *The American Party Systems.* New York: Oxford University Press, 1967.

Clarke, Grace J. *George W. Julian.* Indianapolis: Indiana Historical Commission, 1923.

Cooper, William J., Jr. *The South and Politics of Slavery, 1828–1856.* Baton Rouge: Louisiana State University Press, 1978.

Cross, Whitney. *The Burned-Over District: The Social and Intellectual History of Enthusiastic Religion in Western New York, 1800–1850.* Ithaca: Cornell University Press, 1950.

Curry, Richard G., ed. *The Abolitionists: Reformers or Fanatics?* New York: Holt, Rinehart and Winston, 1965.

Dalzell, Robert F. *Daniel Webster and the Trial of American Nationalism.* Boston: Houghton Mifflin Co., 1973.

Darling, Arthur B. *Political Changes in Massachusetts, 1824–1828.* New Haven: Yale University Press, 1925.

Davis, David Brion. *Ante-Bellum Reform.* New York: Harper and Row, 1967.

Davis, David Brion. *The Problem of Slavery in the Age of Revolution.* Ithaca: Cornell University Press, 1975.

Davis, David Brion. *The Problem of Slavery in Western Culture*. Ithaca: Cornell University Press, 1966.

Dillon, Merton L. *The Abolitionists: The Growth of a Dissenting Minority*. DeKalb, Ill.: Northern Illinois University Press, 1974.

Donald, David Herbert. *Liberty and Union: The Crisis of Popular Government*. Boston: Little, Brown and Company, 1978.

Donald, David Herbert. *Charles Sumner and the Coming of the Civil War*. New York: Alfred A. Knopf, 1961.

Donovan, Herbert D. A. *The Barnburners*. New York: New York University Press, 1925.

Duberman, Martin, ed. *Antislavery Vanguard: New Essays on the Abolitionists*. Princeton: Princeton University Press, 1965.

Duberman, Martin. *Charles Francis Adams*. Boston: Houghton Mifflin and Company, 1961.

Du Bois, Ellen Carol. *Feminism and Suffrage: The Emergence of an Independent Women's Movement in America, 1848–1869*. Ithaca: Cornell University Press, 1978.

Dumond, Dwight L. *Anti-Slavery*. Ann Arbor: University of Michigan Press, 1961.

Dumond, Dwight L. *The Anti-Slavery Origins of the Civil War of the United States*. Ann Arbor: University of Michigan Press, 1939.

Elkins, Stanley. *Slavery: A Problem in American Institutional and Intellectual Life*. Chicago: University of Chicago Press, 1959.

Field, Phyllis F. *The Politics of Race in New York: The Struggle for Black Suffrage in the Civil War Era*. Ithaca: Cornell University Press, 1982.

Filler, Louis. *The Crusade Against Slavery, 1830–1860*. New York: Harper and Brothers, 1960.

Fladeland, Betty G. *James G. Birney: Slaveholder to Abolitionist*. Ithaca, N.Y.: Cornell University Press, 1955.

Fladeland, Betty G. *Men and Brothers: Anglo-American Antislavery Cooperation*. Urbana: University of Illinois Press, 1972.

Foner, Eric. *Free Soil, Free Labor, Free Men: The Ideology of the Republican Party Before the Civil War*. New York: Oxford University Press, 1970.

Foner, Eric. *Politics and Ideology in the Age of the Civil War*. New York: Oxford University Press, 1980.

Formisano, Ronald P. *The Birth of Mass Political Parties: Michigan, 1827–1861*. Princeton: Princeton University Press, 1971.

Formisano, Ronald P. *The Transformation of Political Culture: Massachusetts Parties, 1790s–1840s*. New York: Oxford University Press, 1983.

Friedman, Lawrence J. *Gregarious Saints: Self and Community in American Abolitionism 1830–1870*. New York: Cambridge University Press, 1982.

Frothingham, Octavius Brooks. *Gerrit Smith A Biography*. New York: G. P. Putnam and Son, 1909.

Gatell, Frank Otto. *John Gorham Palfrey and the New England Conscience*. Cambridge, Mass.: Harvard University Press, 1963.

Goodell, William. *Slavery and Anti-Slavery; a History of the Great Struggle in Both Hemispheres; with a View of the Slavery Question in the United States*. New York: William Harned, 1852.

Green, Beriah. *Sketches of the Life and Writings of James Gillespie Birney*. Utica: Jackson and Chaplin, 1844.

Griffin, Clifford S. *Their Brother's Keeper: Moral Stewardship in the United States, 1800–1865*. New Brunswick, N.J.: Rutgers University Press, 1969.

Hamilton, Holman. *Prologue to Conflict: The Crisis and Compromise of 1850*. Lexington: University of Kentucky Press, 1964.

Hammond, Charles A. *Gerrit Smith, The Story of a Noble Man's Life*. Geneva, N.Y.: W. F. Humphrey, 1900.

Hammond, John L. *The Politics of Benevolence: Revival Religion and American Voting Behavior*. Norwood, N.J.: Ablex Publishing Corporation, 1979.

Harlow, Ralph Volney. *Gerrit Smith: Philanthropist and Reformer*. New York: Henry Holt and Company, 1939.

Henle, M. J. *The Making of American Politics, 1750–1850*. New York: Longman, 1977.

Hersh, Blanche Glassman. *The Slavery of Sex: Feminist-Abolitionists in America*. Urbana: University of Illinois Press, 1978.

Hesseltine, William B. *The Rise and Fall of Third Parties, From Anti-Masonry to Wallace*. Gloucester, Mass.: Peter Smith, 1957.

Hesseltine, William B. *Third Party Movements in the United States*. Princeton: Van Nostrand Company, Inc., 1962.

Hofstadter, Richard. *The Idea of a Party System: The Rise of Legitimate Opposition in the United States 1780–1840*. Berkeley: University of California Press, 1972.

Holt, Edgar Allen. *Party Politics in Ohio 1840–1850*. Columbus: F. J. Heer Printing Co., 1930.

Holt, Michael Fitzgibbon. *Forging a Majority: The Foundation of the Republican Party in Pittsburgh, 1848–1860*. New Haven: Yale University Press, 1969.

Holt, Michael Fitzgibbon. *The Political Crisis of the 1850's*. New York: John Wiley & Sons, 1978.

Howe, Daniel Walker. *The Political Culture of the American Whigs*. Chicago: University of Chicago Press, 1980.

Johannsen, Robert W. *Stephen A. Douglas*. New York: Oxford University Press, 1973.

Johnson, Paul E. *A Shopkeeper's Millenium: Society and Revivals in Rochester, New York, 1815–1837*. New York: Hill and Wang, 1978.

Kelley, Robert. *The Cultural Pattern in American Politics: The First Century*. New York: Alfred A. Knopf, 1979.

Kleppner, Paul. *The Cross of Culture: A Social Analysis of Mid-Western Politics, 1850–1900*. New York: The Free Press, 1970.

Kleppner, Paul. *The Third Electoral System, 1853–1892: Parties, Voters and Political Cultures*. Chapel Hill: University of North Carolina Press, 1979.

Kleppner, Paul et al. *The Evolution of American Electoral Systems*. Westport, Conn.: Greenwood Press, 1981.

Kraditor, Aileen S. *Means and Ends in American Abolitionism: Garrison and His Critics on Strategy 1834–1860*. New York: Pantheon Books, 1969.

Lane, Ann D., ed. *The Debate Over Slavery: Stanley Elkins and His Critics*. Urbana: University of Illinois Press, 1971.

Litwack, Leon. *North of Slavery: The Negro in the Free States.* Chicago: University of Chicago Press, 1961.

Ludlum, David M. *Social Ferment in Vermont.* New York: Columbia University Press, 1939.

McCormick, Richard P. *The Second American Party System.* Chapel Hill: University of North Carolina Press, 1966.

McCormick, Richard P. *The Presidential Game: The Origins of American Presidential Politics.* New York: Oxford University Press, 1982.

McPherson, James M. *Ordeal By Fire: The Civil War and Reconstruction.* New York: Alfred A. Knopf, 1982.

McPherson, James M. *The Struggle for Equality: Abolitionists and the Civil War and Reconstruction.* Princeton, N.J.: Princeton University Press, 1964.

Magdol, Edward. *Owen Lovejoy: Abolitionist in Congress.* New Brunswick, N.J.: Rutgers University Press, 1967.

Mayer, George H. *The Republican Party, 1954–1967.* New York: Oxford University Press, 1967.

Mayfield, John. *Rehearsal for Republicanism: Free Soil and the Politics of Anti-Slavery.* Port Washington, N.Y.: Kennikat Press, 1980.

Mazmanian, Daniel A. *Third Parties in Presidential Elections.* Washington, D.C.: The Brookings Institution, 1974.

Morris, Thomas. *Free Men All: Personal Liberty Laws of the North, 1780–1861.* Baltimore: Johns Hopkins University Press, 1974.

Morrison, Chaplain W. *Democratic Politics and Sectionalism: The Wilmot Proviso Controversy.* Chapel Hill: University of North Carolina Press, 1967.

Nash, Howard P. *Third Parties in American Politics.* Washington, D.C.: Public Affairs Press, 1959.

Nichols, Roy F. *The Invention of the American Political Parties.* New York: Macmillan Company, 1967.

Nye, Russel B. *Fettered Freedom Civil Liberties and the Slavery Controversy.* East Lansing, Mich.: Michigan State College Press, 1949.

O'Connor, Thomas. *The Lords of the Loom: The Cotton Whigs and the Coming of the Civil War.* New York: Charles Scribner's Sons, 1968.

Pease, Jane and William. *Bound with Them in Chains: A Biographical History of the Antislavery Movement.* Westport, Conn.: Greenwood Press, 1972.

Perry, Lewis. *Radical Abolitionism: Anarchism and the Government of God in Antislavery Thought.* Ithaca, N.Y.: Cornell University Press, 1973.

Perry, Lewis, and Fellman, Michael, eds. *Antislavery Reconsidered: New Perspectives on the Abolitionists.* Baton Rouge: Louisiana State University Press, 1979.

Potter, David M. *The Impending Crisis 1848–1861.* New York: Harper & Row, 1976.

Quarles, Benjamin. *Black Abolitionists.* New York: Oxford University Press, 1969.

Ratner, Lorman. *Powder Keg: Northern Opposition to the Antislavery Movement 1831–1840.* New York: Basic Books, Inc., 1968.

Rayback, Joseph G. *Free Soil: The Election of 1848.* Lexington: University Press of Kentucky, 1962.

Rice, C. Duncan. The Rise and Fall of Black Slavery. New York: Harper & Row, 1975.

Richards, Leonard. *"Gentlemen of Property and Standing": Anti-abolition Mobs in Jacksonian America*. New York: Oxford University Press, 1970.

Riddleburger, Patrick. *George Washington Julian: A Study in Nineteenth Century Reform and Politics*. Indianapolis: Indiana Historical Bureau, 1966.

Ryan, Mary P. *Cradle of the Middle Class: The Family in Oneida County, New York, 1790–1865*. New York: Cambridge University Press, 1981.

Schlesinger, Arthur M., Jr. *History of U.S. Political Parties*. 3 vols. New York: Chelsea House Publishers, 1973.

Sewell, Richard H. *Ballots for Freedom: Antislavery Politics in the United States, 1837–1860*. New York: Oxford University Press, 1976.

Sewell, Richard H. *John P. Hale and the Politics of Abolition*. Cambridge, Mass.: Harvard University Press, 1965.

Silbey, Joel H. *A Respectable Minority: The Democratic Party in The Civil War Era, 1860–1868*. New York: W. W. Norton & Co., Inc., 1977.

Silbey, Joel H. *The Shrine of Party: Congressional Voting Behavior, 1841–1852*. Pittsburgh: University of Pittsburgh Press, 1967.

Smith, Theodore Clarke. *The Liberty and Free Soil Parties in the Northwest*. New York: Longmans Green and Company, 1897.

Smith, Timothy L. *Revivalism and Social Reform: American Protestantism on the Eve of the Civil War*. New York: Abingdon Press, 1957.

Sorin, Gerald. *Abolitionism: A New Perspective*. New York: Praeger Publishers, 1972.

Sorin, Gerald. *The New York Abolitionists: A Case Study of Political Radicalism*. Westport, Conn.: Greenwood Press, 1971.

Stampp, Kenneth M. *The Imperiled Union: Essays on the Background of the Civil War*. New York: Oxford University Press, 1980.

Stanton, Henry B. *Random Recollections*. New York: Henry B. Stanton, 1885.

Stewart, James B. *Holy Warriors: The Abolitionists and American Slavery*. New York: Hill and Wang, 1976.

Stewart, James B. *Joshua Giddings and the Tactics of Radical Politics, 1795–1864*. Cleveland: Press of Case Western Reserve University, 1969.

Swierenga, Robert P., ed. *Beyond the Civil War Synthesis: Political Essays of the Civil War Era*. Westport, Conn.: Greenwood Press, 1975.

Taylor, Clare. *British and American Abolitionists: An Episode in Transatlantic Understanding*. Edinburgh, U.K.: Edinburgh University Press, 1974.

Trefousse, Hans L. *Ben Wade: Radical Republican from Ohio*. New York: Twayne Publishing, 1963.

Tuckerman, Bayard. *William Jay and the Constitutional Movement for the Abolition of Slavery*. New York: Dodd, Mead and Co., 1893.

Van Deusen, Glyndon. *William Henry Seward: Lincoln's Secretary of State and the Negotiations of the Alaska Purchase*. New York: Oxford University Press, 1967.

Walker, Peter F. *Moral Choices: Memory, Desire and Imagination in Nineteenth Century American Abolition*. Baton Rouge: Louisiana State University Press, 1978.

Wallace, Anthony F. C. *Rockdale: The Growth of an American Village in the Early Industrial Revolution*. New York: W. W. Norton, 1972.

Walters, Ronald G. *American Reformers, 1815–1860.* New York: Hill and Wang, 1978.

Walters, Ronald G. *The Antislavery Appeal: American Abolitionism After 1830.* Baltimore: Johns Hopkins University Press, 1976.

Whittier, John Greenleaf. *The Conflict with Slavery, Politics and Reform: The Inner Life Criticism.* New York: Houghton Mifflin, 1889.

Wilson, Henry. *History of the Rise and Fall of the Slave Power in America.* 3 vols. Boston: James R. Osgood, 1877.

Wright, Elizur, Jr. *Myron Holley and What He Did for Liberty and True Religion.* Boston: Elizur Wright, Jr., 1882.

Wyatt-Brown, Bertram. *Lewis Tappan and the Evangelical War Against Slavery.* Cleveland: Press of Case Western Reserve University, 1969.

ARTICLES

Baum, Dale. "Know-Nothingism and the Republican Majority in Massachusetts: The Political Realignment of the 1850's," *Journal of American History* 64 (March 1978): 959–986.

Benedict, Michael Les. "Free Labor Ideology and the Meaning of the Civil War and Reconstruction," *Reviews in American History* 9 (June 1981): 179–185.

Benson, Lee, Silbey, Joel H., and Field, Phyllis F. "Toward a Theory of Stability and Change in American Voting Patterns: New York State, 1792–1970," in Joel H. Silbey, Allan G. Bogue, and William H. Flanigan, eds. *The History of American Cultural Behavior.* Princeton: Princeton University Press, 1978. Pp. 78–105.

Blue, Frederick J. "The Ohio Free Soilers and the Problems of Factionalism," *Ohio History* 76 (Spring 1967): 17–32.

Bretz, Julian R. "The Economic Background of the Liberty Party," *American Historical Review* 24 (January 1929): 250–264.

Brown, Richard H. "The Missouri Crisis, Slavery and the Politics of Jacksonianism," *South Atlantic Quarterly* 65 (Winter 1966): 55–72.

Curry, Richard Orr. "The Political War Against Slavery," *Reviews in American History* 4 (December 1976): 546–550.

Davis, Hugh H. "The Failure of Political Abolitionism," *Connecticut Review* 6 (April 1973): 76–86.

Dillon, Merton L. "The Abolitionists: A Decade of Historiography, 1959–1969," *Journal of Southern History* 35 (February 1969): 500–522.

Doherty, Robert W. "Status Anxiety and American Reform: Some Alternatives," *American Quarterly* 19 (Summer 1967): 329–337.

Donald, David Herbert. "Toward a Reconsideration of the Abolitionists," in Donald. *Lincoln Reconsidered: Essays on the Civil War Era.* New York: Random House, 1956. Pp. 19–36.

Duberman, Martin. "The Abolitionists and Psychology," *Journal of Negro History* 7 (July 1962): 183–192.

Ershowitz, Herbert, and Shade, William. "Consensus or Conflict? Political Behavior in the State Legislatures During the Jacksonian Era," *Journal of American History* 58 (December 1971): 591–622.

Field, Phyllis F. "Republican and Black Suffrage in New York State: The Grass Roots Response," *Civil War History* 21 (June 1975): 136–147.

Fishel, Leslie H., Jr. "Wisconsin and Negro Suffrage," *Wisconsin Magazine of History* 46 (Spring 1963): 180–196.

Foner, Eric. "The Causes of the American Civil War: Recent Interpretations and New Directions," *Civil War History* 20 (September 1974): 197–214.

Foner, Eric. "Politics and Prejudice: The Free Soil Party and the Negro, 1849–1852," *Journal of Negro History* 50 (October 1965): 232–256.

Foner, Eric. "Racial Attitudes of the New York Free Soilers," *New York History* 46 (October 1965): 311–329.

Formisano, Ronald P. "Deferential-Participant Politics: The Early Republic's Political Culture, 1789–1840," *American Political Science Review* 68 (June 1974): 473–487.

Formisano, Ronald P. "Federalists and Republicans: Parties, Yes—System, No," in Paul Kleppner et al. *The Evolution of American Electoral Systems*. Westport, Conn.: Greenwood Press, 1981. Pp. 33–76.

Formisano, Ronald P. "Political Character, Anti-partyism, and the Second Party System," *American Quarterly* 21 (Winter 1969): 683–709.

Formisano, Ronald P. "Toward a Reorientation of Jacksonian Politics; A Review of the Literature, 1959–1975," *Journal of American History* 63 (June 1976): 42–65.

Freehling, William W. "The Founding Fathers and Slavery," *American Historical Review* 77 (February 1972): 81–93.

Friedman, Lawrence J. "Abolitionist Historiography 1965–1979: An Assessment," *Reviews in American History* 8 (June 1980): 200–205.

Friedman, Lawrence J. "Abolitionists Versus Historians," *Reviews in American History* 5 (September 1977): 342–347.

Friedman, Lawrence J. "Confidence and Pertinacity in Evangelical Abolitionism: Lewis Tappan's Immediate Circle," *American Quarterly* 31 (Spring 1979): 81–106.

Friedman, Lawrence J. "Garrisonian Abolitionism and the Boston Clique: A Psychosocial Inquiry," *The Psychohistory Review* 7 (Fall 1978): 6–19.

Friedman, Lawrence J. "The Gerrit Smith Circle: Abolitionism in the Burned Over District," *Civil War History* 26 (March 1980): 18–38.

Friedman, Lawrence J. " 'Historical Topics Sometimes Run Dry': The State of Abolitionist Studies," *Historian* 43 (February 1981): 177–194.

Gamble, Douglas A. "Joshua Giddings and the Ohio Abolitionists: A Study in Radical Politics," *Ohio History* 88 (Winter 1979): 37–56.

Hammond, John L. "Revival Religion and Antislavery Politics," *American Sociological Review* 39 (April 1974): 175–186.

Holt, Michael Fitzgibbon. "The Politics of Impatience: The Origins of Know Nothingism," *Journal of American History* 60 (April 1973): 309–331.

Howard, Victor B. "The 1856 Election in Ohio: Moral Issues in Politics," *Ohio History* 80 (Winter 1971): 24–44.

Jentz, John B. "The Antislavery Constituency in Jacksonian New York City," *Civil War History* 27 (June 1981): 101–122.

Johnson, Reinhard O. "The Liberty Party in Massachusetts, 1840–1848: Antislavery Third Party Politics in the Bay State," *Civil War History* 28 (September 1982): 236–265.

Johnson, Reinhard O. "The Liberty Party in New Hampshire, 1840–1848," *Historical New Hampshire* 33 (Spring 1978): 123–166.

Johnson, Reinhard O. "The Liberty Party in Vermont, 1840–1848: The Forgotten Abolitionists," *Vermont History* 47 (Fall 1979): 258–275.

Kousser, J. Morgan. "Ecological Regression and the Analysis of Past Politics," *Journal of Interdisciplinary History* 4 (Autumn 1973): 237–262.

Kraut, Alan M. "The Forgotten Reformers: A Profile of Third Party Abolitionists in Antebellum New York," in Lewis Perry and Michael Fellman, eds. *Antislavery Reconsidered*. Baton Rouge: Louisiana State University Press. Pp. 119–145.

Kraut, Alan M., and Field, Phyllis F. "Politics Versus Principles: The Partisan Response to 'Bible Politics' in New York State," *Civil War History* 25 (June 1979): 101–118.

Kremm, Thomas. "Cleveland and the First Lincoln Election: The Ethnic Response to Nativism," *Journal of Interdisciplinary History* 8 (Summer 1977): 69–86.

Latner, Richard B., and Levine, Peter. "Perspectives on Antebellum Pietistic Politics," *Reviews in American History* 4 (March 1976): 15–24.

Lerner, Gerda. "The Political Activities of Antislavery Women," in Lerner, ed. *The Majority Finds Its Past: Placing Women in History*. New York: Oxford University Press, 1979. Pp. 112–128.

Loveland, Anne C. "Evangelicalism and 'Immediate Emancipation' in American Antislavery Thought," *Journal of Southern History* 32 (May 1966): 172–188.

Ludlum, Robert P. "Joshua R. Giddings, Anti-Slavery Gag Rule: History and Argument," *Journal of Negro History* 26 (April 1941): 203–243.

Luthin, Reinhard. "Salmon P. Chase's Political Career Before the Civil War," *Mississippi Valley Historical Review* 11 (March 1943): 517–540.

McElroy, James. "Social Control and Romantic Reform in Antebellum America: The Case of Rochester, New York," *New York History* 58 (January 1977): 17–46.

McFaul, John M. "Expediency vs. Morality. Jacksonian Politics and Slavery," *Journal of American History* 57 (June 1975): 24–39.

McPherson, James M. "The Fight Against the Gag Rule: Joshua Leavitt and the Antislavery Insurgency in the Whig Party, 1839–1842," *Journal of Negro History* 48 (July 1963): 177–195.

Marshall, Lynn L. "The Strange Stillbirth of the Whig Party," *American Historical Review* 72 (January 1967): 455–468.

Morrow, R. L. "The Liberty Party in Vermont," *New England Quarterly* 2 (April 1929): 234–248.

Myers, John L. "The Beginnings of Anti-Slavery Agencies in New York State, 1833–1836," *New York History* 43 (April 1962): 149–181.

Oldham, Ellen M. "Irish Support of the Abolitionist Movement," *Boston Public Library Quarterly* 10 (October 1958): 175–187.

Osofsky, Gilbert. "Irish Immigrants and the Dilemma of Romantic Nationalism," *American Historical Review* 80 (October 1975): 889–912.

Pease, Jane, and William H. "Antislavery Ambivalence: Immediatism, Expediency, Race," *American Quarterly* 16 (Winter 1964): 682–695.

Perry, Lewis. "Psychology and the Abolitionists: Reflections on Martin Duberman and the Neoabolitionism of the 1960's," *Reviews in American History* 2 (September 1974): 309–321.

Rayback, Joseph G. "The Liberty Party Leaders of Ohio: Exponents of Antislavery Coalition," *The Ohio State Archeological and Historical Quarterly* 57 (April 1948): 165–178.

Rozett, John M. "Racism and Republican Emergence in Illinois, 1840–1860: A Re-evaluation of Republican Negrophobia," *Civil War History* 22 (June 1976): 101–115.

Russo, David J. "The Major Issues of the Jacksonian Period and the Development of Party Loyalty in Congress, 1830–1840," *Transactions of the American Philosophical Society* 62 (1975): 4–32.

Shortridge, Ray M. "The Voter Realignment in the Midwest During the 1850's," *American Politics Quarterly* 4 (April 1976): 193–222.

Shortridge, Ray M. "Voting For Minor Parties in the Antebellum Midwest," *Indiana Magazine of History* 74 (June 1978): 115–134.

Silbey, Joel H. "The Civil War Synthesis in American Political History," *Civil War History* 10 (June 1964): 130–140.

Skotheim, Robert Allen. "A Note on Historical Method: David Donald's 'Toward a Reconsideration of the Abolitionists,' " *Journal of Southern History* 25 (August 1959): 356–365.

Stanley, John L. "Majority Tyranny in Tocqueville's America: The Failure of Negro Suffrage in 1846," *Political Science Quarterly* 84 (September 1969): 412–435.

Stewart, James B. "Peaceful Hopes and Violent Experiences: The Evolution of Reforming and Radical Abolitionism, 1831–1857," *Civil War History* 17 (December 1971): 293–309.

Sweeney, Kevin. "Rum, Romanism, Representation and Reform: Coalitional Politics in Massachusetts, 1847–1853," *Civil War History* 22 (June 1976): 309–331.

Van Deusen, Glyndon G. "Some Aspects of Whig Thought and Theory in the Jacksonian Period," *American Historical Review* 63 (March 1958): 305–322.

Walters, Ronald G. "The Erotic South: Civilization and Sexuality in American Abolitionism," *American Quarterly* 25 (May 1973): 177–202.

Wesley, Charles H. "The Participation of Negroes in Antislavery Political Parties," *Journal of Negro History* 29 (January 1944): 32–74.

Woodward, C. Vann. "The Antislavery Myth," *American Scholar* 31 (Summer 1962): 312–328.

Wyatt-Brown, Bertram. "New Leftists and Abolitionists: A Comparison of American Radical Styles," *Wisconsin Magazine of History* 53 (Summer 1970): 256–268.

Wyatt-Brown, Bertram. "Prelude to Abolitionism: Sabbatarian Politics and the Rise of the Second Party System," *Journal of American History* 58 (April 1971): 316–345.

Wyatt-Brown, Bertram. "Stanley Elkins' *Slavery*: The Antislavery Interpretation Reexamined," *American Quarterly* 25 (May 1973): 154–176.

UNPUBLISHED WORKS

Bean, William G. "The Transformation of Parties in Massachusetts, with Special Reference to the Antecedents of Republicanism from 1848 to 1860." Ph.D. Dissertation, Harvard University, 1922.

Benson, Lee, and Silbey, Joel H. "American Political Eras, 1788–1984." Paper presented at the Annual Meeting of the Social Science History Association, 1978.

Benson, Lee, and Silbey, Joel H. "The American Voter, 1854–1860 and 1948–1984." Paper presented at the Annual Meeting of the Organization of American Historians, 1978.

Bruser, Lawrence. "Slavery and the Northern Mind: A Case Study of Free Soil Sentiment, 1846–1850." Masters Essay, Columbia University, 1967.

Davis, Hugh Houck. "The Reform Career of Joshua Leavitt, 1794–1873." Ph.D. Dissertation, Ohio State University, 1969.

Davis, Philip C. "The Persistence of Partisan Alignment: Leaders and Votes in New Jersey, 1840–1860." Ph.D. Dissertation, Washington University, 1978.

French, David C. "The Conversion of an American Radical: Elizur Wright, Jr. and the Abolitionist Commitment." Ph.D. Dissertation, Case Western Reserve University, 1970.

Gienapp, William. " 'Politics Seems To Enter Into Everything': Political Culture In The North, 1840–1860." Paper prepared as part of the Walter Prescott Webb Memorial Lecture Series, University of Texas at Arlington, 1981.

Goldfarb, Joel. "The Life of Gamaliel Bailey Prior to the Founding of the *National Era*: The Orientation of a Practical Abolitionist." Ph.D. Dissertation, University of California, Los Angeles, 1958.

Hendricks, John R. "The Liberty Party in New York State, 1838–1848." Ph.D. Dissertation, Fordham University, 1959.

Imholt, Robert. "Beyond Slavery: The Transformation of Issues in New York Politics, 1852–1860." Ph.D. Dissertation, University of Kentucky, 1974.

Jentz, John Barkley. "Artisans, Evangelicals, and the City: A Social History of Abolitionist and Labor Reform in Jacksonian New York." Ph.D. Dissertation, City University of New York, 1977.

Johnson, Reinhard O. "The Liberty Party in New England, 1840–1848: The Forgotten Abolitionists." Ph.D. Dissertation, Syracuse University, 1976.

Kraut, Alan M. "The Liberty Men of New York: Political Abolitionism in New York State, 1840–1848." Ph.D. Dissertation, Cornell University, 1975.

McElroy, James L. "Social Reform in the Burned-Over District: Rochester, New York as a Test Case, 1830–1854." Ph.D. Dissertation, State University of New York at Binghamton, 1974.

Marsh, Luther. "Alvan Stewart." Manuscript, n.d. Alvan Stewart Collection, New York State Historical Association.

Mooney, James Eugene. "Antislavery in Worcester County, Massachusetts: A Case Study." Ph.D. Dissertation, Clark University, 1971.

Myers, John. "The Agency System of the Anti-Slavery Movement, 1832–1837, and Its Antecedents in Other Benevolent and Reform Societies." Ph.D. Dissertation, University of Michigan, 1960.

Pease, Jane Hanna. "The Freshness of Fanaticism: Abby Kelley Foster: An Essay in Reform." Ph.D. Dissertation, University of Rochester, 1969.

Perkal, M. Leon. "William Goodell: A Life of Reform." Ph.D. Dissertation, City University of New York, 1972.

Peterson, Roger. "Reactions to a Heterogeneous Society: Voting Behavior in Pennsylvania, 1848–1860." Ph.D. Dissertation, University of Pittsburgh, 1973.

Plunkett, Margaret Louise. "A History of the Liberty Party with Emphasis Upon Its Activities in the Northeastern States." Ph.D. Dissertation, Cornell University, 1930.

Rice, Arthur Harry. "Henry B. Stanton as a Political Abolitionist." Ph.D. Dissertation, Columbia University, 1968.

Rietveld, Ronald D. "The Moral Issue of Slavery in American Politics 1854–1860." Ph.D. Dissertation, University of Illinois, 1967.

Stanley, John Langley. "Majority Tyranny in Tocqueville's America: The Failure of Negro Suffrage in New York State in 1846." Ph.D. Dissertation, Cornell University, 1966.

Van Deventer, Carroll. "Free Soil Party in the Northwest in the Election of 1848." Ph.D. Dissertation, University of Illinois, 1968.

Wellman, Judith M. " 'Are We Aliens Because We Are Women?': Female Abolitionist Petitions in Upstate New York." Paper presented at the National Archives Conference, Washington, D.C., April 1976.

Wellman, Judith M. "The Burned-Over District Revisited: Benevolent Reform and Abolitionism in Mexico, Paris and Ithaca, New York, 1825–1842." Ph.D. Dissertation, University of Virginia, 1974.

Wellman, Judith M. "To the 'Fathers and Rulers of Our Country': Abolitionist Petitions and Female Abolitionists in Paris, New York, 1835–1845." Paper presented at the Berkshire Conference on Women's History, June 1976.

Wellman, Judith M. " 'We Do Respectfully Pray': The Social Bases of Abolitionist Petitions from Central New York, 1836–1839." Paper presented at the New York History Conference, April 1980.

Index

Political abolitionists, 4, 74; biographies of, 6; effect of, 16-17; goal of, 225-26; versus moral suasion abolitionists, 3, 15, 207; and republican federalism, 218-19. *See also* Women

Political culture, 154

Political pietism. *See* Religion

Politics, 1, 3; as amusement, 80-81; proper end of, 89; and religion synthesis, 79, 88, 91

Porter, Samuel D., 209, 212, 220, 221

Porter, Susan, 220, 221

Post, Amy, 221-22

Post, Isaac, 221-22

Property ownership, 53-55

Quakers: abolitionist leadership of, 232 n.51; as abolitionists, 60-61, 180, 181, 187, 191; autonomy of, 231 n.47; and male/female equality, 214, 216; women activists, 209, 210

Quincy, Edmund, 118, 242

Radical Abolitionist party, 125, 193; demise of, 195

Radical abolitionists, 6, 10, 12, 30, 32, 92 n.5

Religion: and partisanship, 78; and politics synthesis, 79, 88, 91; and sectionalism, 27, 30

Republican party, 14, 38; abolitionist ideology of, 3-4, 192; abolitionist support of, 125-26; Bay State, 252; and church reform, 192-93; church support of, 193-95; Democratic defection to, 151-52, 163-66, 167; 1860 votes for, 148; and equal suffrage, 14, 128-30, 131-37; evaluation of, 147; and racial change, 127; and third parties, 144; viewed by Eric Foner, 9

Richards, Leonard, 48

Roberts, Seth B., 59

Robinson, William S., *Pen Portraits,* 252-53

Rochester, New York: immediatists in, 237; social environment of, 208

Rochester Anti-Slavery Sewing Circle, 223

Rochester Female Anti-Slavery Society (RFASS): demise of, 228 n.16; membership of, 208-9, 210, 211 (table)

Rochester Ladies' Anti-Slavery Sewing Society (RLASS): ideology of, 213; member profile, 214, 215-16 (table)

Rochester Ladies' Anti-Slavery Society (RLASS), 233 n.61; antislavery fairs of, 223-25; subordinate posture of, 226

Roman Catholic Church, 86

Rome, New York: abolitionist leaders in, 59; economy of, 50; petitioner groups in, 52 (table), 53

Roosevelt, Theodore, 5

Ross, Sidney, 58

Schenectady, New York: abolitionist leaders in, 58-59; economy of, 50; petitioner groups in, 52 (table), 53

School segregation, 112, 114

Scofield, Abishai, 238

Second Great Awakening, 47, 64, 179, 217, 231 n.42

Sectionalism, 146, 157; in Democratic party, 38; final result of, 39; growth of, 33; and Whig party, 26, 27, 30, 33, 34, 36, 37, 38

Seneca Falls Woman's Rights Convention, 210

Sewall, Samuel, 238, 244, 250

Seward, William, 30, 36

Sewell, Richard H., 8, 10, 13-14; *Ballots for Freedom,* 73

Seymour, Horatio, 161

Silbey, Joel H., 2, 8, 14; methodology of, 16

Skotheim, Robert, 7, 235

Slade, William, 30, 34

Slavery: and competitive disadvantage, 244; containment of, 103, 104, 105, 108, 118, 143; defined by Immediatists and Radicals 12; economic impact of, 85, 107; expansion, 35-36; holy war against, 245; and industrialization, 13; means of ending, 80; and modernist views, 238; as national issue, 4; and Roman Catholic Church, 86; as sin, 180, 183; wage, 64

About the Contributors

PHYLLIS F. FIELD is Associate Professor of History at Ohio University. She is the author of *The Politics of Race: The Struggles for Equal Suffrage in New York State, 1846–1869*, which was published by Cornell University Press (1982). She is also the author of several articles on the subject of black suffrage and political behavior.

LAWRENCE J. FRIEDMAN is Professor of History and American Studies at Bowling Green State University and was previously on the faculty of Arizona State University. He is the author of *The White Savage: Racial Fantasies in the Postbellum South* (1970), *Inventors of the Promised Land* (1975), and *Gregarious Saints: Self and Community in American Abolitionism, 1830–1870* (1982). Active in the Group for the Use of Psychology in History, he is interested in applying psychological theories to historical data.

NANCY HEWITT is an Assistant Professor of History at the University of South Florida. She received her Ph.D. from the University of Pennsylvania in August 1981. The issues presented in this article are taken from her dissertation, "Women's Activism and Social Change: The Case of Rochester, New York, 1822–1872." The research for this article was partially funded by a Doctoral Dissertation Research Grant in Women's Studies from the Woodrow Wilson National Fellowship Foundation.

ALAN M. KRAUT is Associate Professor of History at The American University. He is the author of "The Forgotten Reformers: A Profile of Third Party Abolitionists in Antebellum New York," in Perry and Fellman, eds., *Antislavery Reconsidered* and (with Phyllis F. Field) "Politics Versus Principles: The Partisan Response to 'Bible Politics' in New York State" in *Civil War History*. He is interested in the influence of race, religion, and ethnicity upon American society and culture and is the author of *Huddled Masses: The Immigrant in American Society, 1880–1921* (1982).

JOHN R. McKIVIGAN is Associate Editor of the Frederick Douglass Papers and a Lecturer in History and Afro-American Studies at Yale University. He has published articles on the abolition movement in *Civil War History, The Old Northwest,* and other historical journals. His study of the abolitionists' relations with the American churches has been accepted for publication by Cornell University Press.

EDWARD MAGDOL is an Honorary Fellow of the Department of History, University of Wisconsin, Madison, and Associate Professor Emeritus, Potsdam College of Arts and Science of the State University of New York. He is the author of *Owen Lovejoy, Abolitionist in Congress* and *A Right to the Land, Essays on the Freedmen's Community.* He is co-editor (with Jon L. Wakelyn) of *The Southern Common People: Studies in Nineteenth Century Social History.*

RICHARD H. SEWELL is Professor of History at the University of Wisconsin, Madison. A specialist in mid-nineteenth century social and political history, he is the author of *John P. Hale and the Politics of Abolition* and *Ballots for Freedom: Antislavery Politics in the United States, 1837–1860.*

JOEL H. SILBEY is Professor of History at Cornell University. He is author of *The Shrine of Party: Congressional Voting Behavior, 1841–1868* (1967); *A Respectable Minority: The Democratic Party in the Civil War Era* (1977), and co-editor and contributor to *The History of American Electoral Behavior* (1978). In addition he has published articles and edited several anthologies dealing with nineteenth-century party politics and elections in the United States.

JAMES BREWER STEWART is Professor of History at Macalester College, St. Paul, Minnesota. He has written *Joshua Giddings and the Tactics of Radical Politics* and *Holy Warriors: The Abolitionists and American Slavery,* as well as numerous articles on antislavery and pre-Civil War politics.